*The Art of Warfare
in the Age of Napoleon*

The Art of Warfare in the Age of Napoleon

GUNTHER E. ROTHENBERG

Indiana University Press
Bloomington

First Midland Book Edition 1980

Manufactured in the United States of America.

Library of Congress Cataloging in Publication Data
Rothenberg, Gunther Erich, 1923–
   The art of warfare in the age of Napoleon.

   Bibliography: p.
   Includes index.
     1. Military art and science—History.   2. Military
history, Modern—18th century.   3. Military history,
Modern—19th century.   4. Europe—History, Military.
I. Title.
U39.R65   355'.0094   77-86495
ISBN 0-253-31076-8   4 5 6 86 85
ISBN 0-253-20260-4 pbk.

Contents

Illustrations

(between pages 128 and 129)

Line Drawings

Acknowledgments

The Author and Publishers would like to thank The Parker Gallery for their cooperation in obtaining the following illustrations: 1–4, 6–8, 10–14. The remainder are from the Publisher's collection. The diagrams are by Patrick Leeson.

Preface

The era of the Wars of the French Revolution and Napoleon has been one of the favourite topics for historians, writers of memoirs and biographies, and for documentary compilations. Some 12 years ago it was estimated that well over 300,000 works existed on this period and since then several thousand more have appeared. Therefore, it might be reasonably argued that there is little room for another volume. Nonetheless, this vast outpouring of literature has usually dealt with major leaders, specific battles or campaigns, and with certain branches of the service. Moreover, at least in English, the literature tends to concentrate primarily on the French or British armies. There appears to be a lack of works combining a description of the major changes and trends in the art of war, especially at the cutting edge of events, with a discussion of the French military establishment and the armies of the major opponents, British as well as continental. And while this book is only a brief survey, I do believe that it may serve as a contribution towards filling this gap in our historical knowledge of military institutions and fighting men.

It is, of course, necessary to acknowledge the limitations which this approach and considerations of space have imposed. This volume is mainly concerned with the techniques and conditions of warfare on the fighting level. Intricate organizational details, strategic interpretations, and analyses of the major commanders and their decisions have been only lightly touched upon. Also, little has been said about the development of military theory. Although many of the commanders applied calculations of a high order to their planning, they basically were pragmatists. Overall, questions have been covered in accordance with the author's best judgment.

Any survey of so vast a subject is built on the work of many other scholars and I have freely drawn on their many books. In particular I am obliged to Messrs Brett-James, Chandler and Duffy, who have made the Department of War Studies at the Royal Military Academy, Sandhurst, into a major stronghold of Napoleonic scholarship. In this country I am deeply indebted to my friend Professor Peter Paret of Stanford University. I am obliged to the librarians of the US Army Military History Research Collection, Carlisle Barracks, Pennsylvania, and to Dennis Parks of the Purdue University

Library, for bibliographic aid. Beyond this, the book is primarily the result of nearly twenty years of teaching courses in the history of land warfare to undergraduates at the University of New Mexico, Southern Illinois University, and Purdue University. Except for a reduced teaching load in the spring semester of 1967 and for typing help by the secretaries of the Department of History at Purdue University, the support required for completing this volume has been provided by the Rothenberg family. For this, and for their understanding and patience, I am grateful to my daughters Judith, Laura, and Georgia, and above all to my wife, Ruth. Much of the painstaking work involved to bringing this book to press devolved on my editor at Batsford, Mr Michael Stephenson. It goes without saying, that I alone remain responsible for the errors of commission and omission which surely exist in a work of this nature.

I

Armies and Warfare
during the Last Years of
the Ancien Régime

On 20 September 1792 the combined armies of the French Generals Dumou-
reiz and Kellermann faced a Prussian army commanded by the Duke of
Brunswick near Valmy in north-eastern France. After exchanging heavy
artillery fire for several hours, the Prussian infantry formed up for the assault.
Only too aware of the Prussian reputation, even the bravest French soldier
must have felt some apprehension. But, despite the explosion of an ammunition cart, they held their ground. Faced with an unexpectedly resolute enemy,
Brunswick halted the advance before it had come into musket range. 'We are
not going to fight here,' he decided. The cannonade continued for a few more
hours, then heavy rain and early darkness ended the engagement. Ten days
later Brunswick negotiated a peaceful retreat and led his army back across the
frontier into winter quarters.

Although the cannonade at Valmy had cost but a few hundred casualties,
it was a watershed in the history of war. A 'people's army' had defeated the
old order. Two patterns of warfare, the one limited and now becoming
obsolete, and the other, potentially unlimited, had collided for the first time.
That night the young Goethe, who had accompanied the Prussians, commented: 'From this place and day commenced a new epoch in the world's
history.' He was right. 'The wars of kings,' Marshal Foch wrote, 'were at an
end; the wars of the peoples were beginning.' And a noted soldier-historian
put it in even clearer perspective, from the 'military point of view it was the
end of a world'.[1]

The nature of eighteenth-century limited war
During the century before Valmy the wars of the kings had evolved into
formal affairs, pursued with limited means for limited objectives. Monarchs
decided on war and peace by calculating gains and costs in terms of their
interests; the people neither were consulted nor normally expected to contribute much to the fighting which was left to small professional armies. And
in the absence of any national or ideological content it was not in anyone's
interest to seek the total destruction of the enemy. Costly pitched battles were

avoided when possible; manoeuvre not combat were the principal operations of war. The most accomplished strategy, so General Lloyd, author of a *History of the Late War in Germany* (1776–90), advised, was to 'initiate military operations with mathematical precision and to keep on waging war without ever being under the necessity to strike a blow'.[2] Campaigns aimed to place the opponent in an untenable position after which the enemy, accepting the rules of the contest, capitulated on terms. To surrender a fortress or an army in the field was not considered dishonourable; no general ever thought of fighting to the last man. In this framework the Duke of Brunswick, a nephew of Frederick the Great of Prussia, who had conducted an almost bloodless but successful manoeuvering campaign in 1787 in Holland was considered a great strategist and his refusal to fight at Valmy was quite reasonable. He retained the confidence of Prussia's king, commanded the Prussian armies during the campaigns against France until 1795, and in 1806, having aged but changed very little, presided over the destruction of these armies at Jena and Auerstädt.

The limited and formal nature of warfare in the eighteenth century was the result of political, social, economic, and military constraints. No longer raised for one campaign only and then disbanded, most regiments now were permanently embodied, a standing force serving absolute monarchs. Although small by comparison with later mass armies, such an establishment placed considerable strain on the royal treasury and the general economy. More and more resources had to be devoted to maintain a respectable military posture. Prussia, an exceptional case to be sure, spent approximately 90 percent of its revenue for military purposes in 1752, while in 1784 France expended two-thirds of its budget on the army alone.

The armies were regular forces, but not national armies in the modern sense. Their officer corps were composed primarily of aristocrats, natives as well as foreigners, and transfer from one service to another was common. Everywhere the highest positions were reserved for members of the ruling house and the great families; in the lower ranks connections and birth counted for less. Most officers came from the lesser nobility, but a few bourgeois could be found in many regiments and especially in the technical corps, the artillery and the engineers.

Whatever their origins, officers were a world apart from the rank-and-file. Among the population generally service in the ranks was considered neither honourable nor desirable, views reflected in the works of the major literary figures of the age. In Voltaire's *Candide* and in Smollet's *Roderick Random*, for example, the picture of military life is dismal. Although most Continental states had some form of conscription on the books, economic considerations precluded the enlistment of productive and tax-producing elements, so that in practice the soldiery was composed of the socially and economically least valuable, labourers, poor peasants, vagabonds, criminals, and foreigners. Even then it was difficult to find enough soldiers and as difficult to retain them.

Sometimes abject poverty drove men to soldiering and usually the ranks were filled by coercion and deception. Many rulers maintained recruiting agents in foreign countries, and foreign nationals also were enlisted in complete units, often considered elite troops. The most famous, of course, were the Swiss regiments serving France, Holland, and Venice under special contracts, but Irish and Walloon regiments could be found in many armies.

Everywhere governments skimped on the upkeep of their army. Pay was low, quarters wretched, and often soldiers had to look for odd jobs to fill their stomachs. In poor countries like Prussia this was, in fact, a deliberate part of the system, but the practice also was common in England and France, and in other states. British soldiers habitually hired themselves out for menial part-time jobs, while French soldiers hoped for garrison duty at Brest, where 'everyone could find a job', and prayed to be delivered from the 'plague and famine of service at Bergue and Graveline'.[3]

Compounding the misery of a soldier's life was a most ferocious and brutal discipline. Floggings, beatings, and other physical punishments were imposed for trivial offences and the death penalty was prescribed for a wide range of crimes, especially as a deterrent to desertion which in the eighteenth century was common in all armies and reached appalling proportions in wartime. Yet, the need for trained manpower sometimes forced commanders to mitigate these regulations and strenuous efforts were made to entice deserters back into the ranks. Fear of desertion, together with the restricted supply of manpower, imposed real restraints on the conduct of war. The most striking consequence was the reduction in fighting.

The universal adoption of flintlock muskets and bayonets had made fire tactics supreme and pitched battles, fought by infantry shoulder to shoulder trading volleys at distances suited to duelling pistols, could be very costly. At Torgau (1760) the Prussians lost 30 percent of their effectives, while at Zorndorf (1758) the Russians suffered losses of over 50 percent. Such casualties in killed, wounded and missing, could not be replaced easily. To execute the intricate evolutions, to load and volley in cadence, and to perform all this under fire, required an iron discipline that, in the opinion of contemporary commanders, took years to instil. A steady battalion, it was believed, should have no more than a third of its men raw. Therefore, generals avoided accepting battle except under the most favourable conditions, combat often was broken off prematurely, and even the victor seldom dared to launch a pursuit in depth for fear of losing control over his troops.

Similar considerations affected marches and encampments, both rigidly regulated to minimize opportunities for desertion. Field armies moved slowly, encumbered by a huge train of pack horses, wagons, and other conveyances. Tentage took up most of the transport. Even the Prussian army, perhaps the most controlled and frugal of all, allotted 60 pack horses per regiment for tentage. Every company commander was entitled to a carriage and two saddle horses, while staff and general officers took along five to ten times as much. Tents, of course, were not just luxuries. They provided shelter for men and equipment and were considered a necessity to keep powder supplies dry.

But there were other impediments. Most officers, especially French and

Austrian, liked to display their wealth in the field. Foot-men, cooks, servants, hairdressers and other domestics often accompanied field armies together with actors, actresses, mistresses and, occasionally, wives. Camps were like small cities. Sutler's wagons, carriages for the ladies, tents selling all manner of goods and services surrounded the orderly military lines. There were squad tents for the men, wall tents for the officers, and elaborate marquees for senior commanders. To prevent surprise and desertions, camps were well guarded. Usually there were outposts and pickets, camp and quarter guards, and on occasion encampments were protected by small field fortifications. To strike camp and march required time, and usually the marching day was limited to five hours or so.

Fear of desertion and the desire to spare civilian society the ravages of war, demanded that foraging be forbidden or at least sharply restricted. Armies had to be supplied by huge wagon trains which in turn depended on magazines, usually well established in advance of a campaign. To supply 50,000 men 15 miles from their base required some 100 wagons daily and five to seven days marching distance from the nearest magazine, between 50 to 80 miles, was considered the maximum practical operational range. Bad weather, of course, limited the range of wagons even further, and it also hampered the movement of the still heavy field artillery. Therefore, armies normally retired into winter quarters and re-emerged in the spring.

The lines of communications and their magazines thus assumed a paramount strategic importance. To safeguard these, fortifications sprouted up all over Europe, attacked, besieged, defended, and surrendered according to precise rules and customs. Fortresses became primary strategic targets, but they further slowed down the conduct of operations.

Battle tactics of limited war

Field armies, rarely exceeding 50,000 men, were very similar throughout Europe. They did not exist in peacetime but were formed at the opening of hostilities from existent regiments, their component battalions or squadrons providing the basic tactical units. There was little variance in organization or armament, and therefore also in tactics. Although cavalry still was numerous, up to a fourth of the total, its role diminished as infantry and artillery fire became more deadly. Massive volleys rather than the collision of mounted men decided battles. Even so, the flintlock musket remained a highly inaccurate and rather unreliable weapon and there was a common saying that to kill a man required expenditure of an amount of lead equal to his weight. This might appear exaggerated, but it was true. Ammunition expenditure was enormous; Guibert, the famous French theorist, estimated that in an average battle half a million rounds were expended.[4]

The limitations of the musket determined battle tactics. To compensate for the extremely low accuracy of the individual shot, mass fire was required and to achieve this battalions were formed in elongated lines, three deep, firing volleys on command. To form and manoeuvre such an order of battle, as much as 20 battalions wide, required the utmost precision in evolutions. Alignments had to be straight, distances correct, and commands perfectly timed. The drill of the parade ground actually was used on the battlefield and officers had to be competent professionals, while the troops had to be prompt and accurate in executing orders, march in step, usually a stately 75 paces a minute, load and fire in cadence. Bayonets were carried fixed at all times, but shock action clearly was secondary to fire.

Artillery added its weight to the volume of fire. By the middle of the eighteenth century it had become militarized and shed the last remants of its ancient guild status. Generally, armies were well supplied with field pieces, firing 6-, 8-, or 12-pound projectiles, though they still lacked organic transport. Guns and their ammunition supply were dragged to the battlefield by hired civilian drivers. Moreover, until the Seven Years' War (1756–63), pieces remained very heavy and were usually placed in a position from which they rarely moved during action. The effectiveness of artillery support, therefore, depended on the siting of guns previous to battle and, if this was well chosen, they sometimes could exert considerable influence. Smaller pieces, 3- or 4-pounders, 'battalion' or 'regimental' guns, were issued to the infantry and manhandled during the advance, but their effectiveness was limited due to the low weight of their shot. Overall, artillery was undergoing a rapid evolution from the middle of the century on, becoming lighter and more manoeuverable, and equipped with better aiming devices.

In battle, armies deployed in two parallel lines of battalions, the second some 150 to 200 paces behind the first. The cavalry was stationed at the wings and its primary mission was to counter the enemy's horse. On occasion, especially if the opposing infantry was not yet deployed, such as at Rossbach (1757) horse was launched against foot with excellent results. Also, if cavalry drove its opponents off the field and was able to rally, a feat often achieved by Prussia's well-drilled horse under General Seydlitz, it could be hurled against the enemy's unprotected flank or rear. These missions were the duties of heavy battle cavalry, cuirassiers and dragoons, while light cavalry were used to screen the army on the march and during deployment. Pursuit and scouting duties also fell to the light horse.

FIG. 1.   Classic linear formation.

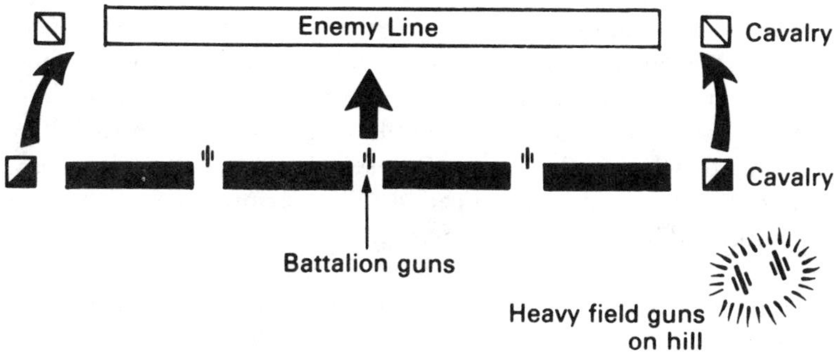

Battles of this type required suitable open and level ground. Hills, ridges, swamps, and woods would break up the formations. Weather also was important. Cannon could not be moved across muddy ground; cavalry was slowed to a walk, even infantry was hampered in its evolutions. Heavy rains, moreover, prevented the discharge of artillery and muskets. Finally, the deployment of an army took time.

The warfare of Frederick the Great

To break completely with the patterns of limited war would require a political and social upheaval, but after 1740 Frederick II of Prussia, better known as Frederick the Great, brought the eighteenth century system to its highest potential. And in many ways his realistic, calculating, and even brutal approach was a departure from contemporary practice. It is perhaps revealing that Napoleon regarded him as one of his main preceptors.

Until the advent of Frederick, France had been considered the leading military power, but now Prussia surpassed her and gained an influence in military affairs out of all proportion to its size and wealth. A remarkable series of rulers laid the foundations for Frederick's achievements. On his accession there existed a well trained and disciplined army, 80,000 strong, a very large force for a country with a population of but two and a half million and no extensive natural resources. When he died in 1786 the army was 200,000 strong, while the population had doubled. To maintain such a military establishment required the concentration of all available resources. Little was spent in Prussia on the luxuries that bankrupted France and Austria; frugality, hard work, and an honest, if sometimes heavyhanded, administration were the hallmarks of the Prussian state. France in 1740 had an army of 160,000 though its population was ten times that of Prussia and its revenues eight times larger, while in the same year Maria Theresa's Habsburg Empire could not muster an army adequate to meet Frederick's attack.

The Prussian army drew its strength from peculiar Prussian institutions and practices. Its officer corps was without rival. Conscripted from the poor landed nobility, the *Junker,* the Corps displayed unmatched dedication, diligence, and professionalism. The Prussian officer entered the army as a boy, was commissioned in his teens, and often remained in the service for the rest of his life. His regiment became his universe and though poorly paid, he was rewarded by membership in the first estate of the Prussian realm. The King, the first soldier of the state, habitually wore the uniform and took a personal, if on occasion capricious interest in each and every member of the corps. Only very few men of non-noble origins were admitted, the King believed that they lacked the requisite sense of honour, and he dismissed them as soon as they were no longer needed. The performance of the army was further improved by the non-commissioned officers, sergeants and corporals, privileged men of unusually high competence.

The rank-and-file was procured from two main sources: conscription of natives and enlistment of foreigners. Since 1735 the Prussian monarchy was divided into regimental replacement districts, called Cantons. In each Canton all men were registered for service, and though wide social groups and indeed whole areas were exempted, each regiment could annually fill its needs from its own district. Those enrolled, but excess to actual requirements, remained on the regimental rolls as a reserve pool, while recruits actually called up received their initial training and then were furloughed to their homes contributing to the economy. These native conscripts, especially those from the Mark of Brandenburg and Pomerania, often revealed a surprising devotion and loyalty to the King that was reinforced by the tenets of the Lutheran faith. And after the victories over the Austrians and the French it became a matter of pride even for a simple peasant's son to serve in the victorious regiments of the great King.

Frederick, however, made little use of these early stirrings of a regional patriotism. On occasion, to be sure, he would appeal to his men in a style later used by Napoleon. At Zorndorf, for instance, he dismounted, seized the colours of the Bülow Fusilier Regiment, and personally led the men forward. But basically he believed that his subjects were of more use as taxpayers than as soldiers. Discipline, he was convinced, could make men fight and foreigners were cheaper than natives. At the onset of his reign natives outnumbered foreigners two to one in the army and though the King did not hesitate to impress entire enemy formations, the series of wars made foreign recruiting more and more difficult. In 1763, at the end of the Seven Years' War, his army comprised 103,000 natives and only 37,000 foreigners. During the following years Frederick set to reverse the ratio. He decreed increased exemptions from military service, vigorously pushed recruiting abroad, lowered standards for enlistment, and provided minor improvement in living conditions. By the time of his death foreigners outnumbered natives by two to one, which contributed to a definite lowering of quality.

Frederick's combat tactics combined the use of all arms. Cavalry and artillery played a major part in almost all of his battles, disrupting the enemy's deployment and supporting the infantry's advance. In several of his victories, above all at Rossbach (1757), his cavalry squadrons 'charging like a wall' shattered the enemy, while later the same year at Leuthen batteries of heavy artillery contributed much, perhaps decisively, to success. Even so, the infantry attack remained his primary instrument with well-aligned ranks advancing, changing front, volleying, and charging with unequalled precision. Like Napoleon, Frederick thought highly of the bayonet. In his early campaigns he ordered his infantry to advance with cold steel only, but experience soon revealed that this was impossible even for his best regiments. Massive volleys became the decisive element of his infantry combat and in his *Military Testament* of 1768 he concluded that 'infantry firing more rapidly will undoubtedly defeat infantry firing more slowly'.[5]

To achieve the highest possible volume of fire, Prussia already before 1740 had replaced the breakable wooden ramrods with iron. Constant drill raised the Prussian rate of fire to three and even four rounds a minute and because speed was all important, the number of movements required to load and fire

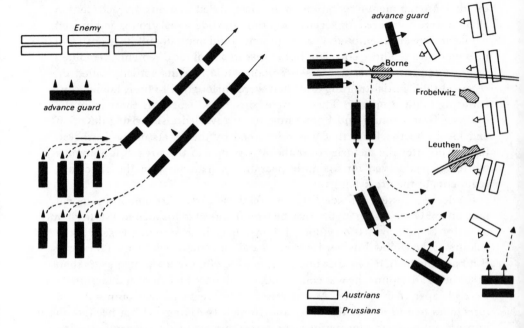

FIG. 2.   The oblique order of battle. *Left:* advance guard screens the main body from the enemy. The main body shifts obliquely in column and forms a line to fall on the enemy's flank. *Right:* Frederick's execution of the manoeuvre at Leuthen, 5 December 1757.

the musket were reduced. In 1777 a double-ended ramrod eliminated the need to reverse the ramrod before reinserting it, and the musket itself was redesigned in 1781 with a conical touchhole which primed itself from the main charge. But, although a slight angling of the butt would have improved accuracy by as much as a third, nothing was done. In fact, aiming, consuming precious time, was forbidden. In any case, the bayonet obscured the rudimentary frontsight.

The rapid fire* of Frederick's 'walking batteries' inflicted casualties and shook the morale of his opponents, but his most important contribution was to restore manoeuvering to the battlefield. By dividing his battalions into platoons he was able to manoeuvre in columns of platoons across the enemy front, the short range of small arms made this a practical move, and he then

---

* These rapid and continuous volleys achieved three or even four rounds unaimed per minute; in practice there are reports of five and even six rounds blank. However, everything depended on the proficiency of the particular unit at that particular time. Moreover, the high rate of fire could be maintained for brief periods only. In theory, the Austrians and French should have achieved the same speed, but due to less dedicated officers and less drill they probably achieved only two rounds per minute – but this is really speculation. Neither Delbrück, *Geschichte der Kriegskunst,* vol. IV, 329–32, nor any other authority has given exact figures. After about 1780, Prussian regulations speak of four rounds per minute, but it is not clear whether this is a goal, or actual performance. The Austrian regulations are mute and merely stress speed.

could wheel them into line against the enemy's weakest flank. This method, in which one wing of his army was reinforced while the other was refused, became his famous 'oblique order of attack'. Of course, it was not new, but only the Prussian army had the precision to execute it successfully.

At the same time, the King was an excellent stategist. His slender military resources induced him to take, whenever possible, the offensive and to destroy the enemy in battle. To achieve the necessary concentration of force, he willingly sacrificed territory, even his own capital. But the total destruction of the enemy's armies often eluded him. He remained tethered to a cumbersome supply system and was unable to exploit the full potential of his victories in a deep pursuit. Facing great odds during the Seven Years' War, he finally was forced to conduct a war of attrition, hoping for the break-up of the hostile coalition. And this, of course, happened. Luck, a prerequisite for a great captain, did not desert Frederick.

After 1763, however, the Prussian army began to decline. Too many promising officers had been killed off in the wars and the King's prejudices barred promising bourgeois from his service. The enlistment of more and more foreigners reduced tactical flexibility and the creation of new Cantons in the territories acquired in the First Partition of Poland (1772) did not add reliable manpower. Above all, however, the Prussian service was no longer forward looking, becoming instead ever more rigid, conservative, and concerned with the punctilio of 'spit and polish' and the perfection and refinements of drill. Officers like General von Saldern, who solemnly pondered whether 76 paces per minute were not perhaps better than 75 paces a minute, came to have much influence.[6] During the last years of the Frederician army, the dark shadows of defeat already loomed on the horizon.

The imitators of Frederick

But for the moment the victories achieved by Frederick were too overwhelming not to invite imitation. Foreign observers flocked to Potsdam to attend the annual reviews and demonstrations, and frequently the exact drill and evolutions were considered as the main secret of Prussia's success. Books extolling the virtues of Prussian drill found a ready sale and in all things military the Prussian example was eagerly emulated. It was a period of considerable ferment and agitation in military circles, yet many disputes were settled by the statement: 'Oh, but I saw it in Prussia'.

Spain and Russia introduced Prussian drill and Austria followed with Daun's regulations of 1769, close copies of the Prussian model. Even the French regulations of 1764 were indebted to Frederick for some details and in the 1770's, Guibert, perhaps the most important of the reformers, borrowed from Prussia the method of deploying from the centre of a formed column into line. This evolution was formalized in the French regulations of 1791 and remained in use during the French Revolutionary and Napoleonic Wars. And the small British army, preoccupied with colonial warfare and indifferently administered, got along without a standard set of regulations for the movement of formed units, until it adopted the *Principles of Military Movement* by Colonel Dundas, another admirer of Frederick.

Light infantry in the eighteenth century

While during the wars of the eighteenth century the rigid patterns of the line and of limited mobility prevailed for the most part, there also arose a need for 'light' troops, capable of both scouting and raiding, and also for employment in situations where the line regiments could not operate. The first requirement was met by the augmentation of light cavalry, a branch that never had gone out of style in eastern Europe. Hussars, *Chasseurs à cheval*, 'Light Dragoons', and others, often wearing elaborate uniforms adapted from the Hungarian light horse in the Austrian service, appeared in western European campaigns and by the middle of the century had become a standard component in all cavalry. And because of the nature of their duties light cavalry troopers had to be reliable men, they were chosen carefully, treated better than ordinary soldiers, and soon came to be regarded as an elite force.

Light infantry also had never disappeared completely. Most European states had retained small bodies of reliable *Jäger*, hunters and rangers of the great forests, usually rifle armed. These acted as scouts, carried messages, and performed other individual missions. But in the use of large formations of light troops the Austrians were the innovators, fielding in the 1740's thousands of troops from the Military Border, the *Militär-Grenze*, a cordon of military settlers along their ever turbulent frontier with the Ottoman Empire. These 'fierce Croatians' greatly astonished Dr Samuel Johnson and his contemporaries by their barbarous costume and manners. More important, their effectiveness in 'small war', raiding and ambushing, forced Frederick to hastily increase his light cavalry and to recruit some 'free battalions'. France also raised light infantry and cavalry, often combining them in irregular legions. In the British service 'independent companies' of Highlanders had been recruited as early as 1729, combined ten years later into the 42nd Regiment of Foot, the Black Watch. But the real development of light troops in the British army began in America where light companies were added to each battalion in the 1750's and in 1756 a light regiment, the Royal Americans, later the 60th Regiment of Foot, was established.

The Seven Years' War brought further increases in the number of light infantry. In the Austrian army of 1756 the *Grenzer*, now better disciplined and formed into regiments, constituted more than one quarter of the effectives, 34,900 foot and 6,000 horse. No longer restricted to small war, they were assigned to support the line. Deployed as skirmishers on the flanks of the battle order, they poured enfilading fire into the Prussian formations at Lobositz (1756) and Kolin (1757). In 1759 Marshal de Broglie, a forward-looking commander, formed foot *Chasseur* companies in all battalions of the French army in Germany and deployed them as skirmishers some 100 paces ahead of the line. Even Frederick, who detested light troops, was forced once again to follow suit. He hastily augmented his *Jäger* and by 1763 raised 23 new free battalions.

Despite their proven value, for reasons more political and social than military, light troops fell into the background during the last decade before the French Revolution. Basically light troops and their warfare contravened many of the fundamental attitudes and conventions of the regular officers, and their discipline, despite improvements, always had left much to be desired. Their scattered and 'disorderly' methods of fighting conflicted with the orderly and rational pattern so admired in the 'Age of Reason'. Above all, there was a reaction against non-aristocratic officers and most nobles considered command of light troops below their dignity. In Prussia, Frederick dissolved the free battalions as soon as hostilities ended, though he retained a number of Fusilier Regiments, armed with a special weapon, the Fusilier Model 1782, differing from the standard pattern by a slightly greater drop at the heel, designed to improve aiming. He also kept one regiment of *Jäger*, equipped in 1787 with a new short rifle.

In Austria too, except for small detachments of sharpshooters, armed with a double-barrelled short musket, the upper barrel rifled and the lower smooth to allow more rapid loading, all *Grenzer* regiments were reorganized and drilled as troops of the line. While this conformed with the spirit of Daun's regulations, it spoiled their 'natural aptitude which once had made them so formidable', and by 1800 one officer complained that 'the ancient *Grenzer* and Pandours, even as late as the Seven Years' War, had constituted a much better light infantry than the present regulated and drilled *Grenzer*'.[8]

Finally, despite the general reduction in forces after 1783, there was a heated debate in England over the proper role of light troops. The lessons of the American War of Independence suggested to many officers who had been employed in America a need for overhauling the army's tactical doctrines. In America skirmishing had been important and the linear order of battle had been much modified. The number of ranks had been reduced to two; the files had been opened up, and all movement had been executed loosely. All this had been necessary because of the terrain and practical because there was no danger from cavalry. On their return these officers and their new concepts collided with officers whose European combat experiences suggested a different approach. Loose order and emphasis on skirmishing aroused the ire of Colonel Dundas who fumed that light infantry 'instead of being considered an accessory to the battalion . . . have become the principal feature of our army'. But Dundas also realized the need for fast as well as precise evolutions and much of the ridicule heaped on the 'pedantic Scot', and 'old pivot', for allegedly trying to cram the entire art of war into 18 evolutions is misplaced. He did prescribe the three-deep line, but this formation was also retained in the French regulations of 1791 and, except for Wellington, practised by commanders on all sides throughout the wars from 1792 to 1815.[9]

The Russian cult of the bayonet

Whether favouring the closed line or more open tactics, expert opinion generally agreed on the supremacy of firepower over shock. The most significant exception was in Russia where General Suvorov advocated shock tactics, well suited to a country with primitive technology and with masses of illiterate, but combative serf-soldiers. Suvorov rejected the linear system and its fire tactics in favour of impetuous column attacks with the bayonet. He composed a collection of maxims, *The Art of Victory*, to raise the morale and striking power of his soldiers. The short range of the musket, which he estimated at 60 paces, Suvorov asserted, made a rapid and violent bayonet attack, delivered in small columns, capable of advancing over all kinds of terrain, the certain way to success. 'The bullet misses,' he maintained, 'the bayonet does not.' Soldiers were indoctrinated in the key points of his doctrine and at the end of each training day they repeated them in unison, shouting: 'Subordination, Obedience, Discipline, Training, Formations, Military Order, Cleanliness, Neatness, Health, Courage, Bravery, Cheerfulness, Formation Exercise, Victory and Glory!'[10]

Suvorov's personal style of leadership and his primitive but violent tactics were well suited to the temper and training of the warrior masses of Holy Russia. Until he came up against the French in Switzerland, he never lost a campaign, though it must be remembered that he usually fought the poorly disciplined and rather backward forces of the Ottoman Empire and Poland, and often enjoyed Austrian support, providing most of his technical services and a good proportion of the troops.

At that, there remained some basic questions about the quality of the Russian army. Suvorov received many honours from his sovereign, the Tsarina Catherine II, but the main direction of the army was in the hands of Prince Potemkin, Catherine's lover, under whom corruption and neglect negated many of the salutary aspects of Suvorov's reforms.

French Military Developments

After the Seven Years' War there was much agitation and ferment in military circles everywhere in Europe. The most important controversies took place in France where the humiliating defeats of the wars unleashed a flood of books and pamphlets that pointed out the defects and suggested reforms in organization, tactics, and weaponry. Many of these were highly impractical, but others were sound and provided the foundations for the armies of the French Republic and Napoleon.

In tactics the debate between supporters of the deep column formation, *l'ordre profond*, and those favouring the linear *l'ordre mince*, resumed. The argument actually dated back to the years after the War of the Spanish Succession (1701–14), and now it was revived. Baron Mesnil-Durand advocated the column and nothing but the column, while others suggested imitating the Frederician tactics. In the end, however, Count Guibert's famous *Essai général de Tactique*, published in 1772, proved most important. Guibert favoured a synthesis of column and line, *l'ordre mixte*, the column for movement and the line for combat. He conceded that the column was also useful for the attack against woods and fortified posts, but for general fire action he preferred the line, three deep. Guibert was not overly concerned with the uniform alignment of the entire battle line, it was sufficient that each battalion should be aligned within itself and roughly level with the others. The main point was mobility and this required that battalions should be able to change rapidly from the column into line and from line into column. After repeated trials his system was adopted. A provisional drill book was issued in 1788, followed in August 1791 by the definitive edition that, though often disregarded due to circumstances or lack of training, remained in use until 1830.[11]

Guibert's concept of 'tactics' embraced virtually all branches of the art of war. In his *Essai* he advocated greater strategic mobility as well as a citizen army. Troops, he advised, should discard the cumbersome supply system and the luxuries of the camp, travel light, and sustain themselves from the countryside. More rapid movement of armies was becoming practicable by the recent invention of the divisional system, first adopted by Broglie in 1759. The divisional organization, standard in France by the 1780's, provided mixed bodies of infantry and artillery, which could march in separate columns and were strong enough to fight independent actions. For battle, these divisions would rapidly unite into an army. The advantage of marching divided, but uniting for battle, particularly useful in mountain warfare, was further elaborated by Pierre de Bourcet's little book, *Principles de la Guerre des Montagnes*, thought to have provided the techniques used in Napoleon's first campaign.[12]

Finally, contemporary improvements in artillery, still considered by Guibert only as a 'most useful auxiliary', enabled guns to keep up with marching troops. Enhanced mobility on the march and on the battlefield led the Chevalier Du Teil to propose a more important role for artillery in battle. He suggested that guns should open the battle and then move rapidly to enfilade the length of the enemy line. Above all, he asserted that 'we must concentrate the greatest quantity of fire on the principal points and on the weak spots that are most threatened'.[13] Napoleon, a gunner by training, almost certainly read Du Teil and was influenced by him.

Guibert also prophesied victory to the first European nation to develop a 'vigorous citizen soldiery'. Taking up a theme then popular among intellectuals, he argued that limited wars had made the governments of Europe weak and the peoples soft. 'But suppose,' he continued in a much quoted passage, 'that a people should arise in Europe vigorous in spirit, in government, in the means at its disposal, a people who with hardy qualities should combine a national army and a settled plan of aggrandizement. We should see such a people subjugate its neighbours.' But Guibert soon realized that such a change involved not only an army but also a government very different from that of the contemporary French monarchy, and this vision went too far for a loyal aristocrat and an admirer of the great Frederick. In 1779 he recanted. 'When I wrote that book I was ten years younger. The vapours of modern philosophy heated my head and clouded my judgment.' In his *Défence du Système de Guerre Moderne*, published in 1779, Guibert stressed the value of the long service professional soldier and emphasized that citizen armies could not stand against regulars. Above all, he praised the system of limited war as the 'most scientific . . . and the most advantageous for governments and nations'.[14]

By this time, though, in distant America citizen armies actually were fighting British and German professionals and not doing too badly at it.

The improvement of artillery

The 'new artillery' that Guibert had mentioned and Du Teil had written about was just then coming into existence. Improved guns and carriages would provide greater firepower and mobility for the warfare of the French Revolution and Napoleon. Although often credited to Gribeauval, who became Inspector General of Artillery in France after the Seven Years' War, the development rested on Austrian, Dutch, English, and Prussian innovations and applications.

Artillery comprised a number of weapons with different characteristics. Cannon, long barrelled, designed to fire a solid round shot along a relatively flat trajectory; howitzers, with a shorter barrel, throwing an explosive shell in a moderately curved trajectory, and finally mortars lobbing an explosive projectile in an extremely curved trajectory. The first two weapons were also capable of firing a variety of anti-personnel scatter projectiles.

We are here concerned with field artillery only, that is guns and howitzers. Field artillery had to be mobile, which required above all a reduction in weight.

In 1742 Benjamin Robins had placed gunnery on a scientific footing, while at about the same time, beginning in Holland, new methods of casting gun barrels were adopted. Previously guns were cast hollow around a core and it was difficult to prevent the core from moving in the mould. A method of drilling a barrel that had been cast solid was devised at the Hague foundry and perfected in 1747. The Dutch tried to keep the process a secret, but without much success and it was generally adopted in Europe. Drilling produced a better aligned bore with closer tolerances, which together with more precise casting of round shot of true sphericity, greatly reduced windage, the difference between the actual diameters of shot and bore. Less gas pressure escaped and this enabled reduced charges to throw projectiles with greater accuracy and the same velocity over the same distances. Lighter charges meant that barrels could be shortened and made thinner, resulting in a significant saving in weight.

Gun barrels were produced both in bronze and iron. Bronze, a mixture of 10 parts copper to one part tin, was lighter and also considered more durable. Well-made bronze barrels could last, so experiments conducted in 1777 in Vienna showed, for 6,000 to 7,000 consecutive firings. For siege and garrison artillery, where weight mattered less, the cheaper iron barrels were commonly utilized.

During the first part of the eighteenth century France led in artillery, possessing the only unified range of artillery, the de Vallière system, comprizing a series of pieces from four to 24 pounds, sturdy but extremely heavy. No other power had such a complete system.[15] Prussia relied primarily on its rapid musketry; English artillery was outdated and of many calibres, mainly light, and the Austrian artillery was weak in numbers and antiquated in design. Encountering the superior Prussian fire during the War of the Austrian Succession (1740–8), efforts were made to improve the Habsburg artillery. In 1744 Prince Liechtenstein was appointed its Director General. He established an artillery school near Budweis, providing both practical and theoretical instruction, as well as designs for a range of light and manoeuvreable field pieces, 3-, 6-, and 12-pounders, supplemented by some excellent howitzers.[16] At the beginning of the Seven Years' War the Austrian army had been re-equipped with new light pieces, so good that other Powers copied them. Prussia adopted the light Austrian 12-pounder, and as late as 1803 France introduced an exact copy of Liechtenstein's field howitzer. Gribeauval, who served in the Austrian artillery from 1756 to 1762, undoubtedly learned much from Liechtenstein and his assistants.

Austrian improvements and the gradual destruction of his veteran infantry made Frederick lean more heavily on artillery. In addition to copying from the Austrians, he introduced a Prussian designed heavy field piece, the 12-pounder *Brummer,* and compensated for the declining quality of his infantry by increasing the number of his guns, reaching almost six pieces to every 1,000 men, a ratio far exceeding that later attained by Napoleon. Although he was primarily an infantry general, he did not shrink from experimentation. To keep pace with cavalry movements, he developed a horse artillery that moved rapidly along with the mounted troops. Of course, ultralight pieces, galloper guns, had been employed by cavalry for some time, but Frederick's horse artillery, introduced in 1759, used light 6-pounders. The innovation caused much comment and was speedily adopted by most European countries.[17]

Frederick also realized that heavier shot was more effective because of its greater hitting power. At Hohenfriedberg (1745) and at Leuthen he employed heavy siege pieces, 24-pounders, to batter Austrian fortified positions; at Rossbach and Burkersdorf (1762) batteries established at important points opened the fight and protected the deployment of his infantry and cavalry columns. He also experimented with howitzers and prescribed their use to search reverse slopes and to shell enemies behind fortifications. In 1763 he ordered production of a medium 10-pound howitzer and assembled an artillery reserve of 70 such pieces.

Prussia, however, could not afford the expense of introducing an entire new system. It continued to employ a wide variety of types and calibres, and Frederick, unhappy about the developing artillery race, repeatedly complained about the ruinous cost of the new armament.

This was the situation when, on his return to France, Gribeauval was called to reorganize the artillery. He created distinct material for field, siege, garrison, and coast artillery, a complete system including weapons, carriages, limbers, ammunition chests, and the tools required to service it. This was the artillery

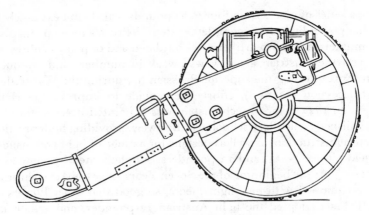

FIG. 3.   Gribeauval howitzer.

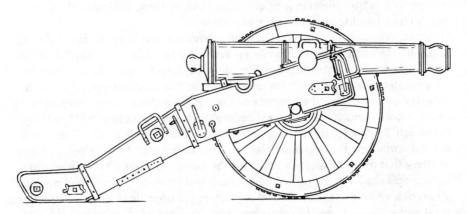

FIG. 4.   Gribeauval 12-pounder.

which was to serve the French armies from Valmy to Waterloo. But the great
reform was bitterly opposed by a group of artillery officers, led by the younger
de Vallière, the 'reds' who opposed the 'blue' proponents of the new system
and delayed its introduction until 1776. The Gribeauval system consisted of
a range of 4-, 8-, and 12-pounder field guns, together with 8- and 6-inch bore
howitzers. It featured standardized carriages with interchangeable parts, iron
axles, limbers, and sights. Weight reduction was achieved by making the
carriage lighter and narrower and by casting the barrels thinner and shorter,
modifications that no longer affected range. Overall the Gribeauval pieces
were about half as heavy as their predecessors. The new 12-pounder, for
instance, weighed only 1,600 pounds, half as much as the cannon it replaced.

For greater ease in transportation, the Gribeauval carriages featured two
positions for the trunnions; the forward position for firing and the rear
position, providing better balance, for travel. Mobility was further enhanced
by the practice of pair-harnessing the draft horses.[18] The Gribeauval system
featured calibrated rearsights and an elevating screw mechanism, two innova-

tions providing greater ease and accuracy in aiming the piece. A solid screw placed under the breech enabled gunners to elevate and lower the muzzle, while the new rearsight, a graduated tangent sight also placed at the breech, could be set to compensate for the drop of the projectile when firing at greater than point-blank range. The tangent sights and the elevating screw have been called the 'most significant improvements in the design of ordnance during the last two hundred years of the smooth-bore era'.[19]

Improvements in carriages, barrels, and aiming devices were complemented by improvements in loading and firing the guns, and in the propellant itself. After 1765 the slow-match or port-fire ignition was generally replaced by the quick-match vent tube. Made of tin, reed, or quill, this tube was filled with an explosive mixture, usually mealed powder, and inserted into the vent of the piece. The port-fire was still required to ignite the tube, but this provided a much stronger ignition flash. By the 1780's it was in general use in all European artilleries, except for the increasingly backward Ottoman service. At the same time, loading was made faster by the use of prepacked charges containing the proper weight of powder, usually one-third the weight of the shot, except for the short British 6-pounder which took a charge of only one-fourth the weight of its projectile. A special tool, the vent pricker, was provided to clear the vent and to break open the serge or flannel powder bags.

Finally, there were improvements in the propellant, blackpowder. It consisted of a mixture of saltpetre, charcoal, and sulphur, the exact proportions varying very little from country to country. British powder in 1781 was made out of 75 parts saltpetre, 15 parts charcoal, and 10 parts sulphur; in Prussia the mixture was 75, 13.3, and 11.5 parts respectively. The English product, manufactured in Crown-owned powder mills at Faversham and Ballincolig, was considered the best due to a suggestion made by Richard Watson, a many-sided cleric, who introduced the technique of making charcoal in closed containers; in part it was due to the superior quality of saltpetre imported from India.

Next to money perhaps the most critical commodity in warfare, saltpetre or potassium nitrate, was in short supply. Formed by the decomposition of organic materials, it flourished best in tropical climates. Continental governments searched for it in stables and cellars, and by the mid-eighteenth century artificial production methods were established. As early as 1748 Prussia and Sweden established *nitrières*, walled enclosures operating like compost pits, and in 1783 the French government offered a prize for the industrial manufacture of this vital material. The final process was invented by Nicolas Leblanc who, sometime between 1791 and 1794, set in operation a factory at St Denis near Paris.

All these technical developments required even better-educated gunners, and in the eighteenth century, though no longer a guild, artillerymen continued to display a distinctive *esprit de corps*, a special pride in belonging to a 'scientific corps'. Unlike the bulk of the soldiers who were drilled to follow orders, even the enlisted gunner had to have at least some rudimentary technical training. In the advanced artillery schools established in Austria and

France, officers and men shared classes and instructions and on the eve of the French Revolution the artillery was the most democratic branch in the armies.

The impact of technical innovations on the art of war

Important as these various improvements were, it has to be conceded that the period from the early eighteenth century to the middle of the nineteenth century showed a remarkable stability in military technology. The tools of land warfare in the most important branch, infantry, remained essentially unchanged, and cavalry weapons remained equally stable. As for artillery the substantial progress in material loading, and aiming, created new tactical possibilities for the more mobile guns. Now they could keep pace with the changing tactical requirements of a battle and be deployed at the decisive point, where outranging musketry, they could produce a very substantial volume of fire. Even so, as a rule this was insufficient to challenge the supremacy of infantry. There now were three major combatant arms, but infantry remained the queen of battle.

This is not to say that the new artillery did not play a considerable role in the French Revolutionary and Napoleonic Wars. But the decisive changes cannot be attributed to technical causes, weapons, formations, or tactics. They can be found in political and social factors that changed the nature of war and of armies and the intellectual premises of their employment.

During the eighteenth century Europe's military potential had increased greatly. There were more men, more food, more metals, and during the wars between 1792 and 1815, governments exercising far greater power than absolutist monarchs, increasingly exploited this potential. Intellectuals like Mably, Voltaire, and Rousseau had attacked the system of limited war and its caste-ridden armies as contrary to Nature, the Rights of Man, and Reason. They advocated a 'natural army', often envisaged as a popular militia that would disband at the end of hostilities. But they failed to foresee that these armies would make wars more bloody and intense than the limited warfare they ridiculed, and that these armies would become a 'nation of the camps', and elevate their own leader, a ruler more powerful and more absolute than the king they opposed.

The pre-Revolutionary crisis of the French army

In the last 30 years of the *ancien régime* some of the ideas advocated by the military reformers actually were introduced to the French by a series of reformist war ministers, Choiseul (1761–70), Saint Germain (1775–7), and Puységeur (1788–9). The list of changes was impressive and included a reduction in the proprietary rights of the colonels, improvement in the soldier's pay, and better housing by the construction of barracks. Military schools and medical facilities were improved. Armament was modernized and the supply system slightly modified.

Many of the reforms were put in their final form by a War Council, sitting in 1787–8, with Guibert as its recording secretary. The Council reduced the enormously swollen commissioned ranks, some 36,000 officers of whom only 13,000 at most were actually on duty (though all received pay), to 9,578 officers with the regiments and another 2,500 either on detached service or retired. It introduced a complete divisional reorganization. The country was divided into 21 divisional districts, corresponding to the number of permanent divisions. It revised regulations and drill manuals, equalized regimental establishments and passed on the final text of the 1791 regulations. All in all, the army was one of the best organized and trained forces of the *ancien régime*.

And yet all was not well. Below the surface of the army, perhaps reflecting the condition of French society as a whole, ran a deep fault that already had damaged its cohesion. As one historian put it: 'On one side of the line were the *bourgeoisie*, and the common people with the non-commissioned officers and the men of the army, on the other side were the King, the nobles, and the officers.'[20] In fact, this oversimplified matters. Within the officer corps an aristocratic reaction challenged the rights of officers who had been promoted from the ranks and those who came from recently ennobled families. In 1781 the old nobility, the *noblesse de race*, managed to obtain a royal edict requiring that in the future officer candidates had to furnish proof of at least four generations of noble ancestors. This exclusionary decree alienated the middle-class officers who had bought commissions and dashed the hopes for advancement of deserving non-commissioned officers, among whom were men destined to rise high in later years – Quartermaster Sergeant Bernadotte, Company Sergeant Major Lefebvre, Murat, Ney, and many others.

In addition there was also a deep rift within the old nobility itself. The court nobles who held most of the higher posts, looked down on the equally ancient, but impoverished, country nobles who filled the regimental posts, especially in the infantry. Under the *ancien régime* it would have been almost as difficult for Napoleon to achieve high rank as a non-noble. All nobles, court or country, started their careers at the lowest rank. But though a sub-lieutenancy was free, higher rank had to be bought, and while the country noble languished in low rank, at most hoping to purchase at long last a captaincy from some elderly incumbent, favour and wealth jumped the court nobles ahead. Some became colonels before they were 20, though they spent much time at court and little with their regiment. At that, these court nobles were by no means devoted to the Crown. In 1788, when troops were sent to put down an aristocratic rebellion against a new and more equitable tax scheme that would have deprived the nobles of substantial benefits, their colonels refused to obey. Powerless to enforce his will, the King had to give way. To procure authorization for new taxes, he now summoned the Estates General to meet the following year.

But the example of high-ranking officers refusing to carry out orders had not been lost on the men. The French army, in contrast with many other contemporary forces, was mainly recruited from native volunteers. About 18,000 new recruits were enrolled annually, almost one-third of them from Paris. These men were by no means isolated from the political currents of the day, and the example of their officers as well as outside agitation eroded their discipline and loyalty and the Revolution turned them into activists almost overnight. The French royal army was the Revolution's first victim.

By that time there was widespread unrest throughout the whole of western and even parts of eastern Europe. Poland simmered with discontent; a popular revolt against the Dutch prince had been put down by Prussian intervention in 1787; a similar revolt in the Austrian Netherlands, however, succeeded. Hungary was restive; the Gordon riots disrupted life in London, there were disturbances in Ireland, discontent in Spain and Italy. But all these disturbances once they assumed proportions threatening the interests of a major power, could be quelled by military intervention such as Prussia carried out in Holland in 1787. But if a major upheaval was to occur in France, despite its internal divisions Europe's strongest power, any intervention would plunge the continent into turmoil. And this is what happened in 1792.

NOTES

1. J.L.A. Colin, *The Transformations of War*, trs. L.H.R. Pope-Hennessy, H. Rees, London, 1912, 206.
2. Cited in G. Ritter, *The Sword and the Scepter*, trs. H. Norden, University of Miami Press, Coral Gables, 1969, 41–2.
3. J. Morvan, *Le Soldat Impérial*, Plon, Paris, 1904, vol. I, 364–5.
4. L. Kennett, *The French Armies in the Seven Years' War*, Duke University Press, Durham, N.C., 1967, 119.
5. Cited in P. Paret, *Yorck and the Era of Prussian Reform*, Princeton University Press, 1966, 14.
6. C. Duffy, *The Army of Frederick the Great*, Hippocrene Books, New York, 1974, 202–3.
7. G.E. Rothenberg, *The Military Border in Croatia, 1740–1881*, University of Chicago Press, 1966, 18–20.
8. Cited in *ibid.*, 94–5.
9. M. Glover, *Peninsular Preparation*, Cambridge University Press, 1963, 117–21.
10. P. Longworth, *The Arts of Victory*, Holt, Rinehart & Winston, New York, 1965, 218–20.
11. Discussion and excerpts in S. Wilkinson, *The French Army before Napoleon*, Oxford University Press, 1915, 54–83.
12. D. Chandler, *The Campaigns of Napoleon*, Macmillan, New York, 1966, 31.
13. In Wilkinson, *op cit.*, 80–1.
14. R.R. Palmer, 'Frederick the Great, Guibert, Bülow: From Dynastic to National War', in E.M. Earle, ed., *Makers of Modern Strategy*, Princeton University Press, 1948, 64–7.
15. M. Lauerma, *L'Artillerie de Campagne Française pendant les Guerres de la Révolution*, Suomalainen Tiedeakatemia, Helsinki, 1956, 10–11, 14–18.
16. A. Dolleczek, *Geschichte der österreichischen Artillerie*, Selbstverlag, Vienna, 1887, 290–2.
17. Duffy, *op cit.*, 112–14, 118–22.
18. Lauerma, *op cit.*, 14–18, 144.
19. B.P. Hughes, *Firepower Weapons Effectiveness on the Battlefield, 1630–1850*, Charles Scribner's Sons, New York, 1974, 18.
20. Wilkinson, *op cit.*, 98.

2

The French Revolutionary and Napoleonic Wars: from Valmy to Waterloo

Introducing the budget in February 1792, Prime Minister Pitt assured the House of Commons that 'there never was a time in the history of this country, when, from the situation in Europe, we might more reasonably expect fifteen years of peace than we may at the present moment'. But that was not to be. There would be no 'peace in our time'. Instead, within a month, there began a series of conflicts which lasted, with few interruptions, until 1815.

For 23 long years the European powers fought against the armies of the French Revolution and Napoleon. As these armies gained ascendency, they employed the organizational, tactical, and strategic techniques developed during the previous decades. To counter them, their opponents had to adopt many, if not all of the new ways, and Europe passed out of the days of the small professional dynastic armies and entered those of national conscription and big battalions. These developments are discussed in some detail in the later chapters; this chapter is designed to provide no more than a historical and chronological background and a condensed analysis of the major campaigns from Valmy to Waterloo.

The coming of war: 1789–92
At the outset, news of the Revolution in France had not caused undue concern in the various European capitals; rather the contrary. France, with its 25 million inhabitants, was by far the strongest continental power and if it was preoccupied with internal troubles, the balance of power and a degree of general tranquility in Europe seemed assured. This, of course, was the basis for Pitt's strange prophecy.

By 1792, however, earlier evaluations of the Revolution had been replaced by apprehension in many quarters. The Estates General summoned in 1789 by Louis XVI to raise new taxes, had transformed themselves in a Constituent Assembly which, backed by a huge armed citizen militia, the National Guard, had forced a reluctant monarch to accept the Constitution of 1791. This document drastically reduced royal power and a ministry, responsible to a Legislative Assembly, now ruled in Paris. Disgusted at this turn of events the King himself had tried to flee in June 1791, but was caught at Varennes and brought back, in plain fact a prisoner of the revolutionaries. Many Royalists, including a considerable number of aristocratic officers, left the country at this time.

During the winter of 1791-2 relations between France and the European courts deteriorated. In particular there was bad feeling between Austria and France. On 7 February 1792 Austria signed a defensive alliance with Prussia. Three weeks later Emperor Leopold II died in Vienna and was replaced by the more bellicose Francis II. Even so, neither Austria nor Prussia really wanted war; they were more concerned with gaining new territories in Poland. However, the decision for war came from Paris. In the Legislative Assembly the powerful Girondins, basically Republican, favoured war in order to consolidate the Revolution, while the remaining Royalists hoped that an external conflict would strengthen the constitutional monarchy. On 20 April 1792, General Dumouriez, an opportunist soldier and then Foreign Minister, and Louis XVI, by that time king in name only, called on the Assembly for a declaration of war. The same evening the Assembly, claiming that Austria was preparing for armed intervention, declared war against the 'King of Hungary and Bohemia', and by implication also on Prussia. This act, so the Assembly declared, was the 'just defence of a free people against the unjust aggression of a King'.

The first campaigns : 1792–3
At this point France was totally unprepared for active military operations. Political conditions were chaotic, the finances in ruin, and the royal army deteriorated. During the early years of the Revolution the doctrines of *'liberté, egalité, fraternité'*, combined with political agitation had eroded discipline. Radical political cells challenged the officers' authority in many units; there were local mutinies, and a great number of desertions. The gaps left by the resignation or emigration of officers had not been filled, and there was mutual suspicion between the officers and the men throughout the army. To strengthen the disorganized and still distrusted regulars, the Assembly had called for 100,000 volunteers from the National Guard. These were to serve for one campaign only, elect their own officers, and receive better pay than the regulars. Even so, the response had not been satisfactory and only about one-third of the required number had come forward; they were poorly disciplined and unreliable.[1]

No wonder then that the first campaign began badly. The three French armies hastily assembled on the eastern frontier, designated respectively as the Army of the North, the Centre, and the Rhine, numbered about 130,000 in all. Dumouriez, who now came forward as the chief strategic planner, pressed for the immediate invasion of Belgium, then the Austrian Nether-lands, where the French expected to be welcomed as liberators. But when on 28 April 1792 elements of the French armies advanced into Belgium, they experienced their first encounter with the enemy. Crying 'treason' they panicked, set upon their officers, and murdered one divisional commander. Further advances brought similar results and by the end of June the invasion of Belgium had collapsed. Austrian troops, in turn, advanced into Flanders to besiege Lille.

News of these setbacks, combined with economic distress, radical agitation, and a threatening manifesto by the Duke of Brunswick, commander of the Austro–Prussian army then assembling on the frontier, triggered a savage radical uprising in Paris. The King's remaining Swiss Guards, some 600 in all, were massacred, the monarchy suspended, and many Royalists arrested. At this, the Marquis de Lafayette, known for his services in the American Revolution and then commanding in Flanders, attempted a *coup d'état*, and, when it failed, crossed over to the Austrians. A few days later Marshal Montesquiou, commanding the southern sector, followed suit. Dumouriez now assumed command of the Army of the North, while Kellermann, a crusty old regular, retained command of the Army of the Centre. The bulk of Dumouriez's troops consisted of volunteers; Kellermann's units were largely regular. In Paris, meanwhile, the Assembly proclaimed the nation in danger, called up more volunteers, and mobilized the National Guards.

But the Austrians and Prussians, joined by the Sardinians in the south, were quite as unprepared for serious operations as the French. The Austrian army had not yet entirely recovered from its last war against the Ottoman Empire (1788–91), there was trouble brewing in Hungary, and large numbers of troops were retained in the eastern provinces. Prussia too was preoccupied with preparations to invade Poland and could employ only a part of her total forces. By mid-summer the Duke of Brunswick had collected some 130,000 men, about half Prussian, one-third Austrian, and the rest Hessian and a rag-tag contingent of French Royalists. A strategist of the old school, Brunswick moved west from his base at Coblentz on the Rhine in slow stages, about five miles a day. On 19 August 1792 he crossed the French frontier. Longwy and Verdun, two border fortresses, capitulated as the Duke continued his methodical advance on Paris. But even at this slow rate, his army dwindled. Garrisons were left behind to safeguard the line of communications, the weather turned bad, and scores of men died daily from dysentery. By mid-September his army was reduced to 50,000 effectives and his resolution was fading.

On 20 September, finally, with about 40,000 men, Brunswick came up against the combined armies of Dumouriez and Kellermann, standing on the defensive in a well-chosen position near Valmy. After an indecisive artillery duel, and surprised at the steadiness revealed by Kellermann's troops, the Duke halted the engagement. Ten days later, without firing another shot, he began to withdraw slowly back to Germany. His decision was quite sound. Even if victorious, his army, enfeebled by sickness and its artillery and supply train mired down by the incessant rains, could no longer hope to attain its objective. Still, his decision, though tactically correct, had enormous political consequences. On the day of Valmy, a newly elected and more radical assembly, the National Convention met for the first day in Paris. The next day it decreed the abolition of the monarchy and proclaimed France a Republic.

Campaigns of the First Coalition : 1793–5

At the cost of a few hundred casualties the Revolution had been saved. French morale soared as Republican armies regained the initiative. From Alsace, General Custine seized Mayence, an important bridgehead on the right bank of the Rhine, and went on to take Frankfurt. In the south, French troops conquered Savoy and Nice from Sardinia, and in the north Dumouriez renewed the invasion of Belgium. On 6 November 1792, with 40,000 men, he surprised 14,000 Austrians in their winter quarters at Jemappes, defeated them, and rapidly occupied most of the country. Exultant, the Convention voted on 19 November to extend its 'aid to all peoples who wish to recover their liberty'. The Revolution was challenging the entire European political and social order, and in a further gesture of defiance, it tried and executed Louis XVI in January 1793. Even more, on 1 February the Convention declared war on England and Holland and the next month it announced the annexation of Belgium. All of which brought together the First Coalition, a rather ill-assorted alliance of Austria, Prussia, Sardinia, Naples, Spain, the minor German states, with England, Holland, and Portugal.

Potentially, of course, the Coalition was very strong, but this hardly worried the French who now considered themselves unbeatable. Many volunteer units disbanded while the Convention, split by bitter factional quarrels between the more moderate Girondins and the more radical Jacobins, allowed the supply system to fall to pieces. For a few months the Coalition held the upper hand but by as early a date as February 1793 an Austrian army under the Prince of Coburg, 40,000 strong, defeated Dumouriez in a series of engagements and then routed him on 18 March at Neerwinden. Forced to evacuate Belgium and worried about the personal consequences of his defeat, Dumouriez opened negotiations with Coburg and tried to rally his troops against Paris. The attempt failed and on 5 April he deserted to the enemy, accompanied by some officers and a cavalry regiment.

France now fell into desperate straits. During the winter of 1792–3 the Convention had decreed a forced levy of 300,000 men. This measure, combined with political and religious discontents, provoked Royalist uprisings in Brittany and in the Vendée region at the mouth of the Loire. The Jacobins' seizure of complete control in the Convention in May (executing many of their political enemies in the process), lead several large provincial cities in the south into armed resistance. Lyon, Toulouse, and Marseilles were lost. In August, Toulon, the main French naval base on the Mediterranean, drove out the Republican authorities and admitted a British naval squadron. Surrounded by hostile armies, torn by savage civil war, the new France faced an unnerving crisis.

But the First Coalition, fragmented by divergent war aims and mutual suspicions, would not seize its opportunity. In January 1793, Prussian and

Russian troops marched into Poland; if Prussia instead had committed her entire army against France, an allied victory would have been likely. As it was, her military effort in the west was limited, while Austria, still hoping to gain Polish territory, also held back a considerable proportion of her forces – ambitions which kept Russia from joining the Coalition. The British meanwhile were busy adding to their colonial empire, 'filching sugar islands', and merely wished to drive the French from the Channel ports. As for the other lesser powers, these counted for little. Throughout the summer of 1793 Allied military operations were few and uncoordinated as the various commanders each pursued his government's separate schemes. On the French side confusion reigned.

Thus the Allies frittered away most of the late spring and summer and provided time for a government of national defence in Paris to take hold. On the central front the Prussians recaptured Mayence in July and a Spanish army advanced some miles into the Pyrenees. However, not all was success for the Allies; on the crucial northern front Coburg was first delayed by some minor frontier fortresses and then, when the Duke of York appeared with a small British contingent, mostly Hanoverians and Hessian mercenaries, he had orders to capture Dunkirk. He was assisted by a Dutch force under the Prince of Orange and Coburg even gave him an Austrian detachment, but, lacking siege guns, the Duke could do very little. The main Austrian army meanwhile marched south to invest Maubeuge, and together the Allies established a thin cordon stretching through Flanders, but without strength at any point.

In Paris the Convention had established a strong executive body, the Committee of Public Safety, in April. This Committee, soon controlled by the fanatic Robespierre, instituted a dictatorship, the 'Terror', enforcing national unity and organization.

Claiming at least 20,000 lives, the Terror saved the Revolution. Its military affairs were handled by Lazare Carnot, a captain of engineers, a superb administrator, the famed 'organizer of victory'. Until Napoleon seized power, eventually driving the austere Republican into exile, Carnot directed military strategy, training, procurement and, when the recruitment of troops lagged, prevailed on the Convention to decree the *levée en masse* of 23 August 1793, calling to arms all unmarried men between 18 and 25 years of age.[2] Although in practice execution of the decree fell far short of its proclaimed principles of universal conscription, it provided Carnot, at least potentially, with numerical superiority over the small professional armies of his adversaries. By September he had concentrated 100,000 men in Flanders; by the end of the year there were over 500,000 men in the French field armies alone. To supervise their enlistment, training, and operations, the Committee and the Convention sent special 'deputies on mission', the forerunners of the Russian military commissars, to each army and each of the French departments.

Although France clearly was becoming more powerful, the Allies still would not make a concerted effort. Quite the contrary, Prussia, angry about Habsburg machinations in Poland, scaled down her operations. By this time, except for the Vendée and Toulon, Republican authority was restored throughout France. Now they were prepared to push the remaining allied forces from the French territory in the north-east. Between 6 and 8 September 1793 General Houchard with the Army of the North defeated a poorly handled British–Dutch–Austrian force at Hondschoote and lifted the siege of Dunkirk. A week later, however, he suffered a setback at Courtrai, and having run afoul of the Deputies, was accused of treason, speedily arrested, tried and executed. The Terror demanded victories; failure was inexcusable and punished. That year 17 generals suffered execution and 67 more went to the scaffold in 1794.

Houchard was succeeded by Jourdan who managed to gain an important victory. The allies, and for that matter the French still used the old cordon strategy of the eighteenth century, that is they distributed their troops in a thin line along the Franco-Belgian frontier, with neither side concentrating strength at a critical point. Despite protests that he was leaving France open to invasion, Carnot ordered Jourdan to collect units from the frontier fortresses and concentrate them south of Maubeuge. In this fashion Jourdan assembled a two-to-one tactical superiority at Wattignies and on 16–17 October gained a major victory that relieved Maubeuge. Further south, in the Alsace, an Austrian offensive under Wurmser had breached the defences of the Wissembourg lines. But new and energetic generals, Pichegru commanding the Army of the Moselle and Hoche that of the Rhine, drove Wurmser back across the river in late December. Also in that month, after a bitter siege that lasted for several months, Republican troops recaptured Toulon. During the operations a young artillery officer, Captain Napoleon Bonaparte, had repeatedly distinguished himself. Rapidly promoted to Major and Lieutenant-Colonel, he was rewarded after the fall of Toulon with the temporary rank of Brigadier-General.[3]

In this fashion France had surmounted the crisis of 1793. It had been saved by the Terror and by its new armies, poorly equipped, often half-starved, and only indifferently armed. But this was no mere rabble in arms. The senior commanders, often non-commissioned or junior officers of the old royal army, were resourceful and active and the Deputies on mission, though many were bloodthirsty and unjust, indoctrinated the troops with a 'Republican spirit', new morale, and determination to fight.

By late 1793 the new armies had improvized tactics emphasizing skirmishing, the use of terrain, and tactical mobility. Lacking cumbersome supply trains, the French lived off the land, bivouacked in the open, and so were capable of more rapid movement. Combining the striking power of mass and mobility, and with human life cheap and heavy casualties easily replaced by conscription, they obeyed Carnot's orders to 'act offensively and in mass . . . and to pursue the enemy until he is utterly destroyed'.

The campaigns of 1794
The capabilities of the French Republican armies further improved when

early in 1794 the so-called *amalgame* combined the volunteer and conscript battalions with the remaining veterans of the old army into new regiments, now styled 'demi-brigades'. Several demi-brigades, together with some artillery and cavalry, formed a division and several divisions, the number varied, were combined into field armies. In 1794 there were 11 field armies as well as an Army of the Interior. The three largest field armies were deployed in the east. On paper, at least, the Army of the North numbered 245,822, that of the Moselle 102,323, and that of the Rhine 98,930. The remaining armies, of the Alps, Ardennes, Italy, Pyrenees, and the Coasts, varied between 60,000 to 22,000 men.[4] Not all of this vast host was effective but the balance in manpower now clearly favoured the French. When strategic or political considerations demanded, new armies were formed. Later that year, for instance, another large force, the famous Army of the Sambre and Meuse, was constituted from units of the Armies of the North, the Ardennes, and the Moselle.

The commanders and the military systems of the First Coalition were hard pressed to deal with the new style of warfare. In 1794 the full power of the French armies made itself felt in a series of offensives that ended the First Coalition. In the north Carnot had prepared a two-pronged attack. Pichegru with the Army of the North, now rated at 160,000, was to make the main effort in the Belgian and Dutch coastal plain, while the army of the Sambre and Meuse, some 60,000 strong, was to press towards Liège. On 18 May 1794 Pichegru defeated an inferior Austro–British force at Tourcoing, suffered a check on 22 May at Tournai, but persisted in the offensive and took Ypres on 19 June. Jourdan, meanwhile, had advanced and besieged Charleroi and on 25 June the garrison capitulated. The next day, Coburg, rather belatedly counter-attacked but failed to concentrate at the decisive point and was defeated by Jourdan at Fleurus on 26 June 1794. Although the French suffered double the number of losses than the Allies Fleurus was a turning point. It marked the end of the threat from Belgium. In July, the Allies evacuated Belgium before the armies of Pichegru and Jourdan.

The end of the emergency brought a political change in Paris. Robespierre and his followers had grown increasingly despotic and became dangerous to all who displeased them and on 27 July the opposition turned on him. He was overthrown and speedily executed. Though staunch Jacobins, the new rulers were forced to relax the Terror. The Convention continued until October 1795 when it replaced itself by a new government, the Directory.

Turmoil in Paris did not halt the march of the French armies. In October, Moreau, commanding the Army of the Moselle, forced the Austrians and Prussians to evacuate the entire left bank of the Rhine, while Pichegru completed the conquest of Holland. Great Dutch fortresses fell with surprising ease, and during the bitter winter of 1794–5 a cavalry detachment managed to capture the Dutch fleet, immobilized in the ice off Texel. Many Dutch cities welcomed the French with genuine enthusiasm, while the Austrians and Germans withdrew to the East. The small British army, sacrificing its foreign units in rearguard actions, retreated across north-eastern Holland into Germany, its discipline and cohesion almost totally collapsed. In April

1795, the Royal Navy embarked 'the officers, their carriages, and a large train', but most of the troops were lost'.[5] Although the Duke of York had achieved much with totally inadequate resources he was widely blamed for the fiasco of the British expeditionary force.

But by the time the British sailed away, the Coalition already had disintegrated. On 5 April 1795, Prussia, tired of the war, signed the Treaty of Basle with France. The agreement ceded all Prussian territory on the left bank of the Rhine, provided for a neutral zone in Germany north of the Main River, and promised Prussia future compensations, presumably at Austrian expense. In July, Spain too made peace, as did most of the minor German states. Holland was proclaimed the Batavian Republic, a French satellite state, and only England, Austria, and Sardinia were left in the war.

The campaign of 1795

Because of renewed internal troubles, France was unable to exploit the disintegration of the Alliance. The great effort of the past year had left her exhausted; the government after the purge of Robespierre and his followers was weak and corrupt and the new constitution creating the Directory, taking effect in October, was detested by Royalists and Jacobins alike. There had been a military victory, but the country once again was divided. The poor, who had shed most of the blood, resented the corruption and luxury displayed by the rich and by members of the government, and as the Terror relaxed its hold, there were schemes both on the Right and on the Left to seize power. Revolt flared up again in the Vendée and in Brittany, supported, albeit half-heartedly, by British gold and British armed royalist *emigré* troops. It took six months of hard fighting to destroy the rebels. On 21 July 1795 General Hoche's Army of the West destroyed the Royalist forces at Quiberon Bay, but even this did not settle the issue for good. The problem of the Vendée was only settled by Napoleon, and even then there were always sporadic resistance activities there.

By far the most serious challenge to the Directory came in Paris. In early October it was facing an aroused populace, potentially backed by some 50,000 armed National Guards now largely sympathetic to the Royalists. Barras, one of the Directors, hastily assembled all available general officers in the capital, including General Bonaparte, as he now styled himself, only recently released from prison because of his suspected Jacobin connections. Napoleon realized at once that artillery would be required to support the 7,000 odd soldiers defending the government. Murat, then a cavalry major, managed to get hold of some guns and when the insurgents attacked, Bonaparte dispersed them with the legendary 'whiff of grape shot' (actually canister). A grateful Directory thanked him by an immediate promotion to General of Division and the promise of command of the Army of Italy during the operations planned for 1796.

Meanwhile corruption and treason had also appeared in the field armies in Germany and this accounted for the poor results achieved in 1795. Here, although fighting single-handedly, the Austrians managed to repulse both the Army of the Sambre and Meuse under Jourdan and the Rhine and Moselle under Pichegru. After initial successes in September, both armies were repulsed and forced back across the Rhine. The defeat has been blamed on Pichegru, a man of expensive tastes and high ambitions, who accepted money from a secret British agent, negotiated with the enemy for the restoration of the Bourbons, and generally did his best to ensure failure of the French operations. Although his activities should have aroused suspicion he retained command of his army until March 1796, when he retired voluntarily, and, even more curious, was well received in Paris. General Moreau then assumed command of the Rhine and Moselle Army.[6]

The campaigns in Germany and Italy : 1796–7

The operations planned by Carnot and his embryonic general staff, the Topographical Bureau, for 1796 reflected new military realities. With the French army short of all manner of supplies, the plains aimed at forcing France's remaining enemies to come to terms. Schemes for rasing Europe and for the overthrow of the entire established order had been quietly shelved. The plan envisaged two distinct, but mutually supporting theatres of operations. French armies were to take the offensive both in Germany and on the long stalled Italian front, thus preventing the Austrians from reinforcing the one from the other. The objective was to bring Austria to accept the new frontiers of France. As for England, Hoche's Army of the West was to invade Ireland as soon as the French navy could provide the necessary transport. For her part, Austria had given up hope of recovering Belgium or of overthrowing the government in Paris. It did plan for a combined Austro–Sardinian offensive to clear the French from their foothold in the Italian Alps. Originally Vienna intended to stand on the defensive in the north, but having received its share in the third Partition of Poland, and under pressure from Archduke Charles, the Emperor's younger brother who had assumed command in Germany in December 1795, substantial reinforcements were dispatched and Charles was authorized to act as he considered advisable.

French planning obviously had given priority to the German theatre and the two armies employed there, Jourdan's Sambre and Meuse with 78,000 and Moreau's Rhine and Moselle with 79,500, were far superior in strength to the Army of Italy, which to be sure, had a paper strength of over 100,000, but in fact had less than half that number of effectives, strung out along the southern slope of the Maritime Alps from Nice to the vicinity of Genoa. And while all French armies then were poorly equipped, the Army of Italy was perhaps in the worst shape, sullen, starved, with some formations even lacking muskets.

In 1796 things did not go as planned by Carnot in Germany. Archduke Charles, whom Wellington considered the ablest Allied commander, drove Jourdan back across the Rhine in June, and when he returned in August, defeated him again at Amberg on the 24th and routed him on 3 September at Würzburg.[7] In turn, this left Moreau, who had pushed through Württemberg into Bavaria, at the end of a dangerously exposed line of communications. Moreau now was forced to retreat and this ended the threat to Vienna from the Danube valley. But Napoleon had prevailed in Italy and in January 1797, Charles was hastily called to the southern front.

*   *   *

Napoleon's Italian campaign of 1796–7 was distinguished by brilliant moves that forced superior enemy forces either to surrender or retreat, though lacking sufficient numbers, especially cavalry, Napoleon failed to achieve the total destruction of the opposing armies. But he inflicted substantial casualties, drove the Austrians out of northern Italy, and established his reputation as a great field commander.

The campaign fell into three major stages. In the first he burst from his positions near the coast and, separating the Sardinian and Austrian armies, forced the first to surrender and obliged the second to fall back to the fortresses of Lombardy. During the second phase, Napoleon remained on the strategic defensive. His army, now supplied by a system that combined requisitions with magazines, blockaded a large Austrian force in Mantua, while utilizing its interior position to defeat in turn several Austrian armies approaching to destroy him. In the final phase, after severely mauling the last attempt to relieve Mantua, and after the fortress capitulated, he moved east into Austria. One year to the date that he had taken command his troops were within striking distance of Vienna and Austria hastily signed an armistice and later a peace.

When he assumed command of the Army of Italy on 27 March 1796 it numbered about 45,000 men and 60 pieces of artillery, divided into four widely dispersed divisions and two smaller detachments. Preparatory to taking the offensive he utilized the superior mobility of his troops to regroup, changed the composition of divisions in accordance with their assigned mission, created a small artillery reserve, and formed his horse, about 4,800, into two cavalry divisions. The object, of course, was to constitute an offensive mass against an enemy who was unprepared to withstand a sudden attack in force at any point. The Austrian and Sardinian commanders moved forward to defensive positions blocking the several passes leading from the coast northward into the Po River valley. During ten days in April, Napoleon defeated the Austrians at Montenotte, 11–12 April, and Millesimo, 13–14 April, penetrated the centre of the Allied cordon and on the 22nd routed the Sardinians at Mondovi. An armistice with the Sardinians followed, while the Austrians retreated east into Lombardy. On 10 May, following artillery preparation, Napoleon led a storming column across the Adda bridge at Lodi, a deliberate act to impress his men with his personal bravery. Five days later he entered Milan, capital of Austrian Lombardy. Part of the Austrian armies fell back to cover the Brenner Pass, while the bulk retreated behind the strong fortifications of Mantua which Napoleon invested.

Four times the Austrians tried to raise the siege, but each time Napoleon repulsed the relief force, taking advantage of his interior lines against an enemy who continued to approach with his forces divided. In the first attempt two

Austrian forces tried a converging offensive with two armies; Quasdanovich with 18,000 coming from the North and Wurmser, 36,000, from the northeast. Together these outnumbered the 45,000 French. Abandoning the siege, Napoleon placed himself to prevent a junction of the two enemy forces, succeeded in concentrating first against the one and then against the other, and defeated them in a series of battles at Lonato and Castiglione, 29 July to 5 August 1796. He then returned to invest Mantua. In September the Austrians tried again with similar results, and it was the same in November. This time, however, the French were hard pressed. At Arcola, 15 to 17 November Napoleon with 20,000 men defeated Alvinczy with 24,000 men in a bloody battle in which no less than 14 French general officers were killed. In January 1797 Alvinczy returned with 42,000 men, which Napoleon could parry only with 32,000, having to leave 8,000 to maintain the blockade of Mantua. However, Alvinczy divided his army into three groups. Two smaller groups were sent against Verona and toward Mantua, while the main force, some 28,000 strong encountered Napoleon with about 22,000 at Rivoli, southeast of Verona. The hilly terrain forced Alvinczy to divide his force into several columns which Napoleon attacked as they emerged from the defiles towards the battlefield. Alvinczy suffered a staggering 43 percent losses in killed, wounded and prisoners. The other two forces also were defeated and with all hope for relief gone the 20,000 strong garrison of Mantua capitulated on 3 February.

With his rear secured, Napoleon ordered an all-out advance. Although reinforced, he was still heavily outnumbered by the enemy, but Austrian morale was shattered and even the redoubtable Charles could not rally them. Leaving 40,000 men behind to guard his communications, Napoleon moved forward with 40,000 more. After a four-week march he was deep in Austrian territory and on 18 April, when the heads of the French columns entered Leoben in Styria, only 80 miles from Vienna, the Austrians accepted an armistice and in October there followed a formal treaty, the Peace of Campo Formio. Austria ceded Belgium and Lombardy, agreed to accept French control of the left bank of the Rhine, recognized the establishment of a French satellite state, the Cisalpine Republic in Italy, and in return received Venice and its territories.

The Egyptian expedition : 1798–1801

After Campo Formio, England, except for Portugal, stood alone against France, unable to confront her on land, but maintained her naval blockade and was ever busy to search out and support new allies on the continent. In December 1796, General Hoche with 14,000 troops, escorted by 16 ships of the line, had managed to evade the British blockade and sailed for Ireland. But, disorganized by storms, only a few small detachments were landed in Ireland and these were quickly rounded up. The Directory was willing to listen to Napoleon's proposal to seize Egypt as a base for further operations against England's oriental empire and trade.

In May 1798, Napoleon sailed from Toulon with a carefully equipped force of 35,000, selected from the Army of Italy. Evading the British Mediterranean squadron, he captured Malta, and arrived off Alexandria on 1 July. After seizing the port, the French marched on Cairo. On 21 July, in sight of the Pyramids, they encountered the Mamelukes, a splendid cavalry force, and the actual rulers of Egypt. Their undisciplined, if superb horsemanship, could not prevail against the efficient volleys of the French infantry and guns, drawn up in a tight checkerboard square formation. Scattering the horsemen, the French army entered Cairo the next day. On 1 August, however, Admiral Nelson destroyed the French fleet at Aboukir Bay and Napoleon's army was marooned.

Undaunted, Napoleon now decided on an advance into Syria. Marching with 13,000 men, along the ancient coastal road across the northern Sinai into Palestine he took Jaffa on 7 March, but further up the coast the walls of Acre, defended by units of the Ottoman New Model Army, the *Nizam i Jedid*, assisted by a British landing force, resisted his assault. Although he defeated with ease a Turkish attempt to relieve the fortress, Napoleon lacked heavy siege artillery which had been sent by sea and intercepted by the British navy. On 20 May he lifted the siege and, making a considerable effort to evacuate his wounded and sick, returned to Egypt in mid-June. It was a defeat, in part compensated by his crushing victory over another Turkish army at Aboukir on 5 January 1799.

By this time Napoleon realized that without control of the seas he could not accomplish his objective. Receiving information that the Directory, facing the Second Coalition, was tottering, he decided to abandon his army. On 22 August 1799 he relinquished command to Kléber and managed to return to France, landing on 8 October. Despite growing unrest and British–Turkish pressure, Kléber managed to beat back a number of attacks, but was assassinated in June 1800. On 8 March 1801, the British under Abercromby executed a spectacular assault landing at Aboukir Bay, defeated the French army under Menou, and with Turkish assistance went on to take Alexandria and Cairo. At the end of their strength, the French still managed to negotiate good terms. Menou capitulated, but his army, almost 30,000 strong, was given free passage back to France in August 1801. The ill-starred Egyptian expedition was over.[8]

The war against the Second Coalition, 1798–1802

Shortly after Napoleon's departure for Egypt in the summer of 1797, the British had put together a new Coalition. This time it included Great Britain, Russia, Austria, the Ottoman Empire, Portugal, Naples, and the Papal states. However, except for Austria and Russia, the new Coalition lacked substantial forces, but the corrupt and improvident Directory had allowed the French army also to sink to a wretched level. Austria declared war on 12 March 1799. Jourdan at once crossed the Rhine and advanced through the Black Forest, while in Italy, Masséna moved north towards the Tyrol. But Jourdan's inferior forces were speedily defeated by Charles on 21 March at Ostrach and again on 27 March at Stockach, while Masséna was repulsed at Feldkirch on 23 March. A Russian army under Suvorov was meanwhile marching towards Italy. Even before it arrived, the Austrians under Kray, gained another victory on 5 April 1799 at Magnano. Together with Suvorov they swept the French out of Italy, while Archduke Charles turned against Massena who had fallen back into Switzerland and defeated him in the First Battle of Zurich, 4–6 June 1799.

But the Russians proved touchy allies and friction between Charles and Suvorov led to the Archduke's recall. Left to his own devices, though reinforced by a second Russian force under Korsakov, Suvorov was beaten by Soult in the Second Battle of Zurich, 26–27 September. The volatile Tsar Paul I now ordered Suvorov and his troops to return to Russia.

At the same time, the Coalition did poorly in the north. A joint British–Russian expedition to the Helder Peninsula in Holland, late in 1799, was hampered by acrimonious quarrels between the Duke of York and the Russian commanders and ended in failure and evacuation. Even so, the French had lost most of Italy, and were barely holding on in south-western Germany. The soldiers were discontented and ready for new leadership, while the Directory, too, was looking for a saviour. At this point Napoleon, with the prestige of his alleged triumphs in the Orient, returned. Within a month he ousted the Directory and established a three-man government, the Consulate, with himself as First Consul.[9]

In the course of the campaigns of 1799–1800 the strength of the French field armies had increased to nearly 227,000 men, divided between the Army of Batavia (Brune with 25,000), the Army of the Rhine (Moreau with 146,000) and the Army of Italy (Masséna with 50,000). In addition, another 100,000 remained in the depots and garrisons in France. But the new replacements, conscripted under the Jourdan Law of 1798, had poor morale; desertion and failure to report were common. Already in January 1800 the First Consul had reorganized some units, formed corps and started to organize a strategic Army of Reserve. To the surprise of the French, however, the Austrians launched an offensive, striking against the Army of Italy. Decimated by sickness and disease, the army was defeated and split. One part, under Masséna, was driven into Genoa; the other, under Suchet, retreated to Nice.

In Germany, on the other hand, the French had done better. On 3 May, Moreau defeated Kray at Stockach, won another victory two days later at Moskirch, and yet another on 19 June at Hochstädt. A few days later and armistice halted fighting until November.

In May 1800 Bonaparte led the Army of the Reserve into Italy. The main body came across the Great St Bernard Pass, while diversionary attacks were launched through the Mont Cenis, Simplon, and St Gotthard passes. Surmounting considerable obstacles the First Consul debouched into the Lombard plain, threatened the Austrians' lines of communication, and occupied Milan on 2 June. He had hoped to relieve Masséna, but came too late. On 4 June, Masséna and his men, weakened by starvation, capitulated after one of the grimmest sieges on record. They did manage, however, to

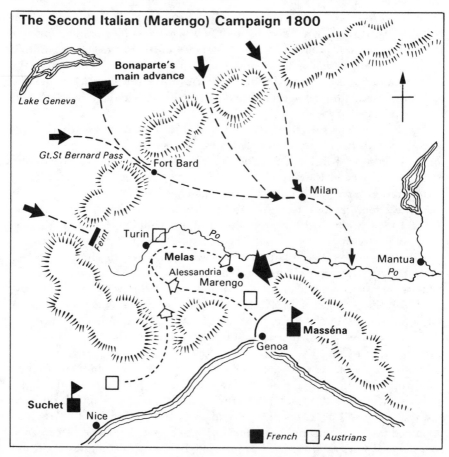

The Second Italian (Marengo) Campaign 1800

Bonaparte's main advance

Lake Geneva

Gt.St Bernard Pass

Fort Bard

Milan

Feint

Turin

Po

Melas

Alessandria

Marengo

Mantua

Po

Masséna

Genoa

Suchet

Nice

■ French □ Austrians

FIG. 5. Manoeuvre in the rear. Instead of marching directly to relieve Genoa, Napoleon's Reserve Army swung eastward toward Milan threatening Melas's line of communications. Melas now had to fight facing rearwards to regain communications and a line of retreat.

receive favourable terms. Moreover, their suffering had not been in vain. Strong Austrian forces had been tied down and this aided Bonaparte in defeating the main Austrian body on 14 June in the plain of Marengo.

The total effectives of the French and Austrian forces operating in north-western Italy numbered 60,000 against 72,000 men. Both sides, however, had dispersed their forces widely. At Marengo, the Austrians mustered superior numbers, 32,000, with 7,000 cavalry and 100 field guns; the French initially had but 18,000, with 3,500 cavalry and only 40 guns. The Austrians attacked first and after heavy fighting the French were driven back, losing a considerable proportion of their artillery. Convinced that the day was won, the Austrian commander, Melas, ordered pursuit and left the field. But the French were not routed and in the afternoon fresh troops under Desaix entered the battle; Bonaparte ordered a counter-attack, surprised the

Austrians forming up in columns of march for the pursuit and turned a near defeat into a resounding victory. The next night a shaken Melas signed an armistice evacuating all of Lombardy as far as the Mincio River and agreed to halt all fighting until Vienna had replied to the First Consul's latest peace offer.

One more victory was required before the Second Coalition collapsed. Moreau provided it when fighting resumed in Germany. In November 1800, the young Archduke John, who had replaced the experienced Kray, ordered a general advance hoping to envelop Moreau's forces. But the mobility of the French frustrated this plan and Moreau, in turn, attempted to envelop the Austrians. After a day of confused fighting in the woods around Hohenlinden on 3 December, the Austrians lost 14,000 men, including 8,000 prisoners, and 40 guns.

Marengo and Hohenlinden broke up the Second Coalition. In February 1801 Austria made peace at Luneville; in March Spain reasserted her old alliance with France, while Britain, left on her own, carried on the conflict. Her position worsened when Tsar Paul I organized a league of northern states, Russia, Sweden, Prussia, and Denmark, to threaten British naval supplies. Great Britain retaliated by an attack against Copenhagen, destroying the major part of the Danish fleet. Soon thereafter, Paul was murdered in a palace revolt and under his pro-English successor, Alexander I, the league was dissolved. Still, England needed a respite, while Bonaparte wished to consolidate his regime. Thus, after prolonged negotiations, the Treaty of Amiens was signed on 27 March 1802.

The war of the Third Coalition : Ulm and Austerlitz

Inevitably, the Treaty of Amiens did not resolve any of the differences between Great Britain and France and war between the two countries resumed in May 1803. For the moment, however, neither side could strike directly at the other. The Royal Navy blockaded France and her allies and English gold supported a Royalist conspiracy, entangling Moreau who, when the plot was discovered, was forced into exile. In the same year, 1803, France invaded Hanover, Britain's only continental possession, and forced the surrender of her army. Having consolidated his position and achieved substantially increased frontiers, on 2 December 1804, Bonaparte, following the popular plebiscite, assumed the title of Napoleon I, Emperor of the French.

For over a year he had been assembling troops and shipping for an invasion of England, establishing the headquarters of his Army of the Ocean Coast at Boulogne, while the troops, organized in seven army corps, were spread out from Hanover to Brest. In the summer of 1805 Britain, Austria, Russia, Naples, and Sweden formed the Third Coalition. By then it was clear to Napoleon that he had but little hope of invading England and in August, having received intelligence of the allied dispositions against him, swiftly deployed his army eastward. The Austrians, greatly overestimating their strength, entered Bavaria, a French ally, and Mack assembled an army, some

50,000 strong, near Ulm. Charles, with a second and much larger army, was to recover northern Italy, while John with 23,000 men was to secure communications through the Tyrol. Mack expected the Russian armies to arrive in time to meet Napoleon but he miscalculated the rapidity and nature of the enemy's reaction.

On 26 August, Napoleon issued orders for the movement of his corps, and the newly designated Grand Army, the best he ever had, swung into action. From Brest to the Rhine and to Hanover the seven corps moved against Mack in a wide arc, their deployment concealed by an effective cavalry screen. By early October, French and Bavarian forces under Wrede, had masked the approaching Russians and surrounded the Austrian concentration at Ulm. Mack waited too long to break out and surrendered on 20 October with 30,000 men. Part of his army under Archduke Ferdinand escaped and retreated eastward to meet the Russians falling back to Bohemia.

With the 'unfortunate General Mack' disposed of, Napoleon marched down the Danube, seized the strategic bridges near Vienna by a ruse, entered the Austrian capital on 15 November, and moved into Moravia and Bohemia. At this point, however, the Grand Army was in a difficult strategic position. The Russians and Austrians with some 90,000 men were at Olmütz with secure communications while Napoleon's forces, 65,000 strong, were vastly overextended and his corps dispersed for logistic reasons. Archdukes Charles and John were already marching towards the Danube with 90,000 men and the Prussian attitude was threatening. Napoleon faced the alternatives of either retreating to Ulm or winning a decisive victory. Calculating time and distance, he decided that Charles could arrive in strength before the end of November. Napoleon now ordered Davout's and Bernadotte's corps to join him in forced marches while he deceived the Tsar by his apparent weakness and lured the over-eager Russians into a premature offensive movement on a carefully chosen battleground near Austerlitz.

On 2 December 1805, the 'sun of Austerlitz' illuminated Napoleon's most meticulously orchestrated battle. By deliberately exposing his apparently weak right wing, even abandoning the Pratzen Heights, a good defensive position, he induced the enemy to attack to overextend their front. Then he assaulted the centre of the enemy line and cut the allied line, while his left wing attacked the enemy flank and rear. By late afternoon the allies had been routed, about 30 percent of their forces killed, wounded, or prisoners. Even more important, their morale was shattered.[10] Two days later Emperor Francis asked for terms and on 6 December an armistice was agreed on at Znaim. The Russians agreed to return their armies home; the Austrians signed the Treaty of Pressburg the day after Christmas which ceded Venetia, Dalmatia and Istria, recognized Napoleon as King of Italy and also conceded royal status to Napoleon's allies, the rulers of Bavaria and Württemberg, preparing the way for the formation of the Confederation of the Rhine in the following year.

In the meantime various other allied operations had also failed. In the north the English and Swedes had achieved little in Hanover; in the south the

British-supported Neapolitans had been driven from the mainland and were now reduced to Sicily. On 27 December 1805 Napoleon's brother Joseph was declared King of Naples; in May 1806 the Batavian Republic became the Kingdom of Holland under Napoleon's older brother Louis. Perhaps the only bright spot in the picture for England was the encounter at Maida in Calabria, 1 July 1806, where a small British expedition fighting in line, defeated a stronger French force, attacking in column, with rapid and accurate musketry. At the same time, and this too was a portent of things to come, throughout southern Italy an aroused peasantry continued to conduct a bitter small war against the French.

The collapse of Prussia : 1806

In 1806 Prussia, trying to act as if it was still the Frederician state, tried to acquire Hanover as a compensation for the changed political situation in Germany. After negotiations broke down the Prussian King, Frederick William III, suddenly gave the French notice to withdraw their troops from Germany. In reply Napoleon concentrated some 200,000 men in southern Germany. A Fourth Coalition was formed. Prussia, Russia, England and Portugal faced Napoleon's Grand Army, now a multi-national force with contingents from the Confederation of the Rhine, Holland, and Italy. As in 1805 the Russians were slow in moving their troops west, while the over-confident Prussians entered Saxony in early September and forced it to join their side. Meanwhile Napoleon's main concentration, some 150,000 men in three columns, moved through the Thuringian Forest and on 13–14 October 1806 encountered the Prussian Army at Jena and Auerstädt. At Jena the Emperor clashed with the smaller part of the Prussian–Saxon forces and routed them, while at Auerstadt, 13 miles north, Davout defeated the main Prussian body. Immediate and relentless pursuit destroyed the Prussian army while the state itself collapsed. Strong fortresses capitulated at the approach of a few French hussars; except for old General Blücher, the remaining Prussian field commanders surrendered without a fight and Frederick William fled to East Prussia. Napoleon entered Berlin on 24 October.

The Eylau and Friedland campaign : 1807

Prussia was smashed, but Napoleon still faced Russia. To launch this campaign Napoleon invaded Poland. On 30 November, Davout's corps entered Warsaw and in mid-December Napoleon almost trapped a Russian army under Bennigsen north-east of Warsaw at Pultusk. But the state of the Polish roads, perhaps the worst in Europe, did not allow rapid manoeuvre. Bennigsen escaped and retired to join the Prussian remnants in East Prussia. Napoleon's army, widely dispersed and suffering much from the cold and wet, went into winter quarters.

In late January 1807, Bennigsen attacked the northern flank of the Grand Army, Ney's corps encamped south of Königsberg. As the Russians advanced deeper into East Prussia, Napoleon moved north with his army to cut off Bennigsen and forced him to retreat. In a blinding snowstorm, on 8 February, he caught up with the Russians at Eylau. After an extremely bloody battle the timely arrival of a Prussian corps under L'Estocq permitted the Russians to retire, though Napoleon retained possession of the field. Thereafter both sides returned to their winter quarters; Napoleon utilizing the pause to improve the equipment of his troops and to call up reinforcements.

When the campaign reopened in June, Napoleon's vanguard, Lannes' corps, pinned down a much larger Russian force at Friedland, trapping them up against the Alle River. Ably supported by an advancing artillery barrage, the guns moving by stages to within 100 yards of the enemy, the French army succeeded in turning the Russian left flank and cutting the Russians from the bridges. An attack along the whole front followed and, despite fierce resistance, the Russians were cut to pieces, losing almost 50 percent of the 80,000 engaged.

Tsar Alexander now sought peace, and was even prepared to become Napoleon's ally. On 7 July at Tilsit Alexander and Napoleon agreed to partition Prussia and delimited their respective zones of influence. Russia, moreover, agreed to join in Napoleon's measures against English commerce and, later that year, even declared war against her.

At Tilsit, Napoleon stood at the height of his power. Only Britain, her control of the seas unchallenged since Trafalgar, remained at war with the French Empire. Napoleon decided to bring England down through an economic blockade, the Continental System, controlling her imports and exports and as Britain's only access to Europe was through neutral Portugal he now turned his attention to the Iberian Peninsula.

In June 1807 the French Emperor told Portugal and Denmark to close their ports to British shipping. England replied by sending a British fleet, an expeditionary force to bombard Copenhagen and seize the Danish fleet, an example which kept Portugal from complying with Napoleon's demands. In October 1807 Napoleon pressured the weak and divided Spanish government to permit a French army under Junot to cross its territory and attack Portugal. The Portuguese were unable to resist and Lisbon fell on 1 December 1807. But to control Portugal and to prevent smuggling of English goods through Spain, Napoleon decided to intervene in the tangled political affairs of that kingdom, opening a campaign that ultimately absorbed a very large proportion of his armies, constituted a constant drain on his resources, and contributed much to his ultimate defeat.

The campaigns in the Peninsula : 1808–9
In March 1808 an army of some 100,000 under Murat entered Spain. Napoleon did not expect much opposition from the poorly trained and led Spanish army. Most of the country was in fact swiftly occupied. Napoleon now forced King Charles and his son Ferdinand to renounce the throne and in May made his brother Joseph, until then King of Naples, King of Spain. Murat, in turn,

received the Neapolitan crown.

The French army, with only 35,000 veterans, easily defeated the Spanish regulars but their unrestrained plundering and outrages against women contributed to the bitter popular resentment against the alien invaders which exploded on 2 May 1808 in Madrid. Although the French under Murat speedily quelled the rising, killing some 2,000 and shooting hundreds more during the night, the revolt spread. Provincial councils, *Juntas*, organized resistance forces and in June a French garrison, 5,000 strong, was driven out of Saragossa, an important city on the line of communications. Even more important, in Andalusia, Dupont's isolated corps was surrounded and on 1 July 1808, at Baylen, it capitulated with 25,000 men. It was the first surrender of a French army in the field for over a decade. Shortly after this disaster, King Joseph abandoned his new capital and withdrew north to the Ebro River.

The Spanish revolt offered Britain, whose army had been retrained by the Duke of York, now Commander-in-Chief, an opportunity of intervening on the continent, and in a region where sea power provided it with better

FIG. 6

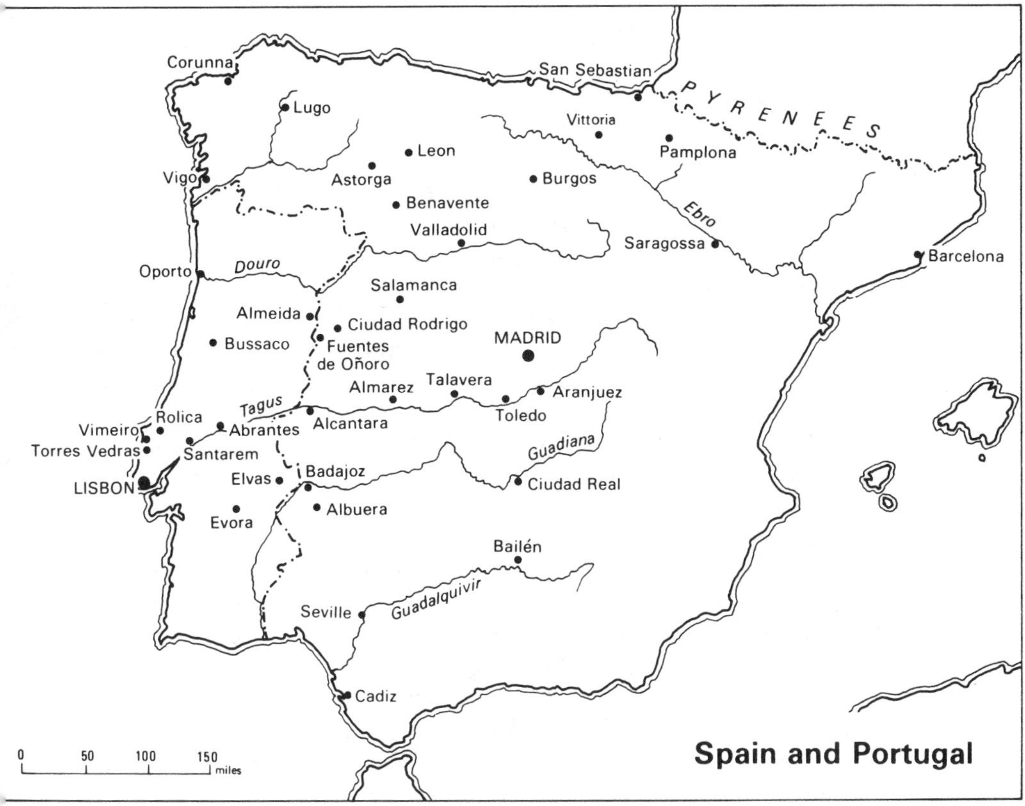

Spain and Portugal

communications than the French. In the first week of August its field commander, Sir Arthur Wellesley, defeated Junot at Vimiero (another victory of line over column). This sparked an uprising in Portugal and Junot, defeated and isolated, signed the Convention of Cintras which repatriated his forces on British ships. Although by that time Wellesley had been superseded by more senior generals, he was temporarily recalled. The British, however, had gained a foothold in Portugal they would not relinquish.

Perturbed, Napoleon rapidly transferred large elements of the Grand Army to the Ebro and at the head of over 200,000 men began an offensive in November that, despite appalling weather and roads, scattered the various regular and irregular Spanish forces facing him. Meanwhile, with British troops in the Peninsula increased to 35,000, Sir John Moore was instructed to move north from Lisbon and cooperate with the Spanish armies and people to drive Napoleon from Spain.

Napoleon entered Madrid in the first days of December but heard that Moore had cut his main line of communications with France. At once he turned against Moore who, unable to face Napoleon and receiving but little Spanish support, started a retreat towards Corunna in north-western Spain. During the retreat hunger and cold broke the cohesion of most units. Moore rallied his command at Corunna and repulsed Soult, thus ensuring an orderly embarkation. Mortally wounded during the battle, Moore came in for much harsh criticism. Nonetheless, Napoleon's plan of conquest had been dislocated; the Spanish revolt gained precious time, while from the base at Lisbon another expeditionary force under Wellesley was preparing operations in conjunction with a reconstituted Portuguese army, trained and commanded by the Marquis of Beresford. Napoleon, disturbed by rumours about a conspiracy in Paris and Austria's warlike preparations, had already departed from Spain in January 1809, leaving the conduct of the war there in the hands of his brother and a group of marshals, who failed to coordinate their efforts and often worked at cross-purposes.

In the summer of 1809 Wellesley, supported by Portuguese elements, and including in his army some excellent German units of the former Hanoverian army, now styled the King's German Legion, advanced into Spain. He was joined by a Spanish army under Cuestas. On 28 July, the British repulsed an attack by the combined forces of Marshal Victor and King Joseph at Talavera, though with appalling losses. But it was a victory and Wellesley now became Viscount Wellington.

The Spaniards proved difficult allies. Cuestas refused to cooperate with Wellington, while the *Junta* at Madrid was quite unwilling or unable, both appear possible, to furnish the British with the supplies promised. Wellington, now threatened by other French forces, and mindful of his government's instructions that the defence of Portugal was his first charge, withdrew back across the frontier. During the winter of 1809–10, British engineers with Portuguese labour built the immensely strong lines of the Torres Vedras north of Lisbon, providing Wellington with a secure, almost impregnable, base against the expected French invasion of Portugal.

The campaign against Austria in 1809

For several years now Archduke Charles had been reorganizing and training the Austrian army for a new war against France. Financial difficulties and the conservatism of many highly placed generals, together with the ever-present suspicions of his imperial brother, had retarded his efforts, but Napoleon's setbacks in Spain gave the upper hand to the war faction in Vienna. As early as June 1808 an imperial patent established the *Landwehr*, a popular militia designed to reinforce but not to supplant the regulars, and in December 1808, the decision for war was taken. On 10 April 1809, the Austrians crossed the Bavarian frontier.

Although a very substantial army, more than 300,000 men, had been raised, three separate theatres, Germany, Italy, and Poland, fragmented the available forces. The main army in Germany amounted to 175,000 men; there were 30,000 in Poland facing Russia, and 50,000 in Italy. The war had been undertaken in expectation of English and German support, but neither materialized in strength. The Confederation of the Rhine remained loyal to Napoleon whilst other German rulers maintained their neutrality. In North Germany only the Duke of Brunswick-Oels and the Prussian Major Schill rallied to Austria's support, while in the South the Tyroleans took up arms against Bavaria. At best, however, these uprisings had nuisance value and could not affect the main issue.

The main army advanced into Bavaria and at first Charles pushed the French and their allies back. But at Ratisbon on 23 April the tide turned. Napoleon entered Austria, occupying Vienna on 13 May against nominal resistance. Charles rallied his army on the north bank of the Danube and on 21–22 May 1809, fighting with stubborn bravery, the Austrians repulsed Napoleon's assaults. The hard-fought battle won by the bravery of the troops of Aspern-Essling was the first major victory on land against Napoleon. Charles, careful as ever, had refused to take any risks and fought a defensive battle aimed at exhausting and debilitating the enemy which, in the end, gave him only a tactical victory. Nevertheless, a deeply impressed Napoleon later told Murat, 'You did not see the Austrians at Aspern, therefore you have not seen anything'.[11]

Charles, however, failed to exploit his success. Both sides spent the next six weeks reinforcing their battered forces. Napoleon was bringing up troops from Germany, while Charles was waiting for the arrival of his brother John with the army from Italy. John, forced to take a circuitous route through Croatia and Hungary, pursued by the French, arrived too late. Napoleon, showed less than his usual skill at Wagram. After repulsing an Austrian attack against his left wing, he launched a dense column of some 30,000 infantry, with strong cavalry on both flanks, in a frontal attack against the Austrian centre. The attack was prepared and supported by a concentration of 100 guns and combined with an enveloping move against the left wing. Charles managed to save a good part of his army, but even so, the battle sufficed to extinguish all sentiment for war in Austria. Except for the Tyroleans, who continued fighting for several more months, there was hardly anyone left prepared to pursue the war. Charles, accused by his brother of entertaining dubious schemes, was abruptly dismissed and held no further command.

In October 1809 Austria had to sign the Treaty of Schönbrunn which deprived her of much territory, including most of the Croatian Military Border, imposed a heavy indemnity and limited her army to 150,000 men. Napoleon had been victorious, though in contrast to his previous operations at Wagram, Aspern, and Essling, displayed no great tactical skill, and relied instead on massed artillery and manpower, neither of which was inexhaustible.

The Peninsular War: 1810–12

In 1809 a British landing on Walcheren in an attempt to seize Antwerp failed when the troops were rapidly decimated by fever, but in Spain, Wellington managed to defeat the French. Even so, when all is said and done, the campaigns, while adding much to his and the British soldier's reputation, did not cause Napoleon's collapse. Even on the Peninsula the continuous drain of the relentless guerrilla war was more damaging to the French, caused more casualties, and loss of equipment, than the intermittent defeats in battle. Wellington's achievements were great, but must be placed in the context of the whole war. Wellington himself realized that Spain would not be saved by roundshot and bayonet, not even by his steady troops, but by the tough guerrilla fighters. In January 1810 he wrote to Lord Liverpool that though the Spanish armies might be routed and the *juntas* dispersed, 'the war of the partizans may continue'.[12] And the French clearly understood the mutual relationship between the British and the guerrillas.

'The bands . . . and the English army mutually supported each other,' one of Masséna's staff officers wrote, 'without the English the Spaniards would have been quickly dispersed or crushed.'[13] In turn, if the French had not been diverted by the guerrillas, the Anglo–Portuguese forces might have been unable to stand against a concentrated French attack.

In 1810, Napoleon reinforced troops in the Peninsula to 370,000 men, and in July the expected invasion of Portugal started. Retiring slowly before Masséna, halting on 26 September to give battle in a prepared position on Bussaco Ridge, Willington withdrew into the Lines of Torres Vedras, applying a 'scorched earth' policy to deny supplies to the French. By October his forces were safely inside the Lines, while Masséna, though unable to force the Lines, maintained himself in Portugal until March 1811. Then he began a slow retreat, destroying, burning, and killing, and being harried by Portuguese irregulars in turn.

Wellington followed slowly. Masséna was in retreat, but other French corps in Spain could easily combine a crushing superiority against him. Moreover, the French still held three of the four vital key fortresses between Portugal and Spain, Almeida, Ciudad Rodrigo, and Badajoz. Masséna, in fact, re-equipped and reinforced turned and advanced to the relief of Almeida with 48,000 men. Wellington met him with 37,000 at Fuentes d'Onoro, 3–5 May, 1811, and halted his advance. Almeida, however, was successfully evacuated by its French garrison. Further south, Beresford with Anglo–Portuguese forces, supported by Spanish regulars under Blake and Castanos was preparing to lay siege to Badajoz. On 16 May, he defeated an attempt by Soult to break through to Badajoz at Albuera, an extremely bloody battle where for one hour British and French infantry traded volleys at ranges closing to 20 yards. In the end Soult failed, but at a cost Wellington could hardly afford.

Following the May battles, operations for the rest of the year revolved around British efforts to take Badajoz and Ciudad Rodrigo, frustrated each time by the lack of an adequate siege train, engineers, and troops. At the onset of winter, Wellington retired to Portugal, waiting for an opportunity to resume offensive action.

The opportunity came early in 1812. Napoleon recalled many veteran formations, including all Polish regiments and all units of the Imperial Guard serving in Spain, about 20,000 men. At the same time, with British aid, the guerrillas had grown stronger and bolder and now tied down a large part of the remaining French forces in eastern Spain. Wellington took the offensive in January 1812. On 8 January he appeared before Ciudad Rodrigo and, as soon as practicable breaches had been made, assaulted the fortress on the night of 19 January. The assault succeeded, but was followed by an orgy of looting and plunder, repeated on a larger and even more atrocious scale after the storming of Badajoz, a stronger and better-defended fortress on 6 April. Even Wellington could not halt the sack that went on for several days. Thereafter, he marched on Salamanca and, following a month of manoeuvring against Soult, defeated him on 22 July thus forcing the French to evacuate most of southern Spain. Wellington's advance, however, was halted at Burgos which withstood a siege during September–October. His supplies failing, he was forced to fall back to Ciudad Rodrigo, suffering some 3,000 casualties during the retreat.

The Russian Campaign: 1812

In 1812, France had been greatly expanded. It included Belgium and Holland, Germany west of the Rhine and along the North Sea, Italy including Sardinia, Genoa, Tuscany, and Rome, as well as the 'Illyrian Provinces' across the Adriatic. These annexed lands were treated as French territory and brought the country's population to 43 million. In addition there were satellite states. The kingdom of Italy, ruled by Napoleon with his stepson Eugene de Beauharnais as viceroy; Spain under Joseph, and Naples under Murat. In Germany there was the Confederation of the Rhine, including almost every German state except Austria and Prussia, with the Kingdom of Westphalia ruled by Napoleon's brother Jerome at its centre. Finally there were two other French satellites, Switzerland and the Grand Duchy of Warsaw. Only Denmark, Austria, and Prussia were outside direct French control, but in all three countries the governments were eager to comply with Napoleon's wishes. Altogether, though there were minor rumblings of discontent, Napoleon's position seemed secure and it has remained somewhat of a mystery why he decided, sometime in 1811, to invade Russia the following year.

To be sure, his relations with Russia had cooled since Tilsit. There was friction over Napoleon's ultimate intention in Poland, the Balkans and even Germany, and demands that Russia enforce his measures against English commerce were resented. Between May and July 1812, Alexander negotiated with England, but it was Napoleon, however, and not the Russian ruler who actively prepared for aggression. By the spring of 1812, Napoleon had assembled an immense army, 614,000 men, including reserves and rear area troops, the 'army of twenty nations' as it was called, for an invasion of Russia. He made great, though as it turned out inadequate, logistical preparation, and on 24 June 1812, without a formal declaration of war, crossed the Niemen with 449,000 men, of whom one-third were French and the remainder Dutch, Westphalian, Polish, Bavarian, Saxon, Prussian, Austrian, Croatian, Dalmatian, Swiss, Italian, and even Spanish.[14]

The very size of the army forced a direct approach along the line of greatest expectation. The main body, including Napoleon and his Imperial Guard, grouped in three converging columns, marched in direct line towards Moscow, hoping to destroy the main Russian forces before he had gone too far into the interior. The strategic flanks, however, were poorly secured. In the north there was an auxiliary Prussian corps under Yorck; in the south an Austrian corps under Schwarzenberg, both of dubious reliability.

Napoleon's movement was remarkably reluctant. He entered Vilna on 28 June and tarried there for two weeks; at Vitebsk again he delayed a fortnight. During the advance from the Saale and Elbe his army, dwindled by about one-third through casualties, desertion, and sickness. Discipline was poor and even the advance guard found no supplies in a country that was impoverished to begin with and had been systematically despoiled by the retreating Russians. On 17 August 1812, Barclay de Tolly, the Russian commander, made a brief stand at Smolensk but evacuated the city before Napoleon could envelop him. Having failed to destroy either the Russian army or Russia's will to resist, Napoleon now had either to advance on Moscow or retreat to the Vilna area. He decided to advance, asserting that 'within six weeks we shall have peace'.

On 7 September, he encountered the Russian army, now commanded by Kutuzov who had superseded Barclay, at Borodino. The Russians stood across the Moscow road, behind a small river, and had reinforced the centre of their position with one large and three small redoubts. Although Kutozov's left flank was vulnerable, Napoleon decided to abandon manoeuvre in favour of a series of frontal attacks, supported by a heavy artillery barrage. At the end of the day, during which all units of Napoleon's army, French and foreign, fought with much bravery against stubborn Russian resistance, the casualties stood at 28,000 killed and wounded for the French and 52,000 killed, wounded and missing, for the Russians.[15] But, although the Russians lost nearly half of their effectives, they nevertheless withdrew in good order during the night.

A week later Napoleon reached Moscow without resistance.

He now was some 500 miles deep into enemy country and still the Russian ruler would not yield. Napoleon's system which depended on mass and mobility which could smash the enemy army soon after the opening of a campaign and force him to come to terms failed against the Russians who bartered space to compensate for their numerical and perhaps tactical inferiority. At the end of a long, vulnerable, and increasingly threatened supply line, Napoleon could not afford to wait forever. Even so, he waited too long. For five weeks he remained in Moscow, a city partially burnt and then, on 19 October, with only 100,000 of the men he had led across the Niemen, he began his catastrophic retreat. Initially he intended to march through the Kaluga district, still well supplied with food and fodder but, after an indecisive battle on 24 October at Maloyaroslavets, he decided to retire through Mohaisk to Smolensk.

Lack of discipline as much as the winter destroyed his army. Over 40,000 vehicles of all kinds, loaded with loot instead of supplies, accompanied his army and slowed down its progress.[16] On November 1st the first snow fell; horses began to die rapidly; much of the cavalry was dismounted, guns and vehicles abandoned. On 9 November the army reached Smolensk, destroying many supplies needlessly. Although the army was still able to brush aside Russian corps barring its retreat, cohesion weakened from day to day. At the crossing of the Beresina, finally, 27–28 November, the army became a straggling mob, and retreat turned into a rout. Only the rearguard, commanded by Marshal Ney, musket in hand, maintained some semblance of order.

In December the remnants of the Grand Army, many of them walking skeletons in rags, straggled into Poland and East Prussia. Hardly 60,000 survived. Napoleon, apprehensive of the European reaction to this débâcle, left the army on 5 December and hurried to Paris to raise a new army.

The campaign in Germany : 1813

The entire political and military situation had changed. On 30 December 1812, General Yorck, who had carefully avoided committing his corps, suspended hostilities with Russia by the Convention of Tauroggen thus forcing the rather reluctant Prussian king to act. Fleeing from Berlin and its French garrison, Frederick William escaped to Silesia, mobilized his army, called out volunteers, and introduced conscription. After concluding an alliance with Alexander (the Treaty of Kalish) he declared a 'war of liberation' against Napoleon on 16 March 1813.

The Emperor, meanwhile, had hastily raised another Grand Army. In all, he wanted some 700,000 men, of which number he had designated 200,000 for the new German front. Already in training was the 1813 class of conscripts and these, together with discharged veterans, troops from Spain, and units of the National Guard combined with drafts of sailors and 12,000 naval gunners, made up a force of 120,000 men. In April, the Emperor moved east to join the 50,000 troops under Eugene still holding the fortresses of the Seale and Elbe river line against a slow Allied advance. At this point the Prussian armies numbered about 80,000, but were rapidly reinforced, and the Russians had 120,000 in Prussia and Saxony. Napoleon's German allies, especially Westphalia, Saxony, and Bavaria remained loyal, but Sweden, now ruled by King Bernadotte, formerly a French marshal, had joined the Prussians, Russians, and Britain, to form the Fifth Coalition. Both sides were short of war material. The French factories produced an adequate supply of arms, but the cavalry was short of remounts and its troopers raw and inexperienced. The Coalition forces lacked all kinds of equipment, but in late spring and summer, British ships had unloaded massive quantities of cannon, small arms, ammunition, clothing, and other supplies in the Baltic ports.[17]

On 2 May 1813, the Prussian–Russian forces attacked Napoleon advancing into Saxony at Lützen. The Emperor personally steadied some of his wavering troops and later that day his artillery blasted a decisive gap into the enemy line. By nightfall the Prussian–Russian forces were retreating – a retreat Napoleon could not exploit for lack of cavalry. On 20–21 May, Napoleon won another victory at Bautzen, but this time the Allies escaped destruction because Marshal Ney, brave but a poor tactician, delivered the final charge in the wrong direction!

On 4 June, the Emperor agreed to an Allied request for a four-week armistice, later extended to 17 August. During this interval the Prussians and Russians re-equipped their forces, trained their fresh levies, and brought up reinforcements. Most important, Austria began to mobilize a large armament, and offered her armed mediation on terms unacceptable to Napoleon. Even by 27 June Austria had joined the Coalition and on 12 August declared war. The very size of her war effort, 480,000 men mobilized and 300,000 combat troops available, entitled her to name the Allied commander-in-chief. Although Tsar Alexander favoured Archduke Charles, the Austrian emperor insisted on Schwarzenberg. On the Prussian side, the rough, hard-drinking Blücher, now 70 years old, emerged as the major commander.

The Allies formed three separate armies: Schwarzenberg in Bohemia, Blücher with a Prussian–Russian army in Silesia, and Bernadotte with Swedish–Russian and Prussian contingents around Berlin. For once, the Coalition had a common strategic plan. During the armistice they agreed not to engage Napoleon alone, but to retire until they could unite all their forces. Gradually they would encircle Napoleon and bring him to battle with much superior forces.

Napoleon detached forces to contain Blücher and Bernadotte and advanced against Schwarzenberg. His strategy was doomed to failure. On 26 August, the Silesian Army defeated MacDonald at the Katzbach; the next day Napoleon defeated Schwarzenberg at Dresden, but Vandamme's corps, pursuing the retreating Austrians, was cut off and forced to surrender on 29–30 August at Kulm and Nollendorf. Although Ney scored some victories in the north, the scales were tipping. Napoleon's Confederation of the Rhine was fast becoming unreliable. In October, Bavaria defected and on the 14th declared war. Plagued by allied raids against his lines of communications and short of supplies, Napoleon made his stand at Leipzig.

The 'Battle of Nations', 16–19 October 1813, was a series of bloody engagements around the city of Leipzig, as the Allies were converging on the French from all sides. Napoleon endeavoured to beat the enemy in detail, but failed to achieve his objective. On the other hand, Allied assaults against his positions also failed, but on the third day, the defection of the Saxons forced him to break off the battle and retreat toward the Rhine, using the only available bridge across the Elster river. During the retreat Napoleon defeated the Bavarians who tried to bar his escape at Hanau on the Main on 30–31 October, and reached France with some 70,000 men still in formed units and with 40,000 stragglers. The Allied pursuit after Leipzig halted at the Rhine.

During the winter of 1813–14, Napoleon mustered yet another army, calling up some 963,000 conscripts, veterans, aged reservists, foresters, policemen, custom officers, and the National Guard. He hoped that this imposing array, reminiscent of the great levies of 1793–4, might give the Allies second thoughts about invading France. The Allies, in fact, were divided. Austria, England, and Sweden were willing to settle more or less for the natural frontiers of France, though Russia and Prussia insisted on removing the 'Corsican Ogre'. This dissention notwithstanding, Napoleon's hopes did not materialize. The large number of conscripts called out did not come forward; junior and non-commissioned officers were in short supply; drafts from Italy failed to appear, and Denmark, his last foreign ally, left the war in January 1814. Even Murat defected and, to keep his throne, joined the Allies.

Wellington's campaign in Spain: 1813–14
In 1813 Wellington, now also commander-in-chief of the partly reorganized Spanish forces, and with much improved artillery, engineering, and medical services, resumed the offensive. The French still had some 200,000 men in Spain, but their position was becoming untenable. Madrid fell on 27 May and Joseph retired north, unable to form a defensive line. Burgos was blown up, and the French finally stood to defend the Ebro line. Wellington, however, turned the position and on 21 June, defeated Joseph and Jourdan at Vittoria, capturing enormous booty on the battlefield. News of Vittoria greatly encouraged Allied morale in Central Europe and contributed to Austria's decision to enter the war.

Soult assumed command of remaining French forces, still holding the fortress of San Sebastian and the town of Pamplona. On 31 August British forces captured San Sebastian and Pamplona capitulated late in October. By this time, Wellington's relations with his Spanish allies worsened and he resigned command of the Spanish army. News of Leipzig reached Wellington on 9 December and the next day he assaulted Soult's line along the river Nive, and after several days of fighting forced Soult back into France. There followed several small engagements in southern France but the French no longer were very active and political instructions from home restricted Wellington. The final battle was fought on 10 April 1814 when Soult was defeated at Toulouse and the British occupied the city. Wellington had indeed come a long way from Mondego Beach.

The defence of France: 1814

France in 1814 was physically and morally exhausted, as three Allied armies, Bernadotte in the Low Countries, Schwarzenberg from the Upper Rhine, and Blücher from Lorraine were pressing against the French capital. Napoleon, however, was far from finished. Although his call-up had produced less than one-seventh of the required number, he manoeuvred his forces skilfully and inflicted some sharp defeats on the impetuous Prussians at Brienne (29 January 1814) and again at La Rothière (30 January). But the other Allied forces were pressing on in ever-increasing numbers and though Napoleon continued to drive Blücher back in February and March, Schwarzenberg, ably assisted by his chief-of-staff, Radetzky, continued to march on Paris. Ignoring Napoleon's threat to their rear the Allies entered Paris on 31 March. The Emperor still hoped for a decisive counter-stroke that would rally the country, but his commanders, eager to salvage their positions, refused to follow him. Marmont deserted with his entire corps. And when Napoleon asserted that the army still would follow him, Ney stingingly replied that, 'the Army will only obey its generals'.

Nothing more was left to be said. Napoleon abdicated on 11 April and was exiled to Elba.

The final act: Waterloo, 1815

On 1 March 1815, Napoleon returned to France and within a few days, without firing a shot, re-established his régime. The Emperor professed peaceful intent, but within a month Britain, Austria, Russia, and Prussia each promised to fight until Napoleon was defeated. But for the moment the Allies were obliged to stand on the defensive because their forces, though greatly superior in numbers, were scattered over a wide area. Only Wellington's and Blücher's armies were in a position to halt Napoleon's first attack. By June both sides were gathering forces: Wellington disposed of some 31,000 British troops, the newly founded Kingdom of the Netherlands provided about as many, and contingents from other north German states, above all Hanover and Brunswick, brought his total to slightly over 93,000 men. It was not his best army. Many of his Peninsular veterans were fighting in America; the loyalty of the Dutch and Belgian contingents was suspect. But Blücher and his superb chief-of-staff, Gneisenau, had assembled almost 120,000 on his left flank. Schwarzenberg was assembling 200,000 near Luxembourg, while another 200,000 Russians were marshalling in Germany and Poland. Against this, Napoleon could muster only 124,000 men for his initial operations, a mix of old and young volunteers.

Napoleon could have stood on the defensive, but measuring the odds forming against him, decided to try and knock out his nearest enemies before the others could come up. Concentrating his army at Charleroi on 15 June he crossed the frontier the next day. There followed three major battles of which the defence of the plateau of Mont Saint Jean, the 'Battle of Waterloo', was the final act.

On 16 June, Napoleon attacked the Prussians at Ligny, while Ney was to occupy the vital crossroads at Quatre Bras and then fall on Blücher's flank. But Ney, for once overcautious, moved too slowly and had to drive out a British defence-force which had established itself. Napoleon, meanwhile, defeated Blücher at Ligny, but the Prussians retired in good order, not east as Napoleon expected, but north to join Wellington. Pushed out of Quatre Bras, the British commander had fallen back to a defensive position – the height of Mont Saint Jean, eight miles south of Brussels.

Napoleon dispatched Grouchy with 32,000 men and 96 guns to pursue the Prussians in an easterly direction, while he moved with his main army against Wellington. On 17 June, soaking rains drenched both armies, making movement difficult, and on the next day, Sunday, 18 June, Napoleon with 71,947 men and 246 guns faced Wellington with 67,711 men and 156 guns. Grouchy, meantime, was still chasing the Prussians who, in fact, were marching fast to support Wellington. The wet ground delayed the opening moves of the battle for some hours. When Napoleon finally moved about 1.30 in the afternoon he hurled massive divisional columns against Wellington's line, deployed as usual on the reverse slopes, with batteries providing fire support and outlying posts held by picked troops. Under heavy attack, the thin defence yielded some ground but did not break. Even Ney's furious cavalry charges and finally the assault of the Old Guard failed to break it. The Prussian troops, already in action during the afternoon, began to arrive in increasing strength: Grouchy did not come. It was the end. As the Guard recoiled, the French wavered, broke, and pursued by Prussian cavalry, dissolved. Only some of the Guard remained fighting, protecting their Emperor's escape.

The long years of war that had opened 23 years before with the cannonade at Valmy finally were over.

NOTES

1. R.W. Phipps, *The Armies of the First French Republic*, 5 vols., Oxford University Press, 1926–39, vol. I, 11–19.
2. R.R. Palmer, *Twelve who Ruled*, Princeton University Press, 1958, 59–61, 78–85, 96–8, 182–5.
3. Chandler, *op cit.*, 19–28.
4. Phipps, *op cit.*, 3.
5. C. Barnett, *Britain and her Army*, Allen Lane, 1970, 235–6.
6. Phipps, *op cit.*, vol. II, 402–4.
7. C. Falls, *The Art of War*, Oxford University Press, 1961, 34–5.
8. Phipps, *op cit.*, vol. V, 352–443.
9. G. Lefebvre, *Napoleon from 18 Brumaire to Tilsit*, Columbia University Press, New York, 1968, 62–3.

10. Chandler, *op cit.*, 421–33.
11. G.E. Rothenberg, 'The Habsburg Army in the Napoleonic Wars', *Military Affairs,* 1973, vol. 37, Febr. 1973, 3.
12. E. Longford, *Wellington, The Years of the Sword*, Harper & Row, New York, 1969, 211.
13. J.J. Pelet, *The French Campaign in Portugal 1810–1811,* ed. D.D. Horward, University of Minnesota Press, Minneapolis, 1973, 31–2.
14. Chandler, *op cit.*, 753–5.
15. G. Bodart, *Militär-Historisches Lexikon*, Stern, Vienna-Leipzig, 1908, 438.
16. *Memoirs of Baron Lejeune,* trans. and ed., A. Bell, 2 vols. Longmans, Green & Co., 1897, vol. I, 201–2.
17. J.M. Sherwig, *Guineas and Gunpowder,* Harvard University Press, 1969, 287–8.

3

The Soldier's Trade

Among the interpreters of Revolutionary and Napoleonic warfare few more clearly recognized the major changes than Karl von Clausewitz. In his famous work, *On War*, he described warfare as an 'act of force', theoretically without limit, and observed that 'experience also leads us to look for a great decision only in a great battle'.[1]

Before 1792 commanders sought to avoid battle; the generals of the Revolutionary Armies and Napoleon pursued it eagerly. Soldiers had been expensive, now they had become cheap and the great increase in the size of armies made rapid decisions both essential and possible. Destruction of the enemy force in battle had become the main objective; manoeuvre but the hand maiden. The number of battles in Europe between 1790 and 1820 was 713, contrasted with 2,659 for the entire period from 1480 to 1790. Frequent battles, of course, meant heavy casualties, but with the resources of whole nations behind them, the French, and eventually their adversaries too, could more easily replace them.

The new face of battle

Armies in the eighteenth century had been small. Although a state might maintain a military establishment of close to 200,000, few individual field armies exceeded 50,000 men. And in specific battles even this figure was rare. Frederick II mustered 77,000 at Hohenfriedberg; 64,000 at Prague, but less than 50,000 in all of his other battles. In contrast, Napoleon commanded more than 100,000 men in seven of his battles – 175,000 at Smolensk; 175,000 at Leipzig; 167,000 at Bautzen; 167,000 at Wagram; 160,000 at Gross Görschen; 133,000 at Borodino, and some 100,000 at Dresden. At Jena, with his army divided, he still mustered 96,000 men. Even his subordinates disposed very large forces in battle. In Spain, for instance, Massena had 70,000 at Ciudad Rodrigo; 60,000 at Almeida, and 58,000 at Bussaco.

To oppose such numbers, the Allied armies also increased in size. Archduke Charles had 130,000 at Wagram; 99,000 at Aspern; 78,000 at Ratisbon, and 74,000 at Eckmühl. Blücher led 100,000 at Craonne and 128,000 at La

Rothière in 1814; the year before he had 80,000 at the Katzbach. Kutuzov fought with over 120,000 men at Borodino. And at Leipzig the Allies brought together 325,000, while at Waterloo, Wellington assembled 67,660 men, with some 25,000 Prussians coming into action later in the day. And even in the Peninsula, Wellington led great numbers in battle, 90,000 at Vittoria and Nivelle; 54,000 at Talavera, and 46,000 at Salamanca.[2]

Despite these large forces, the limited range of weapon kept the battle areas small. At Borodino, for instance, the field was but three and a half miles, and in the final act at Waterloo some 140,000 men and over 400 guns were crammed into an equal space. The British line on the ridge of Mont Saint Jean extended but 3,500 yards. From high vantage points, commanders still could survey the disposition of their troops and those of the enemy, and could control their movements by dispatching mounted messengers, usually junior staff officers to issue orders. But, movement took time. A commander might perceive an opportunity to deliver a blow, he then had to gallop to the troops in person, or send a mounted aide, to give his orders. Then the units had to move to the desired spot and deploy in the required formation. Intervals of one or two hours between a decision to strike and its execution were fairly common and thus a very fine sense of timing was essential for a general.

The problem was further complicated by sharply reduced visibility. After the first few discharges, clouds of black powder smoke, together with the dust raised by thousands of men, horses, and wheels, created quite literally the 'fog of battle'. Men in action saw little. Rifleman Harris remembered that after several firings he was 'enveloped in the smoke I created, and the cloud which hung about me from the continued fire of my comrades, that I could see nothing . . . but the red flash of my own piece'. And this was a rifleman fighting in open order. The smoke, of course, was worse in the lines and for the supporting artillery. 'What was passing to the right and left of us,' Captain Mercer of the Horse Artillery tells in his Waterloo Diary, 'I knew no more of than the man in the moon.' His view of the battle was restricted to his own battery and two adjoining squares of infantry. Even officers commanding larger units lost their bearing and found it difficult to execute orders. Towards the end of the day at Waterloo, Sir Harry Smith of the Rifles was ordered by Wellington to advance but, having completely lost his bearings had to ask: 'In which direction, my lord?'[3]

Few battles, therefore, were as neat, controlled and directed as most historical narratives would have it.

Infantry in battle : arms, equipment and tactics

The great mass of all armies were comprised of foot soldiers who invariably suffered the heaviest casualties and usually decided the outcome of battle. There were three main categories of infantry. Everywhere the bulk was composed of the infantry of the line, though this category, too, was subdivided. In most armies grenadiers were chosen from the bravest and strongest men while, in theory at least, the light companies of the line were composed of men of superior agility but small stature. Secondly, there existed various guards formations, elite troops selected for bravery, stature, and experience, and usually held in reserve for particularly difficult assignments. Both line and elite troops commonly manoeuvred and fought in close formations, though during the early Revolutionary campaigns, the French used their ill-trained masses *en debandade*, that is as loose skirmishing swarms. By 1800, however, this had become primarily the task of the third category, the light infantry, variously styled as *chasseurs à pied, voltigeurs, flanqueurs, Jäger,* and riflemen, who were deployed ahead of the line. During an attack their fire was supposed to shake and demoralize the enemy line, while in the defence they were to break up the pace of the enemy advance. To carry out these functions, light infantry were issued with special weapons, sometimes rifled, more often improved smooth-bore muskets. As the wars continued, line infantry often detached a considerable portion of its strength to fight as skirmishers, while light troops acquired the capability to fight in line so that gradually an all-purpose infantry emerged.

Throughout the campaigns of the French Revolution and Napoleon, the great majority of infantry continued to be armed with a smooth-bore flintlock musket of large calibre. This weapon, remarkably similar in all armies, continued to determine tactics, training, and even uniform. The British Land Pattern Musket series, a 'pinned' type, standardized about 1740, as the Long Land Pattern with a 46-inch barrel and a .75-inch bore, may serve as a typical example. By the end of the Seven Years' War it had been slightly modified as the Short Land Model with a 42-inch barrel but retaining the same calibre. When the outbreak of war with France found England desperately short of arms and failing to procure adequate supplies from continental sources, the government approached the East India Company and obtained considerable quantities of the India Pattern, a plain 39-inch barrelled musket firing the standard ball. By 1797 this serviceable piece had been adopted as the standard weapon, and eventually put into mass production; it armed not only British troops but also was furnished in very large quantities to the various continental allies. In 1802, the Board of Ordnance began production of a new model, the 42-inch barrel New Land Pattern, but few were issued before 1814. Finally, and also in limited production only, there was a short 39-inch barrel Light Infantry Model. Although notoriously inaccurate, of which more later, the British Land Pattern series, affectionately nicknamed the 'Brown Bess', was well received by the troops and especially liked in the Russian army where 60,000 muskets were distributed to particularly meritorious soldiers in 1806.

Armament of other countries varied only in detail. The French utilized the Model 1777 musket, with a 44-inch barrel, but a smaller calibre, .69-inch, an overall length of 59.5 inches, and weighing slightly less than the British piece, about 10 pounds. With its reinforced cock, brass priming pan and with barrel bands designed for easy removal and field maintenance, the Model 1777, only slightly modified during the Revolution, remained the standard French weapon and was issued in many versions – infantry, dragoon, musketoon, and carbine – differing in length and furnishing, but sharing the same lock and calibre.

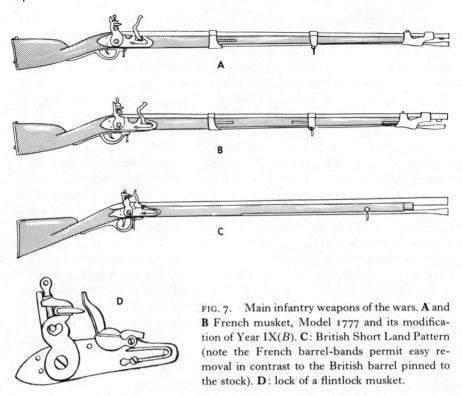

FIG. 7.   Main infantry weapons of the wars. A and B French musket, Model 1777 and its modification of Year IX(B). C: British Short Land Pattern (note the French barrel-bands permit easy removal in contrast to the British barrel pinned to the stock). D: lock of a flintlock musket.

Weapons of the other major combatants included the Prussian Model 1782, the Nothardt musket of 1805, and the New Prussian Model of 1809, though after the disaster of 1806 Prussia had to rely heavily on captured weapons and British material. The main Austrian weapon was the Model 1770, replaced after 1798 by a new model equipped with a slightly improved lock mechanism. The Russian infantry, finally, carried no less than 12 different types, of which the 1810 model, produced at Tula Arsenal, was perhaps the best.

A great disadvantage of all flintlock smooth-bore muskets was their inaccuracy and unreliability, the product of a combination of design and tactical factors. There was the slow lock time, that is the appreciable delay between the falling of the cock and the ignition of the main charge, causing the heavy piece to waver. This, of course, interfered with accuracy, a drawback compounded by the absence of rear sights. A small blunt projection serving as a front sight was provided but was usually obscured by the fixed bayonet, while accuracy was further compromised by the continued tactical requirement for speed and volume of fire. Balls had to be loose-fitting in black powder arms, otherwise the barrel would have to be cleaned after a few shots, a difficult procedure in the field. Therefore balls were always cast smaller than the bore, the windage amounting to between 0.07 to 0.10 inches. Attempts to reduce windage and make the weapon more accurate failed. The Prussian Nothardt musket had reduced windage of 0.04 inch, but this caused extensive fouling and much greater recoil. Previously troops had complained about recoil after 20 shots, now complaints came from the start. Flinching became more acute and accuracy was not much improved.

At that, accuracy also suffered because of the need for rapid fire. With a rate of two to three shots a minute, the first usually was the most accurate as the piece had been loaded with care. Later discharges were less effective and also a great many things could go wrong in the process of loading and firing. The powder might flash in the pan, but fail to ignite the main charge. Sometimes in the noise and excitement of battle this went unnoticed and a soldier might continue to load additional charges, often with disastrous results. As firing continued, flints became worn and had to be replaced, and vents became clogged and had to be cleaned. During a prolonged fire fight as high as 20 percent misfires could be expected.

All this, of course, lowered the capability of the weapon. Although the killing range of a musket was about 300 paces, this was far from its effective combat range. According to Prussian tests, the 1782 musket hit a 10-foot wide and 6-foot high target about 60 times out of 100 at 100 paces, only 40 times at 200 paces, and only 25 times at 300 paces. The French 1777 musket had slightly better performance, but this was under test conditions.[4] In 1814 a British ordnance officer concluded that 'a soldier's musket, if not exceedingly ill-bored as many are, will strike the figure of a man at 80 yards . . . but a soldier must be very unfortunate indeed who shall be wounded by a common musket at 150 yards, provided his antagonist aims at him, and as for firing at 200 yards you might as well fire at the moon'. Prussian, French, and British tests indicated that 500 men firing two volleys against an attacking infantry column over a range narrowing down from 100 yards could, in theory, expect to obtain between 500 and 600 hits. Actual combat experience, however, indicated that due to the thick smoke, careless loading, and various malfunctions, the number of hits, at best, ranged between 6 and 15 percent of the rounds expended. The first volleys were the most deadly; thereafter effectiveness declined sharply.[5]

Writing in 1811, an American officer observed that considering the number of rounds fired, 'the little execution done by muskets in some engagements almost surpasses belief'.[6] Soldiers in most Continental armies carried between 50 to 60 rounds in their pouches, and normally were expected to use no more than 20 during a battle. At Vittoria, however, the British fired over 3,500,000 rounds, about 60 per man, and calculations show that it required some 450 rounds to inflict one casualty.[7] The British were lucky. By this time Wellington had an efficient ammunition train and soldiers were able to replenish their supply. At Marengo, on the other hand, Captain Coignet reports that his battalion ran out of ammunition and was saved only by the timely arrival of the Consular Guard carrying extra rounds.

One additional reason for the large expenditure of ammunition in combat at such close ranges was that musketry training remained extremely sketchy in most armies. Although the French Revolutionary forces often had used hordes of *tirailleurs* in 1793–4, these men had little training, and this did not change much in later campaigns. Coignet, a writer assiduous in detail, reports that he learned to shoot only after Napoleon became First Consul, and in 1800 Berthier, Napoleon's chief-of-staff, ordered that 'all conscripts ought to fire a few rounds, and also learn how to load, hold, and aim their muskets properly'.[8] But there never was enough time or powder for intensive training in the Revolutionary or Imperial armies, or for that matter in those of their various adversaries. Only the British, universally admired for their musketry, did better. Even so, regulations allowed but 30 rounds of ball and 50 blank cartridges annually for practice, and only light infantry and riflemen received a larger allowance and were expected to hit a mark.

Prussian experiments revealed that a slight angling of the stock would have greatly improved accuracy, but tactical doctrines still called for the highest volume of fire possible in a short time and not for individually aimed fire. This was provided by riflemen, present in most armies. The French had experimented with them, but in 1807, Napoleon had ordered all rifled weapons withdrawn. Other armies had small bodies of *Jäger* as well as light infantry, two separate types, though interchangeably used for skirmishing. The all important difference was in their weapons. Both could be used in open order, but while light infantry, usually carrying a more accurate version of the issue musket also could fight in line, riflemen were armed with a weapon of greater range and accuracy, but one which suffered from a much reduced rate of fire and fouled very rapidly. When these factors were combined with the high initial cost of the weapon and the longer time required to train a competent rifleman, the disadvantages seemed to outweigh the advantages. In most Continental armies, therefore, the numerous *Jäger* units (Russia had 20 regiments) were simply light infantry and usually only partially equipped with rifles. In the British army there were two rifle-armed regiments, the 60th and the 95th, though the famous Light Brigade, later the Light Division, in the Peninsula for the most part carried modified issue muskets.

Rifles and muskets shared the common flintlock and flints were a small, but important, item of equipment. Flint was quarried from layers of chalk, preferably in damp weather, and dried before skilled workmen, knappers, processed them. Some of the best gun flints came from English quarries and were supplied in large quantities to Britain's allies. Fine-quality flints were produced in Champagne and Picardy and there were also good deposits in Saxony. Prussia, however, was short of flints and in 1813, before English supplies could arrive, the Royal Porcelain Manufacture was ordered to make some *ersatz* supplies.

Being vital for ignition, flints were taken very seriously in all armies. Every soldier carried at least one spare, while additional supplies were held in the battalion baggage. Worn flints would cause misfires and soldiers were forbidden to snap their locks during exercises unless the flint had been replaced by a wooden dummy 'snapper'. Before battle, flints were a vital piece of equipment to be checked. On the eve of Austerlitz, Coignet remembered, Napoleon personally told his guard, 'put new flints in your guns, tomorrow morning you will need them'.[9]

Another item to be checked frequently was cartridges, made out of strong paper and containing some 150 grains of powder and the ball. Usually these were made up in arsenals, packed in paper-lined boxes, about 1,000 to a box, and issued to the troops in packages of 10 to 15 rounds. The French normally carried 50 cartridges, the British 60, except for the Rifles who carried 80 rounds. Because dampness would spoil the powder, waterproof cartridge boxes were essential and company officers in all armies checked the ammunition supply of their men every morning.

Fire tactics : column against line

Given the limitations of the musket and the conditions of the battlefield, the most important improvements in the effectiveness of fire depended on tactics.

During the early Revolutionary campaigns the French discovered that their new volunteers and conscripts lacked the discipline and training to fight according to the 1791 Manual. Therefore they adopted loose skirmishing tactics; employing clouds of *tirailleurs* who moved forward supported by battalion columns. As the French armies became better trained and disciplined, both the attack column, a deep rectangular formation, and the line were used as the tactical situation demanded, and again preceded and screened by skirmisher swarms. Beginning in 1807, Napoleon finally reduced the emphasis on skirmishers and relied more and more on massive attacks, carried out by large columns, sometimes divisional formations.

The various powers fighting the Revolution and the Empire continued to rely initially on the eighteenth century linear formation both for attack and defence. 'Regular, well drilled, and steady infantry,' the Austrian army instructions of 1796 maintained, 'cannot be impeded by skirmishers. All the individual firing and skirmishing decides nothing.' Still, the outcome of the campaigns forced the Austrians to modify their practices and after 1800 they came closer to the French system. They retained the three deep linear formations, though often part of the third rank was detached as skirmishers. Moreover, after 1806, they too began to use columns for the attack. Similar changes were made in Prussia after 1807 and in Russia after 1810.

Only the British retained confidence in the line. While official doctrine directed infantry to be formed in three ranks, in practice Wellington and other British commanders formed their troops only two deep in order to present the broadest possible front. It should be remembered, however, that the short range of the muskets restricted the number of files that could engage an attack column from either side of its direct frontage. Still, given equal numbers, the line had greater firepower than the column and sometimes it was possible for the wings to swing inward to enfilade the attackers. The French certainly were impressed by the volume of British fire. General Marbot contended in his *Memoires* that this was based on 'superior accuracy achieved by training and on their two rank formation'. Napoleon added fire-discipline to the factors contributing to British victories, but he also realized that the third rank was not functional and shortly before Leipzig he sup-

pressed it. 'This,' he wrote, 'will give a 500 men battalion the firepower of
750 men.'[10]

The classic examples of encounters between the column and the line are
recorded during the Peninsular campaign where highly trained British troops
met French attack columns, often unseasoned troops, who failed to deploy in
time when coming up against a skirmisher-screened and at least partially
concealed line. Under those conditions, it was often difficult for the French
officers to judge the right moment and distance for deployment from column
into line, still the manoeuvre called for by the Regulations of 1791.

The first clash between the two tactical formations had already taken place
on 1 July 1806 at Maida in southern Italy where Sir John Stuart's small
British force, 5,200 in all, defeated a roughly equal French force under
Reynier. During this action some 700 British light infantry, formed two deep
on a front of 200 yards, routed a French regiment surging forward in columns
of division – that is on a two company frontage each three deep, a formation
about 50 yards wide and 12 ranks deep. At about 120 yards the first volley
inflicted casualties; at 80 yards the second volley cut a deep swath, and the
third volley, delivered at 20 yards, broke the attack. 'The 42nd of the Line,' a
French participant recorded, 'suffered from the terrible fire of the enemy . . .
the British battalion fire, unfortunately for us, is executed perfectly.'[11]

The story was repeated many times in the Peninsula where Wellington
again and again placed his infantry on the reverse slope of a hill to protect it
from the French artillery, a practice he also followed at Waterloo. A young
British officer tells what it was like: 'The regiment stood about forty paces
below the crest of the position, so that it was nearly or quite out of fire. The
roar of round shot still continued, many just clearing our head – others striking the top of our position and bounding over us.' Meanwhile, the French
were forming up for the attack and the British line waited and listened. 'The
drummers were beating the *pas de charge*, which sounded as well as can
recollect, very much like this, the rum dum, the rum dum, the rummadum,
dummadum, dum, dum, then *Vive l'Empéreur*! This was repeated again and
again.'[12] As the French column approached, the British line rose, waiting for
the command. Then the muskets moved up as the column closed shouting
and firing, a volley crashed out, once, twice, or more, and then followed a brief
British charge before which the column retired. After that the line reformed
and resumed its previous position.

Wellington always chose his positions most carefully to secure his flanks,
but when his guiding hand was missing, such as at Albuera, French infantry
or cavalry might charge into the flank of the line and inflict very heavy
casualties. But when he was present, from Vimeiro to Waterloo, the British
line usually repelled columnar assaults.

The myth of cold steel: bayonets in combat
Although all armies cherished the bayonet, a triangular blade about 15 to 18
inches long fastened to the muzzle by a ring socket, it is doubtful that this

weapon was very effective. Still, its use appealed to Republican and Imperialist alike in France. Carnot's instructions of February 1794 had ordered 'action with the bayonet on every occasion', and Napoleon, too, liked cold steel. 'To be killed regularly,' Captain Blaze claimed sardonically, 'one had to be killed by the bayonet . . . the Emperor had an extreme fondness for those who perished in this manner.'[13] More importantly, official doctrine, as expounded by Gay de Vernon, at the École Polytechnique, claimed that only the first musket volley was effective, 'after which the bayonet and the sword may charge without sustaining great losses'.[14] For that matter, Austrian and Prussian regulations also stressed the role of the bayonet in the attack, and even the reforming Archduke Charles regarded it as the best weapon for hand-to-hand combat. As for the Russians, General Wilson reported in 1810, that the 'bayonet is a truly Russian weapon', and the *Precepts for Infantry Officers on the Day of Battle*, issued in the summer of 1812, still advocated the bayonet charge delivered in deep column formation.

Yet, few soldiers actually fought each other with cold steel. At Austerlitz, the Russian Guards made a classic 300-yard charge, but were exhausted after breaking through the first French line and driven back by fire. Generally, it was the threat of the bayonet, and not the actual clash that decided an issue. After studying the casualties suffered by units in a number of hand to hand combats, Surgeon General Larrey of the Grand Army found only five bayonet wounds and concluded that the effect of the weapon was primarily psychological.[16] And one of Wellington's senior medical officers, George J. Guthrie, asserted that formed regiments 'charging with the bayonet *never* meet and struggle hand to hand and foot to foot; and this for the best possible reason, that one side turns and runs away as soon as the other comes close enough to do mischief'.[17] The observations of the medical men are supported by experienced officers. Commenting on bayonet encounters, General Lejeune pointed out that these were 'very rare in modern warfare, for as a rule one of the corps is demoralized to begin with by the firing, and draws back before the enemy is near enough to cross muzzles', while Jomini declared that 'I never saw such a thing on a regular field of battle'.[17]

Though rare, hand to hand fighting occurred when troops were struggling for a battery or redoubt, or when rain made firing impossible. At the Katzbach, in 1813, Prussian infantry attacked in a driving rain with bayonet and musket butt, inflicting heavy casualties on the French. Above all, the bayonet affixed to the long musket constituted a defence against cavalry and to offset the shortness of their weapons, riflemen carried an even longer blade, 25 inches, in the form of a sword bayonet. However, in contrast with line infantry which carried their bayonets fixed at all times, the Prussians even discarding the scabbard, riflemen 'fixed swords' only when forming squares or preparing to receive an attack in closed formation. Rifleman Costello believed that without it the slow loading rifle-armed troops would be helpless at close quarters against bayonet-equipped infantry or cavalry.

Defence against charging horse was also one of the arguments produced in 1792–4 for the reintroduction of the pike in France. The shortage of firearms, combined with the Republican emphasis on the attack with cold steel, were alleged to make this ancient weapon a useful instrument of war in the hands of untrained but enthusiastic soldiers. Early in 1792 pike production began in various French cities, and in August 1792, the Legislative Assembly decreed the manufacture and distribution of a national pike, roughly 10–15 feet long. Many of the new units rushed to the threatened frontier carried these weapons and as late as the summer of 1793, General Custine of the Army of the North advised one of his subordinates that lacking muskets, 'we must make up for this with pikes; you are not the only one who suffers from the arms shortage'.[18] But despite the alleged advantages of the pike for close action, upheld among others by Carnot, the pike disappeared from the inventory as soon as the supply of firearms improved. Similar sentiments were voiced from time to time throughout the next 20 years in England, Ireland, Russia, and finally in Prussia, but in all cases the pike was considered as a mere expedient and abandoned as soon as muskets and bayonets became available.

Infantry in combat against cavalry

Cavalry, as can be imagined, was a major threat to foot soldiers. Although fighting in line made infantry formidable against frontal assault, its flanks and rear were vulnerable to sudden cavalry charges. The best defence against this was to form squares, a difficult manoeuvre that had to be carried out precisely but when completed, presented an all around hedge of bayonets against the swords and lances of the horse. At Albuera, Colborne's brigade, deployed in line, was blinded by a sudden rain squall and when it lifted, two French light cavalry regiments fell on its flank. Within five minutes three of its battalions, lacking time to form squares, were annihilated. Out of a total 80 officers and 1,568 men, 1,248 were dead, wounded, or captured.

Squares, however, had certain inherent weaknesses. As long as it remained firm, its ranks steady and holding their fire until the attacking cavalry was at close range, it generally could stand off and inflict heavy cavalry losses. But if the square wavered or broke before the psychological impact of the cavalry, losses were terrible. Moreover, well-trained horse could confound a square. For instance, in 1812 at Garcia Hernandez, the Dragoons of the King's German Legion broke a steady French square, while at Wagram, Colonel Castex of the 20th *Chasseurs à cheval*, inclined his charge from the square assigned as his target and fell on a neighbouring square that had just discharged its muskets against the 7th *Chasseurs*.

Then too, squares drastically reduced the firepower of infantry and in the presence of hostile foot, commanders hesitated to adopt this vulnerable disposition. Finally, and worst of all, squares constituted prime targets for artillery. At Waterloo, Mercer recalled seeing two squares punished by French fire. 'The Brunswickers,' he remembered, 'were falling fast – the shot every moment making great gaps in their squares, which the officers and sergeants were actively employed in filling up by pushing the men together.'[19] To keep a square compact was vital, but it meant that most shots and balls found their target.

A variant of the square was the 'mass' introduced after 1806 by Archduke Charles in the Austrian army. The mass was a closely packed column, with only minimal intervals between the ranks and files. The battalion mass had a company front and was 18 ranks deep. Such formations could, though with difficulty, manoeuvre on flat ground and at Aspern, for example, made local advances in the presence of French cavalry and shattered the charge of six Cuirassier regiments with volleys at 15 paces. Nonetheless, the mass, essentially a revival of the tactics employed against the Turkish hordes of horse on the Hungarian plain, had little flexibility. It was rarely employed after Aspern, but remained on the drill books for over half a century.[20]

During the Egyptian campaign, Napoleon, with an army composed only of infantry, and having to contend with a numerous cavalry, adopted deep and close orders of battle, flanked by cross fires of horse artillery. And for his advance into Palestine, he introduced pikes in the Army of Egypt. Before setting out across the Sinai, five-foot-long pikes, with chains to link them together as portable obstacles against expected cavalry charges, were issued to the infantry. However, most of this cumbersome gear conveniently disappeared during the march.[21]

Cavalry on campaign and in battle

The increased size of armies led to a decline in the proportion of mounted troops. Whereas in Marlborough's armies horse constituted between 20 to 40 percent of the total, and comprised from 23 to 42 percent of Frederick the Great's effectiveness, Napoleon's armies had much smaller percentages of cavalry. At Austerlitz about 23 percent of the Grand Army was cavalry, but, due to the losses sustained in Russia, mounted troops amounted to only 5.2 percent of his forces at Gross Görschen. In the Peninsula, Wellington, suffering from the difficulties of transporting horses by sea as well as the shortage of forage, operated with a high of 18.5 percent mounted troops at Talavera, but with only 5.7 percent at Fuentes de Onoro. On the average, mounted troops constituted about 12 percent of his forces.[22]

Cavalry was divided into two major categories, heavy and light. Sometimes an intermediate type, line, is mentioned. Heavy cavalry comprised the armoured Cuirassiers and Carabiniers, as well as Dragoons; light cavalry included *Chasseurs à cheval*, Hussars, Lancers, and irregular bodies of Russian Cossacks.

Light horse retained its traditional reconnaissance and security roles, but in every army the overriding ambition of all horse, light or heavy, was the mounted charge delivered in line two deep. On rare occasions cavalry might charge with squadrons in echelon at 30–50 paces intervals, but this was not recommended. During the early campaigns, cavalry was still positioned on the wings of the battle line, but Napoleon developed the arm as an instrument for shattering the enemy line, a *masse de rupture*. In the Grand Army he massed mounted regiments and used them as a tactical reserve under his own control for a charge or counterstroke, or for the pursuit after victory. 'Without cavalry,' Napoleon concluded, 'battles are without result.' No Napoleonic victory was complete without the cavalry thundering in hot pursuit of the beaten enemy. The most famous example was the pursuit after Jena, when Murat led the cavalry reserve in a 24-day chase covering 500 miles. Few cavalry units could match the French after 1805, though the British and Hanoverians were their equal in individual combat. But the British cavalry, so Wellington found, was too undisciplined and too unpredictable for his liking and he was always short of mounted troops and often had to put up with incompetent cavalry commanders. The Hanoverians, on the other hand, were excellent, but there were few of them. As for the Russians, they were numerous and their irregular cavalry was skilled, but in the opinion of most French cavalry officers not as well trained in the use of arms as the French.

If time permitted, the mounted charge was preceeded by some prepara- tions. All fodder bags, bales of hay, and other encumberments were discarded and in the French army at least, *Chasseurs* and other unarmoured troopers rolled their cloaks before action and slung them across their chests as a partial protection. The charge itself was delivered with gradually increasing speed, usually starting out at about 600 paces with the trot, changing at 400 to a canter, the next 150 at a restrained gallop, and only the last 50 paces before impact at full career. When cavalry met cavalry in a countercharge there was much noise and commotion, but surprisingly few casualties. 'When cavalry meets cavalry,' General Marbot concluded, 'the slaughter is much less than when it is opposed by infantry.'[23] At Waterloo, Captain Mercer witnessed the clash of two cavalry regiments. They rode at one another, but the ranks opened and the men passed through, slashing and stabbing, but with little effect. While cavalry combat often saw units passing through each other with little damage, heavy casualties occurred when weapons were unequal or when one side was driven to flight.

For all cavalry – *les armes blanches* – sword, sabre, and lance were the principal armament. Heavy cavalry was equipped with a long straight sword, sharpened at both the edge and point, while the light regiments carried a curved sabre. The French, light or heavy, usually used the point of their weapons in cavalry action, while in the British army the merits of the cut over the thrust were hotly debated in the heavy regiments. The light cavalry sword was considered a poor weapon, 'equally ill adapted for either the cut or the thrust'. Yet, if British troopers in the Peninsula found it difficult to cleave through the stout cloth of the French uniforms, their comrades of the King's German Legion, using the same weapon, had no such trouble and one suspects that training had much to do with it. The French were impressed by the British sword, Captain Parquin of the *Chasseurs* recorded that though the British blows missed most of the time, 'if the edge of the blade found its mark only once, it was a terrible blow and it was not unusual to see an arm cut clean from the body'.[24]

The heavy lance had been the main weapon of mounted men until the sixteenth century and it had survived in eastern Europe where a lighter version was carried by Cossacks and Polish Lancers. The Polish Partitions had introduced lancer units, designated as Uhlans, into the Austrian and Prussian service, equipped with 12–14 foot light lances. During the Polish campaign of 1806, the French encountered Cossacks and Napoleon was so impressed that he raised some Polish Lancers to counter them, and after the Lancers distinguished themselves in Spain, overrunning some British infantry at Albuera, he equipped several more light regiments with this weapon, nine-foot long in the French cavalry.

Yet the value of the lance was disputed. Petre maintains that the Cossacks were more than a match for mounted opponents armed only with a sword. But by 1812, French cavalry officers seemed less impressed. In line, lancers were formidable, but in a *melée* Marbot found that the 'length of the lance is an encumbrance when their bearers are closely pressed by adversaries armed with sabres . . . which they can handle easily, while the lancers find it difficult to present the point of their poles'. And British cavalry meeting French lancers in the Peninsula also reported little difficulty in dealing with them.[25] Nonetheless, after 1815, the British converted several light regiments into Lancers and lance-equipped units were retained in many major European armies into the post-World War I era.

Almost every cavalry trooper was also equipped with a firearm, a pistol, carbine, musketoon, or short musket. These, of course, could not be reloaded in action and often were discarded by troops as a useless and unnecessary weight. Still, on occasion, they were useful. According to Parquin, in 1807 a *Chasseur* regiment stopped a Russian Dragoon advance with a carbine volley. But the bayonets issued with these carbines were useful only for digging up potatoes, and Parquin relates that 'we threw them away before we went into action'. In the end, the troopers had to pay for them, 7 francs and 50 centimes, but considered it worthwhile. The British cavalry also was not fond of its firearms, a variety of pistols and carbines. A standard weapon, the Paget carbine, with a ramrod attached to the piece on a swivel, was introduced after 1811, but used little.

Constituting a major shock instrument, cavalry was increasingly hurled against infantry and artillery, and it was here that it took its heavy losses. At Wagram the French attacked Austrian masses (Parquin called them squares) with three cavalry regiments. 'At one hundred paces a terrible volley . . . caused the most fearful confusion,' killing one general, several officers, and over 50 troopers. And artillery could cause even more damage. Perhaps the classic description was given by Mercer who watched the French deploy for a frontal charge. 'On they came in compact squadrons, one behind the other, so numerous that those of the rear were still behind the brow when the head of the column was but some sixty or seventy yards from our guns.' As the French approached the battery stood ready, the guns double shotted, that is with round-shot first and canister over it, a practice that was damaging to the tube and only used in an extremity. At 50 or 60 yards Mercer opened fire: 'The effect was terrible. Nearly the whole leading rank fell at once; and the round-shot, penetrating the column carried confusion throughout its extent.'[27] The first salvo, Mercer observed, reduced the attackers to a walk, while the second and subsequent firings heaped up carcasses that the survivors could not pass.

Artillery materiel and organization

Guns were not always as effective as Mercer described, in fact much of their effect was psychological. Yet, during the era of Revolutionary and Napoleonic warfare, in the words of the official French officer-instruction text, they 'now ranked among the constituent elements of a complete army; they vary the power of the arms, and render practicable to the latter, operations otherwise impracticable'.[28] Artillery had become one of the three main combat arms and on many a battlefield its fire, outranging musketry, was decisive. Smoothbore artillery's effectiveness was much influenced by proper siting and ability to target, and few commanders appreciated its full potential. A real gap was developing between the 'scientific' artillery specialists and the field generals. Frederick II already had complained about the technical jargon and the 'pretensions' of his artillery officers; Wellington's alleged dislike of his gunners was notorious, and Archduke Charles did not comprehend that his mass formations were extremely vulnerable in the face of long-range artillery fire. For that matter even Napoleon, a trained gunner who exploited artillery mobility to achieve maximum concentrated fire at the decisive point, failed to grasp the possibilities of reverse-slope fire by howitzers, perhaps a major factor in his defeat at Waterloo.

Although the total number of pieces increased greatly, proportionately artillery remained at or slightly below the level achieved by Frederick. In Napoleon's armies the ratio of guns to men stood at two per 1,000 in 1800 and by 1812, to compensate for the declining quality of his infantry, had risen to five per 1,000 soldiers, though many were light battalion or regimental pieces.

There were now fundamental changes in the types or designs of guns during this period, and except for the introduction of spherical case, shrapnel, no major advances in ammunition. Field and siege artillery continued to be divided, though except for the horse artillery, their personnel often was interchangeable. With mobility becoming more important, there was a considerable increase in this branch. But, though extremely effective in supporting an attack or covering a retreat, it also was very expensive, and therefore an authoritative French text concluded that the 'main body of the troops of this arm [i.e. artillery] should be composed of foot artillery; these troops are more patient in their duties and works, more careful of their equipages and implements, and the effects of their efforts are more certain'.[29]

The last statement referred to the fact that despite the requirement for mobility, the weight of the projectile remained of paramount importance. European armies utilized two basic ranges of field artillery. The French and Spanish employed 4-, 8- and 12-pounders; the Austrian, British, Prussian, and Russian artillery 3-, 6- and 12-pounders. The heavier 8- and 12-pounders far outranged the lighter pieces and their effect on impact was more devastating. While there was little difference in muzzle velocities between the various weights, the heavier shot, due to the kinetic energy which varies directly with the weight but according to the square of the velocity, had much more hitting power and finally the heavier pieces produced a much more terrifying noise. As a result, Napoleon increased the number of his beloved *belles filles*, the 12-pounder field pieces, and partially replaced his 4-pounders with 6-pounders. (It has to be remembered here that the French pound was a tenth heavier than the English.) To counter the French guns, the British introduced a 9-pounder as the standard field piece, and Wellington eventually armed many of his horse-artillery batteries with the heavier piece, considering that the greater effectiveness was well worth the small reduction in mobility. Despite the improvements in the designs of barrels and carriages, guns were still far from light. Napoleon's 12-pounders weighed one and a half tons without their ammunition chests and required 12 horses to move them; the British 9-pounder weighed 29 hundredweights and was supposed to be pulled by six horses, though over rough ground eight were better.

Field howitzers, with a shorter and less solid barrel, were of course lighter. The French and British service classified them by calibre, the British fielding $4\frac{2}{5}$-inch, $5\frac{1}{2}$-inch, and 8-inch howitzers, while the French had 6- and 8-inch howitzers. The other European armies clung to an obsolete measure, designating their howitzers by the weight of a stone projectile that would have fitted their bore. Prussia, Austria, and Russia mainly had 7- and 10-pound field howitzers.

For tactical purposes field artillery was divided into two main categories – those in direct support of the infantry and those in an artillery reserve. At the outset of the war the small 3- and 4-pounders constituting the first category were standard in all armies. Nominally these guns were served by detached gunners, but in practice they were operated by hastily trained foot soldiers. The efficiency of this arrangement, flouting the principle of concentration, was questioned by many. Napoleon, for example, suppressed them in 1800, but reintroduced them after 1806 to shore up his infantry; whilst in 1802 they were discarded in the British army, and after 1805, Archduke Charles concentrated them in a brigade artillery reserve.

The tendency to centralize field artillery, especially the foot batteries forming its bulk, at the division, corps, and army level was pronounced. Usually organized in mixed batteries of six to eight pieces, typically four cannon and two field howitzers, they were used to lay down fire concentrations at the decisive point. This was the practice followed both by Napoleon and Archduke Charles, and adopted in the Russian army following the reforms of 1810. In Prussia, however, the Regulations of 1812 placed artillery reserves at the brigade level, but the Prussian brigade was a heavy formation, roughly equal in size to divisions elsewhere, and it combined all three combat arms. Finally the British army, numerically weak in artillery, usually distributed its guns in batteries or divisions, that is half-batteries, in support of their line, though commanders retained control over its disposition and Wellington sometimes sited the pieces by himself.

Artillery fire tactics and projectiles

Ranges of field guns and howitzers varied according to elevation, loads, wind conditions, and projectiles fired, but the practical outer limit for the 12- and 8-pounders was 800 to 900 yards, 800 yards for 6-pounders, and 700 yards for 4-pounders. The range for field howitzers, firing shells over a curved trajectory, was lower, between 500 and 600 yards, and about the same when fired in line of sight with canister or shot.[30] An authoritative French text provided slightly larger range tables, though the author cautioned his readers 'Never to make use of fire, but within the distances established for effective ranges'.[31] Austrian tests indicated that at 800 yards cannon could expect 40–70 percent hits against a company in line. As one would imagine effectiveness diminished with range or when the target was protected. Although the 12-pound round shot could penetrate six-foot-thick earth ramparts, at Chiclana (1811) one French redoubt received 93 hits in 15 minutes without sustaining a single casualty, and at Bautzen a French regiment manoeuvred under heavy long range fire with only two men killed and a dozen or so wounded. The results of long range fire were further reduced by the smoke and dust of the battlefield making targeting difficult.

Additional range could be obtained by means of ricochet fire, allegedly invented by Vauban. Here the round shot, fired with a reduced charge, glanced off the ground, bouncing in repeated jumps for as much as an additional 50 percent of the range. Its final effect depended on the weight of the projectile, but it was most deadly when employed against the heads of columns or in enfilading a line.

MEAN RANGES OF ARTILLERY PIECES OF ALL CALIBRES

Calibres	Mean Ranges in Meters	Mean Ranges in English yards
24- and 16-pounders	about 1,000–1,200	about 1,120–1,340
12- and 8-pounders	800– 900	900–1,000
4-pounders	500– 600	560– 670
Field howitzers	400– 500	450– 560
Mortars	600–1,500	670–1,670
Muskets	200– 250	222– 280

Table adapted from S.F. Gay de Vernon, *Treatise on the Science of War and Fortification*, New York, 1817, p. 169.

Artillery projectiles and fire tactics

Cannon and howitzers fired solid round shot, common shell, spherical case, and canister; mortars were limited to shell. The ranges provided in the table above are for solid round shot, which was probably fired more than any other type of ammunition. Solid shot was effective against formed troops in direct as well as ricochet fire, and could cause great havoc in a column, though it generally was less effective against troops in line. But for the individual soldier, long range bombardment by round shot, against which he had no chance to reply, was terrifying. Coignet graphically describes such a situation when at Essling in 1809 a regiment of the Imperial Guard, supported only by some small battalion pieces, came under the fire of a large Austrian artillery concentration. 'To the left of Essling,' he recounts, 'the enemy planted fifty pieces of cannon. The fifty pieces thundered upon us without our being able to advance a step, or fire a gun . . . The balls fell among our ranks and cut down our men three at a time . . . [eventually] we had to place the guard all in one rank so as to keep up the line in front of the enemy.'[32] Despite such casualties, the French, Prussians, and Russians habitually deployed in the open, while Wellington wisely always tried to place his troops behind the crest of a ridge.

Common shell, the second type of round projectile, could, of course, reach the reverse side of a slope. Frederick the Great Already had used his howitzers for this purpose and on 10 August 1813, Prussian army instructions repeated this principle. 'Should the enemy be on the reverse side of a slope,' the instructions read, '. . . it will be advantageous to concentrate the howitzers, as a large number of shells thrown on one spot will produce a fearful effect.' Napoleon, however, did little to exploit the potential of his howitzers. As for the shells themselves, they were hollow cast-iron spheres filled with powder and equipped with a fuse. The fuse was a hollow reed, filled with strands of quickmatch, about five inches long and cut to varying size according to the distance and time required. To cut a fuse correctly required experience and in the heat of battle fuses sometimes were cut too short and exploded the shell in the air, others, cut too long, left the shell smouldering on the ground where it might be extinguished by a brave man. Unless muffled by soft wet ground, a bursting shell had a danger radius of about 25 yards.

Spherical case shot, first proposed by its inventor Lieutenant Henry Shrapnel of the Royal Artillery in 1784, represented a new type of projectile and was used only by British artillery during the Napoleonic wars. Shells depended for their effect on the bursting of their charge. Shrapnel's spherical case, by contrast, contained only enough of a charge to open the sphere so that its contents, from 27–170 musket balls, depending on size and calibre, could continue to travel forward in the same direction and with the same velocity as the burst case. In the words of its inventor, the new projectile made 'the fire of case shot effective at all distances within the range of cannon'. This, of course, was of great value for hitting formations, but it took 20 years for the British army to adopt and use it in the field. After 1804 it became a standard part of ammunition supply in the field, amounting to between 13 and 19 percent of the rounds for field guns and up to 50 percent for field howitzers. Although extensively used for long-range fire against troops, its effectiveness was disputed and records are scanty. Wellington, after some misgivings, pronounced it of 'great benefit', and the French, having no means to reply, detested it. The main drawback was the tendency to premature explosion, thought to be due to the unreliable fuses. Only after extensive tests in the 1850s was it discovered that these were due to the friction heat developed by the intermingling of the balls and the powder in flight.[33]

At closer range, used both offensively and defensively, the most common anti-personnel ammunition was canister or case. The name comes from its canister or case, a cylindrical container of thin metal which was filled with musket balls, pellets, or scrap. The container merely held the projectiles together during their passage through the bore. When it emerged, the canister disintegrated, while the individual projectiles continued to fly forward spreading out. The size of the balls or pellets varied. Austrian and French canister contained three different sizes; the British employed two, ranging from $1\frac{1}{2}$ ounce to $3\frac{1}{4}$ ounce balls. The exact number of the projectiles as well as the range varied with the calibre of the gun and the size of the projectiles, but the British limited its use to below 350 yards, while the French, lacking spherical case, used the heaviest type up to 600 yards, and one authority claims that the 12-pounder field gun could fire the heaviest pellets over a distance exceeding 800 yards.[34]

At short ranges canister was highly effective. British records indicate that under test conditions 41 percent of the British 6-pounder canister was effective at 400 yards and 23 percent at 600, meaning that a battery firing 500 light pellets in a single volley could expect to obtain some 300 hits, about equal to a 500-man battalion volley delivered at 100 yards.

As the table below shows, heavy canister sometimes was referred to as grape, but this type of projectile, nine heavy balls weighing from 8 to 16 ounces, and wired together around a stand, was not employed in the land service during this period. Heavy canister was used much more effectively and more extensively, but solid round shot remained the predominant projectile.

CANISTER SHOT

	12-pounder			8-pounder			4-pounder			6-inch howitzer		
	ins.	lins.	pts.	ins.	lins.	pts.	ins.	lins.	pts.	ins.	lins.	pts.
Diameter of balls No. 1, or heavy grape shot	1	5	0	1	2	9	0	11	10	1	5	0
Diameter of balls No. 2, of small grape	1	0	0	0	10	6	0	10	9	0	0	0
Diameter of balls No. 3, or smallest grape	0	11	6	0	10	1	0	0	0	0	0	0
Length of the charge of powder	12	0	0	11	0	0	10	0	0	10	0	0
Exterior length of the canister of large grape	8	3	0	6	9	0	5	7	0	7	4	0
of the canister of small grape	7	6	0	6	8	0	6	6	0	0	0	0
No. of balls No. 1, in the large canister	41 balls			41 balls			41 balls			60 balls		
No. of balls in the small canister { of No. 2 / of No. 3 }	2 total balls { 8ob / 32b } 112			{ 8ob / 32b } 112			No. 1 4 / No. 2 59 } 63					

Adapted from S.F. Gay de Vernon, *Treatise on the Science of War and Fortifications*, New York, 1817, p. 123.

Ammunition scales reflected the preponderance of round shot. While the exact figures varied, the table for the French field artillery was average. The British 9-pounder was supplied with 88 round shot, 12 spherical case, eight heavy and eight light canister, while the 6-pounder carried 132, 20, 14, and 14 respectively. This was an adequate supply immediately available to the guns in their firing positions, with the ammunition caissons usually some 30 yards behind the guns. Only if caissons were destroyed, or if a long bombardment of the enemy's position was required, did batteries have to watch their fire.

CONTENTS OF LIMBER BOXES AND CAISSONS

	Limber boxes	Caissons	Total No. of rounds for each piece
For *12-pounders*			
Rounds of shot or ball	9	48 ⎫	
of large canister		12 ⎬ 68	
of small canister		8 ⎭	
Three caissons to each piece		204	213
For *8-pounders*			
Rounds of shot	15	62 ⎫	
of heavy canister		10 ⎬ 92	
of small canister		20 ⎭	
Two caissons for each gun		184	199
For *4-pounders*			
Rounds of shot	18	100 ⎫	
of heavy canister		26 ⎬ 150	
of small canister		24 ⎭	
One caisson for each gun		150	168
For *6-inch howitzers*			
Rounds of howitz or shell		49 ⎫	
of heavy canister	4	3 ⎬ 52	
Three caissons to each howitzer			160

Adapted from S.F. Gay de Vernon, *Treatise on the Science of War and Fortifications*, New York, 1817, p. 123.

When on the defensive, it was not considered profitable to engage in counter-battery fire, and ammunition was conserved for the main mission, to repel enemy cavalry and infantry charges. Offensively, artillery was used to soften up the enemy positions, though again the main targets were troops rather than guns. Counter-battery fire here was rare, but not unknown. Once the attack went in, artillery advanced trying to enfilade the enemy or to find profitable targets in deployed squares. A different version of artillery support during an attack was first practised by Senarmot at Friedland, where 38 guns advanced, unlimbered, fired, and then repeated the process at ever narrowing ranges. Guns could be brought into action in about a minute, and limbered up ready to move in two or three minutes. Horse artillery was the fastest, and heavy foot artillery the slowest. In all cases, the guns far out-ranged the musket and above 100 yards the crews were reasonably safe from infantry fire.

Guns often came into position partially loaded, with the primer wire stuck through the vent to prevent the charges from slipping. The ignition tube usually was not inserted until the actual firing and projectiles often were left out unless it was certain what type of target was to be engaged. Once in action, the first shot was very rapid, thereafter the rates of fire varied. Two to three round shot per minute was high average, and in an emergency four rounds of canister, for which the gun did not need to be sponged out between firings, could be delivered. As the action continued and as casualties and fatigue took their toll of the gun crews (7–15 men), the rate of fire diminished. The labour of running a gun back into position after each firing was exhausting and not always possible. At Waterloo, Mercer relates that it became more and more difficult to run the guns in his battery back after each round and when the action ceased they were all together in a confused heap.

With guns and howitzers at their most effective at closer ranges, the old doctrine that guns had to be preserved from capture regardless of circum-stances had to be modified. While there is the famous story of a captured Russian officer, deeply perturbed by having lost his guns, and being consoled by Napoleon, Wilson reported in 1810 that the Russian 'think that it is better to fight to the last moment, and let an enemy gain it dearly [the cannon], than withdraw it too soon for a preservation that also preserves the enemy'.[35] And before Borodino, Kutuzov confirmed these instructions. At Waterloo, Wellington ordered his gunners to fire to the last moment and then make a dash for the nearest square. If actually overrun by cavalry, gunners some-times saved themselves by taking refuge under their carriages and, after all, guns overrun and abandoned could, when recovered, be returned to service. Although in theory guns could be disabled by driving a long soft-iron spike into the vent, this rarely was done by either defenders or attackers and no such implements were issued to assault formations.

The Congreve rockets
Neither Napoleon, Archduke Charles, nor Wellington had much faith in new inventions. On one occasion, when after much pleading he failed to receive 12-pounders, and was instead offered some 24-pounder carronades which, so he was assured, were particularly suited to the new spherical case shot, Wellington somewhat testily replied that 'I do not consider this to be a proper time period to alter the equipment of the army or to try experiments'.[36] Not surprising then, that he was little impressed by the war rockets developed by Sir William Congreve and introduced into the British service after 1806.

These missiles ranged in size from 5–32 pounds with different warheads for case, shell, or carcass. They could be fired from a wheeled frame, more usually from a copper tripod, and in an emergency from a sloping embankment. Their accuracy was at best poor, though they served well against non-fortified targets in area bombardment.

At Copenhagen, one observer remembered that 'they rushed through the air in the dark like so many fiery serpents, creating, I should think, terrible dismay among the besieged'.[37] And at Flushing, Major Beamish, the historian of the King's German Legion, claims that they destroyed houses, churches, and killed many civilians.[38] Wellington, who had witnessed some rocket demonstrations in southern France in 1814, was not impressed. 'I do not want to set fire to any town,' he remarked, 'and I do not know of any other use for the rockets.'

On the other hand, an eye-witness at Leipzig claimed that the 2nd Rocket Troop, Royal Horse Artillery, had great effect at Leipzig, and that 'entire French columns ran away and abandoned everything', when they saw a rocket coming in.[39] So, after much initial opposition, Wellington allowed the 1st Rocket Troop to carry their missiles in 1815, provided they also brought their conventional pieces. His suspicions about the rocket were confirmed, however, when during the retreat from Quatre Bras, after first scoring a surprise hit on a French battery, the succeeding rockets fell wide, 'some', so Mercer tells, 'actually turned back upon ourselves . . . which put me in more danger than all the fire of the enemy'.[40]

Losses in battle

Although modern studies tend to show that Napoleonic battle losses have been much exaggerated, they also confirm that the carnage was real enough and represents a considerable jump over most, if not all, of the losses suffered in the battles of the limited wars. Overall, the estimate of 1,000,000 men killed or died of wounds in all European armies has been widely accepted. Deaths from disease, exhaustion, cold, and hunger probably claimed many more. Treatment of casualties and military medicine, will be treated in the last chapter, here we are concerned with the battlefield only.

The largest battles, as could be expected, also produced the heaviest losses. Leipzig, with 500,000 engaged, resulted in 140,000 killed, wounded, or missing; Borodino with 246,000 combatants some 80,000, while at Waterloo 192,000 men suffered 63,000 casualties. On the other hand, losses were lower at Bautzen where 264,000 lost 36,000; at Gross Görschen where the figures were 237,000 and 34,000, and Jena where 150,000 sustained a loss of 33,000. Proportionate to the number of participants, Eylau with 49,000 casualties for 158,000 engaged was one of the bloodiest battles, the percentage being slightly higher than at Borodino. Smaller battles could be even more sanguinary.[41]

In pitched battles such as at Aspern, Wagram, Austerlitz, or at Talavera, Albuera, and Bajadoz, some regiments lost up to 80 percent of their effectives. The British suffered the most at Albuera, 44 percent casualties, as against 24 percent at Waterloo and 23.7 at Talavera. The French also lost 44 percent at Albuera, perhaps the most intense encounter; 34.8 percent at Waterloo;

30.6 percent at Eylau; 26 percent at Auerstädt, and 23 percent at Marengo. Prussian losses, however, were consistently below the level suffered in the bloody battles of the Frederician era, 22.3 percent at Jena; 20 percent at Auerstädt, and 26 percent at Leipzig. The Russians suffered 35.2 percent losses at Borodino, 31.1 percent at Leipzig, and 27.7 percent at Eylau. Finally, the Austrians had 21.7 percent losses at Apern, 18.3 percent at Wagram, and 20 percent at Leipzig. The lowest losses in a decisive battle were the five percent sustained by Moreau at Hohenlinden.

Losses sustained by officers also serve as an indication of the intensity of fighting and the prowess of individual armies. In the French army, where conspicuous bravery in action was one sure way to promotion, officer casualties were by far the most severe, and they also were extremely high among the contingents of Napoleon's Saxon and Westphalian allies. All in all, between 1805 and 1815, the French army had some 15,000 officers killed and 35,000 wounded. Proportionate to the forces raised, Great Britain came next, followed by Austria, Prussia, and Russia. At Leipzig, a unique battle in many respects, officer losses were heavy on all sides. The allies had 29 generals and 1,896 officers killed and wounded, while the comparative figures for the French were 66 and 2,414. All in all, losses in senior officers were highest in the French army. During the Republic, 80 generals were killed in action, and during the Napoleonic wars 139 more suffered the same fate. While these figures are not totally conclusive, they nonetheless may be taken as indications of the 'Follow me' quality of French combat leadership.

The armies on the march and in bivouac

The new style of mobile warfare introduced by the fast moving French armies abandoned the use of tents and reduced the vast amount of baggage and supplies previously carried by all armies. In 1794, Carnot had already decreed that armies should always bivouac on campaign, and Napoleon, too, favoured his men living hard. 'The first quality of a soldier,' he stated, 'is fortitude in enduring fatigue and hardship,' and he also asserted that 'tents are not healthy; it is better for the soldier to sleep out', with his feet to the fire and a windbreak constructed from some plants and a bundle of straw. The troops did not necessarily agree, though they made the best of it. Moving light did give armies a decided advantage and tents, considered essential in the eighteenth century, disappeared in most field armies by 1800, and bivouac in the field became the standard practice not just of the French, but also of their adversaries. Prussia, however, retained a considerable baggage train, 8–10 times as large as the French, until the débâcle of 1806, when reforms put an end to this and by 1813 the Prussian field armies were fully as mobile as the French.

In contrast to tent cities with their well ordered lines, the bivouac was irregular, though units were always kept together. The Imperial Guard often camped in a huge square with Napoleon's coach or tent in the centre. Before Eylau, Coignet tells that 'the emperor ordered us to light his fire in the midst

of our battalions and asked that each mess should give him a log and a potato
. . . He seated himself in the midst of his "old grumblers", on a bundle of
straw.'[42] Sergeant Cooper of the 7th Fusiliers described a British bivouac:
'Tents we had none, nor yet blankets. We slept in the open air and this was
the mode: the greatcoat was inverted and our legs thrust into the sleeves;
one half was put under us, and the other half above. The knapsacks formed
our pillow. Thus arranged . . . we rested as we could.'[43] Rain added to the
soldier's troubles. Lacking waterproof sheets or coats and 'lying out on the
sod in all weather', General Bell remembered that the men frequently were
soaked to the skin. But worst of all was the morning-stand-to, 'up and armed
ready for anything one hour before daylight, and never dismissed until we
could see a white horse a mile distant. This always was a very long hour, just
unrolled from one's blanket to stand shivering in the early chill of a drizzly
morning.'[44]

Contrary to Napoleon's assertion that tents were unhealthy, bivouacs,
especially in cold, wet weather, did little to improve troop health and often
raised the sick rate alarmingly. Therefore, whenever the situation permitted,
troops were billeted in towns and villages, or, as in Poland during the winter
of 1806–7, built wooden hutments. These often became large encampments,
constantly improved by the ingenuity of the men and by the vigour of inspect-
ing generals. The British also abandoned their exclusive reliance on the
bivouac. In 1810, Wellington asked for prefabricated hutting to be shipped
to Portugal and for his final campaign he made some efforts to procure tents.
Still, bivouac was the rule and encampments the exception in the field for all
armies.

Doing away with battalion transport inevitably threw a great amount of
weight on the men's shoulders and in any army courage, fortitude, and above
all stamina were necessary to be a soldier. Although the French infantry
during the Revolutionary wars was lighter equipped, by 1800 loads had
returned to the 60-pound average of the eighteenth century, with only small
differences in weight due to variations in uniforms and muskets. The only
real alleviation was that the *sabre-briquet*, the short infantry sword, of no
particular utility in battle, was withdrawn in the British army by 1783,
abolished but for the grenadier companies in Austria by 1798, and by the
Prussians after 1806. The Russian army, however, retained this item of
equipment, while in the French army all Grenadiers, *Chausseurs* and *Voltigeurs* carried this weapon in addition to their bayonets.

The French infantryman's load may be taken as typical. In Davout's corps,
perhaps the best administered, great care was taken that the soldier only
carried the most necessary items. But two spare shirts, two pair of shoes, a
spare pair of pants and half-gaiters, 60 rounds, and marching rations for one
week, added to the basic weight of the uniform, equipment, and arms, still
came to over 58 pounds.[45] Some units were even more burdened. The
Imperial Guard carried about 65 pounds, but this included their full-dress
uniform, considered essential for the great parades that Napoleon was wont
to stage in conquered capitals. And the weight carried by the British Rifles

exceeded the tolerable. Riflemen Harris and Costello complained of the excessive weight carried by 'these troops, considered the lightest in our service', about 80 pounds. Harris claimed that men died needlessly during the retreat to Corunna because they were not permitted to discard their packs, and matters had not improved during the marches preceeding Talavera 'when four hundred of the battalion died a few months after our arrival, without a single shot being fired'. The number of dead seems exaggerated, but the weight 'sufficient to impede the free motion of a donkey', as Harris put it, was real enough.[46]

Harris was a tradesman, a cobbler, and he carried an extra load of tools, but even when one considers 60 pounds as the average load, the marching performance of the armies inspires respect. To be sure, routinely the French and other armies covered only 10–12 miles a day, but in 1796, Napoleon fought two engagements and one battle within one week during which Augerau's division marched 114 miles, and Masséna's division 100 miles. And when the Grand Army left the Channel coast to attack the Austrians, the corps of Lannes and Soult marched 152 miles in 13 days over secondary roads, while Davout's corps covered some 175 miles, partly over mountain roads, in 16 days. In those days a common saying among soldiers was that 'Our Emperor makes war not with our arms but with our legs'.

Such marches not only demanded much from the troops, they also ruined the mass-produced boots, glued or pegged rather than stitched together, faster than it was possible to replace them. When the Grand Army reached Bavaria, shoes had to be procured from many sources – some were captured in the Austrian magazines, others taken off prisoners, others requisitioned in Württemberg and Bavaria. Still, it was not enough. Before Austerlitz, Napoleon had to give his army a week to recuperate and repair its equipment; battalion cobblers were valuable men and, if at all possible, they were kept out of the firing line. This was true of the British army also. Before Vimeiro, Rifleman Harris, the regimental cobbler, was given special instructions to keep out of harm's way.

Shoes, however, were not the only item of equipment that suffered during campaigns, bivouacs and, of course, battles. Historians of the Napoleonic wars always describe the splendid uniforms of the troops – the bearskins of the Grenadiers of the Guard, the dolmans of the Hussars, the glittering helmets of the Cuirassiers, and the many other impressive uniforms. Yet, these splendid uniforms, except for the guard, existed in regulations only. Few, if any regiments, were ever clad according to regulation, and even at its zenith, that is between 1805 and 1809, the Grand Army did not present a uniform appearance. On 11 October 1805 Berthier wrote to Marmont that 'in an offensive war such as the Emperor wages it is up to the commander of the army corps to obtain for themselves such supplies in the countries they conquer'. How well they managed depended on the state of the local resources. Austria, for instance, was an excellent resupply area and its military magazines and civilian manufactures in Vienna, Styria, and Bohemia furnished shoes, equipment, and clothing in great quantities both in 1805 and again in 1809.

Moreover, it was not just a question of making up wastages. French industry was unable to keep up with the demands of the campaigns and many soldiers departed lacking basic items of clothing. In January 1806, for instance, the Emperor met 1,200 conscripts at Rastatt, 'entirely nude and dressed in peasant smocks'. And at Strasbourg, then the main replacement depot for the Austrian campaign, there were only 3,000 uniforms for 15,000 conscripts.[47] By the end of the campaign of 1805 some French soldiers were seen 'dressed in peasant blouses, sheepskin cloaks, or wild animal skins', and 'carrying long strips of bacon, hams, or chunks of meats dangling from their belts'.[48]

For that matter other armies were little better. Wellington cared little about the colour of his soldiers' trousers as long as they came on the battlefield with 60 rounds, and even after the short Waterloo campaign the uniforms of the British infantry, Mercer tells, were 'dirty, shabby, mean', their colours faded and the shakoes out of shape. The Russian troops looked business-like enough under Suvorov in Italy, but hardly military, and, except for the Guard, they often did not look much better in 1805 or in 1812. And even the meticulous Prussian armies wore a great variety of gear, some civilian, in 1813 and 1815, and the Austrian field armies in 1813 lacked boots and overcoats.

The soldier's rations

Rations, like uniforms, were quite different in practice than in the regulations and field orders. The subject of logistics will also be treated in the last chapter, and here we are again concerned with what actually was done in the field. On paper, at least, the ration scales were generous, far above the daily consumption of the great masses of the people. Under Napoleon the basic ration constituted of one pound of 'munition' bread, four ounces of meat, two ounces of dried vegetables, two ounces of vinegar, and one ounce of brandy, while the British ration included three-quarters of a pound of beef, one pound of bread, and a gill of rum. The Austrian and Prussian scales were similar to the French.

In practice, however, the supply system was defective and usually broke down in all armies, and soldiers lived by requisition, foraging, and often outright theft.

The preparation of food also left much to be desired. Napoleon asserted that every soldier should be able to cook his own food, but there were few individual mess kits. Cooking was usually done by sections, forming a six- to eight-man mess, which had among its prized possessions a camp kettle, weighing two to three pounds, and holding nine quarts. Larger kettles and cauldrons, were carried with the regimental train. These items were easily lost and often replaced from enemy stores. In 1807, for instance, the magazines of Potsdam, Spandau, and Berlin furnished 49,000 large camp kettles and 47,000 stew pans for the Grand Army.

Only a few soldiers had mess kits, others a plate or a bowl, but everyone carried a spoon and a knife, rarely a fork, in his haversack or decorating his hat. Canteens were also individual issue and much prized. In the British army the standard issue was wooden, in France tin with wicker covers, though

improvizations from gourd or leather were common. Captured supplies and
civilian substitutes frequently were pressed in the service. Although a vital
item, canteens were in short supply and the French in Egypt and Spain
suffered immensely.

The marching ration, issued for movements independent of magazines or
bases, was bulky and heavy and often was eaten up during the first day, leaving
the troops hungry for the remainder. In the Grand Army orders were issued
that officers check their men each day to see that they still had the required
amount. This availed little. In 1812, Gunner Wesemann of the Westphalian
artillery remembered, that though five days' rations, two days' bread and five
days' flour were issued, most infantrymen ate the bread and threw away the
flour so that 'for part of the way the path looked as if it had snowed'.[49] Whenever possible, the bread ration was issued in the form of biscuits, hard but
durable, which foot-soldiers carried on a string around their neck.

Meat rations were more difficult and usually were provided by beef on the
hoof driven along, or rather behind, the marching armies. But cattle, if it was
allowed to feed by grazing, could under best conditions hardly move more
than ten miles a day, and so it usually fell behind. If available, they were
usually slaughtered either early in the day or late at night so that the meat
could be hung for a few hours. Much was wasted in the haste with which this
was done. A cow was considered the equivalent of 1,000 rations, and supplemented by such other supplies as the troops could procure.

In the British army foraging was strictly forbidden, and severely punished
by Wellington; yet, on occasion, necessity forced him and his officers to turn
a blind eye to the practice. In the French army foraging was elevated to a
system, and troops showed considerable ingenuity in finding supplies. In
central Europe the potato had become an important crop by the end of the
eighteenth century and offered soldiers a prime source of food when they out-
marched their supply organization. During the Ulm campaign, the various
corps were actually allotted foraging areas, though digging up the new crop
certainly ruined the villages along the route of march. Peasants tried to hide
their supplies upon the approach of armies, but the French veterans soon
ferreted them out. 'The inhabitants,' Coignet reports, 'had buried everything
underground in the forests and in their houses. After much searching we
discovered their hiding places. By sounding with the butt ends of our guns
we found provisions of all sorts.' Another method was to push ramrods into
the ground and to dig where the earth appeared less closely packed.[50]

The result of all this generally was a stew, mainly endless variations of the
pot-au-feu among the French, with soup stock carried in canteens and soup
bones wrapped in cloth in the knapsacks. At night messes gathered around
their pot and emptied into it everything they had, adding what was issued or
otherwise procured. Another French staple was vegetable soup and olive oil
and bread soup. The first required boiling bacon, potatoes, carrots, salt,
beans, and meat, if available. The second consisted of boiling water, to which
oil, meat, vegetables, and condiments were added. Finally munition bread or
biscuits were put in and stirred. Other armies also had their stews. Parquin

relates that during the 1814 campaign his troop captured some Russians together with an 'enormous cooking pot in which some thirty chickens, a number of hams, and other ingredients were stewing', while Mercer found Prussian troop stew, 'potatoes, turnips, onions, etc., . . . [and] a very carrion-like meat' distinctly unappealing.[51] The British army in the Peninsula, despite the Duke's effort, often went hungry and raw corn, and even acorns, were eaten. But in France, Private Morris recorded that his section snared a hare, stole some hens and a turkey, and the whole boiled together with flour and vegetables made a rich stew.[52]

But these occasions were probably remembered because they were so rare, and on the whole the soldier's fare was poor, unappetizing, and there was little of it.

The soldier's women

Throughout history soldiers have seldom been celebate and camp followers represented a serious problem for all armies. Under the *ancien régime* officers had their mistresses, and attempts were made to provide for the rank and file by tolerating, even encouraging, soldiers to marry or have permanent liaisons with local girls. The prevailing economic theory, Mercantilism, held that the strength of a state depended on population as well as economic resources, and the children of these affairs, *les enfants de troupes* as the French called them, were often brought up with an eye towards joining their father's regiment. In peacetime and in garrison towns the soldiers' families presented few problems, but for overseas campaigns the number had to be limited. British army regulations permitted only 60 women for every 1,000 men, entitled to half-rations and selected by lot before embarkation. And separation, of course, meant not only a final farewell, but also destitution for the wife and children since the government provided no marriage allowance for the regulars, though it paid one for the militia. No wonder that the authorities tried to discourage marriage. 'Officers must explain,' the regulations of 1795 stipulated, 'to the men the many miseries that women are exposed to and by every sort of persuasion they must prevent their marrying if possible.'[53]

Women did indeed suffer in the field, marching with the troops, sharing their privations and dangers. Sometimes they carried the packs for their men, nursed them when wounded or sick, and, as Harris tells us, often a devoted wife would search a battlefield hoping to find her husband alive. During retreats women and children, the weakest, suffered the most. Many died in the wet and cold of Holland in early 1795; others perished when Moore fell back on Corunna in 1808–9, and some who were evacuated drowned in the wreck of the *Smallbridge* off the Scilly Islands. They equally suffered during Wellington's marches, often lagging behind their husbands in the main body.

There were, to be sure, women who caused trouble, Costello tells of the wife of a Grenadier who deserted her husband for a sergeant in the 95th and was murdered by her former mate, and other women became, largely by necessity, expert foragers and looters. 'It is well known in all armies,'

Wellington wrote, 'the women are at least as bad, if not worse, than the men.'[54] He wanted to have them sent back to England or at least confined to the base at Lisbon, but for once the Iron Duke failed. Even the most draconian measures failed to keep the women from following their regiment.

A French combatant in the Peninsular War, General Marbot, observed in his memoirs that women had been a great encumbrance of the British army, but perhaps he forgot that the French armies had similar, and perhaps worse, problems. During the Revolution the austere Carnot had been shocked by the large number of prostitutes congregating at the barracks at Douai and had evicted more than 3,000 of them. Napoleon, too, though neither he nor his generals did without female company, disliked having women with the army. Some, of course, he had to tolerate, especially the *cantinières*, but in 1797 he issued orders that unauthorized females were to be 'arrested, daubed over with black, and so exposed in some public place'.[55] And as First Consul he ordered that the prostitutes, *les chattes*, who attached themselves to the armies were to have their carriages overturned. But to no avail. In Spain especially, where Napoleon was far away, marshals and generals brought their mistresses into the field, some like Massena and Fournier several at the same time. Lower-ranking officers had dancers or actresses and the rank and file had native girls. In starving Spain, parents sold their daughters to the soldiers, others were abducted by force, and there 'were a great number following the regiments, and even a few at headquarters. They were quite free and were attracted by this new type of life'.[56] And while one may question the last statement, made by Major Pelet, Massena's adjutant, it is quite true that there were many devoted camp followers. Women of many nationalities followed the Grand Army into Russia as wives, mistresses, or *cantinières*, and they and their children were among those who died there.

The *cantinières*, uniformed and attached to a particular regiment, were unique to the French army. Appointed by the *conseil d'administration*, a body of officers and men presided over by the colonel, which ran the internal affairs of the regiment, and often married to a sergeant, the *cantinière* kept her wagon stocked with small luxuries and comforts, cognac, tobacco, and suchlike. The trade was profitable, but also dangerous. The women often developed a strong attachment to their unit. Hearing that the well-liked Brigadier Simon had fallen wounded into British hands, the *cantinière* of the 26th declared that 'we shall see if the English will kill a woman'. She crossed the lines, nursed Simon, and 'though she was young and very pretty', as Marbot records, returned unharmed to her regiment. And then there was Catherine Baland of the 95th, who encouraged men in battle and distributed her goods free in the firing line. She received the coveted Légion d'Honneur in 1813.[57]

Of course, not all women were as heroic as Catherine Baland or as lucky as the *cantinière* of the 26th. In the French army, too, there were complaints about women looting and plundering, and in Spain women were exposed to the guerrillas who raped, tortured, killed, and mutilated women following the French army.[58] The war brutalized women as well as men in all armies. Both Marbot and Pelet tell of a band of English, Portuguese, and French deserters who, together with their women, established themselves in the mountains and engaged in indiscriminate fighting against all sides as well as 'unrestrained debauchery'.[59]

Prisoners of war and their treatment

The introduction of ideological and national hatreds into warfare caused a definite deterioration in the treatment of prisoners of war. During the dynastic wars prisoners had been reasonably well treated, often in the hope of securing their transfer into the captor's army. And while this was not completely unknown, especially during the heyday of Napoleon's victories, there is little doubt that much cruelty, often deliberate, was practised by all sides.

The Convention had ended the mutual goodwill existing between professional soldiers for if the Revolution was prepared to show no mercy to its own officers and men, it saw no reason to give quarter to its enemies. Ransoming of prisoners, one of the common practices of limited war, was forbidden by decrees of September 1793 and May 1794. At the same time, the Convention declared that no prisoners were to be taken. At first this policy was directed against the Royalist *emigré* troops, but it soon was extended to British, Hanoverian, and Spanish soldiers. Commanders and troops in the field, if only for fear of reprisals, usually evaded these commands, but some 3,000 Royalists and over 8,000 Spanish prisoners were massacred. And in the Middle East, warfare degenerated even more. Here French prisoners often were tortured, killed, and mutilated, which in part explains the fury of the sack of Jaffa where the troops 'spared neither the lives of men or the honour of women'.[60] But Napoleon added little to his stature by ordering the execution of 7,000 Turks of the surrendered garrison.

During the siege of Genoa in 1800, Masséna calmly allowed several thousand Austrian prisoners to starve to death on prison hulks in the port, but on the other hand, Russian prisoners taken at Zurich were well received in Paris and offered small comforts by the civilians. In general, during the years of Napoleon's ascendency, that is from 1805 to 1811, the treatment of prisoners improved somewhat. The Emperor intended either to incorporate them into his own forces or to have them return as friends to their own countries. After Jena, he released the Saxon prisoners to their homes, and after Tilsit he returned Russian prisoners, freshly equipped and uniformed, to impress Tsar Alexander.

In Spain, however, things went badly almost from the start and the responsibility rested on both sides. Most of the captured Spanish regulars were sent to France and put to work there, while the civilian *Junta* broke its word after Bailen and sent the surrendered French to the prison hulks of Cadiz or to the Balearic island of Cabrera where most died of hunger, disease and maltreatment. And in the guerrilla war few prisoners were taken by either side, and bloody atrocities were followed by equally horrible reprisals. Yet, here too there were exceptions. Both Parquin and Lejeune relate that some *guerrilleros* were chivalrous and offered decent treatment to captives. Still, on

the whole, the French much preferred to surrender to the British than to
either the Spaniards or Portuguese.

In the field, the British usually treated their prisoners of war correctly and
would not hesitate to use force to 'preserve our French prisoners from being
butchered', by the Spanish or Portuguese irregulars.[61] But in the rear areas
and in England the picture changed for the worse. During the early years of
the war, the British had treated prisoners well. Men were employed as farm
labour, officers paroled and quite frequently exchanged. But as the wars
continued, the British adopted a harsher way of war. French soldiers were
confined to prisons and prison hulks, and while conditions in the zone of
operations, especially at Lisbon, were tolerable, conditions in England, both
afloat and ashore were bad indeed. By 1811, Great Britain held some 44,000
French prisoners, and small contingents of Danes, Dutch, and other French
allies. There were numerous complaints about conditions on the prison hulks,
especially the nine at Chatham where some 7,000 men were reported to have
died of malnutrition and disease. All in all, 30,000 French died in British
captivity. At this date France held some 88,000 prisoners of war, including
40,000 Spaniards, 10,526 English, and 932 Irish. Napoleon was very sus-
picious of the English prisoners and ordered them tightly guarded, confined
to the 'strongest and most distant fortresses'.

The invasion of Russia in 1812 brought new atrocities, as usual, committed
by both sides. Already during the opening phases of the campaign, after the
battle of Borodino, Russian prisoners too exhausted to keep up with the
column, were shot by their escort, while French prisoners marched through
Moscow were abused by the civilians with the guards doing nothing to inter-
fere.[62] And General Wilson, the English military representative to the Tsar,
reported that during the retreat French prisoners were 'stripped stark naked
and marched in columns in that state, or turned adrift to be the sport and
victims of the peasantry'.[63] Protests to the Tsar were of no avail, though one
Westphalian prisoner reports that Russian officers tried to intervene and
protect the victims.[64] Those who survived were sent to Siberia and often
managed to live reasonably well there.

In 1813, finally, Russian treatment of prisoners improved, but the aroused
Prussians often gave no quarter, while the Austrians marched their prisoners
into Hungary and there confined them in fortresses at half-rations.

Fraternization between opposing forces

Although the Revolutionary and Napoleonic wars led to the indoctrination of
troops with a previously rare hatred of their enemies, there nonetheless persisted incidents of traditional behaviour both among officers and men of the
opposing armies.

It was still considered unsporting to fire deliberately at enemy commanders.
At Wagram, when Napoleon's personal staff came under Austrian long range
shell fire, Oudinot exclaimed 'Sire, they are firing at the General Staff!' To
which Napoleon calmly replied, 'In war every accident is possible!' And on

the other side, when asked by an eager gunner for permission to fire at Napoleon during the battle at Waterloo, Wellington is supposed to have replied that one could not conduct war if generals shot at each other.

Lower-ranking officers also attempted to carry on the chivalrous traditions of the past. In the Peninsula British and French officers tried to take care of each other. For instance Bell relates that when the French occupied a village and found there the wounded colonel of the 24th, the French commander, Count D'Erlong, visited him to express his sympathy and placed a sentry on the house so that the wounded men would not be disturbed. And Lejeune tells how after he had been stripped by Spanish irregulars, he was clothed, provided with money, and entertained by British officers before being sent on to captivity in Lisbon and later England. Junior officers met to exchange small tokens, trade cognac for rum, discuss their past exploits, boast a bit, and arrange for letters to be forwarded to a fellow officer prisoner in France.[65]

Similar incidents also occurred in other theatres. Blaze writes that before the 1809 campaign Austrian and French officers along the Bohemian frontier exchanged addresses and made arrangements for mutual help in case one or the other was taken prisoner. Even in Russia there were occasions when officers of the opposing armies exchanged drinks and news. Particularly the Poles, serving on both sides were eager for contacts. Freemasonry, strongly represented in both the French and Russian officer corps, provided another common bond, and Russian officers recognizing the Masonic distress signal given by some French officer prisoners hastened to see that they received better treatment.

But no such amenities existed on the battlefield and they rarely extended to the rank and file. Except for the British soldier, who often would treat a defeated enemy with kindness, fighting had become much more cruel. At Austerlitz, up to the last hour, the French refused to give quarter, and during pursuit after battle, cavalry would hack at a retreating foe, showing little mercy for the wounded and often taking no prisoners. But even in the bloody Peninsular Campaign the British showed little animosity towards the French. Forward pickets between the two armies generally gave each other notice of imminent attacks, sometimes shaking hands before battle, and recognizing that the French before Torres Vedras were half starved, they even shared their ration biscuit with them.[66] Neither the French nor the English liked the Spanish and Portuguese, and Rifleman Harris records with distaste that Portuguese cavalry pursued and cut down a solitary Frenchman fleeing for his life.[67] On occasion, troops elsewhere made similar accommodations. In the winter of 1806–7, Russian and French pickets in Poland made an agreement not to fire on each other, and when a Russian did loose a shot at a French officer, his regimental commander came and apologized profusely.

But such occasions were rare and became rarer as the wars continued. The new European armies became more nationalistic, egalitarian, and larger. If democracy made all men equal in theory, it was conscription which did so in fact, but at a price. With the manpower resources of entire nations behind them, commanders could hold human life cheap, no longer capital to be saved as much as possible, but income to be expended. At the same time, to make the continual sacrifices acceptable to the population, propaganda was pressed into the service of war; the enemy became evil incarnate, and the soldier's trade became more cruel, demanding and devastating.

NOTES

1. C.v. Clausewitz, *On War*, trs. O.J.M. Jolles, Infantry Journal Press, Washington, D.C., 1950, 210.
2. Bodart, *op cit.*, passim.
3. Longford, *op cit.*, 479–80.
4. Lauerma, *op cit.*, 32–3; tables in C. Jany, *Die Gefechtsausbildung der Preussischen Infanterie von 1806*, vol. V of *Urkundliche Beiträge und Forschungen zur Geschichte des Preussichen Heeres*, Ernst S. Mittler & Son, Berlin, 1903, 36–8.
5. Hughes, *op cit.*, 26–8, 64, 126–7; S.F. Gay de Vernon, *Science of War and Fortification*, trs. J.M. O'Connor, J. Seymour, New York, 1817, vol. I, 62, 88–9.
6. E. Hoyt, *Practical Instructions for Military Officers*. J. Denio, Greenfield, Mass., 1811, 117.
7. Glover, *op cit.*, 140–1.
8. H. Delbrück, *Neuzeit*, vol. IV of *Geschichte der Kriegskunst im Rahmen der politischen Geschichte*, Georg Stilke, Berlin, 1920, 466.
9. *The Narrative of Captain Coignet*, ed. L. Larchey, trs. M. Carey, Thomas Y. Crowell, New York, 1890, 122.
10. Morvan, vol. II, 329–30, 349–50.
11. Lieutenant Chevalier, *Souvénirs des Guerres Napoliennes*, eds., J. Mistler and H. Michaud, Hachette, Paris, 1970, 82.
12. Ensign Leeke in J. Naylor, *Waterloo*, Batsford, 1960, 168.
13. E. Blaze, *Recollections of an Officer of Napoleon's Army*, trs. E.J. Meras, Sturgis & Walton, New York, 1911, p. 222.
14. Gay de Vernon, *op cit.*, 62.
15. Sir R. Wilson, *Brief Remarks on the Character and Composition of the Russian Army*, Egerton, 1810, 7; Duffy, *Borodino*, 42.
16. Chandler, *op cit.*, 343–4.
17. Lejeune, *op cit.*, vol. II, 66; Henri Jomini, *The Art of War*, G.H. Mendell and W.P. Craighill, trs., Lippincott, Philadelphia, 1862, 276.
18. Cited by J.A. Lynn, 'French Opinion and the Military Resurrection of the Pike, 1792–1794', *Military Affairs*, vol. 41, no. 1, 1977, 51–5.
19. C. Mercer, *Journal of the Waterloo Campaign*, intro. M. Glover, Praeger, New York, 1970, 170.
20. M. Rauchensteiner, *Die Schlacht von Aspern am 21. und 22. Mai 1809*, vol. 11 of *Militärhistorische Schriftenreihe*, Österreichischer Bundesverlag für Unterricht, Wissenschaft und Kunst, Vienna, 1969, 11–12, 21–2.
21. Phipps, *op cit.*, vol. V, 392–3.
22. Bodart, *op cit.*, 813–15.
23. *Mémoires du Général Baron de Marbot*, Plon, Paris, 1891, vol. III, 124.
24. L. Cooper, *British Regular Cavalry 1644–1914*, Chapman Hall, 1965, 121–2; C. Parquin, *Napoleon's Army*, trs. and ed. B.T. Jones, Archon Books, Camden, Conn., 1969, 143.

25. F.L. Petre, *Napoleon's Campaign in Poland, 1806–7,* Hippocrene Books, New York, 1975, 35; Jomini, *op cit.,* 203.
26. Parquin, *op cit.,* 41, 53.
27. Mercer, *op cit.,* 172–3.
28. Gay de Vernon, *op cit.,* vol. I, 107.
29. *Ibid.,* 110.
30. Chandler, *op cit.,* 358–9.
31. Gay de Vernon, *op cit.,* vol. I, 168.
32. Coignet, *op cit.,* 175–7.
33. O.F.G. Hogg, *Artillery : Its Origin, Heyday, and Decline,* Archon Books, Camden, Conn., 1970, 180–1; Hughes, *op cit.,* 34, 38.
34. Lauerma, *op cit.,* 18–19, 26.
35. Wilson, *op cit.,* 24–5.
36. Cited in Longford, *op cit.,* 401–2.
37. *Recollections of Rifleman Harris,* ed. H. Curling, R.M. McBride & Co., New York, 1929, 12.
38. N.L. Beamish, *Geschichte der Königlich Deutschen Legion,* Hahn, Hanover, 1832, vol. I, 241–3.
39. A. Brett-James. *Europe against Napoleon. The Leipzig Campaign, 1813,* Macmillan, 1970, p. 188.
40. Mercer, *op cit.,* 153.
41. Bodart, *op cit.,* passim.
42. Coignet, *op cit.,* 143.
43. Cited in S.F. Johnston, *British Soldiers,* William Collins, 1944, 28.
44. G. Bell, *Rough Notes of an Old Soldier,* Day & Sons, 1867, vol. I, 14, 67.
45. Duffy, *Borodino,* 30–1.
46. Harris, *op cit.,* 18, 150; E. Costello, *The Peninsular and Waterloo Campaigns,* ed. A. Brett-James, Archon Books, Camden, Conn., 1968, 18.
47. Morvan, *op cit.,* vol. I, 136–7.
48. Cited in Chandler, *op cit.,* 408.
49. H.H.C. Wesemann, *Kanonier des Kaisers. Kriegstagebuch des Heinrich Wesemann, 1808–1814,* ed. H.O. Wesemann, Verlag Wissenschaft und Politik, Cologne, 1971, 26.
50. Coignet, *op cit.,* 148–9.
51. Parquin, *op cit.,* 174–5; Mercer, *op cit.,* 279.
52. T. Morris, *Memoirs of a Soldier in the 73rd Infantry Regiment,* ed. J. Selby, Archon Books, Camden, Conn., 1967, 98.
53. Cited in Glover, *op cit.,* 221.
54. Cited in Longford, *op cit.,* 201. Cf. Bell, *op cit.,* vol. I, 74–5.
55. Phipps, *op cit.,* vol. IV, 177.
56. Pelet, *op cit.,* 125–7, 313.
57. Lejeune, *op cit.,* vol. II, 69.
58. Blaze, *op cit.,* 53–4; Parquin, *op cit.,* 128.
59. Pelet, *op cit.,* 314–15; Marbot, *op cit.,* vol. II, 439–40.
60. Phipps, *op cit.,* vol. V, 393.
61. Costello, *op cit.,* 44.
62. Marbot, *op cit.,* vol. II, 594; Wesemann, *op cit.,* 33–4.
63. Cited in A. Brett-James, *1812 Eyewitness Accounts of Napoleon's Defeat in Russia,* St Martin's Press, 1966, 224.
64. Wesemann, *op cit.,* 68–9.
65. Bell, *op cit.,* vol. I, 109; Lejeune, *op cit.,* vol. II, 103–4; Parquin, *op cit.,* 130–1.

66. Costello, *op cit.*, 48.
67. Harris, *op cit.*, 59.
68. F.v. Schubert, *Unter dem Doppeladler. Erinnerungen eines Deutschen im Russischen Offiziersdienst 1789–1814*, Koehler, Stuttgart, 1962, 211.

4

The French Revolutionary Armies and their New Art of War

The armies of the French Revolution represented a new departure in military organization and the art of war. Based on the principle of the 'nation in arms' the Revolution raised huge citizen conscript armies and, lacking the time to give them combat discipline, resorted to large scale political indoctrination. All had to believe in the fight they were to make and all had to accept authority. For a few crucial years the enthusiasm of the nation communicated itself to the French soldiers and gave them a sense of daring and enterprise that confounded their conventional adversaries. At the same time, the Revolution brought forward leaders who put into practice the theories of open order fighting, movement and fire, and the swift and deadly concentrations later called 'Napoleonic'.

The dissolution of the royal army : 1789–91
At the outbreak of the Revolution the French army, like all other armies in Europe, was a 'voluntary' long-service force, augmented in time of war by militia drafts. It consisted of 182,000 regular and Household Troops, supported by 72,000 militia selected from the unmarried peasantry. The foot, 134,236 strong, was organized into 79 regiments of French Infantry, 11 Swiss, 8 German, and 8 Irish Regiments, and 12 battalions of light infantry. The Household Troops, or *Maison du roi*, comprised of the senior regiment of *Gardes françaises* and the Swiss Guards, together with a small mounted body-guard, a total of 8,560 men. The mounted arm, 35,000 in all, was organized in 62 regiments: 2 regiments of Carabiniers, 24 of the Line, 18 of Dragoons, 6 Hussars, and 12 *Chasseurs à cheval*. The artillery consisted of 7 foot artillery regiments, each with 20 companies, and there were 6 companies of miners attached to this corps. Finally, there was a small, all officer Engineering Staff. Altogether, following the reforms of 1788, there were 9,478 officers on active duty.[1]

This establishment, improved by recent reforms, was considered by many observers the best in Europe. On the eve of the Revolution, however, there were deep divisions within the officer corps; the noncommissioned officers were disaffected, and the discipline of the rank and file eroded. Late in 1788, Marshal de Vaux warned Louis XVI that it was 'impossible to rely on the troops', and this prediction came true when during the disorders accompanying the transition of the Estates General into a Constituent Assembly in June 1789 the French Guards, the pride of the *Maison du roi*, defected. On 24 June two companies refused to obey orders and four days later, when called out for riot duties, the entire unit mutinied.

An alarmed government ordered 17 regiments, mainly Swiss and German, to the vicinity of the capital where their arrival in the first week of July caused great alarm. On 13 July mobs broke into various locations searching for arms to 'defend the Assembly'. The next day elements of the French Guards spearheaded an assult on the Bastille, the state prison. To prevent further bloodshed, the king agreed to remove the foreign regiments and placed the security of Paris into the hands of a hastily formed middle-class militia, the National Guard, with the Marquis de Lafayette, a hero of the American War of Independence, as commander. Moreover, the king pardoned the French Guards, though the regiment was disbanded, most of the men joining the National Guard.

Revealing the weakness of established authority, these events were the signal for civil disorders and a score of mutinies on the provinces, reaching such proportions that a radical deputy exclaimed 'there is no more king, no more justice, no more army!' The threat to the 'most sacred property and even the harvests', became so great that on 11 August the Assembly, having assumed legislative functions, decreed the formation of National Guards throughout the kingdom and these eventually restored order.

Clearly control over the army was slipping out of the king's hands, but the Assembly was not yet prepared to pick it up. Not that it lacked interest in military affairs which had figured prominently in the lists of grievances, the *cahiers*, brought by the deputies elected to the Estates General and on 30 October 1789 the Assembly established a permanent Military Committee. Among the issues debated were demands for the reduction of the Household Troops, the dissolution of the foreign regiments, and equal promotion opportunities for bourgeois and petty noble officers. There were also demands for reforms in recruiting and improvement in the condition of the rank and file. Above all, there was widespread aversion to the militia, described as an institution which 'devastates the country, takes workers away from husbandry, produces premature and ill-matched marriages, and secret and arbitrary taxes upon those subject to it'.[2]

Some of these issues were resolved quickly. The dissolution of the French Guards had reduced the Household Troops to one regiment of Swiss Guards, while the establishment of the National Guards had replaced the militia, formally abolished the following year. The renunciation of feudal privileges passed by acclamation during the night of 4–5 August specified that 'all citizens may be admitted, without distinction of birth, to all ecclesiastical, civil, and military employments', and opened the officer corps to all. In 1790 the Assembly abolished proprietary rights and purchase, and decreed that one-fourth of all sub-lieutenant vacancies be reserved for deserving non-commissioned officers. There was also general agreement that the army should take an oath to the nation as well as the king and to cement this relationship the Assembly, on 1 January 1791, abolished the old royal or territorial titles of the regiments and replaced them with plain numerals. In July of the same year the foreign regiments were assimilated into the new order and by 1792 had largely lost their foreign character.

But on the basic issues, the character of the army and its methods of enlistment, the Assembly could not make up its mind. Servan, an officer of Engineers and later War Minister, attacked the abuses of 'voluntary' recruitment; Condorcet, wanted to destroy 'military despotism' and demanded that soldiers should judge the legality of orders, while Mirabeau called for the total abolition of the standing army. As early as October 1789 the word 'conscription' was heard in the debates, but the Assembly refused to consider this seriously, feeling that 'free enlistment' alone befitted a free people.

Increasingly the Assembly regarded the National Guard as a counterforce to the royal army. And during 1790-1 the character of the National Guard changed. Promising better pay and treatment than the regulars, it lost its character as a bourgeois volunteer militia and incorporated many former non-commissioned officers and men of the royal army. It obtained artillery and in Paris, where it was charged with maintaining public order as well as the protection of the Assembly, Lafayette disposed of 6,000 permanently enrolled men, backed by another 60,000 part-time volunteers. Overall the National Guard continued to swell in size, reaching their maximum strength of two million in August 1791 and by providing an alternative to the royal army, contributed to the deterioration of that force.

The royal army, shaked by the defection of the French Guards and by the mutinies of 1789, was subject to political agitation which created near anarchy in many units. A few regiments maintained order, but in most soldiers formed political clubs, established soldiers' councils, challenged the authority of their commanders, and even demanded control of the regimental funds and the ousting of unpopular officers. On 4 June 1790, La Tour du Pin, the War Minister, reported the sad state of the army to the Assembly. He urged that soldiers be forbidden to engage in politics and that the clubs and councils be suppressed. Failure, he warned, would create a 'military democracy, a sort of political monster which always ended up by devouring the empires that produce them'. But the deputies would not listen and some blamed 'reactionary officers' for the unrest in their units.

The Assembly's lack of will encouraged further excesses. In August 1790 there was a major mutiny at Nancy, involving the French Regiments de Roi and Mestre de Camp, as well as the Swiss Chateauvieux Regiment. This time Lafayette persuaded the Assembly to act and it authorized Lieutenant-General Bouille, commanding at Metz, to put down the 'military revolution'. After heavy fighting the mutiny was suppressed. The Swiss, subject to their own military jurisdiction, were promptly court-martialled: 33 were executed and 44 sent to the galleys. But when it came to the French mutineers the

Assembly, eager to gain favour with the soldiers, insisted that they be pardoned. Bouille was accused of acting too hastily and La Tour du Pin was dismissed a few months later. The Assembly reaffirmed the right of soldiers to be politically active and introduced juries of privates and non-commissioned officers into the military court system. During the winter of 1790, in garrisons large and small, there were confrontations between troops and their officers. Commanders had difficulty enforcing even the most rudimentary order. Desertion went unchecked and there were few recruits. By 1791 the army fell below 110,000 men.

The disruption of the army was accelerated by the exodus of experienced officers. Some aristocrats emigrated after the fall of the Bastille, but the majority were prepared to serve a moderate Revolution. Continued disorders induced other officers to follow, and their number became very large when after Louis XVI's abortive flight in the summer of 1791, the Assembly imposed a new military oath which omitted all references to the king. Between July 1791 and the end of 1792 over 6,000 officers left. Some, to be sure, were glad to see them go. Radicals like Robespierre advocated that all officers should resign so that new men, loyal to the Revolution, could be appointed. And the Assembly seemed to agree with him. In the summer of 1791, clearly violating the royal prerogative, it appointed 69 colonels and 124 lieutenant-colonels, the first time that commissions had been issued without the king's signature.

Finally, in September 1791 the Constituent Assembly presented its new Constitution. Although the king gave his reluctant assent, it clearly alterred the character of the army. Although still nominally under the command of the King in his capacity as the nation's chief executive, the army was no longer described as 'royal', but designated as a 'public force', to be used only against foreign enemies.

Raising the Revolutionary Armies : 1791–8

By September 1791, however, the army was a shadow of its former self and military power, while easily dissipated, is hard to rebuild, a fact driven home to the Assembly when war drew near. As early as 2 January 1791 the Assembly, lacking reliable troops, called for 100,000 National Guards to volunteer as 'auxiliaries' for the Line, but this appeal was ignored. During July and August 1791 the Assembly called first for 26,000, then for 97,000, and finally for 101,000 'one campaign only' volunteers. Response was disappointing again. Instead of the 169 battalions envisaged only 60 were mustered by October. Still, the 'Volunteers of 91', were the best the Revolution would find. They were genuine volunteers and many of them had previous military experience.[3]

But even the accession of these volunteers left the army under-strength. In early 1792 there were but 150,000 men, while the three field armies mustered only 82,000 effectives. With war imminent, the Assembly decided in April 1792 to draft men by lot. These impressed levies were, of course, hardly enthusiastic, but the *requisitionnaires* were accorded the same privileges as the original volunteers, including the right to elect their own officers.

Election produced a goodly number of incompetents, but also brought forward good men. Among the officers elected in 1791–2 there were no fewer than nine future marshals of the Empire and many senior commanders of the Republic. The continued presence of almost 1,000 noble officers, patriotic but suspect in the prevailing political atmosphere, caused tension. In 1793, when France appeared in mortal danger, the Committee of Public Safety suspended almost all of them without a hearing.

The same atmosphere of suspicion led to the formation of a third volunteer force, the *fédérés*. On 8 June 1792, the Assembly, eager to have a reliable force in Paris, decreed that 20,000 *fédérés* (so called because they ostensibly were to represent their departmental National Guards at the great Feast of the Federation scheduled for 14 July) were to assemble in the capital. To prevent the infiltration of unreliable elements, all *fédérés* had to provide certificates of political reliability. Most of them were more noted for their revolutionary ardour than for their military qualities, though some units were outstanding. The famous Marseilles Battalion left its home 500 strong on 2 July and after marching about 18 miles a day, dragging along two light pieces, arrived in Paris on the 30th with every man present.

The majority of the federals considered military discipline incompatible with the concepts of 'Liberty and Egality'. Sent to camp at Soissons, they informed their superiors that 'we do not have to be in camp; we do not like rice; we want our 20 sous a day or we shall not serve'. And though they usually elected old soldiers as their officers, they would, in good revolutionary fashion, not obey them. The 1st Battalion of the Pas de Calais, for instance elected a regular sergeant, Godart, as their lieutenant-colonel. But when Godart, later a general under Napoleon, tried to drill them, they denounced him as a 'despot who despises Liberty and Egality', and attempted to hang him.[4]

Without discipline and training, short on equipment, arms, and even clothing, the new levies saw little action in 1792 and the repulse of the Prussians at Valmy and the defeat of the Austrians at Jemappes was accomplished by the regular battalions and the Volunteers of 1791. But during the winter the army dissolved. Now that the campaign was over many volunteers decided to go home. One volunteer tells that his company commander, a lieutenant, asked the lieutenant-colonel for permission to march his company home. That worthy wavered, but finally urged the volunteers to wait. 'We then decided to leave the same day.'[5] By early 1793 Dumouriez's armies had lost 10,000 men in combat, while over 25,000 had deserted and his army was reduced to little more than a skeleton force. On 23 January 1793, Dubois-Crancé, speaking for the Military Committee of the Convention, warned that the situation was critical. Voluntary enlistments had failed and he urged the mobilization of additional men, by conscription if necessary. One month later, on 24 February, the Convention resolved that 'all French citizens from the age of eighteen to fully forty years, unmarried or widowers without children, are in a state of permanent requisition'. To meet the immediate threat it called for 300,000 men, a number estimated to equal that which the enemies were mustering, to join the armies as soon as possible.[6]

Although the decree established the principle of general liability for the military service, the Convention hesitated to apply conscription. Instead, each department was assigned a quota and was instructed to fill it with volunteers if at all possible. If this could not be done, then the necessary number was to be made up by local designation or the drawing of lots. Moreover, the decree provided for numerous occupational exemptions. Public officials were excused and the National Guard declared 'mobilized in place', while 'any citizen summoned to march' was allowed to provide a substitute. Finally, realizing that volunteers were prone to go home, the decree concluded with a stern admonition that 'no volunteer may leave his battalion', and that 'permission may no longer be granted for the defenders of the *patrie* to leave their colours'.

In some places enough volunteers turned out in response to patriotic appeals. In Rennes the mayor appealed to the students at the local college. 'The Law Schools,' he told them, 'are prepared to march! Who amongst you will follow their example and leave tomorrow for the army?'[7] But overall the decree failed to attract sufficient volunteers and even with compulsion it added only 180,000 men to the army. At that, it rekindled in western France all the old resentments against compulsory service and helped to bring on the civil war in the Vendée.

But invasion, civil war, defections, and defeat forced the Convention into desperate measures. The ruthless Committee of Public Safety assumed virtual control of the government, while the Republican Constitution of the Year I (24 June 1793) declared that the 'general force of the Republic is composed of the entire people . . . all Frenchmen shall be soldiers; all shall be trained in the handling of arms'. The nation in arms was born.

On 23 August 1793, the Convention implemented the principle of the nation in arms by passing the decree of the *levée en masse*. The decree itself was proposed and framed by the Committee of Public Safety.

> From this moment until that in which every enemy has been driven from the territory of the Republic, every Frenchman is permanently requisitioned for service with the armies. The young men shall fight; married men will manufacture weapons and transport stores; women shall make tents and nurse in the hospitals; children shall turn old linen into lint; the old men shall repair to the public squares to raise the courage of the warriors and preach the unity of the Republic and hatred against the kings.

Although the decree continued that 'the levy shall be general', France could not hope to produce arms and equipment for all. Therefore, stipulated the decree, 'unmarried men and childless widowers from eighteen to twenty-five years shall go first'. Units were to be formed on a territorial basis and each battalion 'shall be gathered around the flag bearing the inscription: *The*

French people risen against the tyrants'.

In September recruiting under the *levée en masse* decree began and provided some 450,000 men for the armies. By 1794 the Republic had over 700,000 men under arms, though the figure is only approximate. For the greater part of the 1790's the French did not know exactly how many men they had in their service. In the winter of 1793 the Committee ordered 15,000 men detached from Jourdan's army and sent to the Vendée. Jourdan protested, claiming that his force was already dangerously weakened. The Committee then demanded to know what had happened to the 140,000 men on his ration strength and Jourdan replied that whatever the books stated, the number of his men was nowhere near 140,000. Eventually, as the methodical Carnot began to bring order out of the chaos, there was some better accounting for manpower. The decrees of 11 and 31 October 1795 established norms for the French army – 323,000 infantry of the line, 96,960 light infantry, 59,000 cavalry, 29,000 gunners, and 20,000 engineers, miners, and sappers. But these numbers also represented nominal rather than actual strength and as late as 1798 the Ministry of War complained that it was unable to rely on its records.[8]

Whatever the exact figure, the *levée en masse* provided the necessary manpower to build up the huge French armies which checked invasion, suppressed insurrections, and carried the Revolution across the frontiers. But it was not popular. It had been introduced and enforced in a national emergency, but the victories of 1794, the end of the Committee of Public Safety, and the break-up of the First Coalition in 1795, all tended to favour a return to the volunteer system. The Constitution of the Directorate in the Year III (22 August 1795) declared that 'the army shall be constituted by voluntary enlistment, and, in case of need, by the method determined by law'. In practice, men in service were retained and, except for medical reasons, there were to be no discharges until after the Peace of Amiens in 1803. Wastage was replaced by local draft, voluntary enlistments encouraged by bounties and, on occasion, plain chicanery. It was an unfair system and desertion again assumed alarming proportions.

In 1798, finally, the Directory passed the so-called Jourdan Law, an act combining volunteer enlistments with conscription. 'Every Frenchman,' the act began, 'is a soldier and owes himself to the defence of the *patrie*'. Then, however, it continued that substitutes were permitted, though not encouraged, and that volunteers, provided they presented a certificate of good conduct from their local authorities, would be accepted for an initial four-year engagement. Conscription was to be limited to single men between the ages of 20 and 25; the youngest class to be called first. The Directors fixed a quota of 200,000 men to be drawn from this age group, but never succeeded in procuring more than 37,000. In any case, the annual levies between 1799 and 1804 required less than a third of the available manpower, and substitutes were cheap. In practice therefore few well-to-do young men served unless they had a taste for adventure and wanted to enter a profession in which rank, honours, and even riches could be obtained. Still, the Jourdan Law was resented. The Directory was afraid to apply it in the Vendée, while elsewhere, despite threats of punishment, there was widespread evasion. The act was one of the final legacies of the Directory to Napoleon and, in its essentials, remained the basis of the French army's recruiting system until after 1870.

The organization of the armies: infantry, cavalry, artillery

Infantry constituted the bulk of the revolutionary armies. At the outset of the war it consisted, on paper at least of 94 numbered regiments, each with 2 battalions and each battalion with 9 companies. One company in each battalion was designated as grenadier and the regulation strength of each company was 56 men including three officers. In addition there were 12 light infantry battalions, their number rising to 25 by May 1793 and more than doubling the following year.

In addition the various levies had produced about 750 battalions, legions, and corps, of widely differing strength and quality. One battalion, for instance, had 27 officers and only 13 men. Even worse, perhaps, was the friction between the *blancs* of the former royal regiments and the *bleus* of the new formations, the names referring to the circumstances that the former still wore their tattered white uniform while the new units were dressed in the blue of the National Guard. Regular soldiers resented the partiality shown by the government to the citizens in arms. They called themselves 'men of porcelain' because they had been tempered in the crucible of fire and looked down on their untested compatriots as mere 'soldiers of clay'.

And with the infusion of additional manpower by the *levée en masse* re-organization clearly became imperative. Carnot realized that a combination of old and new units would not only provide rapid training, but equally indis-pensable, provide combat units of uniform size and strength. Lafayette, recalling his experiences in America where militia frequently had been brigaded with the Continentals of the Line, as well as Kellermann had already tried similar measures, and Dumouriez and Dubois-Crancé also had advocated such combination. The solution was the famous *amalgame* of 1793–4. It consisted of two distinct operations. First came the combination of the different kinds of voluntary and requisitioned troops into a single body, followed by the merger of this force with what was left of the old army.

The operation was opposed by some officers who feared losing their positions and by some soldiers who disliked the idea of changing uniforms. It also was denounced by radicals who alleged that the reorganization would sacrifice 'Republican Liberty'. But Carnot persisted and by the end of 1793 he had successfully carried out the first part of the programme. There now existed 213 battalions of former regulars and 725 of volunteer and requisi-tioned troops. On 8 January 1794 the Convention, satisfied with the progress, sanctioned the immediate implementation of the next step, the combination of 426 of the new with 213 of the old battalions into three battalion demi-brigades, a designation replacing the old title regiment. Remaining units either were split up to bring weak battalions up to strength, or formed into supernumerary reserve demi-brigades.

A second *amalgame* took place in 1796–9. This time the total number of units was reduced, but individual demi-brigades were enlarged. There now were 110 demi-brigades of the Line and 30 of light infantry, each with an establishment of 3,277 men, and differing only in that in the light demi-brigade a carabineer company was substituted for the grenadiers of the line unit.

STRENGTH OF A DEMI-BRIGADE OR REGIMENT OF THREE BATTALIONS

STAFF					*Officers*	*Soldiers*
Chiefs of Brigade or Colonel					1	
Chiefs of Battalions or Lieutenant Colonels					3	9
Adjutants (Majors)					3	
Quarter-Masters					2	
Sergeant-Majors of Battalions					3	
Surgeon and Assistant Surgeons					3	
Drum Major					1	20
Drum Corporal					1	
Musicians					8	
Master Workmen					4	
BATTALIONS						
	1st	*2nd*	*3rd*	*Total*		
Captains	9	9	9	27		
Lieutenants	9	9	9	27	81	
Sub Lieutenants	9	9	9	27		
Quarter Master Sergeants (Fourriers)	9	9	9	27		
Sergeants	36	36	36	108		
Corporals	72	72	72	216		3117
Grenadiers	71	71	71	213		
Privates	824	824	824	2472		
Drummers	18	18	18	54		
Strength of each battalion	1066	1066	1066	3198	90	3137
Total strength of the Demi-Brigade					3227 men	
Number of Combatants					3208	

Adapted from S.F. Gay de Vernon, *Treatise on the Science of War and Fortification*, New York, 1817, vol. I, p. 43.

Under the *amalgame* of 1794 one out of every three lieutenants and captains were chosen by the men, while two were promoted by seniority. In the higher ranks seniority could be, and was, overruled by the Committee of Public Safety which in turn entrusted many appointments to Jean-Baptiste-Noel

Bouchotte, an old soldier risen from the ranks, War Minister from April 1793 to April 1794. Bouchotte held that a people's army had to have popular generals and gradually a new officer corps replacing the old. The new generals were young indeed, 33 years on average, though the regimental officers were middle-aged. Between 1791 and 1794 the medium age for lieutenant-colonels was 42 and for captains about 30 years of age. At that, though the average age declined during the next ten years, the officer corps was not as youthful as has sometimes been imagined. Seniority was increasingly important in the lower appointments, especially after April 1795 when the election of officers was abolished. Still, there was promotion for bravery, and the opportunity to gain advancement from the ranks remained an important incentive in the Republican and Napoleonic armies.[9]

As soon as a unit had been formed under the *amalgame* it was, whenever possible, activated with great ceremony. There were speeches; a new flag was presented; the bands played the *Marseillaise*; then the troops broke ranks and embraced each other. After that ranks reformed and the demi-brigade paraded past its commander and civilian functionaries. Despite earlier opposition and misgivings, the operation was a success. The last traces of the army of the *ancien régime* vanished along with the remnants of the old regimental uniforms and traditions. Friction between the regular and the national troops was eliminated and replaced by republican and national spirit.

The *amalgame* applied to the cavalry in modified form only. There were far fewer mounted units and the old regiments managed to retain many of their traditions and even particulars of uniform. Historians have differed in their appraisal of the cavalry of the Revolution. 'The French cavalry of this period,' Chandler pronounced, 'was generally abysmal. This arm suffered most from the exodus of officers.'[10] Moreover, the lack of time to train good horsemen and the shortage of suitable mounts affected its efficiency adversely. In contrast, Rogers claimed that 'the cavalry of the French army suffered much less than the infantry from the upheavals of the Revolution'.[11] Recognizing the difficulties of improvising mounted troops, Rogers argued that the Revolution accepted those noble officers willing to serve it. A compromise is presented by Phipps, whose multi-volume account of the French Revolutionary armies often is considered the standard work. In the earlier campaigns, he wrote, the French horse certainly was not equal to the Austrian or Prussian squadrons, but the French learned from their opponents and combat experience provided better training than more formal instruction.[12]

In any case, while cavalry expansion did not equal that of the infantry, the arm was considerably augmented. There were 62 mounted regiments in 1789 and 84 in 1798. The heavy cavalry, where replacements for men and mounts were most difficult, showed the smallest increase, only one regiment of the Line and two regiments of Dragoons. In contrast the *Chasseurs à cheval* and Hussar regiments doubled in number to 24 and 12 regiments respectively. Light cavalry, with its individualism and panache and wide appeal, produced, during the early revolutionary campaigns, a number of irregular formations which, in the *amalgame*, were used to make up new regiments. *Les Guides de l'Armée d'Allemagne* became the 7th Hussars, the *Hussards de la Liberté* became the 9th Hussars and other irregular units were broken up and distributed among the existing regiments.

There were only minor changes in organization. In 1791 the heavy cavalry and the Dragoons had formed three squadron regiments, while the light regiments had four squadrons each. By 1798 Carabineer regiments fielded four squadrons, a total of 703 men, while the four squadron Dragoon regiments had an establishment of 943 officers and men. Light regiments had the same establishment, while the Line regiments, with only three squadrons, numbered 531 officers and men each. Altogether, including artificers, armourers, bootmakers, and farriers, the mounted arm in 1798 had a regulation strength of 68,432 officers and men.[13]

Despite the infusion of new elements, some of the regiments jealously clung to their old customs and uniforms. The Hussars especially retained as much as they could of their extravagant uniforms together with their long hair plaited at the back of the head. Other regiments too, except for a *tricoleur* cockade introduced in 1791, continued to wear the old Bourbon uniforms for several years. And Marbot recalled that when he joined the 1st Hussars, the former Bercheny Regiment in 1799, the unit, primarily recruited among the Germans of the Alsace, still maintained its old customs, uniforms, and language.

By 1796 the performance of the French horse, admittedly mediocre until then, though hardly a 'patent disgrace' as Chandler also called it, showed much improvement. Able leaders were coming forward and in 1796, when he started operations on the North Italian plain, Napoleon formed a small cavalry reserve. Commanded by Murat this routed a larger body of Neapolitan horse. Napoleon later commented that 'this was the first time that the French cavalry, seeing the bad state in which it had been, measured itself with advantage against the Austrian cavalry'.[14] Strictly speaking, this, of course, was not true. The Neapolitians were not Austrians, but Napoleon wanted to encourage this arm. His faith was rewarded when his cavalry defeated a large Turkish force at Mount Tabor in 1799, and again at Marengo when the younger Kellermann's sudden charge against the flank of a superior force may well have won the battle.

Other commanders, too, were beginning to use concentrated cavalry to deliver a decisive shock. When Hoche took over the Army of the Sambre and Meuse in 1797, he withdrew one cavalry regiment from each division and formed separate cavalry divisions by categories. The Hussar Division, responsible for strategic reconnaissance, was entrusted to Ney.[15] The use of concentrated cavalry masses for break-through and pursuit became a standard feature only during the Napoleonic campaigns.

The third combat arm – artillery – flourished during the Revolution and maintained high morale and technical competence. In 1789 this corps was organized in seven regiments of foot artillery, each with 20 companies. Named after their home stations – La Fère, Metz, Strasbourg, Grenoble, Besançon, Auxonne, and Toul – regiments were numbered in 1791. As a 'scientific' corps, always considered less feudal than either the infantry or the cavalry, the artillery initially displayed enthusiasm for the new order. In return, on 29 October 1790, the Constituent Assembly designated the corps as one of the main combat branches, no longer merely the 'useful auxiliary', as Guibert had described it. Its demonstrated loyalty as well as its battlefield performance continued to gain the approbation of successive governments and in 1797 it was accorded precedence as the senior arm in the army, ranking ahead of the infantry and cavalry.[16]

The artillery suffered less than the other arms from the exodus of officers. Between September 1791 and July 1792 some 107 officers left the corps and several hundred more departed after August 1792. In all it is estimated that the corps lost about one-third of its officers, but this was only half as much as the rest of the army. Many able officers remained including some who achieved high rank during the Revolutionary and Napoleonic Wars – d'Aboville, d'Anthouard, Baltus, Dommartin, Duturbie, Du Teil, La Martillière, Lariboisière, Lespinasse, Pernetty, Sénarmont, Songis, and Sorbier. Vacancies and new positions created by expansion were filled largely by the promotion of deserving non-commissioned officers. By 1793, for instance, more than half of the captains in the 1st Artillery, the former La Fère Regiment, had been promoted from the ranks.

In 1792, with their establishment virtually intact and their materiel still in excellent shape, the batteries played a prominent part at Valmy and their thunder was heard at Jemappes. During the subsequent campaigns in 1793–5, however, artillery had only a modest role. According to regulations the foot regiments were equipped with Gribeauval pattern field guns of which there was a serious shortage. Many pieces had been issued to the National Guard, while battalions guns, which had been abolished after the Seven Years' War, were reissued to the new volunteer units in an effort to give these raw troops more firepower. Many of these pieces were lost during the early defeats, but the infantry divisions, formed on a permanent basis in 1793, also had been allotted one or more batteries.

As a result, the theories regarding the concentration of artillery, already developed before the Revolution, had to be disregarded. The proportions of guns to men dropped to about 2 per 1,000 in most Republican armies and by 1793 all manner of materiel, from obsolete 16-pounders to ineffective 2-pounders, were pressed into service. Few batteries, then also designated as divisions with two to a company, could muster the eight cannon of the same type and calibre prescribed by regulations and numbered anywhere from 2 to 12 pieces, the majority fielding some five to eight cannons or howitzers. Expertise declined due to the loss of many regulars, killed, wounded or detached to the new units and during the siege of Charleroi in 1794, Phipps described the gunners as 'young and inexperienced'.[17]

The great rearmament effort directed by the Committee of Public Safety brought results. In 1792 howitzers constituted but 1 in 40 pieces, by 1798 they numbered 1 in 4, and every battery was equipped with at least one of these useful weapons. By this time, moreover, the artillery had been reorganized, or more accurately, returned to its pre-war organization. Artillery officers had always opposed allocating valuable guns to the inexperienced volunteers, but until 1795 it had not been politically expedient to halt this misuse of valuable materiel. In 1795, however, the volunteers had to give up their modern guns and in January 1796 the volunteer batteries were abolished. Instead an additional foot regiment, the 8th, was formed. Pressure to abolish the battalion guns continued and these disappeared in 1798.

One innovation, however, became a permanent part of the artillery establishment. This was the horse artillery. Experiments with such formations had been carried out in the late 1770s and in 1791, General Mathieu Dumas had formed two 'flying batteries' at Metz, utilizing the Austrian system which employed light caissons, the famous Wurtz design, to carry the gunners along with their guns. In the spring of 1792, Lafayette proposed the introduction of true horse artillery (with all personnel mounted) to the Assembly which passed the necessary measure on 17 April 1792. The new companies, three to each of the armies of the North, the Centre, and the Rhine, were manned with gunnery instructors from the foot artillery and volunteers from the grenadier battalions. Many commanding officers availed themselves of the opportunity to get rid of their worst disciplinary cases. Horse gunners became renowned throughout the army both for their fighting qualities and for their love of quarrels. Most of them were poor horsemen, but owing to the shortage of horses, only one company in each army was mounted, the remainder used Wurtz caissons.

The new branch made its debut at Jemappes and performed very well. Every commander asked for the new batteries and the prestige of the horse artillery rose sharply. The Convention was impressed and on 7 February 1794 it constituted an independent corps of 'Light Artillery', with an establishment of nine regiments, each with six batteries, and its own instructional and administrative staff. Each battery had 6–8 pieces, usually 6–8-pounders and a light howitzer, and establishment of four officers and 72 men. The prestige of the new branch appealed to young and zealous men and to commanders like Debelle, Foy, Sorbier, and Sérurier who demonstrated its potential. To be sure, there were drawbacks. Too many horse artillery officers were cavalrymen, without proper knowledge of gunnery; discipline was always shaky. In 1797, during the defence of Kehl, a horse battery had to be deployed in a fixed position. Annoyed at this unaccustomed role, the horse gunners refused to construct emplacements against enfilading fire. 'We are,' they boasted, 'horse artillery, meant to fight in the open field and not behind entrenchments.' Permitted to have their way, their guns soon were smashed and the crews almost wiped out.[18]

In 1795, again at the insistence of the artillery specialists, the separate corps was abolished and horse artillery returned to the general artillery establishment. At the end of the Revolutionary Wars this was organized in eight foot and eight horse artillery regiments. Foot regiments, with 20 companies each, had a total of 1,899 officers and men, including a number of artificers and workmen; horse regiments, formed with only six companies, numbered 574 officers and men. Including maintenance personnel, as well as the two regiments of pontooneers, a branch remaining under the control of the artillery throughout the Revolutionary and Napoleonic Wars, the total establishment was 21,846 of all ranks.[19]

ALL FORCES OF THE ARM OF ARTILLERY ON THE WAR ESTABLISHMENT

	Officers	*Soldiers*
Inspector Generals, Directors, Sub-Directors, Brigadiers etc.	116	
12 Companies of Artificers	48	900
2 Regiments of Pontooneers	38	960
3 Regiments of Foot Artillery	1,040	14,152
8 Regiments of Horse Artillery	320	4,272
	1,562	20,234
Total	21,846	
Number of combatants, about	17,600	

Adapted from S.F. Gay de Vernon, *Treatise on the Science of War and Fortification*, New York, 1817, Vol. I, p. 51.

Artillery personnel had doubled in numbers and this expansion, as well as field wastage, required trained officer replacements. Until the war each regiment had provided basic gunnery training with advanced instruction conducted at the Artillery School at La Fère. From 1792 on officer training was centred at Chalons and after 1794 the new *École polytechnique*, though established to train civil engineers, sent most of its output either to the artillery or to the military engineering staff. To avoid duplication between the two schools an order of 16 December 1799 assigned basic instruction in military science, defined primarily as organization, fortification, and ballistics, to the *École polytechnique*, while advanced schooling for gunners continued at Chalons and for the military engineers at Metz.

Before the Revolution the French army had no separate engineer troops, though, as already noted, there existed a small, all-officer, engineering staff. In addition, six companies of miners and six of sappers were attached to the artillery. During the early campaigns some of these were transformed into foot artillery companies and on 15 December 1793 the Convention decreed the establishment of 12 sapper battalions, with eight companies each, part of a separate Corps of Engineers, reduced in 1798 to four battalions.

Moreover, steps were taken to remedy the greatest shortcoming of the foot artillery, the problem of transportation. During the Revolutionary campaigns the foot regiments did not have any organic transport; guns and vehicles were hauled by civilian drivers, partially provided by civilian contractors, partially by regimental arrangements. Often exposed to danger, these men were not subject to any military discipline and proved unsatisfactory. At Valmy, for instance, the explosion of two caissons in the great battery, caused many drivers to flee along with their animals, and similar incidents plagued the gunners on numerous other occasions. To do them justice, however, the drivers had reason to complain. They were neglected by the military as well as the civilian authorities, were furnished the poorest clothing and equipment, and often they did not even receive the rations to which they were entitled. During the winter of 1796 their condition became so wretched that they declared that while they were prepared to risk their lives in the common cause, they would rather go to prison than continue to serve under their current arrangements.[20]

The obvious remedy was to organize and treat them as soldiers, a status they already held in the horse artillery. In 1799, Marmont suggested the formation of artillery train battalions and this was implemented by 1800. Drivers and wagoneers became uniformed soldiers, subject to military discipline, though their number always remained inadequate and complaints about their behaviour continued.

During the Revolution, finally, there evolved permanent higher tactical formations combining all arms. Although the theory of the divisional system, developed by Bourcet, had been adopted in the French army in 1779, its tactical employment became standard only in 1793 when Carnot gave divisions the form in which they endured until the First World War. Two demi-brigades were combined into a brigade and two or more brigades, usually including line as well as light infantry, together with some cavalry, field artillery, a divisional park, service troops, and a small staff formed a mixed division, commanded by a General of Division, a title replacing that of lieutenant-general. The divisional establishments fluctuated greatly, and even in the well administered Army of the Sambre and Meuse they varied between 8,000 to 12,000 men.

There also were great differences at the army level. Armies, formed on specific fronts and for specific missions, varied in size. Several had overly large numbers of divisions and in March 1796 Moreau introduced a provisional *corps d'armée* organization into the Army of the Rhine and Moselle to facilitate better control. But this was experimental only and the corps structure did not become a permanent feature in the French army until its reorganization under Napoleon.

Command and control of the Republican armies

From the outbreak of war in 1792 to Napoleon's reorganization after 1799 the French supreme command structure was ill-suited for the conduct of a major war. In the latter years of the eighteenth century the French system of command had been perfected and in October 1790 the Assembly passed legislation which provided for a number of adjutant-generals to conduct the staff work for the operational armies. But this, essentially, was a paper reform only. When the war came in 1792 both coordination and leadership were lacking. There had been no preparations, no rations, no field trains, and the fortresses were in poor condition. The army commanders did not cooperate

during the first months, though at Valmy, Dumouriez ably assisted Keller-
man in blocking Brunswick's advance. By the fall of 1792 Dumouriez had
become the actual commander-in-chief of the armies, but in the spring of 1793
he engaged in a conspiracy to overthrow the Republic and this, perhaps more
than any other single event, convinced the Revolutionaries that it was unwise
to entrust any general with too much power. The Constitution of 1793
reflected this point of view. 'There shall be,' it stated, 'no generallissimo.'

The defection and removal of numerous senior officers, between 1791 and
July 1793 made it necessary to replace 593 generals, had ruined the old staff
system and that summer the National Convention, a loosely structured body
of some 700, was quite unable to deal with the emergency. The Committee of
Public Safety took on most of the executive and military functions and in June
divided up its work among sections dealing with various affairs. The Military
Section was directed by Lazare Carnot, who joined the body just nine days
before the declaration of the *levée en masse*. His principal assistant was another
engineer, Prieur of the Côte d'Or, the inventor of the decimal system and
author of an instruction manual for all branches of the service. Carnot
directed the disposition of the armies and planned strategy; Prieur organized
the supply of arms and munitions, while Lindet, the third member of the
Section, acted as Quartermaster General. The Section was ably assisted by the
Minister of War, Bouchotte, who from April 1793 to April 1794, transacted
much of the routine business.

During the early months the Committee acted as a whole in the determination of major strategy, and its instructions often were contradictory. After the
victory at Wattignies in October 1793, it sent orders to Jourdan instructing
him to pursue the beaten Austrians but not to do anything risky, to surround
the enemy, but not to divide his forces, to carry on the offensive, but not to
venture too far into Belgium.[21] Eventually Carnot came to dominate the
direction of strategy and relying only on a small staff, the *Bureau topographique*
housed in the Tuileries, he acted as actual commander-in-chief. The introduction of a rapid means of communication, the Chappe visual telegraph,
assisted in the rapid transmission of his orders. Installation of signalling
stations was begun in 1793, the first line connecting Paris with Lille. Under
good conditions the system could transmit messages at 120 miles per hour,
though bad weather could render it inoperable. News of the fall of Quesnoy
on 15 August 1794 was the first signal sent, reaching Paris within one hour.

As a strategist Carnot stressed the concentration of large mobile masses, if
necessary by depleting some parts of the line, and lacking supplies he ordered
them to live off the countryside. These, of course, were important departures
from the practices of the *ancien régime*, but his most important contribution,
in which he had the full support of his colleagues and of Bouchotte, was not
in the realm of strategy, but in his resolution of the conflict between revolutionary ideals and military discipline.

In 1793 the French Republic confronted the fact that the success of the
Revolution had been achieved by the disintegration of the old army. The
Revolutionaries had advocated insubordination, undermined the authority

of the officers, created numerous irregular formations, and called to arms enthusiastic but totally untrained volunteers. The earliest Revolutionary armies were noted for their indiscipline and disorganization. A core of the old regular army still remained, but there were thousands of volunteers with decided political ideas regarding 'Liberty and Egality', and even more conscripts, unwilling to serve, hard to train, and prone to panic in the field. The volunteers, one account tells, were 'persuaded that they saw the enemy. They fired on their own friends and then, frightened by the sound of their own guns they took off for the rear, led in their flight by their officers.'[22] And Dumouriez complained that the enthusiastic volunteers 'might be wolves, but still ran like sheep'.[23] Cannon and other valuable war materiel was abandoned or neglected, while the breakdown of the supply system turned many units into unrestrained bands of marauders, plundering friend and foe alike.

Once in power, the Revolutionaries discovered that any military force, no matter what regime and ends it served, could not ignore the fundamentals of discipline and order. The *amalgame* provided a solution to the organizational chaos and a rapid means of integrating raw troops into tactical formations, but it neither resolved the morale problem nor the threat posed by ambitious or obstructive generals. The still controversial solution to this dual problem was the appointment of deputies on mission.

Appointing civilian commissioners to the armies had been a practice of the old order and as early as 1790 the Assembly had dispatched representatives to investigate the Nancy mutiny. During the invasion of 1792, Carnot and several other deputies had been sent to help organize the armies on the frontier, and after August 1792 the commissioners, or deputies, sent out by the National Assembly had authority to suspend, and if necessary arrest, disloyal generals. The Convention retained and expanded these practices. On 9 April 1793 it resolved that 'three representatives of the people shall be deputized to each and every army of the Republic', and on 30 April a second decree elaborated their duties and powers. Depending on the size of the army, their numbers were raised up to twelve. They were to keep a constant vigil over the generals, officers, and government contractors, to 'fraternize with the soldiers . . . inspire their zeal . . . and cause them to realize the advantages of discipline'.

Dressed in a theatrical martial costume, a blue coat with brass buttons, a *tricoleur* sash, and a soft plumed hat, the deputies sat beside the generals in the councils of war and rode beside them into battle. With 'unlimited powers' and the backing of the Committee of Public Safety they effectively outranked or intimidated commanders in the field during 1793–4. Their activities have aroused considerable controversy. Conventional soldiers have denounced them as frequently incompetent, cowardly, and bloodthirsty doctrinaires, who knew nothing about the business of fighting and whose actions often were detrimental to the conduct of operations and morale. Civilian historians, mindful of similar experiments in the Russian and Chinese Revolutions, have been more favourable.

The soldier-historians have shown that, on occasion, at least the deputies on mission identified themselves with their part of the army and objected when a commander wanted to redeploy troops for strategic reasons. In September 1793, Houchard could not shift his right wing because the deputy on mission refused to release it. Many deputies regarded all generals as suspect. During his mission to the army in the Alsace, Saint-Just asserted that for the good of the army at least one general had to be executed. 'Up until now, he declared, 'there have been at the head of our armies only imbeciles and rogues', and this, he continued, had been the major cause of the French setbacks. The victim in this instance was Isambert, a man of 60, who had surrendered a position to a handful of Austrian cavalry. He was executed before the assembled troops, and within a short time other officers, including a brigadier, shared the same fate. Defeat now meant execution, but even victory, as Houchard found out, would not save a general if he was accused of insufficient zeal.[24]

Even lower ranking officers were not safe from the wrath of the all-powerful deputies. In 1794, during the siege of Charleroi, Saint-Just demanded that a battery emplacement be completed the next morning, and when despite an all-out effort this proved impossible, he had the officer in charge, a captain, executed. There are numerous other such instances, some not quite as absurd and Saint-Just also ordered that officers were to stay with their troops and that surgeons accompany forward elements into battle. He stopped the practice of soldiers leaving their encampments and repeatedly pressed Pichegru, then commanding the army to which he was attached, to drill his troops.

Many of the aberrations occurred because the deputies, ardent and zealous Republicans, usually lacked military qualifications. Levasseur tells that he was summoned by Carnot and instructed to proceed on mission to the Army of the North. His protests that he lacked military expertise were brushed aside. 'Your strength of character and devotion to the Republic are our guarantee.' And when he asked for specific orders he was told that they were in his 'heart and head; they will come out when needed. Go on, and succeed.'[25]

And in the opinion of many civilian historians they did succeed. There is no doubt about their ruthlessness, or for that matter the atrocities and injustices they committed. But the deputies understood the imperatives of revolutionary warfare. They understood that the troops had to feel that they fought for a cause, the salvation of the Republic, and that they had to have faith in the men who commanded them in battle. The public executions warned generals that they did not have to fail, lack of energy or commitment was sufficient. Victory at any price became all important and this propelled new and energetic officers into high command over the heads of senior but less daring men. Many of these young officers were selected and appointed provisionally by the deputies and later confirmed by Carnot. Among them were Bonaparte, Jourdan, Hoche, Pichegru, Masséna, Moreau, Davout, Lefebvre, Perignon, Sérurier, Augerau, and Brune – a formidable array of talent seldom matched in military history.

New leadership combined with inspiring revolutionary propaganda gave new heart to the dispirited troops. The French conscripts, one historian wrote, were 'driven in their thousands to the frontiers, trembled as they reached them, and then made all of Europe tremble'.[26] The transformation of young peasants, artisans, and workers into formidable soldiers was one of the major achievements of the Revolution and changed the nature of warfare.

But the very success of the deputies on mission eventually led to their decline and ultimate downfall. After the Committee of Public Safety was replaced by the Directory their powers declined. By September 1795, Lefebvre rudely overruled the objections of a deputy to a divisional deployment, and the following year General Bonaparte bluntly informed the Directory that the civilian deputy, now styled war commissioner, was a coward and that there were plenty like him. Instead of inexperienced civilians, the general asserted that commissioners should be men who 'have served in several campaigns . . . and have given proof of their courage. No man ought to belong to the French Army who values his life more highly than the glory of the nation and the opinion of his comrades.'[27] And Carnot, who had survived the fall of the Committee and who for a short time served as one of the Directors, agreed and gradually the deputies and commissioners were withdrawn from the armies.

Bonaparte's communication to the Directory expressed the new style of a neo-professional army. By 1796 the war had lost its unique ideological character. France had been saved; large areas had been annexed. The French citizen soldier was still patriotic, but from the viewpoint of the conscripted peasant or worker, the great adventure of the Revolution was over. Even new recruits were no longer receptive to political indoctrination. Coignet, conscripted in 1799, remembered that when he reported to barracks at Fontainebleau, he was 'received by some very unenthusiastic officers'. Even before his new unit was formed, more than half of the recruits departed and had to be brought back by gendarmes. Then training started. Every tenth day, the revolutionary *decadi*, there were speeches and 'we had to sing 'La Victoire', and the officers flourished their sabres. . . . Then we shouted 'Vive la République'. It was, he commented, 'very entertaining', but made very little impression on him.[28]

Revolutionary propaganda had even less appeal to the battle-tested veterans. Patriotism there still was, but it expressed itself in group solidarity and bravery in combat. As a body, the army opposed the Royalists who would despoil the new officers of their ranks and the army of its prestige, but they also opposed a return to extreme Jacobinism which had attempted to impose civilian control on the soldiers. Officers and men, as La Tour du Pin had prophesied, became a self-willed 'nation of the camps', obedient only to its own commanders. And the Directory, weak, corrupt, and increasingly dependent for its survival on the army, could do nothing to restrain them.

On occasion, even senior officers had trouble in handling troops and compared with other contemporary forces the French armies remained undisciplined. Late in 1798, facing a series of minor mutinies in the Army of Italy, Sérurier complained that this 'manner of serving cannot be suitable for a man of my age', and he asked the Directors to relieve him.[29]

Discipline in the French army was maintained by various devices. There was a strong aversion to corporal punishment, abolished in 1789. For capital offences the penalty was shooting or transfer to a penal unit. Lesser offences were punished by loss of rank, extra fatigues, and drills. In addition there existed a unique and extra-legal punishment, the *savate*, a beating with the sole of a shoe administered to stragglers or shirkers by a soldier's squad or mess-mates, a procedure more humiliating than painful. As a contemporary American officer observed, 'dread of shame and hopes for reward operate more powerfully in their system of discipline than fear of punishment'.[30] Glory and riches became the major motivating impulses and commanders who knew to appeal to these feelings, Napoleon or Hoche for example, exerted extraordinary power over their men.

As the wars continued, relations between the French army and its opponents changed; both sides began to appreciate the qualities of the other and to render the usual professional courtesies. In September 1796, when General Marceau of the Sambre and Meuse was fatally wounded and had to be abandoned to the Austrians, Archduke Charles sent his own surgeon to treat him. And his funeral became an occasion for both armies, French and Austrian cannon joining in a last salute.

The Revolutionary armies at war : tactics

The development of tactics during the wars of the French Revolution was not uniform. The early battles were fought according to the Manual of 1791 which called for a combination of line and column; the line, three deep, for fire action and assault, and the column for the approach and the bayonet charge against fortified posts. As long as the field armies were composed of regulars or of the Volunteers of 1791 who had received a year's training, this remained possible. At Valmy, Kellermann's Army of the Centre was, except for two battalions, all regular, as was a large proportion of Dumouriez's Army of the North. And later that year, at Jemappes, reports show the French fighting in accordance with the Manual.

Maréchal du Camp Dampierre, commanding on the right wing, recounts that he began the attack with the infantry marching in columns formed on the centre companies. Then, coming into artillery range, he deployed his battalions into line. After firing a few volleys, he continued, 'we took the first line of entrenchments with the bayonet'. In the centre, Dumouriez ordered an assault in columns against the village of Quaregnon. Both forms of attack were those prescribed in the Manual. Of course, the troops here included many regulars, among them the 5th Regiment of Infantry, formerly Navarre, shouting its old battle cry *'En avant Navarre sans peur!'* and the 18th Regiment, formerly Royale-Auvergne, shouting *'Toujours Auvergne sans tache'!*

By the following summer the old cadres had been submerged by the new levies of volunteers and conscripts. These no longer could operate according to the Manual, retaining only its 'quick march' of 120 paces a minute. For the rest the improvised French armies temporarily abandoned all formal tactics and during 1793–4 relied primarily on the 'natural' combativeness of a highly politicized army. Saint Just declared that 'the French armies must stress shock tactics', and Carnot gave his endorsement in his famous order of 2 February 1794. 'The general instructions,' he told his generals, 'are always to manoeuvre in mass and offensively; to maintain strict, but not overly meticulous discipline . . . and to use the bayonet on every occasion.'

The substance of these instructions was essentially derived from Carnot's experience in the field at Wattignies the previous autumn. There, despite a French superiority of nearly two to one, 26,000 allies had repulsed attacks on a fortified position. That night Carnot transferred 8,000 men from his defeated left to the right wing, and the next morning attacked in loose columns, beaten back twice, but successful on the third charge. In practice these charges combined skirmishing and the use of mass. Marching columns, as distinct from attack columns, were used to bring troops into range. Then they broke up into a ragged skirmishing line, taking cover behind hedges and in ditches. After their fire unsettled the enemy, the bulk of the troops, kept out of the demoralizing range of direct fire, were brought forward and with their officers and deputies leading them, often singing revolutionary songs, they rapidly charged the enemy. The preparatory firing and the speed of such an advance greatly discommoded more conventional adversaries who scorned these 'horde tactics'. A French Royalist officer denounced this 'hellish tactic' in which 'fifty thousand savage beasts foaming at the mouth like cannibals, hurl themselves at top speed upon soldiers whose courage has been excited by no passion'.[31]

But the use of columns and masses was not typical. Many battles in 1793–4 were fought in open order, with the French relying heavily on individual fire and movement, attacking with whole brigades deployed in skirmishing order, *en débandade*. Another emigré officer described such an attack by Ferino's division of the Army of the Moselle in 1794. 'We saw,' he recalls, 'the whole plain suddenly covered by an immense number of soldiers scattered over the ground . . . who made at full speed for the village of Berstheim. Hardly had they got into pistol range when they formed . . . to rush the attack of this post. This bold stroke nullified in an instant all the effects of our artillery fire.'[32] Indeed, some observers felt that fighting in open order was the major tactic employed by the French armies. 'One can truthfully say,' observed General Duhesme, 'that by the end of 1793 the French armies had only light infantry.'[33]

But such tactics, lacking the support and coordination of cavalry and artillery, were vulnerable to counteraction. At Kaiserslautern in November 1793, for instance, several French brigades surging forward *en débandade*, were driven back by Prussian volleys and sharp counter-attacks. As the French armies and their commanders gained more experience and discipline, their tactics became more sophisticated. Neither the horde attack nor the individual fire action provided adequate tactical control, and by 1795 the French moved to a flexible combination of linear formations, attack columns, skirmishing, and sniping. Line infantry adopted some of the methods formerly

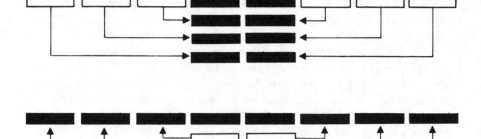

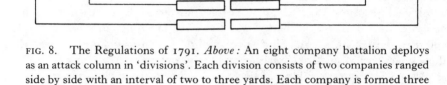

FIG. 8.   The Regulations of 1791. *Above:* An eight company battalion deploys as an attack column in 'divisions'. Each division consists of two companies ranged side by side with an interval of two to three yards. Each company is formed three deep with deploying intervals between divisions. *Below:* The attack column resumes linear formation.

reserved to light troops, while light troops acquired some of the steadiness of the line, producing the decisive element in the modernization of tactics. In many ways, of course, this had already been the aim of the Manual of 1791.

In 1795 the French armies in Germany began to deploy about one-fifth of a division's strength, light troops, *voltigeurs*, *tirailleurs*, or *chasseurs* if available, line infantry if necessary, ahead of the main body, and kept the mass of battalions behind, ready either to reinforce the skirmishing line or, if the skirmishing line had shaken the enemy sufficiently, ready to pass through for a massed attack, delivered in either single or double company columns of battalions, with maximum speed and little regard to the alignment of ranks or units. In Italy, too, General Scherer favoured this disposition, though his subordinates often fought in linear order. And when Napoleon took over, though in the whole he had little interest in the refinements of infantry tactics, he usually employed some variation of Guibert's *ordre mixte*.[34]

Of course, the allied adversaries of the French also had their own skirmishers, often as many or more than the French. The Austrians had their *Grenzer* and the Prussians had their fusiliers, while both armies also fielded small units of rifle armed *Jäger*. The fundamental difference was that the Austrian and Prussian armies continued to depend primarily on the exact movements and rapid volleys of infantry fighting in close order and continued to regard light troops essentially as auxiliaries. Their tactics, therefore, had much less flexibility than those of the French.

An additional element, giving the French greater flexibility in the field, came from necessity rather than from any designs. Lacking magazines, tents, and supply wagons, the French were more mobile, could concentrate their troops in smaller areas, and exploit the divisional system to the fullest degree.

Despite the introduction of the divisional system of combined arms, the development of cavalry and artillery tactics did not keep up with the infantry.

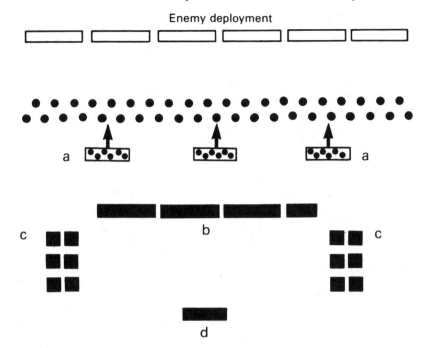

FIG. 9. French tactics – the *ordre mixte*. A three battalion French regiment or demi-brigade deployed with (a) one company from each battalion, *voltigeurs* or line, deployed in skirmish order; (b) one seven-company battalion deployed in line for fire; (c) six companies of the other two battalions deployed in columns of 'divisions', and (d) the three grenadier companies in reserve. On occasion, the grenadier companies would form the 'heads of the column' and lead the attack. (Depth of column is exaggerated in this diagram and deployment of column shown at close intervals.)

Throughout the Revolutionary Wars infantry carried the main burden of combat; artillery and cavalry, despite organizational improvements and gradually increased numbers, played a subordinate role.

Cavalry tactics remained essentially unchanged. As for artillery, despite the already existing theories concerning the concentration of fire and the mobile use of guns, such use remained exceptional rather than the tactical norm. At Wattignies the French were supported by what an English officer who was present described as an 'immense artillery', and in the autumn of 1794 the Army of the Sambre and Meuse began to mass guns in an artillery reserve. But usually there were not enough horses to haul either guns or supplies.

In several battles mobile guns were used, as Du Teil had advocated, against a decisive point in the enemy line. At Arlon, 9 June 1793, Captain Sorbier's horse battery performed an artillery charge; unlimbering and commencing fire at 800 yards, and then repeating the manoeuvre at continually closing ranges to pour canister into the Austrian line. Marmont executed a similar manoeuvre at Castiglione in 1796 with 19 guns, and again at Marengo. On that occasion, when Desaix's counter-attack was checked by an Austrian grenadier battalion, Marmont's guns which had accompanied the infantry unlimbered four light guns and fired canister at close range. Together with the explosion of an Austrian ammunition cart and with Kellermann's perfectly timed mounted charge, this decided the battle. Even so, these daring feats, later repeated on a larger scale during the Napoleonic Wars, remained exceptions during the Revolutionary Wars.[35]

The Revolutionary armies at war : counterinsurgency

The French Revolutionary Armies also became involved in a number of bitter guerrilla wars both at home and abroad, foreshadowing some of the problems later encountered on an even larger scale in Spain. At home they faced insurgencies in western France; abroad they met with guerrilla activities in southern Italy and in Switzerland.

The great uprising in the west of France, the War of the Vendée, was the most threatening to the Revolution. Since the summer of 1792 the rural population of the Vendée had been restive and the conscription decrees of February 1793 provoked a widespread rebellion. In March, armed with improvized weapons, scythes, pitchforks, pikes, and fowling pieces, the peasantry rose and quickly overran the small Republican garrisons. By June, reinforced by additional recruits and equipped with captured arms, the 'Whites' controlled a substantial area, including the cities of Saumur and Angers. But the 'Royal and Catholic Army', did not develop a military character or strategic capabilities. It remained an unstable assembly of local units, capable of protracted defence and of short but massive efforts. As one observer described it, their leaders 'could never organize the Vendeans into a permanent army or keep them under arms. . . . They eagerly entered battle, but were equally prompt to return home; they generally fought with courage, but they never became soldiers.'[36] They excelled in ambushes and raids, taking advantage of cover and terrain, but in the open field or in their attempts to seize defended towns, their disorganization and lack of discipline put them at a hopeless disadvantage.

Their initial successes against the government forces, the 'Blues', were against a motley force of National Guards, hastily raised internal security battalions, free corps, legions, stiffened by a few regulars. Most of these were of poor quality; they 'paraded abominably, marched anyhow, and had not the slightest idea of small arms drill'.[37] But by the end of June, the Convention had 30,000 men in the Vendee and an insurgent assault against Nantes was repulsed. Thereafter their army, in reality, a large mass of men, women, children, animals, and carts moved north into Brittany, hoping to receive English assistance. But coordination failed. They attempted to storm a port, Granville just inside Normandy, but failed and the British squadron arrived too late. Then, still an inchoate body, they fell back to their home base.

Meanwhile the Convention had sent in strong reinforcements, including

15,000 veterans by the capitulation of Mayence. Although the guerrillas, described as 'fearsome enemies . . . in the front rank of warrior peoples', by General Turreau, beat back the first Republican advance, they were unable to withstand the massive concentric drive. Just before Christmas their remaining force was smashed by Generals Marceau and Kleber at Mans and Savenay; about 15,000 Vendeans perished in these battles.

This was the end of the great war, but not the end of the insurgency. Now followed a punitive regime that lasted through the winter. While search and destroy columns, the notorious *colonnes inferneles*, scoured the countryside, sparing neither women or children, and turning the Vendée into 'heaps of ashes, death, and famine', in Nantes the bloodthirsty Carrier, deputy of the Convention, executed several thousands of suspects in such a brutal fashion that he was recalled by the Convention.

Repression proved counterproductive and in the spring of 1794 the Vendeans reopened the guerrilla war. The task of pacification fell to Hoche, an able and energetic general. He covered the Vendée with a network of fortified camps, pursued the bands with rotating columns which kept his troops fresh and tired out the enemy, and, avoiding bloody reprisals, he disarmed the inhabitants by seizing hostages as well as the cattle and grain. After the fall of the Committee of Public Safety negotiations began and finally led to an amnesty and the Treaty of La Jaunais in February 1795.

But even Hoche could not prevent the escalation of guerrilla actions north of the Loire. In Brittany several small bands, *Chouans* as they were called, had been operating since the winter of 1793. They too were in contact with the emigrés and the British government and received occasional supplies. However, the *Chouannerie* never assumed the proportions of a civil war; it remained confined to a low level of endemic insurgency. An attempt to fan it into a larger undertaking came in July 1795, when, after months of quibbling, a British squadron landed a royalist force at Quiberon Bay. Composed of some emigré units, as well as some reluctant French prisoners of war pressed from the hulks, and joined by local bands, the royalists mustered altogether 20,000 men. Poorly led, the royalists hesitated too long on the beaches and on 22 July 1795 Hoche crushed them, taking between 4 to 5,000 prisoners of whom some 750 were executed.[38]

These developments led to a renewed flareup in the Vendée, while even after Quiberon Bay, Chouan bands continued to be active in Brittany. By 1796, however, in both cases these activities could be contained by gendarmerie and National Guard units.

The insurgencies in the Vendée and in Brittany had been provoked by a long standing series of grievances. In contrast, the outbreaks of guerrilla war in Italy and in Switzerland were the direct result of the French system of living off the countryside, though religious and even primitive national resentments played a role too. In 1798 the Neapolitan lower classes, fearful of French intentions towards their religious customs, revolted against the occupation forces. After some fighting, the local commander, General Championnet, quieted the uprising by promising the *lazzaroni* freedom for their city and respect for their religion. He was successful in the city, but French requisitioning in the countryside, together with the Allied advances during the War of the Second Coalition, led to a peasant uprising the following year, which dragged on into guerrilla warfare and at its height tied up about 40,000 French troops. In northern Italy and in Switzerland, meanwhile, the exactions of the French garrisons provoked savage uprisings, equally brutally suppressed. In September 1798, at Stanz in Switzerland, the French massacred about 1,200 men, women, and children.

Engaged in what was still perceived as an ideological crusade, the French generals did not display the temperament or understanding to apply the careful political and psychological measures to contain or eliminate popular insurrections. Even Napoleon, whose handling of men had no rival, when encountering native uprisings in Italy and later in Egypt, had no other answer than brutal reprisals.

Arming the Republic

Throughout the Revolution the French armies were at best indifferently supplied and equipped. With stocks already depleted at the onset of the war, French financial and industrial resources were hard pressed to arm, equip, and sustain the vast numbers in the new armies and to replace the wastage of constant and hard campaigning.

Clothing and footwear were the first to give out. The regular regiments went to war in their old uniforms, while the Volunteers dressed in the blue of the National Guard. But already after the first few months the army was short of shoes and pouches, and during the first winter of the war Carnot told the Legislative Assembly that 'some of these brave fellows have no shoes, socks, or shirts, and are almost without breeches or coats'.[39] The look of the army changed. Aversion to the Prussian styles which had become fashionable before the Revolution did away with powder and queues, and long, unkempt hair became all the rage. As clothing wore out, blue or red striped loose pants, wooden clogs, and red woollen 'Liberty caps', began to replace regulation issue. Unable to provide uniforms, in February 1793, the government instructed local authorities to furnish their volunteers and conscripts with 'one coat, one vest, two pairs of breeches, three shirts, two pairs of stockings, two collars, and two pairs of gaiters . . . a hat, two pair of shoes'.[40] Needless to say that few recruits received their full issue and that uniformity vanished. Officers, on the other hand, began to affect the most extravagant sartorial styles, coats encrusted with gold embroidery, tricolour sashes, feathered hats, high boots, and whatever accoutrements caught their fancy. By 1800, however, the wear and tear of campaigning had led to the abandonment of much unnecessary ornamentation, though senior officers continued to dress in expensive style, and even the uniforms of the rank and file showed a tendency to return to the more highly adorned dress of former years.

But this was yet in the future. The Committee of Public Safety, armed with unprecedented powers, managed to remedy the worst shortages, but it naturally gave highest priority to procuring arms and ammunition. Still,

Lindet's efforts managed to obtain blue cloth for new and simplified uniforms and by the end of 1794 few battalions remained barefoot. Shortages, however, persisted. Some, no doubt, due to corruption and thievery, much was the result of inadequate transportation facilities. In 1797 the Directory acknowledged that it could do little about the situation and informed commanders that it could supply only 'men, arms, and ammunition', the rest would have to be requisitioned in conquered areas. Napoleon's famous proclamation to the Army of Italy in 1796, 'Soldiers, you are naked, ill-fed. The government owes you much; it can give you nothing,' was not far from the truth. Even the armies closer to the supply depots and the manufacturies were little better off. Both the Armies of the Rhine and Moselle and the Sambre and Meuse were short of many items and early in 1797, Hoche specifically promised his troops that 'you shall have mess tins, platters, and shoes'.[41] However, it was not until the interval of peace following the Treaty of Lunéville that the French armies were fully equipped.

The record of the Revolution in providing arms and ammunition was much better, even though the escalating intensity of the fighting required an enormous increase in output and demand often continued to outrun supply. At the outbreak of hostilities there was a shortage of arms in France. The Seven Years' War and the shipment of 100,000 muskets to America had depleted the arsenals, while arming the National Guard had taken the rest. At the end of 1791 available stocks comprised of 245,466 muskets, musketoons, and carbines, including only 158,233 infantry muskets of the 1777 pattern. Yearly production of the factories at Maubeuge, Charleville, and Saint Etienne amounted to only 42,000 pieces and early in 1792 the French government placed large orders for muskets in Birmingham. Of course, few of these ever reached France.

In August 1792 the National Assembly decreed the establishment of additional facilities at Autun, Clermont-Ferrand, Montauban, and Paris. But little was achieved until the decree of 23 August 1793 which not only conscripted the nation's manpower, but, in theory, at least, also requisitioned all means of production. Although in the end the Revolution did not abolish private enterprise, for a time the government itself entered into the manufacture of arms on a large scale. Prieur de la Côte d'Or, assisted by some of the ablest scientific and managerial minds of the time, including Gaspar Monge, headed the effort. It was decided to centralize musket production in Paris. Public workshops, eventually numbering 258, were set up in the parks and squares of the city and lacking skilled craftsmen, especially pattern makers, sculptors and wood carvers were drafted. Starting out with a small labour force of about 600, by August 1794 more than 5,000 men were employed in these workshops and output had reached almost 750 muskets a day. In addition, private workshops were pressed in service and in September 1794 a great plant was opened on the great commons of the Versailles Palace. By this time, however the changed political climate no longer supported the operation of public workshops and manufacturing was returned to private contractors.[42]

Paris had produced an unprecedented quantity of small arms, though quality suffered only slightly the modified muskets produced in the Paris workshops sometimes were substandard. Mass production was still in its infancy and though the concept of interchangeable parts had already been demonstrated by Le Blanc in 1785, nothing had come out of it. Mass production was achieved by employing as many workers as possible. Machines were utilized in boring cannon and for grinding metal parts, but fitting remained handwork and unless there were large tolerances no interchangeability was possible.[43] The greatest bottleneck was the production of gunlocks and in the end, old and obsolescent locks had to be reworked. By 1795, however, the breakup of the First Coalition decreased the need for muskets, and the lull in fighting permitted additional factories to come into operation at Tulle, Culembourg, Liège, and later Turin. These provided some, but not necessarily much, increase in production. At Liège, already a major centre for arms manufacture, for instance, French occupation actually reduced production and restricted it to making lockplates only. But from 1795 on most French armies had a sufficient supply of small arms, though the following year the Army of Italy found itself short of weapons and after the battle of Montenotte (12 April 1796) captured Austrian muskets had to be pressed into service to arm the 1,000 men of Augerau's division who had advanced without weapons.[44]

Providing the required quantities of gunpowder and artillery was equally difficult. Normally, large amounts of saltpetre were imported from Turkey, but this source now was cut off. Before the Revolution government agents also had the right to search in barns and sheep enclosures for deposits, but the Assembly had abolished this as an invasion of privacy. By August 1793 the shortage of gunpowder was acute; the army had only 14 million pounds of powder on hand, and its requirements were 80 million. On 1 September 1793 the right of search was reinstituted and citizens were exhorted to search 'in the name of patriotism' in houses, cellars, stables, and caves for the precious saltpetre. In the end, enough was found and the powder was ground up in requisitioned flour mills, equipped with a simple counter attached to the wheels which rang when the required number of turns had been reached. In addition, a large new powder factory was set up at Grenelles, producing 30,000 pounds of gunpowder a day.

The manufacture of cannon was, of course, the most difficult. A special committee, headed by Monge, attacked this problem. Although some 10,000 pieces of artillery were in hand in 1791, the vast majority were garrison guns. Only 1,300 pieces were suitable for field service, and 4-pounders, required as regimental guns, were in short supply. In late 1793, Monge estimated that, counting guns for the fleet and for coast defence, France needed 6,000 additional pieces of artillery. To speed up manufacturing, Monge invented a simplified casting method, substituting sand casting for the clay forms previously used, built furnaces in converted churches, and taught the new processes to selected workers in evening classes.[45] The necessary copper for bronze cannons was obtained by requisitioning church bells and through a tacit trade with the enemy. French cattle, destined for the Austrian army, were traded for Carpathian copper in Switzerland.

Although many of the pieces were not up to the pre-war standard, Monge and his assistants succeeded in producing an astonishing quantity of artillery. During the critical year 1793–4 almost 7,000 new cannons and howitzers were cast. By the end of 1795, France disposed of 4,816 bronze siege and garrison guns, 2,851 iron siege guns, as well as 2,543 bronze field pieces. At that, the supply never caught up with the demand.[46] During the next year, the Army of Italy began to utilize captured Austrian materiel. Despite the fact that the Austrian pound was lighter than the French, so that an Austrian 12-pounder was equal to a French 11-pounder, Napoleon was well impressed with the captured pieces, except for the Austrian 3-pounder regimental gun which he considered too light. In addition, limited numbers of Sardinian and Venetian cannon were taken into service.

The revolutionaries were eager to employ all scientific developments. Already before the Revolution the brothers Montgolfier had ascended successfully in a hot air balloon, and in 1793 one of the brothers proposed to destroy Toulon by having an enormous balloon carry a 30-ton explosive charge into the city.[47] The Committee of Public Safety established a research centre at Meudon and there conducted development pyrotechnics and experimental weaponry. The most celebrated product was an observation balloon and the first balloon company was formed by decree of 2 April 1794.

Already before that date the French armies had made use of hot air balloons during the sieges of Valenciennes and Condé in 1793. Here besieged French garrisons used small balloons and also had a carrier pigeon for return messages, but when the balloon drifted into the Austrian lines the pigeon was eaten by its captors.[48]

The new balloon company, *aerostatiers*, was formed for service with the Army of the Sambre and Meuse. It had a strength of 26 officers and men, and was equipped with a silk balloon filled with hydrogen gas, about 12 yards in diameter. The first use on the battlefield came in June 1794 at Fleurus, where the Austrians allegedly were frightened and the French encouraged by the sight. Its effectiveness as an observation platform was, however, limited. Although messages were relayed to the ground by the use of red, yellow, and green flags, and by written notes dropped down in weighted bags, the two passengers either were too high or too inexperienced to make accurate observations.

Even so, immediately after the battle a second balloon company was formed and some 20 other balloons, with names such as *Céleste, Intrépide, Hercule, Martial,* and *Aigle,* were sent to the armies. Napoleon used balloon observation during the Italian campaign of 1796 and took a balloon company with him to Egypt two years later. But the difficulties of transporting the cumbersome gas generating apparatus, and the time required to inflate the balloons, between 36 to 48 hours, outweighed their dubious value. Moreover, when most of the French balloon equipment sent to Egypt was captured off Alexandria by the British fleet, Napoleon became convinced that this innovation was of no practical value and soon after he took power in France he disbanded the balloon companies.

Observation balloons were one of the few innovations of the French Revolution that Napoleon rejected outright. For the rest, he accepted substantially what he found ready to his hand – the armament, the drill, the tactics, the recruitment system, and promotion through the ranks. After he became master, he made changes which increased the striking power of this great war machine, but otherwise he remained faithful to the methods of the Revolution.

NOTES

1. Gay de Vernon, *op cit.*, vol. I, 36–9.
2. Cited in J.H. Stewart, *A Documentary Survey of the French Revolution*, Macmillan, New York, 1951, 82.
3. Phipps, *op cit.*, vol. I, 16–17.
4. *Ibid.*, 17–18; H. Nickerson, *The Armed Horde*, Putnam's Sons, New York, 1940, 74–5.
5. M. Bricard, *Journal du Cannonier Bricard,* Hachette, Paris, 1894, 52.
6. Stewart, *op cit.*, 402–3.
7. M. de Jonnès, *Adventures in the Revolution,* trs. C. Hammond, Praeger, New York, 1969, 19–20.
8. P. Mahon, *Études sur les armées du directoire,* Paris, 1905, vol. I, 31–2 as cited in Paret, *op cit.*, 71.
9. Morvan, *op cit.*, vol. II, 427.
10. Chandler, *op cit.*, 69, 351.
11. H.C.B. Rogers, *Napoleon's Army,* Hippocrene Books, New York, 1974, 55.
12. Phipps, *op cit.*, vol. IV, 134–5.
13. Gay de Vernon, *op cit.*, vol. I, 45–9.
14. Phipps, *op cit.*, vol. II, 134–5.
15. *Ibid.*, 414–15.
16. Lauerma, *op cit.*, 93.
17. Phipps, *op cit.*, vol. II, 156; Lauerma, *op cit.*, 107–9.
18. Phipps, *op cit.*, vol. II, 394.
19. Lauerma, *op cit.*, 122–8; Gay de Vernon, *op cit.*, 48–51.
20. Lauerma, *op cit.*, 143–4.
21. R.R. Palmer, *Twelve who Ruled,* Princeton University Press, 1941, 104.
22. M. Weygand, *Histoire de l'armée française,* Flammarion, Paris, 1961, 210.
23. Phipps, *op cit.*, vol. I, 156.
24. Palmer, *op cit.*, 94–6, 183.
25. *Ibid.*, 82–3.
26. Cited in L. Madelin, *The French Revolution,* W. Heinemann, 1933, 360.
27. J.M. Thompson ed., *Napoleon's Letters,* Dent & Sons, 1954, 55.
28. Coignet, *op cit.*, 52–3.
29. Phipps, *op cit.*, vol. V, 259.
30. Hoyt, *op cit.*, 107.
31. Cited in Nickerson, *op cit.*, 91.
32. Cited in Phipps, *op cit.*, vol. II, 117.
33. Cited in Paret, *op cit.*, 73.

34. R. Quimby, *The Background of Napoleonic Warfare*, Columbia University Press, New York, 1957, 332.

35. Lauerma, *op cit.*, 287–8.

36. J. Clemenceau, *Histoire de la güerre de la Vendée*, ed. F. Uzureau, Nouvelle Librairie Nationale, Paris, 1909, 8.

37. De Jonnès, *op cit.*, 23.

38. Phipps, *op cit.*, vol. III, 42–3; De Jonnès, *op cit.*, 93.

39. Phipps, *op cit.*, vol. II, 33.

40. Stewart, *op cit.*, 408.

41. Phipps, *op cit.*, vol. II, 414, 416, 435.

42. Palmer, *op cit.*, 237–8.

43. J. Mirsky and A. Nevins, *The World of Eli Whitney*, Macmillan, New York, 1952, 222.

44. Chandler, *op cit.*, 66.

45. G. Monge, *Description de l'art de fabriquer les cannons*, Imprimerie du Comité de Salut publique, Paris, 1794, iv–v, 67–72.

46. Lauerma, *op cit.*, 115.

47. Phipps, *op cit.*, vol. II, 171–2.

48. *Ibid.*, vol. I, 184.

5

Napoleon's Armies

From the Revolution, Napoleon inherited huge conscript armies, led by young and ambitious commanders, accustomed to a mobile, offensive, and ruthless way of war. As First Consul and later Emperor, Napoleon imposed his own genius and personality on these armies. He inspired Frenchmen and foreigners like with fierce loyalty and devotion. As a soldier he stood among the great captains, and under his leadership his armies swept aside all opposition. He won unsurpassed victories and his campaigns, strategy, and style of command are to this day studied by soldiers everywhere. In the end, of course, both his overweening ambitions and his overcentralization, coupled with a neglect of logistics and supply, proved his undoing and he was defeated by attrition and greater numbers.

The Grande Armée
Napoleon's main military instrument was the *Grande Armée*, the Grand Army, designating from 1805 on the principal body of French and allied forces operating under his personal command. Concentrating the bulk of his strength to deliver the decisive stroke at the crucial point, its tremendous offensive impact gave Napoleon a considerable advantage over his enemies. At the same time, the formation of the Grand Army manifested in the military sphere the goal that Napoleon already had attained in the political sphere – the concentration of all power in his hand. But it also imposed an important handicap. As an absolute autocrat, Napoleon could not brook any competing authority. Therefore there could be only one main army, and when this was engaged in one theatre of operations, makeshift command arrangements would have to do elsewhere. And in Spain, where except for a brief appearance in the winter of 1808–9, Napoleon did not exercise direct command, the consequences would be costly.

The development of the Grand Army took several years. When Napoleon returned from Egypt and established the Consulate, he carefully observed the Republican injunction against the head of state commanding the field army and this was the major reason for designating the army of Marengo as the 'Army of the Reserve'. Marengo, and Moreau's victory at Hohenlinden, brought peace and allowed Napoleon to begin restructuring the military forces.

The victories had come just in time. By 1799 the French armies had deteriorated, numbers were down to about 230,000, desertion was rampant, and morale was low. The general inspection held in August 1801 revealed additional shortcomings. 'The officers,' the report noted, 'are apathetic. They know their trade fairly well, but they are sullen and without spirit. And the non-commissioned officers are even worse. The majority is ignorant, pretentious, and slack. These men between 25 and 35 act as if they were 80.'[1] A major cause of the low morale was the intense rivalry between the various French armies. Under the Republic and the Directory 'each of these armies acquired a history, style, prejudices, and reputation of its own'.[2] Especially dangerous was the ill-feeling between Moreau's old Army of the Rhine and the troops who had served with Napoleon in Italy and Egypt. Bad blood, in fact, survived for many years. As late as 1811, Napoleon observed that Marmont would make an excellent replacement for Ney who had clashed with Masséna in Spain, because 'both are from the same family; they are of the Army of Italy, while Ney is from a foreign [i.e. the Army of the Rhine] army'.[3]

Moreau, the victor of Hohenlinden, was Napoleon's most bitter rival and his troops sullen. Soon after the Treaty of Amiens, Napoleon despatched a considerable portion of these units to reconquer San Domingo. A short time later, he discovered Moreau's involvement, together with some other generals, in a plot implicating royalist elements. There followed executions and prison sentences; Moreau was sent into exile. These events paved the way for Napoleon to assume supreme power. In May 1804, France received a new constitution with Napoleon as hereditary emperor.

Since March 1803, Napoleon had been concentrating large forces, designated as the Army of England, in camps and cantonments along the Channel and the North Sea. For the first and only time, troops received intensive training, practised new tactics, and received new equipment. Incompetents were weeded out, deserving officers promoted, and higher formations organized; shortages, however, persisted. There was inadequate transport and too little artillery. Even so, when it went to war in 1805, the Grand Army, as it was now styled, was a finely honed weapon and Napoleon could properly boast that 'surely there is no finer army in Europe than mine today'.[4] The army of 1805 was the first Grand Army and fought at Ulm, Austerlitz, Jena, and Friedland. In 1808 it shifted a considerable part of its forces to Spain, but was hastily reconstituted in early 1809 to battle at Aspern and Wagram. In 1812 it assembled its greatest strength for the invasion of Russia. After its destruction there, a new Grand Army arose in 1813–14. When Napoleon conducted his last campaign in 1815, he no longer used the title Grand Army; instead his forces were known as the Army of the North.

Organization of the Grand Army
At the end of 1804, according to a semi-official source, the French military

establishment numbered a total of 610,976 officers and men, 472 battalions, 320 squadrons, 8 regiments of foot and 6 of horse artillery, as well as staff, engineer, and supply elements. A modern writer, however, gives a lower estimate. 'Including garrison and second-line troops,' Chandler states, *'La Grande Armée* probably comprised some 350,000 men by 1805'.[5] The lower figure seems closer to the mark.

For strategic and grand tactical purposes, Napoleon institutionalized the corps organization, used experimentally by Moreau. The corps became the smallest force of all arms. Primarily an infantry organization, each corps combined two to four infantry divisions, a brigade or division of light cavalry, several artillery batteries, and a small number of engineer and support troops. The exact number of divisions and guns allocated to each corps varied purposely, both to confuse enemy intelligence and to reflect its assignment and the talents of its commander. In 1805, for example, it ranged from Soult's IV Corps with 41,000 to Augerau's VII corps with 14,000 men. Ney's VI Corps, 24,000 strong, three infantry divisions and one of cavalry, supported by 36 guns, was about average. Each corps was to be capable of defeating approximately equal numbers and able to hold against superior forces until reinforced. The system was adopted by Napoleon's allies and imitated by almost all of his opponents.

In 1805 the Grand Army's order of battle comprised seven corps, with one additional allied corps formation. In addition, there were three major formations which Napoleon kept under his own control. There was the Army Cavalry Reserve, six heavy mounted divisions; the Army Artillery Reserve, concentrating almost a quarter of all available guns, and finally the Imperial Guard, the *corps d'élite* of Napoleon's forces, numbering over 7,000 men. For the 1812 campaign, Napoleon modified the army organization, introducing the army group. On that occasion, operating with over 400,000 men exclusive of support formations, the Grand Army moved in three army groups. The central, led by the Emperor, consisted of three mixed corps, two cavalry corps, the Imperial Guard, 47,000 strong with 112 guns, as well as allied contingents. This central group was flanked by two other army groups, the Army of Italy under Eugene and the Second Support Army commanded by Jerome. One Prussian and one Austrian auxiliary corps operated on the extreme northern and southern flanks, while additional corps were in reserve and along the line of communications.

Command and control of the Grand Army was exercized by Napoleon who practised a personal, highly centralized style of command. Imperial Headquarters was constituted of three major divisions. By far the most important was Napoleon's separate personal staff, the *Maison*, performing political as well as military functions. The General Staff of the Grand Army proper, presided over by the efficient Berthier, formed the second major division. The third division, and never able to function as smoothly as the others, was the staff of the Commissary General. Altogether with its subsidiary staffs, bureaus, escorts, and attached personnel, Imperial Headquarters became extremely large, looking, when drawn up for review in 1812, 'like a small

1   *Battle of Friedland, 14 June 1807*: French grenadiers in column charging Russian Guard Grenadiers (distinguished by their old-fashioned mitre caps). Note the mounted French officers leading the attack as well as the light gun brought up in direct support.

2   *Entrance of the French into Turin, May 1796*: Following his early victories over the Sardinians, Bonaparte's army entered the capital. This picture shows cavalry and light guns and also illustrates the lengthy marching columns. The uniforms, however, are those of a later period.

3 *Revolt at Pavia, 30 May 1796*: The French advance into Lombardy was opposed by local citizens. Pavia shut its gates against Bonaparte. An assault column under General Dommartin breached the gate, there followed a massacre and Bonaparte ordered execution of the town council. Street fighting usually brought out the worst in troops.

4 *Battle of Mount Tabor, 16 April 1799*: Bonaparte with 4,000 men and 16 guns defeats 26,000 Turks. The scene depicts French squares, supported by artillery, breaking Turkish cavalry charges. In the centre right, Bonaparte with his escort. Uniforms are those of a later period.

5 '*1805*' *by Meissonier :* Cuirassiers of Napoleon's cavalry reserve waiting for the order to charge. Note the foot artillery moving up for the preparatory bombardment.

6 *Jena, 14 October 1806 :* Napoleon and his staff during the battle. The grenadiers of the Imperial Guard drawn up on the right, while a battery of medium guns dominates the field from a position personally chosen by the Emperor. Horse artillery is moving forward on the left.

7 *Battle of Wagram, 7 July 1809* : After being initially repulsed by Archduke Charles at Aspern, Napoleon reorganized his forces and defeated the Austrians at Wagram. The Emperor, his staff, and escort are in left centre. A column of infantry is moving up on the right, while elements of the great artillery concentration are firing in the background.

8 *Battle of Talavera, 28 July 1809* (from *Campaigns of the British Army in Portugal, 1812*): British and Spanish forces under Wellesley and General Cuestas defeat strong French forces under Victor. While the Spanish forces occupied a position affording considerable cover, the British for once fought out in the open in a bloody see-saw battle. In the centre, French columns assault the stretched British line while light guns are providing supporting defensive fire.

9 *French army in the Sierra de Guadarama, 22–24 December 1808:* After the Spanish rising and the dispatch of British troops to the Peninsula, Napoleon transferred elements of the Grand Army to Spain and in December, despite appalling weather, crossed central Spain to turn against Sir John Moore's forces.

10 *Baggage Wagon, Peninsular War:* Women followed Wellington's army in Spain, though the four-wheeled wagon is not typical of the transport which commonly consisted of oxcarts and mules.

11 *Russian Cuirassiers, 1812*: Following the army reforms of 1812, Russian Cuirassiers were organized in two divisions and provided the army with a strong striking force. The helmets consisted of a tall leather skull with side bars, while the front and back peaks were bound with brass. Cuirassiers were equipped with black front and back pieces, held by black leather strappings.

12 *Russian lancers, 1812*: Lance-armed light cavalry, in this case Cossack regulars, formed an important part of the Russian army. Of interest in this picture are the shaggy, light horses, and the peasant and his light cart in the centre. Carts like this formed a considerable part of the Russian train.

13 *Battle of Dresden, 26–27 August 1813 :* In a bitterly fought battle Napoleon repulsed the Austro–Russian forces under Schwarzenberg. This panoramic picture shows Schwarzenberg and his staff on the right, cavalry and infantry in reserve, while others are moving up to the line in columns, and strong artillery concentrations are firing in the background.

14 *Cossacks stripping a body, Leipzig :* Soldiers of all nations tended to rob the dead and, on occasion, the wounded on the·field. Valuables were preferred, but clothing, especially boots also were considered useful.

15 *A square of the 28th of Foot withstanding a charge of French lancers at Quatre Bras:* Forming squares against cavalry charges was the best defence for infantry. Fire control and unbroken lines of bayonets commonly were able to ward off charges. Note the regimental colours in the centre of the square and the dead French cuirassier in the foreground.

16 *A British battery in action:* British artillery commonly was employed in direct support of their infantry and rarely concentrated in grand batteries. The gun shown here seems to be a light 6-pounder with a single block train, firing canister up to 300 yards. French guns generally tended to engage at longer ranges.

army'.[6] In the field, Napoleon repeatedly tried to reduce the size of Imperial Headquarters and in battle he usually surrounded himself with only a few trusted subordinates and a small escort.

For all practical purposes Napoleon was his own operations officer and he made all decisions. Berthier did not participate in the planning. In 1806, Napoleon instructed him to 'adhere strictly to my commands. I alone know what I have to do,' and Berthier, in turn, told Ney in 1807 that 'the Emperor needs neither advice nor plans of campaign. No one knows his thoughts and our duty is to obey.' Although Berthier was extremely efficient in his executive functions, this did not shield him from occasional outbursts. 'Not only are you no good,' his master stormed at him in 1812, 'but you are in the way.'[7] Berthier's passive role was further underscored by Napoleon's use of a pool of trusted officers attached to his personal staff to serve as observers and to carry out special missions. Staffs also existed at corps and division level, where on occasion, as in the case of Ney and Jomini, an effective partnership developed between a commander and his chief of staff.

Napoleon, as chief of state and at the same time supreme commander, had distinct advantages in maintaining control of planning and operations. At the same time, however, the system had severe limitations. The forces under his command grew from less than 50,000 to over 400,000 men, but he never changed his command system. His system did not produce capable leaders on the highest level, though at the intermediate level he always had a hard core of excellent divisional and brigade commanders. Napoleon was almost unbeatable as long as he could exert direct control over his armies, but he refused until 1813 to nominate a supreme commander in Spain, although very large forces were fighting there. In 1813 and again in 1815 his command control failed, and despite his subsequent complaints about slow or faulty execution of his orders, Napoleon's refusal to train his subordinates to act independently was largely responsible. 'Wherever Napoleon was,' Fuller commented on the 1813 campaign, 'success was assured; wherever he was not, it was disaster.'[8]

There was one more crucial shortcoming in Napoleon's system of war – his improvised and ramshackle logistics. Although he did not entirely rely on 'living off the land', and frequently, such as in 1800, 1807, and again in 1812, laid down great magazines for the supply of the army, and also made considerable efforts to provide his troops with bread and hardtack, the problem of bringing these supplies forward remained. Napoleonic strategy was based on rapid movement forcing the enemy into a decisive battle. Large wagon trains, even if they had existed, could not have kept pace. The army that marched to the Danube in 1805 carried with it but eight days' rations, bread or hardtack to be used only when the enemy was close and forces had to remain concentrated. During the approach march the various corps, spread over a wide frontage and each allocated a specific sector for foraging, were able to subsist on the country, but in the restricted area around Ulm this method did not work well. And in poor countries – Poland, Spain, or Russia – such arrangements could produce calamities.

Foraging and requisitioning, moreover, aroused local resentments and had adverse effects on discipline. In October 1805, Davout demanded authority to shoot all marauders, and on 14 May 1809, Napoleon decreed that 'all stragglers who under the pretext of fatigue have left their units to maraud, shall be rounded up, tried by summary provost courts, and executed within the hour'.[9] Even so, march discipline remained poor. Before Wagram, in rich wine country, the French, according to Captain Blaze, broke into the cellars and a considerable part of the army was drunk during the battle. And in Spain, the French alienated the population by their indiscriminate looting. As early as 1807, when Spain was officially an ally, Junot's corps, admittedly mainly recruits, lost all cohesion and looked, so Marbot tells, 'more like an evacuated hospital than an army coming to conquer a kingdom'.

Napoleon made some efforts to improve his supply arrangements. During the operations of 1806–7 the inadequate system of field transportation provided by civilian contractors broke down completely. In 1807 the French militarized transport and formed nine transport battalions. In addition, Napoleon introduced a network of military staging areas, the *étapes*. However, he always maintained that the security of the rear areas depended upon success at the front and so he did not allocate the *étapes* much manpower. In 1808, for example, there were some 200 such posts between the Rhine and the Vistula, manned by some 75 commissaries, 90 officers, and about 1,000 gendarmes.

Having suffered from short supplies in Poland, Napoleon made his most extensive preparations for the invasion of Russia. Huge amounts of provisions were accumulated in Prussia, but once again it proved impossible to bring these forward to the fighting troops. Moreover, neither Napoleon nor most of his subordinates, except for Davout, took care to preserve supplies. Already on the march to Moscow, provisions ran short and men weakened by hunger and fatigue became an easy prey to disease, losing one-quarter of their combat effectives before ever coming into contact with the enemy. And when he left Moscow, Napoleon allowed his army to depart with over 40,000 vehicles, most of them carrying loot instead of supplies.[10] In fact, it was this tail impeding the French, which allowed the slowly moving Russians to close. And finally, the total breakdown of discipline in the rear areas, especially at Smolensk and at Vilna, where the advance elements of the retreating troops wasted or destroyed the accumulated supplies, completed the destruction of the Grand Army.

Despite his often quoted pronouncement that 'an army marches on its stomach', Napoleon remained essentially an improviser. He could never free himself from the experience of his first Italian campaign when a small, highly motivated army, moving rapidly in a rich countryside had sustained itself from local resources and captured supplies. Failing to acquire a substantial logistical capability, his strategy remained geared to the quick knock-out blow, dictated, at least in part, by the problem of how to keep huge forces in the field without an adequate supply organization.

Officers and men

The larger armies as well as the corps system required commanders of higher rank than that of General of Division. In 1804, Napoleon reinstituted the title of marshal, discontinued during the Revolution. Altogether he created a total of 26 marshals, 18 in 1804 and the remainder between 1807 and 1815. Four of the original appointments were 'senatorial', that is they went to honour deserving officers of the Revolution – Kellermann, Lefebvre, Perignon, and Sérurier. A fifth went to Brune, an undistinguished soldier, but with excellent Republican connections. None of these five saw much field service. The remaining 21 were chosen primarily for their military capabilities. All had merit, though except for Davout, whose appointment in 1804 caused some surprise, few of them had the capacity for independent strategic command.

Davout, a noble who had thrown his lot in with the Revolution and had served as a brigadier under Napoleon in Egypt, was the best all-around commander. A cold, dedicated, and efficient soldier whose corps always was the best disciplined, supplied, and equipped in the army, he was not much liked by his peers but admired by his soldiers who appreciated his concern for their welfare. Always dependable, he deployed his corps at Austerlitz without waiting for a last minute change in orders; at Auerstädt he engaged and defeated a Prussian force more than double his own, and at Ratisbon, commanding more than twice the numbers he ever had led before, he performed well among a confusion of orders and counter-orders from Napoleon and Berthier. In 1812 his corps retained good discipline and order. Altogether, the little, bald, unpretentious officer served Napoleon better than his more flamboyant peers. He alone remained completely loyal to the end.

All marshals had one common quality, conspicuous physical bravery. Ney, a fine cavalry commander, earned the application 'the bravest of the brave', for his conduct in a series of skilfully fought rearguard actions during the retreat from Moscow, though afterwards his mind seemed disturbed and his performance during the Waterloo campaign erratic. The other marshals all excelled in a particular combat speciality. Murat was a renowned cavalry commander; Marmont a gunner of distinction and an excellent administrator; Bessières, who usually commanded the Imperial Guard, as well as Augerau, Mortier, Oudinot, Soult, and St Cyr were able tacticians. Lannes, 'as brave as he was intelligent', did exceedingly well at Friedland, but was killed in 1809. Masséna, a distinguished soldier in Italy, declined in Spain and became too dominated by love of money. Berthier was a devoted and able chief of staff, but no longer the enterprising soldier of earlier days. Suchet showed talent for counter-insurgency operations and did well on his own in Italy in 1814. Grouchy was a fine corps commander, but fatally indecisive at Waterloo. Poniatowski did well as an independent Polish commander, but received his baton only two days before he was killed at Leipzig. Bernadotte was able, though always more interested in politics than in war and as king of Sweden eventually commanded an army against Napoleon.

At the intermediate and lower levels the Napoleonic officer corps had a hard cadre of veterans from the royal and revolutionary armies. Of the 5,000 officers in the first Grand Army, nearly all had combat experience. Only 100 came from the new military school at Fontainebleau. The majority of the regimental officers, on average older than the generals, had served in the old Royal Army. By contrast most of the 140-odd generals had made their careers under the Republic. One quarter had been officers of the king; another quarter had seen enlisted service in the Royal Army, but the other half had begun their service after 1792. These remained the mainstay of Napoleon's senior officer corps. Overall, Napoleon promoted far fewer generals than the Republic. Guided mainly by merit in his appointments, he once confided to Gourgaud that 'I cannot abide promoting a desk officer . . . I only like officers who make war'. Seniority alone counted for little, and intellect alone for even less. Outstanding bravery and success were the all important considerations. Favour, however, played a role; Napoleon always retained a special fondness for those who had served with him in Italy and Egypt.

Entrance into the officer corps was possible in a number of ways: by spot promotion on the battlefield, through the military schools, and special training regiments, and by transfer. Napoleon continued the Revolutionary practice of promotion from the ranks. After a battle, subaltern casualties were replaced at once, usually on the recommendation of the colonels commanding the various regiments. They would present their most deserving sergeants to the Emperor who asked each some personal questions – service, wounds, awards – before commissioning him with the words 'I make you an officer'. When the new lieutenant returned to his old platoon, his messmates ceremonially would shoot his pack to pieces, for he would no longer need to carry one. Beginning in 1809, when casualties became substantial, about one-fourth to one-fifth of all Napoleonic officers came from this source, although few rankers promoted on the battlefield rose beyond the grade of captain. However, if there was no marshal's baton in every private's pack, opportunities for advancement in Napoleon's forces were far greater than those in any other contemporary army and served as a potent morale booster.[11]

Another increasingly important source for new officers was the military schools. During the Revolution the Royal Military Schools had disappeared and Robespierre's experimental *École de Mars* had been disbanded soon after his fall. There remained the specialist establishments for the artillery and the engineers, above all the *École polytechnique*. Napoleon founded new schools, primarily the *École speciale militaire*, established in 1803 at Fontainebleau and moved in 1808 to Saint Cyr. On paper this school continued the strong intellectual and mathematical orientated curriculum of its royal predecessors, but in practice the pressing need for junior officers forced drastic changes. The objective became to produce the maximum number of reasonably competent infantry and cavalry subalterns in the shortest possible time. Originally designed to graduate 100 officers a year, with the normal course set at two years, in practice hundreds of young men spent only a few months or even weeks at the school before they were posted to their regiments. By 1815, one way or the other, the school had produced 4,000 officers.

Pressed for junior officers, Napoleon also accelerated the training of artillery and engineer cadets at the *École polytechnique*. He denied that two years for an engineer and one year for a gunner were necessary. 'There is no need,' he wrote in September 1807, 'that these men know all about ballistics and construction; all that is necessary is that they can serve in the field and in the trenches.' And when the shortened programme failed to meet the demand, Napoleon decreed in 1811 that veteran artillery sergeants be given direct commissions.[12] Finally, the Emperor encouraged young men from well-connected families to enter the army as volunteers. He formed a number of training units, including the *velites* of the Guard, from which, after spending a short time in the ranks, these volunteers were commissioned in the line.

By 1813, however, Napoleon faced both the problem of quality and quantity and he found it extremely difficult to provide enough competent junior leaders. Inexperienced cadets and promoted non-commissioned officers did not always work out and to lead the huge levies of men conscripted to reform the Grand Army, Napoleon recalled invalids, and used officers from the colonial battalions, the National Guard, and the Customs Service. It was not a satisfactory solution. 'These officers,' he wrote to Clarke, the Minister of War, 'are the laughing stock of their men. . . . I shall have to dismiss them all and send them home.'

The final source of officers was by the transfer of entire units into the French army. These included contingents from areas annexed to the growing French Empire, Holland and parts of Italy, or units like the Polish regiments and squadrons taken directly into the French service after 1807. On occasion, individuals like Jomini entered the corps as aides-de-camp. The inclusion of new units did not always mean an accession of commissioned strength. For example when the Dutch kingdom and its army was absorbed in 1810 the Emperor fumed that its regiments were short of officers and its non-commissioned officers 'had no brains'. French officers had to be diverted to these units. In addition, the Emperor also insisted that the senior ranks of his satellite forces, like those of Westphalia, be commanded by French officers.

Napoleon opposed corporal punishments as degrading. Soldiers, he believed, should be inspired, not driven to fight and his officers were not only expected to know their men but to lead by example. Supreme disregard of danger was the hallmark of Napoleonic combat leadership at all levels, exacting a rising toll as bravery and mass compensated for lower quality. Officer losses mounted steadily in the years after Wagram. Among senior officers, 1 general was killed and 13 wounded at Austerlitz; 8 were killed and 15 wounded at Eylau; 12 were killed and 37 wounded at Borodino, and 16 were killed and 50 wounded at Leipzig. Casualties among the regimental officers were even greater; some units lost 80 percent of their officers at Borodino, the Katzbach, and the Beresina. Overall, according to Martineau, the military historian, the Imperial Army suffered some 50,000 officer casualties, 15,000 killed and 35,000 wounded, between 1805 and 1815. By arms, infantry sustained the greatest losses, 34,770 dead or wounded. Cavalry suffered 8,073 casualties, and artillery 1,698. Staff officers, at imperial, corps, and divisional level, suffered an amazing 3,024 casualties, while the small corps of engineers lost 501 officers. Remaining losses were distributed among the various smaller corps.[13]

Relations between officers and men were much closer and less formal in the French army than elsewhere. As early as 1796, Ney complained that 'contrary to good order . . . officers mingled with soldiers and drank with them in cabarets', and fraternization continued. An American officer observed in 1811 that 'French officers have been noted for their easy and familiar conduct with their soldiers'.[14] Sergeant Coignet of the Imperial Guard Grenadiers relates being invited to his company commander's house, there meeting other officers and their fashionably undressed ladies. 'I must say,' he recalled, 'that I never before had seen the ladies of Paris, half-naked, so near. I did not like it.'[15] The last statement may be doubted.[15]

Although its flags bore the motto 'Valour and Discipline', the conduct of the French on the march, in bivouac, and in garrison left much to be desired. Professor Lefebvre concluded that 'few armies have tolerated insubordination to such a degree where mass demonstrations, isolated rebellions and mutinies were common currency'.[16] Some officers, especially Davout, were appalled at this state of affairs, but most, like Major Pelet of Masséna's staff, accepted it, arguing that the French soldier had an innate combativeness that needed to be 'contained more with the help of confidence and the influence of talent than with that of rank'.[17] After Waterloo, however, there were some second thoughts. Among the papers in the *Archives de la Guerre* there is an unsigned memorandum to Drouot, dated a few days after the battle, insisting that lack of 'discipline was the cause of all our misfortunes'. The shameful incidents in Russia where officers had deserted their men to save themselves, had done great damage to morale and discipline.[18] The soldiers of 1813–15, even the prematurely conscripted 16–17-year-old *Marie Louises*, fought well, but the rot among the senior officers, many too concerned with preserving their wealth and position, could not help but affect the rank and file.

Under Napoleon recruitment continued to follow the system laid down under the Directory. In theory all able-bodied Frenchmen were liable for military service. Those between the ages of 20–25 could be called for the field army; all men between 20 and 60 were included in the National Guard serving within the French frontiers. The numbers of men actually conscripted, though large by the standards of the *ancien régime*, was not excessive. Between 1800 and 1815 a total of 2,543,357 men were mustered, but only some 1,500,000 enlisted. This came to less than seven percent of the population of France proper, and with the Empire steadily expanding and new areas becoming subject to conscription, the percentage was even lower. Recruits were mustered by age groups and service was for five years. But the continual wars after 1805 prevented discharges. Re-enlistments were encouraged with service stripes, bonuses, and better pay. In 1804 the army still had some 170,000 men, conscripted or enlisted between 1792 and 1799 in its ranks, their service far from over.

The number of recruits taken each year was determined by a quota levied against each department. After rejecting the medically unfit, the required number was selected by lot. The quota was always less than the total number eligible and substitutes could be provided. As manpower requirements escalated, the percentages conscripted rose, but up to 1812 the annual average was only about 85,000. And even including the total levies of 1813–14, the number of men actually serving did not exceed 41 percent of the eligible male population.[19]

Deferring men created a reserve on which Napoleon could, and did call later. As early as 1805 he called for 30,000 men from each of the classes 1800–4, and from 1806 on he called annual classes in advance. In 1813, however, he made an all-out effort to rebuild the Grand Army. Before leaving for Russia, he had organized a number of special National Guard units, 'Cohorts' as they were styled. These battalion-sized units contained about 78,000 men, fairly well drilled and disciplined, and in January 1813 they were incorporated into the army. In addition, Napoleon called up all deferred men from the classes 1808, 1809, and 1810, as well as the complete quotas for 1813–14. Finally, he activated the so-called Guards of Honour, composed of the sons of wealthy families, who had been organized in various places to receive and attend the Emperor. Although inexperienced and unfit for service, these units became part of the cavalry. All this should have provided some 360,000 men, but evasion and desertion, which between 1806 and 1810 had dropped to about three percent, rose alarmingly. In all, only 200,000 men were mustered in the spring of 1813. Napoleon supplemented this by recalling veteran units from Spain, converting marines into field artillery, and withdrawing troops from Italy. By the summer of 1813 another Grand Army was ready.

Of the 1,500,000 men conscripted between 1800 and 1812, about three-quarters came from the old France, the burden falling most heavily on the lower classes. The balance came from the annexed areas. Many 'French' units, therefore, were multi-national. In 1812, for instance, the 5th *Tirailleurs* of the Imperial Guard had soldiers from Genoa, Amsterdam, Mayence, and Erfurt, all 'Frenchmen' in its ranks. In 1802 Napoleon had asserted that only a national army protected the liberty of the nation and that 'one should not allow any deserters, foreign or French, into our forces'.[20] But he soon changed his mind and in fact enrolled numerous deserters, Hanoverian, Irish, Spanish, Prussian, and others, usually formed into 'legions' in his army. These, of course, should not be confused with the national contingents furnished by his satellites and allies, or with the volunteers such as the Poles.

The Napoleonic soldier received little formal instruction. Normally recruits were assigned to their regiments at once and departed for the front without more than a week's instruction. Marched to the front in short stages, they received uniforms, arms, and equipment *en route*, and often received some drill in the afternoon. With the average number of marching days from 50 to 60, they arrived in the field in good condition and fairly well trained. They picked up further proficiency in the field, a process perpetuating the *amalgame*. 'A soldier,' Napoleon declared, 'is trained after two month campaigning.' By dispensing with long periods of formal training, the French armies obtained replacements in the shortest possible period of time and as long as enough veterans were available to absorb the recruits the system worked well. It did, of course, not permit units to perform complex manoeuvres, and contributed to the marked changeover to mass tactics after 1807. And after the bulk of the veterans perished in Russia, the Grand Army was in dire straits. In 1813, three-quarters of the soldiery had no military training. Colonel Fezensac for one complained that his regiments consisted of 'young soldiers who had to be taught everything', and of 'non-commissioned officers who did not know much more'. And the next year, so some reports claimed, some units did not even know how to shoulder arms, cavalry troopers did not know how to ride, and gunners could not load or aim their pieces.

These reports seem exaggerated. These young and half-trained troops fought magnificently, for, as Wellington once suggested, that while such troops were inferior to veterans in manoeuvring, they were superior in fighting because they had not yet learned caution. The disenchanted Captain Blaze, who served in the Imperial Army from 1806 to 1815, put it differently. 'The soldiers,' he wrote, 'fought for their own account, to defend themselves. . . . They fought because it was impossible to do otherwise.'[22] Most authorities, however, give Napoleon a great deal of credit for the performance of his troops. Wellington calculated that Napoleon's presence on the battlefield was worth several divisions, not only because of his tactical skills, but because his very presence inspired men to do their utmost. The devotion of his men was one of the most important ingredients of his success. From the day that he took command of his exposed battery at Toulon, Napoleon perfected an intensely personal style of leadership. He once indicated to Metternich that, having grown up in the camps, he knew what motivated soldiers. According to Baron Odeleben, a Saxon officer on his staff, he carefully cultivated the morale of his men. 'The military,' he is reported to have said, 'are a freemasonry, and I am its Grand Master.' His frequent inspections, reviews, and his presence the battlefield enabled him to establish a close rapport with the troops. 'One appeals to men through their honour,' he declared in 1805 and to his brother Joseph he wrote that the 'morale and opinions of the army are more than half the battle'.

Besides a remarkable memory, he utilized extensive files on the performance and characteristics of his units and carefully appealed to their corporate feelings. On St Helena he told Gourgaud that 'the 32nd Demi-Brigade was prepared to die for me because I wrote to them after Lonato "the 32nd was there; I was tranquil"'. In 1807, Marbot tells, that he told the 44th of the Line that 'your three battalions count as six in my eyes', and the men responded shouting 'and we shall prove it'. During battle he encouraged troops with exhortations. At Eylau, again according to Marbot, he galloped along the marching columns shouting 'this is a lucky day. The anniversary of Marengo'! The results were demonstrated by the performance of his men and in the receptions he received. Even the wounded and dying raised themselves up to shout a last *Vive l'Empéreur*, while neither great losses nor defeat diminished the veneration in which the survivors held him.

Napoleon reinforced his personal appeal by tangible rewards and symbols of córporate and individual achievements. 'One does not,' he commented in 1805, 'reward bravery with money.' Instead, he provided decorations and the eagles. Already in 1795 the Republic had begun to award weapons of honour, *armes d'honneur*, for outstanding gallantry in action. Napoleon regularized the awards on 29 December 1799. Swords, carbines, muskets, and the like, all finely made and with an inscription relating the act for which they had been earned, were presented in limited numbers, 30 for an infantry regiment and 15 for a cavalry regiment.

Even more significant was the award of the *Légion d'honneur*, instituted on Napoleon's order on 19 May 1802. In contrast to other armies, the *Légion* was open to all ranks. Altogether some 40,000 awards were made between 1804 and 1815, casualties among the members were heavy; by 1815 only some 25,000 bearers were alive.

There was occasional grumbling about the distribution of the awards. The *Grande Armée* fared better than troops serving in distant theatres; relatively few awards went to the units in Spain. Initial distribution was lavish. Even by 1807 some 15,000 had been awarded. Another 1,000 were given after the 1809 campaign. Few were distributed in 1810–11, and there were none in 1812 which were supposed to be awarded at the close of the campaign, but the lists of nominations were lost with Berthier's carriage. In 1813–14 awards were handed out lavishly. After Bautzen, for instance, Girard's division alone received 260 decorations. Victories at Champaubert and Montmirail in 1814 resulted in 1,750 awards, the majority to the Imperial Guard. With such baubles, Napoleon once remarked, men are led.

For units there were the bronze eagles topping the regimental colours or standards. The eagle was the symbol of the Emperor's presence and the regiment's rally point in battle. Sergeant Thirion of the 2nd Cuirassiers, who carried one in Russia, described it thus: 'At the end of a fairly long staff was a bronze eagle with open wings. Under the eagle, and nailed to the staff, was a square flag of white satin surrounded on three sides by a gold fringe.'[23] From 1804 on the eagles were ceremoniously presented to all guard and line regiments by the Emperor in person and they became objects of worship. Their loss was a disgrace which severely shook the morale of a regiment and hence great precautions were taken to prevent their loss. In 1806 and again in 1807, Napoleon issued orders that the light cavalry and infantry regiments, both often in poor condition to defend their eagles, should leave these precious objects with their depots before going on campaign. The order, however, was widely ignored. On 18 February 1808, the Emperor decreed the establishment of special 'eagle bearing parties'. A *porte aigle*, ranking as an ensign, was added to the establishment of all infantry regiments. Napoleon specified that he had to be veteran of no less than 10 years service and to have fought at Ulm, Austerlitz, Jena, and Friedland. This 'first eagle bearer', was to be escorted by two veteran senior sergeants, the second and third eagle bearers. All were personally approved by the Emperor, who also designed their special weapons, a spontoon, short sword, and two pistols carried in an open breast-holster.[24]

During the retreat from Moscow orders were issued to break the eagles into pieces and bury them, while the flags were to be burned. But Colonel Fezensac of the 4th Line could not bring himself to do this. 'I had the staff burned and put the eagle in the haversack of one of the eagle bearers, and I always marched beside him.'[25] After Napoleon's first abdication many regiments destroyed their eagle, but the *Garde chasseurs* had theirs and proudly displayed it to the Emperor when he returned to Paris.

Napoleonic combat arms: infantry, cavalry, artillery

In general the combat arms followed the main line of development which emerged during the late Republic and the Directory. Infantry, nominally divided into line and light, remained the backbone of Napoleon's armies and by far the most numerous arm. A Consular order dated 24 September 1803 reintroduced numbered regiments. The actual establishment, however, fluctuated considerably and the numbering was not necessarily consecutive. In 1804 there were 89 regiments of line infantry, numbered 1 to 112, and 26 of light infantry, numbered 1 to 31. Both line and light regiments had much the same organization and equipment. Up to 1806 the typical regiment was composed of three battalions with nine companies each, including one elite company, designated as grenadiers in the line and carabineers in the light units. By order of 4 September 1806, Napoleon reorganized the regiments into three battalions of eight companies each, converting one of the centre companies, called fusiliers, into an elite *voltigeur* battalion. Grenadiers were selected from the bravest and strongest men with at least two years service. They were employed, sometimes in composite battalions, for specially difficult missions and drew extra pay and were excused from fatigues. The *voltigeurs* by contrast were chosen from small and agile men and given a skirmishing role. Two years later, Napoleon once again changed the regimental organization. An order dated 18 February 1808 stated that 'in future line and light infantry regiments will consist of a staff and five battalions; the first four will be designated as combat battalions, and the fifth as the depot battalion'. Each of the combat battalions was to consist of six companies, one grenadier, one *voltigeur*, and four fusiliers, all of equal strength.[26] The overall strength of a regiment was set at 3,970 all ranks, though in practice, this was rarely achieved. Seldom were more than two or three battalions actually present for action and wastage reduced field strength to about 600 for each battalion.

By 1808, except for minor differences in uniforms, the distinction between line and light infantry had disappeared. The two types usually were brigaded together and the light regiments were employed in conventional infantry roles. As the French began to adopt more massive assault formations, these were sheilded by the *voltigeurs* drawn from the entire brigade or division, and if necessary entire line or light regiments were deployed as skirmishers. Of course, the elite status of the *voltigeurs* had become nominal. Although Napoleon wrote to Eugene in December 1805 that 'it is not enough that a soldier shoots, he must shoot well', little was done towards this goal.[27] Even the *voltigeurs* received no special musketry training and they carried basically the same weapon, albeit in the two-inch shorter dragoon pattern, as did the line companies. Light troops, *voltigeurs*, and line all picked up their trade in the field.

Lack of training and the adoption of massed formations reduced the firepower of the French infantry, and yet firepower became more and more necessary to prepare the way for the assault. Napoleon now reversed his stand on regimental artillery. 'Every day,' he declared, 'I become more convinced that great damage was done to our armies by the abolition of the battalion guns.'[28] And with a great stock of Austrian and Prussian guns available, he had two 4-pounders issued to each regiment in late 1809. Served by hastily trained infantrymen detached from their regiments, these pieces were none too efficient, but they bolstered the morale and firepower of the foot. Regimental guns were not issued in Spain and when most of the pieces were lost in Russia they were not replaced.

Except for the reintroduction of the battalion (or regimental) guns, Napoleon retained the tactical formations based on the 1791 regulations. But many discrepancies had developed and the manual also did not fit the new regimental organization. In 1809, Napoleon ordered an overhaul of the infantry manual, but the result, largely drawn up by General Dumas did not please him. In 1812, General Preval produced another set of regulations, but circumstances did not permit its adoption. Napoleon, however, did try to abandon the conventional arrangement of infantry in three ranks. Combat reports convinced him that the presence of the third rank interfered with rapid reloading, and one observer, St Cyr, even claimed that a quarter of all casualties were inflicted by the third rank on the first two. Moreover, the two-rank deep British line had more firepower and frontage than the equivalent number of French troops. On 13 October 1813, Napoleon instructed Marmont that 'it is my intention that you form your troops in two ranks instead of three. The third rank does no good firing and is even less useful with the bayonet.'[29] Although at Leipzig some units fought in two ranks, it was obviously difficult to change basic formations in the middle of a campaign. Then too, there was opposition. Ney, for example, preferred to keep the third rank as a reserve, and the adoption of the two-deep line remained partial in the last year of the war.

French infantry maintained its reputation for marching. Ordinary marches were performed at the rate of 10–12 miles per day. Troops would form up at dawn and covering about three miles an hour, would halt early in the afternoon in time to forage, cook, and rest. The traditional head of the column was formed by a squad of leather-aproned pioneers with felling axes, followed by the drum major, the drummers, and musicians. Many regiments hired a civilian band master and band out of their own funds. During a long march the band was often divided into sections playing at the head, centre and rear of the column, each section striking up in turn. If artillery accompanied the movement, the regiment would march in files along the sides of the road, leaving the roadway free for the guns to pass. While marching at ease, soldiers sang or told stories such as the exploits of a mythical private, La Rammée who, though on leave, walked 400 miles to his unit to collect his bread ration. But forced marches, an integral part of Napoleonic strategy, were quite different. Daily mileage would double or even triple, troops might march night and day. 'We had not a moment of sleep, marching by platoon all day and all night, and at last holding on to each other to prevent falling.' Coignet remembered, 'those who fell could not be wakened. Some fell into ditches. Blows with the flat of a sabre had no effect on them. The music played, drums beat a charge; nothing got the better of sleep.'[30]

Only highly motivated and well-disciplined troops could make such marches; inferior units suffered great losses through straggling, and finally even the elite units were no longer capable of such efforts. Napoleon, however, refused to take this into account. Perhaps the memory of the extraordinary endurance and stamina shown by his men in Italy led him to expect too much of his later armies. As Phipps pointed out, had his troops in 1813 been capable of 'anything like the feats of fighting, marching and again fighting, performed by the Armée d'Italie, he would have dealt in fine style with the strategy of the Allies'.[31]

On occasion, such as early in 1809 when hastily reassembling the Grand Army to meet the Austrian threat, Napoleon would move key units by wagon. With careful staging of relays, frequent changes of teams, prepared food, and gendarmes to escort the convoys, 50–80 miles could be covered in a day over good roads. But with each wagon carrying from 12–20 men at best, and with vehicles and horses always in short supply, only relatively small numbers could be transported in this fashion. In 1809, for example, Napoleon moved part of his Old Guard infantry from southern France to the Rhine by wagon.[32]

There was no change in the armament of infantry during this period. Napoleon had little faith in the slow-loading rifles and only a few selected officers and sergeants were so armed. The ordinary *fantassin*, Guard, line, or light, carried the smooth-bore 1772-pattern musket, or the variations of 1794 and 1802. The French musket had standard range and accuracy, though compared with the British its main shortcoming was that it was used with a coarser powder, fouling more rapidly, and requiring cleaning after every 50 rounds. Arms were procured through a mixture of state control and private enterprise. The Directorate had abolished the national workshops and returned the production of small arms to various private manufacturers who undertook to supply certain quantities of weapons at a certain price and of a quality acceptable to the government. Inspectors, usually artillery officers, supervised fabrication and tested the arms before acceptance. Excluding satellite production, the Grand Empire manufactured a grand total of 3,926,257 small arms of all kinds, but even this was inadequate to fill needs.[33]

When Napoleon became First Consul the French armies were short of weapons. The Army of the Reserve, he complained, had regiments 'with half of their muskets in poor shape; others were 300 muskets short'. He demanded accelerated production and by 1803 annual output rose to 125,000 weapons. Purchases were also made in the satellite states. Hanover provided 40,000 non-standard pieces in 1804; a smaller quantity was procured in Turin. But Napoleon never obtained the great reserve of three million muskets he considered essential.

In 1805 first-line units of the Grand Army were adequately armed, but second-line formations had shortages. Many weapons were lost in combat; Austerlitz alone cost 12,000 muskets. Seizure of the large Prussian arsenals alleviated the situation in the following year, but from 1808 on Spain created a constant drain. More and more captured weapons, Prussian and Austrian, were pressed into service and in 1809, Napoleon notified Clarke, the war minister, that 200,000 new muskets were required by 1 July 1810. The 1812 campaign resulted in a critical situation. Non-standard calibre foreign arms were issued, obsolete weapons restored, and muskets collected from the German allies. But major musket reserve supplies were locked up in the besieged fortresses along the Vistula and Elbe, and on 25 November 1813, Napoleon was forced to order the disarmament of all foreign corps, except the Poles. And in 1814, during the last battles in France, his infantry was short of weapons.[34]

The second combat arm – cavalry – was completely transformed by Napoleon. He found some good regiments, but as a whole the arm was not equal to the Austrian or Prussian horse. Convinced that it was not possible to fight anything but a defensive war without at least parity in cavalry, Napoleon made great efforts to turn this branch into a powerful striking force, capable of rupturing the enemy front, while retaining its ability for exploitation, pursuit, and reconnaissance.

Unlike the foot where there was a definite trend toward an all-purpose infantry, Napoleon's reorganization of September 1803 emphasized the distinctions between heavy line, and light cavalry. He valued heavy cavalry above all. 'Cuirassiers,' he wrote on one occasion, 'are more useful than any other cavalry.'[35] Starting with a single regiment, this category eventually numbered 15, including one regiment of Dutch origin. In 1809 the two Carabineer regiments, the second component of the heavies, received steel helmets and breast plates and were used in the same fashion as Cuirassiers. Heavy cavalry was supposed to ride down opposing horse and exploit its success against enemy infantry. Its regiments, about 1,000 all ranks, and considered the best in Europe, composed a large part of Napoleon's cavalry reserve and justified his expectations at Austerlitz, Jena, Eylau, Essling, Borodino, Ligny, and Quatre Bras. Big men on big horses, with cuirasses and helmets, and wielding a straight heavy sword, they presented an awesome sight. At Waterloo, Private Morris felt that his regiment, formed in a two-deep square, 'would not have the slightest chance with them', yet, their armour was not ball-proof and firing at 12 paces, the steady square repelled their repeated charges.[36]

The cavalry of the line was composed of Dragoons whose number fluctuated between 20–30 regiments. In practice they were increasingly used as battle cavalry, though they also acted as flank guards, and when needed, as in Spain, in their original role as mounted infantry. The regiments were some 1,200 strong and the Dragoons were well armed, carrying in addition to the cavalry sword a shortened musket, a bayonet, and two pistols. They saw extensive mounted and dismounted service on all fronts.

The light regiments – Hussars, *Chasseurs à cheval*, and Lancers – constituted the largest and most dashing part of Napoleon's mounted arm. In addition, there were also a number of smaller subsidiary units, the *Gendarmes d'élites*, the *Éclaireurs à cheval*, and the Mamelukes, performing specialized functions. The establishment of the light cavalry fluctuated as new units were formed, sometimes by conversion from other regiments. The Hussars numbered 10–13 regiments, the *Chasseurs* attained a strength of 30, and at their greatest expansion there were 30 Lancer regiments. Without a doubt, the Hussars were the most showy, adventurous, reckless, hard-drinking and swearing organization. Their ideal was General Lasalle, a superb leader of light horse, who allegedly said that 'any hussar who is not dead at thirty is gold-bricking'. Born in 1775, he was, with a neat sense of timing, killed at Wagram in 1809. Light cavalry participated in battle, screened the army during marches, performed reconnaissance, outpost, and picket duties. It successfully covered the French advance to the Danube in 1805 and its great pursuit after Jena has become a model of strategic exploitation. Led by Murat, the French light cavalry covered over 600 miles in two weeks, and by giving the beaten enemy no opportunity to reform, contributed decisively to the collapse of Prussian power. Except for the Lancers, light cavalry was armed with sabres, carbines and pistols. It usually engaged in mounted action, though it could do a limited amount of dismounted work if necessary. To execute its different missions, light regiments were large, 1,800 all ranks at full strength.

Napoleon formed his cavalry in homogeneous brigades and divisions of light and heavy regiments at the corps and army level and also established independent cavalry corps. He used large cavalry masses, though he realized that cavalry alone could not overcome unshaken and supported infantry or artillery. Normally, cavalry charges were preceded by a heavy bombardment and supported by horse artillery. Murat's great charge at Borodino was accompanied by 100 horse guns. Unsupported charges such as Murat's charge with over 10,000 sabres against the Russians at Eylau, or the epic dash of the Polish light horse at the Somosierra Pass in 1808 were exceptional. At Waterloo, unsupported mounted charges, five in two hours, were repulsed with heavy losses by steady British squares.

French cavalry greatly improved throughout the Napoleonic era. After Eylau its heavy regiments were 'the dread of Europe and the pride of France', while the light horse excelled in panache, daring, and gallantry. Still, it suffered important administrative shortcomings. For example, it always was difficult to procure suitable mounts, especially for the heavy regiments, though the capture of a great many Austrian and Prussian chargers alleviated this problem. The French, however, were not good at caring for their animals. During the Russian campaign, for example, the allied German and Polish cavalry managed to preserve many more horses than the French who often neglected the most basic care. And in 1813, the situation became worse. The raw recruits did not know how to saddle or care for their animals. Many horses were disabled before battle and one could tell the approach of a French mounted unit by the smell of the infected sores of its horses.

Napoleon, a gunner by education, attached more and more importance to firepower and therefore to artillery. 'It is with artillery alone,' he told Bernadotte in 1806, and he repeated much the same to Eugene in 1813. 'Great battles,' he wrote, 'are won by artillery.'[37] Between 1804 and 1814 there was a considerable increase in the French artillery establishment. In 1804 there were eight foot and six horse artillery regiments, the first with 20 and the latter with six companies each. Successive increases in the establishment brought the strength up to nine regiments of foot and six of horse artillery, each foot regiment now 28 companies strong. In addition there were 21 foot and eight horse companies of the Imperial Guard. The term 'company' was synonymous with 'battery', each company normally comprizing six guns and two howitzers in the foot, and four guns and two howitzers in the horse artillery.

For all that, Napoleon's artillery was quite small. The original Grand Army had only two pieces for every 1,000 men, and the artillery ratio rose only slowly. In 1807–9 it stood at three per 1,000 men, and the introduction of regimental artillery finally brought it to 3.5 to every 1,000 men. But Napoleon never reached his target of 5 per 1,000 and in many campaigns he actually faced an enemy with an artillery ratio superior to his own. At Eylau, for example, the Russian artillery outnumbered the French almost two to one; at Leipzig the Allies had a three to two advantage.

The shortage of artillery was, in part, due to Napoleon's attempt to replace the 4-, 8-, and 12-pounders of the Gribeauval system with 6- and 12-pounders. On 29 December 1801 he charged an artillery committee headed by Marmont with designing a new artillery. However, the result of their work, known as the System of the Year XI (1803) was of little consequence. The renewal of war interrupted efforts to recast the artillery and only a new light 6-pounder was rushed into production. In practice, though, the new piece was too fragile and it was eventually abandoned.[38] Meanwhile the Grand Army was under-gunned and relief was achieved by utilizing captured Austrian as well as Prussian material. 'The siege artillery,' Napoleon commented, 'is poor . . . but the field pieces are useful and should be employed.' By 1807, for example, out of 48 guns in Soult's corps, 42 were of Austrian origin. Generally 6- and 8-pounders were employed at the divisional level, while 12-pounders were concentrated in the artillery reserve. There never were enough of these powerful pieces, between two and six per corps and slightly more in the Guard, and they were not used in Spain.

From 1809 on, Spain constituted a steady drain on Napoleon's artillery resources, though the Russian campaign was the greatest single blow with some 1,200 guns lost and many abandoned during the retreat for lack of horses to pull them. Even so, stripping his arsenals, coastal batteries, and allies, Napoleon fielded 1,300 pieces in 1813–14. He was, however, unable to provide enough ammunition. The escalation of fire demanded an ever-increasing supply of gunpowder and projectiles. Normally, Napoleonic artillery was provided with between 200–300 rounds per gun depending on calibre, carried in two caissons for each 4-pounder, three for each 6-pounder, and four for each 12-pounder. Additional ammunition was carried by divisional and corps parks. But in battle, expenditure outstripped supply. At Wagram the French artillery fired 96,000 shots, 91,000 were expanded at Borodino, and at Leipzig, Napoleon's ammunition ran out. 'If on the eve of the 18th I could have had 30,000 cannon balls,' he complained to Eugene, 'I would be master of the world today.'[39] By early 1814 he estimated his requirements at 400,000 charges and projectiles, and his available stock at only 100,000. Makeshift arrangement, inferior powder and scrap projectiles were used, until in the final battles batteries were silenced for lack of ammunition.

The deficiencies were in part due to the ill-timed 1803 conversion project, compounded by the limitations in production. Another important factor, as in the army in general, was inadequate transport. Artillery drivers had been militarized by the First Consul but the artillery train remained inadequate. To be sure, the artillery of the Guard acquired by 1807 two train battalions, 12 companies each, but the entire artillery of the line had only 11 battalions in 1805, 13 in 1808, and 14 in 1810. The numbers could be doubled by raising second battalions, designated as *bis*, but there was a shortage of specialized vehicles, limbers, ammunition carts, and caissons. For field maintenance and repair there existed from 1807 on an equipment train, eight battalions, ultimately increased to 22 battalions. But given the growing scale of operations and the greater frequency of battles, the artillery's logistical apparatus was hard put to keep up with requirements.

Napoleon always displayed a considerable interest in artillery tactics and often sited batteries himself. During the Austerlitz campaign artillery did not play a major role, though the night before Jena, Napoleon personally supervised the placement of his guns. From 1807 on, he used massed artillery to pave the way for the assault. The artillery of the Guard, commanded by Drouot, came to constitute the army artillery reserve. At Eylau, the Guard artillery, supplemented by the horse batteries of the cavalry reserve, covered the deployment of the French army against an initially superior enemy. At Wagram and Borodino, his big guns helped decide the issue, with Drouot, as usual, performing admirable service. Drouot, faithful and efficient, stood his ground against Napoleon. When during the advance to Dresden an enemy artillery concentration seemed to impede passage of the Elbe, the Emperor ordered up the artillery of the Guard. Drouot posted them and opened fire, but when the effects of the fire did not become evident at once, Napoleon stormed at Drouot for not placing his guns better. Drouot calmly replied that 'the guns could not be better placed', and in fact, within a short time the enemy's batteries were silenced.

From 1809 on, at least in the French army, artillery dominated the battlefield. 'Fire,' Napoleon proclaimed, 'is everything; the rest does not matter.' Even so, he remained strangely unaware of the difficulties of using artillery against an entrenched enemy or against formations deployed on a reverse slope. As late as 1809, for example, he remarked that 'I could do just as well without howitzers', but after his first and only experience against an English reverse-slope position he changed his views. In his 'Notes on Artillery', dictated on St Helena, he declared that howitzers were most useful against enemies in entrenched positions.[40] But this realization came too late, for in artillery matters, as indeed in almost everything else, Napoleon was an improviser, and the strength of his army could be found primarily in his flexible genius and in the individual valour of its soldiers.

The Imperial Guard

The combination of improvization and courage manifested themselves most clearly in the Imperial Guard, the *corps d'élite* of the Grand Army. The most famous of all of his formations, the Imperial Guard, was officially established in 1804, combining elements from the personal escort of Guides which had accompanied General Bonaparte in Italy and Egypt, the Guard of the Directory, and the Consular Guard formed in 1799. Purged of unreliable Republican elements, and with some new units, including marines, added, in 1804 the Imperial Guard numbered a mere 5,000 foot, 2,000 horse, and 24 guns, about 8,000 men. Napoleon constantly added new and different units and the Guard grew into a corps of all arms, and eventually into an army within an army, complete with its own administrative and support services. With men from many nationalities, Frenchmen, Belgians, Dutchmen, Poles, Mamelukes, and others serving in its ranks, it embodied Napoleon's rising ambitions and was evidence of his continental empire. By 1805 its strength had risen to over 12,000; during the Russian campaign the Guard numbered 56,000, and in 1814 it attained its greatest expansion, some 112,482 men in all of its many formations. When he abdicated in 1814, his last order to Drouot was to 'lead the Guard to Louis XVIII', but few of the guardsmen were happy in the royal service, and when Napoleon returned from Elba the Imperial Guard was hastily reconstituted. Around the core of 700 veterans who had accompanied the Emperor into exile, there rallied units from the Bourbon Royal Guard, retired officers and men. This time, however, it only reached a strength of 25,000 men. Its combat spirit, however, was high and its final stand in the dark hours of defeat after Waterloo aroused universal admiration. When its remnants, covering Napoleon's escape, where summoned to capitulate, General Cambronne defiantly replied 'the Guard dies but it does not surrender'.

The Imperial Guard was made up of three major and distinct elements. First and most prestigious were the regiments of the Old Guard, picked men with at least four years service and two campaigns. The second element, the Middle Guard, was also highly selective and included some excellent foreign units. Finally there was the Young Guard, composed of the best recruits of each annual conscript class. The Young Guard never quite attained the standards of the prestige of the more senior regiments, and it was less carefully conserved by Napoleon. Its combat record in Spain, Russia, and in 1813–14, was excellent, though it suffered severe losses.

Napoleon separated the Imperial Guard in many ways from the rest of the army, and he developed an intimate personal relationship with its officers and men. Especially he liked to talk with his Old Guard, asking them details of their service, wounds, decorations. It was Napoleon who nicknamed the Old Guard grenadiers *les grognards*, the grumblers, and he frequently shared their camp and their food. Defeat and suffering could not break these bonds. At Essling in 1809 the Guard refused to fight unless the Emperor retired out of danger; during the retreat from Moscow the Guard maintained discipline until the Emperor left the army, only then did it break ranks and joined the other stragglers.[41] In more tangible fashion, every guardsman ranked one grade higher than his counterpart in the line and he received substantially higher pay, better quarters, uniforms, and rations. Decorations were more lavishly awarded to the Guard than to other formations, its medical service was superior, and when other troops went hungry, the Guard often had its own provisions, enjoying the only permanent supply train in the French army. As line troops caustically observed, even the mules of the Guard rated as donkeys.

Napoleon hesitated to commit the Guard, especially his cherished grenadiers of the Old Guard, to combat. He preferred to hold them back as a last reserve and the sight of thousands of grenadiers in their tall bearskin caps, complete with plumes and white cap-lines (the Guard always fought in full-dress uniform) standing ready behind the French line served as a potent threat to enemy commanders. In some major battles, Austerlitz and Borodino for example, they never were committed, and sometimes they were engaged too late. But when the Old Guard advanced, the climax of battle had arrived and it always was assumed that its intervention assured victory.

Even so, the value of the Imperial Guard, as indeed that of all such élite formations, is debatable. The Guard provided an example for other troops and it often earned its extra pay and privileges. On the other hand, the Guard drained the line of much valuable manpower, depriving it of many potential junior leaders, and it also caused a morale problem. Constantly held up to the army as an example, its failure in action would have grave consequences. When, for the first time in its career, the Old Guard wavered and broke at Waterloo, and in the opinion of many critics it was kept in reserve far too late in the day, the cry '*La Garde recule!*' swept through the French army. Its repulse was the last straw for the French line troops who had fought well all day. Seeing with their own eyes the defeat of the allegedly invincible Guard, the other units were seized by near panic and disintegrated rapidly.

Napoleonic strategy

Napoleon frequently paid respect to the great captains of the past, to Alexander, Hannibal, Caesar, Gustavus Adolphus, Eugene, and above all, Frederick the Great. He also studied the writings of recent military theorists,

Bourcet, Du Teil, and Guibert, and acknowledged his debt to these men. But in his strategy he was basically a pragmatist. Although he often wrote and talked about the so-called principles of war, he never enumerated them. In fact, he once confessed that in war there were 'no precise or definite rules'. Fundamentally, he told Gourgaud, the whole art of war was 'just like all beautiful things, simple; the simplest manoeuvres are the best'.[42] Despite his denial of any system, later strategic analysts have tried to deduce meaningful patterns from Napoleon's generalship. Yorck von Wartenburg declared that the operations before Marengo illustrated Napoleon's major strategic principles. They were the use of one major line of advance, careful attention to security in order to screen his intentions from the enemy, the selection of the enemy's main body as his objective, manoeuvre against the flank or rear of the enemy's communications, while safeguarding his own. And Fuller summed it up more succinctly. He reduced the elements characteristic of Napoleon's strategy to three: unity of command, generalship and soldiership, and planning.[43]

The destruction of the enemy's main field force, rather than the mere occupation of territory or the capture of the enemy's capital was Napoleon's main objective. 'There are in Europe,' he once observed, 'many good generals, but they see too many things at once. I see only one thing, namely the enemy's main body. I try to crush it.'[44] Carefully planning a short campaign of annihilation, and able to direct both the strategic and political aspects of the war personally, he made use of the corps system and the well-developed road network of central Europe to force his opponents into one decisive confrontation, '*une grande bataille . . . une affaire décisive et brilliante*', to be followed by vigorous pursuit which completely shattered the opponents capacity and will to resist while raising the morale of his own troops. This approach, of course, could exact heavy casualties, but Napoleon could draw on the almost unlimited replacement pool provided by conscription while for some years his opponents found such losses unacceptable. The potential of this strategy was most brilliantly demonstrated in the Ulm–Austerlitz and Jena–Auerstädt campaigns. However, if the enemy eluded destruction and if he was able to fall back on strategic depth and reserves, then Napoleon faced severe problems.

Napoleon's strategic deployments were carefully planned to set the stage for the great and decisive battle. Even before hostilities had begun, the Emperor's intentions were carefully shrouded from the enemy. Newspapers were censored, borders closed, travellers detained. Then, when the Grand Army moved, its advance was preceded by swarms of light cavalry, screening its line of advance, protecting its communications, and gathering intelligence about the location of the enemy. The self-contained corps would march along separate routes, deployed to encompass the entire area of operations. At the outset this strategic net would be quite large, about 170 miles wide in 1805–6, and over 300 miles wide in 1812. Then, when the main body of the enemy was located, Napoleon pulled his corps closer together, adopting a loosely quadrilateral formation known as the *bataillon carrée*. Frontage was reduced to about one day's march between the corps, until finally the corps' first contact with the enemy engaged him at once and pinned him, while the other corps would hurry to its support. Final concentration was achieved either before or during the climactic battle. When concentration had been achieved, Napoleon's forces often outnumbered those of his adversaries. He could fight and win when the odds were against him, at Austerlitz, the Beresina, and Dresden for example, but he always attempted to gain local superiority, achieved by exact calculations of time, distance, and the mobility of his forces.

Within this strategic scheme, Napoleon practised two major manoeuvres against the rear. The first he used when facing a numerically stronger foe. He divided his force into an advance guard, two wings, and a reserve. Then he rapidly advanced to seize a central position dividing the hostile army and while pinning down one part of the enemy, moved his reserve to gain local superiority against the other part and defeat it. If, however, the enemy was in equal or inferior strength, Napoleon adopted an envelopment strategy – the manoeuvre on the rear. He induced the opponent to advance against what he was led to believe to be the main French force, conducted a holding action on that sector, while the bulk of the army swept around the enemy in forced marches, compelling him either to surrender or to give battle with no satisfactory line of retreat.

FIG. 10.   The *bataillon carrée*. Napoleon's strategic march order in which several corps marched independently but within supporting distance. The first to contact the enemy became the advance guard and engaged while the others moved to its support. All corps were self-contained and the direction of march could be changed rapidly. *Left* Bernadette's I Corps is the advance guard and, *right* is relieved by Darout's III Corps and Lanne's V Corps as direction changes.

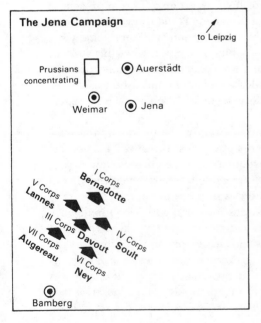

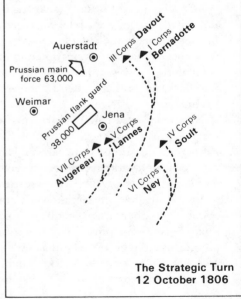

Both manoeuvres were delicately timed affairs, depending on tight security, good intelligence, precise planning, and troops capable of stout holding actions and great marching feats. The last was especially important. In September–October 1805, for example, when executing the famous manoeuvre at Ulm, the Grand Army moved from the Rhine to the Danube and east in 11 days. Soult's corps covered 275 miles in sustained marching. And in December, when Napoleon had lured the Russians and Austrians to attack him on ground of his own choosing at Austerlitz, Davout's urgently summoned corps covered over 70 miles in little over 48 hours. To appreciate such mobility it should be realized that, in round numbers, 30,000 infantry on the march took up five miles of good road; 60 guns with their caissons required $2\frac{1}{2}$ miles, and 6,000 cavalry, riding four abreast, extended for about four miles. The length of such a column made it mandatory to move along several parallel roads, keeping in mind the need for lateral communications if the situation required such a change.

With good commanders and troops, and with an ample network of roads, the *bataillon carrée* formation was capable of rapid large scale manoeuvres. Pouring into Saxony and Prussia in 1806, and discovering that the main Prussian body was west of the Saale River instead of north towards Leipzig as had been assumed, the huge mass of 140,000 men shifted its line of advance 90 degrees without confusion and delay. But when roads were poor or nonexistent and when the opponent had learned to counter Napoleon's moves, the *bataillon carrée* was no longer effective for trapping the enemy. This had become the situation in 1812–13.

Napoleonic tactics

Napoleon's entire strategy was directed towards the decisive battle and his grand tactics were closely linked and in fact very similar to his strategic practices. Throughout his military career he favoured the offensive both strategically and tactically. In all of his battles he stood only three times on the defensive, at Leipzig, and at La Rothière and Arcis in 1814. Each time he took the defensive only after his initial attack had failed. Basically his battle plan was offensive movement supported by massive fire, but Chandler, the most recent historian of his campaigns, distinguished three major variations, repeating the pattern of his strategy.

These variations include the manoeuvre on the rear, the central position, and the frontal attack. Manoeuvre on the rear involved the classic flanking attack and envelopment, exemplified by Marengo, Ulm, Jena, Friedland, Smolensk (where, however, it failed) and Montmirail. A variant was the massive turning manoeuvre in which a rather large portion of the French army engaged the enemy's front, while a sudden attack crushed his exposed flank. This shattered Napoleon's opponents at Austerlitz, but did not succeed at Eylau. The second major variant was the 'central position', dividing the enemy and defeating him successively in detail. Finally, if time, terrain, or enemy disposition made either of these approaches impossible, Napoleon

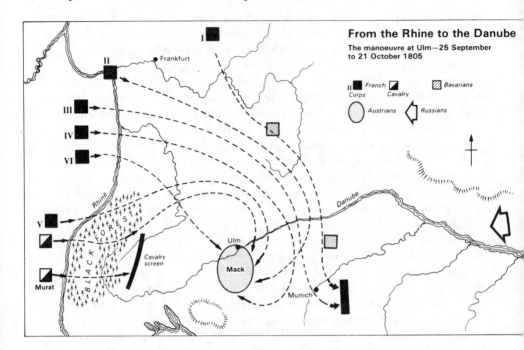

From the Rhine to the Danube

The manoeuvre at Ulm—25 September to 21 October 1805

FIG. 11. The manoeuvre in the rear. A cavalry screen both protects the advance and confuses the Austrians under Mack. Before the Austrians can recover the Grand Army swings around the Austrian northern flank and envelops them from the rear. Meanwhile, a re-inforced French corps and Bavarian allies shield the flank and interpose themselves between the encircled Austrians and their slowly approaching Russian allies.

resorted to the direct frontal assault. Even here, he would try to draw out the enemy by mounting an attack on one wing, hoping to weaken the centre and engage his reserves, and when the opponent was stretched, Napoleon with a superb sense of timing would launch the breakthrough force, the *masse de rupture*, using elite troops carefully concealed until this moment. The artillery reserve would gallop to within 400 yards of the enemy and batter him with canister, while the infantry columns advanced, drums beating the *pas de charge*. The assault would be accompanied by cavalry charges which forced the opponent into squares, thus reducing his defensive firepower at the critical moment. When the enemy finally broke, light cavalry would move through the gap to pursue and complete his destruction. Such a combined arms attack would need careful orchestration and could be prohibitive in casualties. Moreover, it rarely succeeded – Borodino was a Pyrrhic victory and Waterloo a failure.

Indeed, as historians have observed, Waterloo revealed a major weakness in Napoleon's grand tactics. Although none of his battles was exactly the same, the pattern of his moves had become predictable, while his adversaries had learned much and were able to turn his own methods against him. After

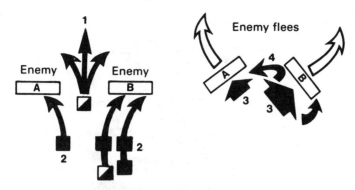

FIG. 12. Napoleonic strategy: the central position. *Left:* facing two strong forces the French cavalry and supporting troops (1) from the advance guard move between the two hostile forces. The main body detaches one corps (2) which, together with the advance guard, pins the enemy, while the main body turns against the other enemy and defeats it (3). Then (4) it shifts to assist the pinning force to defeat the second enemy army while a corps pursues the first. This manoeuvre almost succeeded at Waterloo where Napoleon pushed Wellington out of Quatre Bras and Blücher out of Ligny. It failed, however, when Blücher, not closely enough pursued, rejoined Wellington.

FIG. 13.   Waterloo

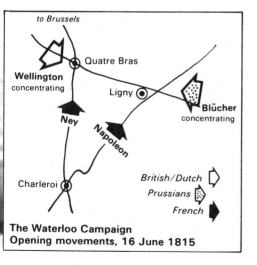

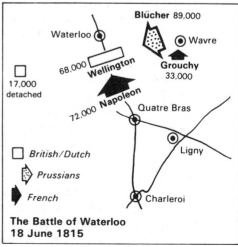

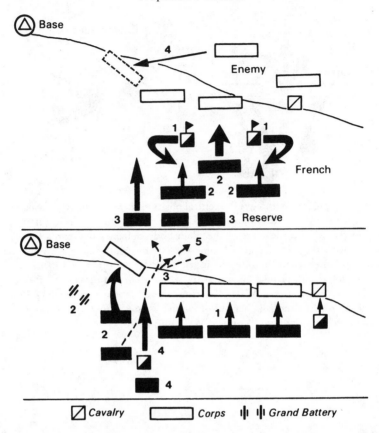

FIG. 14. The flank attack. *Above :* Cavalry (1) pins enemy and advance guard
(2) immediately attacks. The reserve (3) comes up to threaten enemy flank and
line of communications. Enemy shifts its reserves (4) to meet the threat. *Below :*
Enemy is now attacked in front (1) while part of the reserve (2) threatens his flank.
Additional troops and grand battery hammer away at his flank. Enemy now shifts
reinforcements from the centre and is stretched thin (3). The reserve can now
break through into the enemy rear (4). The reserve cavalry can now pursue (5).

the battle Wellington remarked to Creevey that the 'French have always
fought the same way since I first saw them at Vimeiro'. In fact the observation
referred to the column attacks with which Wellington was familiar and
perhaps gives too little crédit to the Prussian intervention whose gradually
escalating pressure against the French right flank contributed so much to
victory. But in a larger sense, Wellington certainly was correct. The Prussian's
arrival, marching to the sound of the guns, was another adaptation of Napoleon's grand tactics.

Napoleon generally left tactics at unit level in the hands of subordinates.
He had great powers to gauge a situation and to estimate speedily, the dispositions and numbers of whole corps. But the divisional formations, now
constituting his basic manoeuvre units, and fought as a whole, as well as the

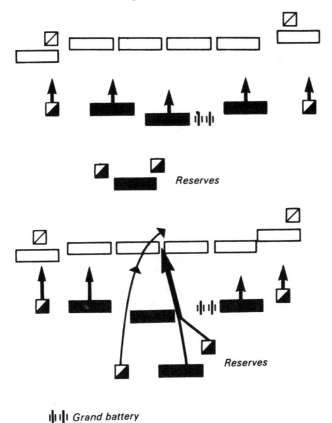

ǁ₁ǁ₁ *Grand battery*

FIG. 15. The frontal attack. Not favoured by Napoleon but resorted to when time or space did not permit manoeuvring. In position a grand battery followed by infantry and cavalry assaults. Meanwhile reserves are assembled which might include the heavy cavalry and the Imperial Guard. When enemy weakened, the reserves moved forward to penetrate the enemy front while one or two heavy supporting attacks pinned the enemy. After reserves had broken through, light cavalry moved to exploit.

problematical communications during a large and violent battle, made personal intervention in tactical detail impracticable. Napoleon rarely informed his subordinates of his overall plans, and in turn he exerted little tactical control during battle. Austerlitz was an exception. The night before the battle he held a staff conference and issued detailed tactical dispositions, essentially that synthesis of column and line – the *ordre mixte*. Even so, the next day, Soult attacked with his divisions in three waves. On other occasions, the absence of prescribed tactical formations produced odd results. At Friedland, one division attacked in deep column whilst another advanced in line, perhaps reflecting the different training levels of the units involved.

Whenever Napoleon issued detailed tactical instruction, he preferred the *ordre mixte* with some battalions in line and others in column. This formation combined the advantages of both and was highly flexible. Fighting in *ordre mixte*, Morand's division at Auerstädt executed five different deployments within a short time, but this required well trained and experienced troops. As casualties mounted and standards of training and experience declined, this sophisticated formation became difficult, while in Spain, where there always was a large proportion of raw troops, it was almost impossible.

The Peninsular experience induced some historians, notably Fortescue and Oman, to assert that the standard French attack formation was a deep column, covered by skirmishers. A later school, led by Colin and Becke, held that generally speaking the French used the marching column for the approach and usually intended to deploy into line for fighting.[46] Some misunderstanding is also due to the use of the term 'column' itself. The marching column was a formation of narrow front and considerable depth, while the attack column, developed in the French armies and then adopted by most other European services, was a rectangle, its front far more extensive than its depth. Only in terrain that did not permit deployment on a broad front, in mountain warfare, in street fighting, and in siege operations, marching and attack columns became essentially identical.

The declining standards of training, however, increased reliance on the attack column in the French army after 1807. The French infantry battalion usually formed an attack column with a front of one company and a depth of four, that is, on average, a mass of 40 men wide and 12 deep. On occasions double columns called 'divisions' were deployed, and columns by sections which halved the front and doubled the depth also occurred, but were rare. In major battles fought on relatively level ground the columns might be considerably enlarged. Such attacks would be delivered by a score of battalions, forming columns side by side or in echelon, sometimes in a wedge-shaped formation, or a large hollow square.

At Wagram, Macdonald's attack column was a huge hollow square, formed with eight battalions in double line three deep, sustained on the right wing by eight battalions in column and on the left by four battalions in column. The rear of this square was formed by three battalions in column side by side. Altogether there were 23 battalions, albeit of very reduced strength, some 8,000 men, with a front of 1,200 yards and a depth of about 750. At Waterloo, d'Erlon's attack in the early afternoon was carried out by four columns of 6, 7, 8, and 9 battalions respectively, each with a frontage of about 200 yards, the width of a battalion formed in three ranks, and a depth of 25 to 35 yards, not counting the space occupied by the skirmishers who preceded the closed formation. This unwieldy body, unsupported by artillery and cavalry, advancing uphill against a firm defensive line, had little chance of success. Several contemporaries as well as later historians have argued that this was not the intended attack formation, but that the British fire prevented the French from forming smaller columns or deploying into lines as they had planned. There is some substance to these speculations. While an attack column could bring men in close order rapidly to the enemy, success depended largely on adequate fire preparation by artillery and skirmishers and

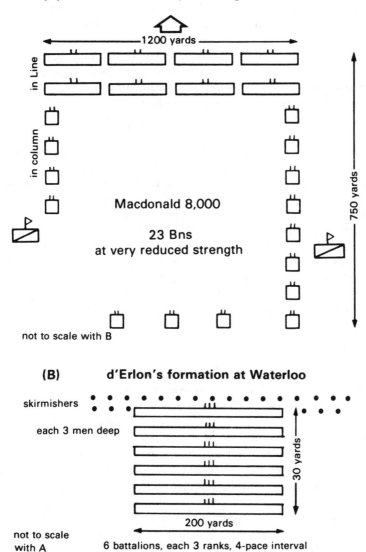

(A) Macdonald's Corps at Wagram

1200 yards

in Line

in column

Macdonald 8,000

23 Bns
at very reduced strength

750 yards

not to scale with B

(B)   d'Erlon's formation at Waterloo

skirmishers

each 3 men deep

30 yards

200 yards

not to scale
with A

6 battalions, each 3 ranks, 4-pace interval
between battalions, depth about 30 yards

FIG. 16. French tactics: the massive column, 1809–15. Casualties of trained
officers and troops forced Napoleon to adopt larger formations in closed column.

it was their fire, rather than the column itself which possessed little or no firepower once it started to move, that made a breakthrough possible. In the Napoleonic period bayonet charges actually driven home against an unshaken enemy were rare.

The great tactical value of the column lay in its flexibility and versatility. It permitted rapid movement of large numbers on the battlefield and it could easily change into different formations. Skirmishers could be detached without major readjustments, two or three-rank firing lines could be formed, as could squares. A battalion in attack column thus was able to act to some extent on its own, and the need to maintain tight flank connections was reduced. But the column in its pure form, was not adequate on the battlefield, especially when it no longer could provide its own fire preparation. The columns of the Revolutionary Wars had often served as a *masse d'usure*, an attrition mass, to use Napoleonic terminology. The column sent out skirmishers to begin the firefight, served as a replacement pool for the skirmishers, and as their immediate tactical reserve. Only after the skirmishers had shaken the enemy line did the column move forward. After 1807, however, and this was true not only in Spain, French skirmishers no longer had the power to shake enemy lines and artillery had to take over the job. 'Wherever a regiment goes,' Napoleon concluded, 'one needs artillery.'[47] The column became part of a complex combined tactical system, requiring coordination with artillery and cavalry.

The counter-insurgency problem in Spain

In 1808, Napoleon removed the unpopular Bourbons from their throne and installed his brother Joseph as king of Spain. But the Emperor miscalculated the reaction of a proud, xenophobic people. The uprising of 2 May 1808 in Madrid marked the opening of a war of national liberation, setting a classical pattern that is familiar today. Even though for a brief period, in the winter of 1808–9, Napoleon took personal charge, smashing the Spanish regular units and chasing a British expeditionary force out, the combination of guerrillas, another British army, and the eventual revival of Spanish and Portuguese forces, all sustained by an uninterrupted flow of seaborne supplies, produced the famous 'Spanish ulcer', a constant drain on French manpower and resources for the next six years.

From the summer of 1808 on the insurgent bands waged a typical hit-and-run guerrilla war. Major Pelet described it. The guerrillas, he wrote, 'attempted to destroy us in detail, falling upon small detachments, massacring sick and isolated men, destroying convoys, and kidnapping messengers'. When they encountered superior force, they dispersed, often hiding their arms and pretending to be peaceful peasants. On the whole, he concluded, they were 'more bothersome for the individual soldiers in our army than dangerous to the army itself'. These individual casualties ran about 100 men daily, but the main French dilemma was that to defeat the British they would have to concentrate their forces, and to do this they would have to relinquish control over the rear areas, endangering their supply link to France. But this link was essential. In Spain large forces could not hope to live off the land, and from the outset French foraging and looting had been one of the main causes of Spanish hatred. As Pelet perceived it clearly, 'the bands of Spanish insurgents and the English army mutually support each other'. Without the British, the bands might have been crushed, and if the French had not been forced to disperse a great number of troops to guard their communications, they might have pushed the British into the sea.[48] As it was, although outnumbering the British five times, when Masséna launched his all-out invasion of Portugal in 1810 he mustered but 65,000 out of some 250,000 French troops in Spain. And even when, late in 1811, the French heavily reinforced their forces, logistic and security reasons, as much as Wellington's skill, prevented them from achieving a decisive victory.

For that matter, the marshals Napoleon sent to Spain did not have any of the qualities required to deal with the situation. Masséna, Napoleon conceded, was a good fighter, 'but had not talent for civil administration', while Augerau in Catalonia, faced by sporadic incidents of terrorism, resorted to wholesale and indiscriminate executions. By the time Napoleon realized that this policy was counter-productive and sent Macdonald to replace him, the damage had been done. Then too, the marshals often were more intent on looting than on fighting with only Ney remaining aloof from this corruption. Finally, the rivalries among the marshals and between them and King Joseph prevented any effective cooperation, but Napoleon refused to appoint a commander-in-chief until 1813, by which time it was far too late.

Corruption, terror, and looting did not make an alien rule more palatable, and Joseph's feeble efforts at reform and the enlistment of a Spanish army met with failure. He would repeatedly enlist Spanish troops, only to discover that as soon as they were armed and equipped, they would desert to the guerrillas. His efforts earned him the nickname '*El capitan vestuario*' and sarcastic letters from his brother.[49] Only Suchet, commanding in Aragon, had success against the guerrillas, combining military action with political reform. He sent out strong columns to search and destroy the bands, but he rigorously suppressed all looting and plundering by his men. He provided an efficient and honest administration in the cities and security in the country-side. Gradually the guerrillas lost ground; they became isolated from popular support, and some villages even took up arms against them. Aragon was pacified and it was the only area in Spain where French soldiers could move about alone and unarmed.

Elsewhere the guerrilla war continued, escalating in a spiral of murder, torture, atrocities and reprisals. At times French counter-guerrilla tactics were inventive. From garrisons established along the main routes, columns went out after the bands, the troops rotated to wear down the enemy with fresh forces. 'Baited' convoys were used to lure the bands into traps. Even psychological warfare was tried; faked messages were sent and rumours circulated to turn one guerrilla chief against another; clemency was alternated with reprisals. All this, however, did at best achieve temporary and local results; it did not solve the basic problem. By 1812, in fact, the guerrillas were able to move about in strength, sometimes in groups of 2,000 to 3,000 men with artillery, and they no longer evaded encounters with strong French forces.

Spain not only set the pattern for future wars of national liberation, more immediately it provided encouragement and inspiration for other national risings. Although these had only limited success, Tyrolean resistance was put down by French and Bavarian troops, and an uprising in northern Germany never got off the ground, the spirit of nationalism spread, undermining the Napoleonic Grand Empire. The commitment of over 300,000 men, by this time the largest French army, containing only about 60,000 allied soldiers, to the Spanish theatre seriously weakened Napoleon's subsequent operations and forced him to rely more and more on allied troops.

Napoleon's allied troops

Every state and nation in continental Europe was in turn the enemy and the ally of the French and several of them furnished troops of excellent quality for Napoleon's armies. Although as First Consul, Napoleon repeatedly emphasized the great virtue of a national army, as Emperor he was a pragmatist and a large proportion of his armies were composed of foreign troops. Although these elements were numerous and diverse, they can be roughly categorized into four main groups. First were troops from areas incorporated into the Grand Empire, usually, except for the Dutch regiments and the Croats, serving as conscripts in French units; the second category consisted of contingents contributed by the satellite states – Italy, Naples, Westphalia, and the Grand Duchy of Poland. In the third category were the troops of the allied states, above all those of the Confederation of the Rhine. Austria, Prussia, and Spain were also allies for a short time. The first two each contributed a corps to the invasion of Russia; Spain furnished a division for coastal defence duty in Denmark. The loyalty of these units, however, was rightly suspect. Finally there was a great host of lesser units in the French service, usually battalion or regimental size, Irish, Hanoverian, Portuguese, Prussians, and others. These were formed and disbanded with bewildering frequency and their combat performance, though not necessarily poor, varied greatly. One calculations shows that 25 nations contributed troops to the Russian campaign and that well over half of the force that crossed the Niemen in 1812 were foreigners.

Altogether these troops constituted a considerable accession of strength to the French armies. When the Batavian Republic was converted into the Kingdom of Holland in June 1806, Napoleon made his brother Louis king with instructions to form an army of 30,000 men. But Louis moved slowly and by 1807 his army numbered only 20,000; the infantry and the cavalry mainly German mercenaries, while the artillery and the engineers were Dutch. But Louis stubbornly refused to introduce conscription. He did, however, supply 3,000 men for service in Spain in 1808–9 and also in 1809 a regiment defeated the insurrectionary Prussian Schill Hussars at Stralsund. Even so, Dutch troop strength was disappointing and when the British landed at Walcheren, Louis had few troops to oppose them. This was the last straw; Napoleon forced his luckless brother to abdicate with the consequence that Holland was incorporated into France and her army became part of the French forces; the Royal Guard was transferred to the Imperial Guard, the foot becoming the 2nd and 3rd *Grenadiers à pied*, while the cavalry joined with French elements to constitute the 2nd Light Horse, later the famed 'Red Lancers'.[50]

A few months earlier Napoleon had incorporated another existing military organization. On 1 December 1809 the French took over six regiments of the Austrian Military Border in Croatia, ceded as part of French Illyria. Although at first Napoleon intended to demilitarize this singular institution where every peasant was a soldier and every soldier a peasant, representations by Marmont and others changed his mind. The military framework remained unaltered. The *Grenzer* continued to guard the frontier against Turkish raids and provided garrisons for the Dalmatian coast. Late in 1811 they mobilized three field regiments, styled *Chasseurs d'Illyrie*, for the invasion of Russia, but saw only limited service. Other units remained in Croatia, where attachment to the French was eroding. In August 1813, when Austria entered the war against Napoleon, the *Grenzer* returned to their old allegiance without offering much resistance.[51]

In contrast to the limited contributions of the Dutch and the Croatians, the assistance provided by the satellite states was very substantial. Westphalia, a synthetic state created after Tilsit out of Hessian, Hanoverian, and Prussian territories, and ruled by Napoleon's brother Jerome, 'contributed to Napoleon's military strength far out of proportion to her size', and Westphalian troops 'served with distinction everywhere'.[52] As early as 1809 Jerome had raised a conscript army of 27,000 – 20,000 foot, 3,500 horse, 1,500 artillery, and 2,000 Guards – organized on the French pattern. At Napoleon's insistence, the senior officers were French, but the regimental officers and sergeants German. The Westphalians suffered heavy casualties in Spain and altogether drafted 70,000 men, with an additional 3,000 entering as volunteers. In 1812 the army reached its peak strength, 38,000, and sent a strong corps to Russia. Most of the Westphalians fought at Borodino and took heavy casualties. The army was decimated in Russia and never fully recovered, though new units were raised and remained loyal until the country was overrun in the late summer of 1813.

Westphalians earned 14 *Légions d'honneur* in Spain and 93 in Russia. Many were captured there, but remained loyal. Gunner Wesemann of the 1st Westphalian Artillery recorded that when the Russians approached Westphalian prisoners of war to join the Russo–German Legion, then being formed, the men refused, holding it to be incompatible with their military honour.[53] Jerome's success in building an effective army was based on a shrewd combination of combining military tradition with self-interest. The expansion of the Westphalian army afforded opportunities for the professional officers incorporated from existing formations, while the introduction of the merit principle appealed to the educated middle class and offered opportunities for the non-commissioned officers.

The performance of the two major satellites in Italy varied. There was the so-called Kingdom of Italy, with Napoleon's step-son Eugene as viceroy, and the Kingdom of Naples, first ruled by Joseph and later by Murat. The Neapolitans proved of little value to the French. During the Revolution, Neapolitan troops had been sent to aid Toulon against the Jacobins, but had done poorly. Their Bourbon sovereign is supposed to have exclaimed when it was proposed to reuniform them, 'dress them in red or blue, dress them in green, they will run away just the same'. With such encouragement it was not surprising that the regular troops gave little trouble when the French invaded the kingdom in 1798, but the peasantry rose and fought with bitter hatred, a foretaste of what was to recur on a larger scale in 1806 and again in Spain. When the French returned to Naples in 1806, the regular army withdrew to Sicily, though the fortress of Gaeta, commanded by a dapper and feisty German mercenary, the Prince of Hesse-Philippsthal, held out from February to June 1806. Hesse would go out on the bastions and shout 'Gaeta is not Ulm, Hesse is not Mack!' In the end, he was wounded and evacuated, and only then did the fortress surrender.

Under Joseph and Murat, Naples raised a considerable number of troops. Conscription was introduced in 1807 and the army formed on French lines. Naples sent troops to Spain, two regiments of infantry and one of light horse in 1809, augmented to divisional strength in 1811. It also contributed one division and one additional brigade to the invasion of Russia. Drawn from the poorest classes which did not receive any political or social benefits from the French regime, the Neapolitan soldiers showed little enthusiasm for a cause many of them disliked. Their desertion rates were high, and their combat value low.

In marked contrast, the army of the Kingdom of Italy fought well wherever it served. 'The Italians,' Napoleon observed in 1805, 'are full of spirit and passion, it should be easy to make them good soldiers.'[54] Northern Italy had been under French rule or influence since 1796 and Eugene inherited an army of 23,000 raised by conscription from the peasantry. While soldiering was still held in low esteem by the middle and upper classes, the mercenary tradition of many centuries was still strong, the Viceroy introduced reforms and for many educated Italians the French conquest meant an altogether desirable liberation from obscurantist and priest-ridden governments. Capitalizing on these feelings, Eugene created military academies at Pavia, Bologna and Lodi and was able to create an efficient and dedicated corps of officers. His Royal Guard, founded in 1805, had especially high morale, as did the *velites* regiments.

The army was enlarged to 44,000 in 1808 and reached its maximum strength, 90,000 men, in 1812. During the course of the Peninsular War, some 30,000 Italians fought in Spain, of whom only 9,000 survived. Losses were even more severe in Russia where 20,000 out of 27,000 perished. During the retreat from Moscow the Royal Guard distinguished itself at Maloyaroslavets, but was almost wiped out. Eugene managed to reconstitute the army in 1813 and contributed a division to the Grand Army forming for the last time in Germany. In addition, he formed three corps, two divisions each, to defend Italy from the Austrians. In his kingdom, Eugene was able to enlist support of considerable elements of the population for although imposed by the French, the Kingdom of Italy provided an expression for the rising national-ism of the population and the prospect of returning to Sardinian and Austrian rule was disliked.[55]

Finally there were the Poles who had been allied with the French cause since their country had been partitioned and Dombrowski had led Polish emigré forces in Italy. After many vicissitudes, Dombrowski's legionaries were formed into the Legion of the Vistula, three infantry and one lancer regiment, in 1807. A second Legion was formed the next year, and both units were combined for service in Spain. When Napoleon established the Grand Duchy of Warsaw in 1808, a new national Polish army was organized, com-prising 20 infantry, 18 cavalry, and 2 artillery regiments. At the same time, other Polish formations continued to serve directly in the French army, one infantry division and several mounted regiments, including the Polish light horse, later the Lancers of the Guard. The Grand Duchy supported Napo-leon's war against Austria in 1809 and in 1812 provided V Corps under Poniatowski and one brigade each in IX and X Corps, supported by a light cavalry division.

The Polish forces suffered extremely heavy losses in Russia, but already in late 1812 the Grand Duchy raised new units, including the three small *Cracus* regiments, modelled on the Cossacks, which fought with the French until 1814. More important, perhaps, the Grand Duchy contributed VIII Corps and one additional division to the Grand Army in Germany, though most of these troops were lost after Leipzig. But few Poles deserted and Napoleon took a squadron of Polish lancers with him to Elba and they returned with him to France in 1815.

No foreign troops fought more valiantly for the Emperor, none were more trustworthy than the Poles but, except for the Neapolitans, Napoleon re-ceived considerable support from all of his satellite forces. Whatever short-comings there were in the Grand Empire, many young Europeans fell under Napoleon's spell and where French rule brought desirable political and civil changes that coincided with national aspirations, military cooperation usually followed. This was the case in Westphalia, Italy and Poland and this explains the staunch adherence of these troops to the Napoleonic cause.

Such changes were, of course, much less pronounced in the allied German states of the Confederation of the Rhine. Yet these too were a valuable accession of strength and the fact that they deserted Napoleon in the late summer and autumn of 1813, does not diminish their contribution. Con-federation of the Rhine troops fought against Prussia in 1807, against Austria in 1809, they shed their blood in Spain, and constituted a large part of the Grande Armée in 1812. At Borodino soldiers from many nations fought with great valour – but the Confederation of the Rhine forces, especially the Saxons, Bavarians, and Wurttembergers, were outstanding and suffered some of the highest unit losses for the entire Napoleonic period.

All of the Confederation of the Rhine states had their armed forces, mainly professional, before 1806 and maintained many of their old traditions, though conforming to the French corps and divisional system. The Bavarians, however, took it hard when they were forced to reduce their lavish transport to the French scale. Although it is dangerous to generalize, these German troops, largely professional cadres and conscripts, provided better-than-average soldiers for Napoleon's armies. They generally cooperated well with their French comrades in arms, though on occasion they complained about French arrogance and pretensions.[56] The French thought well of them. Two Bavarian divisions had participated in the Ulm campaign and Saxon fighting spirit in 1806 so impressed Napoleon that after Jena he released all Saxon prisoners at once. Marbot contended that the Saxon cavalry was equal to any, perhaps the best, in Europe, but that the Saxon infantry was not as solid or as well organized. But German troops tended to rely too much on their leaders; they needed orders and would not act on their own. 'Unlike the French discipline,' General von Scheler, commander of the Wurttemberg brigade in 1812, commented, 'the German system lacked the many motives to awake the soldier's ambition, goodwill, and pride.'[57] The German allies did their soldierly duty, but Napoleon's cause did not engage their imagination.

Napoleon's armies : a summing up

As has been often pointed out, Napoleon's system of warfare was based on theories developed during the *ancien régime* and put, at least partially, into practice during the Revolution. He also profited by the advances in manufacturing, population, and road building. As Liddell Hart stated, eighteenth-century commanders, Marlborough, Frederick, and Saxe, 'understood like Napoleon, that rapidity of movement, security of movement, ease of manoeuvre, and efficient supply are the primary conditions for victory'.[58] They lacked, however, the physical means to translate their theories into practice.

Napoleon, absolute head of state and commander in chief, was able to achieve the realization of these theories and his short and relentless campaigns restored decisiveness to land warfare. His corps organization was adopted throughout Europe and his strategy became a model for future generations of planners. Both the central position and the manoeuvre on the rear, the indirect approach as Liddell Hart called it, were the basic models for many successful modern operations.

Yet, there were substantial weaknesses in Napoleon's approach and in his armies. Combining all aspects of government and war in one hand led to over-centralization and neglect of detail. When Napoleon failed or when he was absent, difficulties arose that could not be compensated. He had little interest in technology and considering the scope and duration of his wars, there was remarkable little technological change. Communication on the battlefield and in the period of concentration remained haphazard; several of his victories were won only by the fortuitous arrival of detached forces – Marengo, Eylau, and Friedland were examples. The chronic indiscipline and the neglect of proper administration could well have been overcome. Davout's corps, with its efficient administration and attention to detail, suggests how the entire army might have been run.

Like all other military institutions, Napoleon's army was to a large degree the product of its historical experience, transformed and made more powerful by the charismatic genius of its leader. It served him well, sometimes better than he deserved, and even in extreme adversity, the hard core of the army remained loyal to him. His memory lived on, and his legend grew, and there were thousands upon thousands of veterans whose greatest experience had been to have served the Emperor.

NOTES

1. Morvan, *op cit.*, vol. I, 281–2.
2. Phipps, *op cit.*, vol. I, 4; vol. IV, 145.
3. Pelet, *op cit.*, 504.
4. S.J. Watson, *By Command of the Emperor: A Life of Marshal Berthier*, The Bodley Head, 1957, 9.
5. Gay de Vernon, *op cit.*, 56; Chandler, *op cit.*, 333.
6. M. de Fezensac, *The Russian Campaign of 1812*, trs. L. Kennett, University of Georgia Press, Athens, 1970, 10–11.
7. Watson, *op cit.*, 193.
8. J.F.C. Fuller, *Decisive Battles*, Charles Scribner's Sons, New York, 1940, 642.
9. E. Picard ed., *Préceptes et jugements de Napoléon*, Berger-Levrault, Paris-Nancy, 1913, 92.
10. Lejeune, *op cit.*, vol. II, 201–2.
11. Morvan, *op cit.*, vol. I, 470–1; vol. II, 437.
12. *Ibid.*, vol. I, 317, 332; Picard, *op cit.*, 164–5.
13. Bodard, *op cit.*, 862, 870–1.
14. Hoyt, *op cit.*, 106.
15. Coignet, *op cit.*, 105.
16. Lefebvre, *op cit.*, 218.
17. Pelet, *op cit.*, 360–1.
18. H. Lachouque, *The Last Days of Napoleon's Empire*, trs. L.F. Edwards, Orion Press, New York, 1967, 30–1.
19. Lefebvre, *op cit.*, 214–18; Morvan, *op cit.*, vol. I, 4–120, *passim*.
20. Picard, *op cit.*, 15.
21. Morvan, *op cit.*, vol. I, 385.
22. Blaze, *op cit.*, 217.
23. Brett-James, *op cit.*, 238.
24. Lejeune, *op cit.*, vol. II, 2–3.
25. Fesenzac, *op cit.*, 101.

26. Picard, *op cit.*, 141.
27. *Ibid.*, 106.
28. *Ibid.*, 26.
29. *Ibid.*, 107.
30. Coignet, *op cit.*, 117.
31. Phipps, *op cit.*, vol. IV, 223.
32. Coignet, *op cit.*, 168–9; Chandler, *op cit.*, 340.
33. Glover, *op cit.*, 47, n. 4.
34. Picard, *op cit.*, 18; Morvan, *op cit.*, vol. I, 186–204, *passim*.
35. Picard, *op cit.*, 55.
36. Morris, *op cit.*, 77.
37. Picard, *op cit.*, 212.
38. Lauerma, *op cit.*, 314.
39. Picard, *op cit.*, 28.
40. *Ibid.*, 29–30.
41. M. Dupont, *Napoleon et ses grognards*, Hachette, Paris, 1945, 193–5; Morvan, *op cit.*, vol. II, 22.
42. Picard, *op cit.*, 23.
43. Yorck v. Wartenburg, *Napoleon as a General*, Kegan Paul, 1902, vol. I, 168; J.F.C. Fuller, *The Conduct of War, 1789–1961*, Minerva Press, New York, 1961, 44–7.
44. Chandler, *op cit.*, 141.
45. *Ibid.*, 178–85.
46. *Ibid.*, 350. Discussed in detail by R. Quimby, *The Background of Napoleonic Warfare*, Columbia University Press, New York, 1957, 331–44.
47. Picard, *op cit.*, 26.
48. Pelet, *op cit.*, 31–2.
49. Marbot, *op cit.*, vol. II, 479–80.
50. O. Connelly, *Napoleon's Satellite Kingdoms*, Free Press, New York, 1965, 166–7.
51. Rothenberg, *op cit.*, 110–19.
52. Connelly, *op cit.*, 196.
53. Wesemann, *op cit.*, 90.
54. Picard, *op cit.*, 219.
55. Connelly, *op cit.*, 50–2, 274.
56. Wesemann, 85. Cf. the accounts in B. Hildebrand ed., *Drei Schwaben unter Napoleon*, Konrad Theiss & Co., Aalen, 1967, *passim*.
57. Brett-James, *op cit.*, 55.
58. B.H. Liddell Hart, *The Ghost of Napoleon*, Faber & Faber, 1933, 33.

6

Opponents of the French

Although taken together the various European powers opposing the French Revolution and Napoleon were clearly capable of matching, even surpassing, the manpower mobilized for the French, for the first dozen years a general lack of enthusiasm and coordination, combined with outdated strategy and tactics, resulted in almost constant defeats. Gradually, however, new men, methods, and in Prussia at least, limited social and political reforms, transformed the armies of the opponents of the French. From 1809 on the fortunes of war were reversed until at last, combining in a rudimentary joint strategy, the European powers brought Napoleon down. Although many countries contributed to this end, the present chapter deliberately concentrates on the four major powers – Austria, Great Britain, Prussia, and Russia. This is not from any indifference to the contributions made by the smaller European armies, but because the increased reliance on mass armies, supplied by the production of mass industry, led to a progressive concentration of military power in a few major states. And their forces alone counted in the final analysis. Only Austria, Prussia and Russia could raise the numbers and only Great Britain could supply the industrial capacity to fight the French successfully.

The European armies reacted in different ways to the challenge of the French wars. As the Republican armies swept from victory to victory the contention that the 'old methods of warfare had collapsed', gained wide acceptance among military thinkers.[1] To withstand the French, so they argued, it was necessary to imitate their innovations, to raise large armies animated by a spirit of patriotism. But to do so, of course, required political and social readjustments which Austria and Russia, and for that matter England too, were unwilling or unable to make. In the end, only Prussia changed the nature of her society to raise a national mass army; Austria and Russia made limited military reforms only, while England retained her reliance on a small but highly trained expeditionary force, supported by various allied contingents, a superior navy, and a constantly growing industrial capacity.

The Habsburg army in the French and Napoleonic Wars: 1792–1805[2]
The Austrian army was the largest force continually engaged against the
French Revolution and Napoleon and carried much of the burden. Despite a
certain amount of experimentation and organizational, tactical, and strategic
change, it underwent no radical modification in its character and remained
essentially a typical eighteenth century dynastic organization. The reasons
for this conservatism stem from the preoccupations of the rulers and the very
nature of the Habsburg Empire with its diverse political institutions and
nationalities all inhibiting radical changes. Yet, this old-fashioned army gave
a good account of itself. One military historian, Cyril Falls, called it the 'most
formidable army which the French had to face in the last years of the eighteenth century and the first few years of the nineteenth'.[3] Repeatedly crushed
by superior forces and superior generalship, it always managed to find the
strength to rise and fight again, and in the end it contributed the major contingent in the defeat of Napoleon.

The Austrian army of 1792 was created by Maria Theresa and Joseph II.
On her accession in 1740, Maria Theresa inherited a ruined treasury and a
disorganized and indisciplined army. To maintain herself against her enemies
the queen initiated a series of military reforms, continued after 1765 by her
son, co-ruler, and successor, Joseph. Organization and administration,
recruitment and training, arms and fighting methods were overhauled and
recast on the Prussian model. By 1792, despite reverses sustained in the
Turkish War of 1788–91, Austria had a considerable military establishment.

It was not, however, a national army. Its officer corps, aristocratic and
international, had only personal and professional loyalties to the monarch.
The highest command positions were reserved for members of the dynasty
and from the great noble families, but in the lower ranks, wealth, family
connections, and birth mattered less. Officers, including many sons of the
lesser nobility and even the bourgeoisie, came from the military academies
established by Maria Theresa, but since the number of graduates was dis-
appointingly small, about 100 a year, others came by direct entry or transfer
from foreign armies. Although since the end of the seventeenth century all
officers above the rank of major had to be appointed by the monarch, appointment to the lower grades remained the prerogative of the colonel proprietors
of the various regiments. Only the artillery and technical services, as well as
the regiments of the Military Border were exempt from this practice. Promotion from the enlisted ranks was possible, though infrequent. A notable
exception was General Feldzeugmeister Karl Leiberich Baron Mack, the
'unfortunate Mack' of Ulm, a Protestant who enlisted in the army and gained
a commission for bravery in the field. By and large the Habsburg officer corps
was unimaginative, devoted to routine, and the typical officer looked no
further than the orders of his immediate superior or the appropriate military
regulations. But on the other hand, the corps was courageous, honest, trustworthy, and faithful to its personal concept of loyalty to the sovereign.

The rank and file came from the lower classes, both by a system of selective
conscription and voluntary enlistment. The hereditary lands, Austria,

Bohemia, and Galicia were subject to conscription, while in Hungary and the Tyrol enlistment was voluntary. In practice, however, the many exemptions kept the system from working well. The people disliked military service and evaded it whenever possible. Voluntary enlistment too met with many difficulties and the authorities often had to use subterfuges and compulsion to fill their quotas. An important source of manpower was recruiting in the smaller states of the Holy Roman Empire and up to one-third of the personnel of the so-called 'German' infantry regiments came from this area. Except for foreigners, service was for life and competent company officers and drill sergeants produced excellent fighting men from the heterogeneous mass.

In addition, the Habsburg Empire possessed a singular institution, the Military Border in Croatia and Hungary, which furnished a very considerable number of soldiers, the *Grenzer*. Originally light troops, after the reforms of Maria Theresa the *Grenzer* were trained and utilized as line infantry. Finally, there survived two relics of the medieval military organization. In Hungary the nobility was still liable for knight service and formed the *insurrectio* in defence of the kingdom, while in the Tyrol the free peasants constituted militia sharpshooter units. On paper, not counting the *insurrectio* or the militia, the Habsburg Army in 1792 consisted of almost 300,000 men, 57 regiments of line infantry, 17 *Grenzer* regiments, 32 cavalry regiments, 3 regiments of field artillery, and small contingents of sappers, miners, and pontooneers. The composition reflected the decline of cavalry since the days of Maria Theresa when cavalry had reached its greatest expansion, 45 regiments, and had constituted between one-fourth to one third of the army. Now its strength was down and, even when the regiments were at full strength, a state rarely achieved, it constituted only about one-seventh of the total, a ratio roughly maintained until 1815. It should also be noted that in contrast with other European armies, there were no special Guard formations in the army. On paper the war strength of the Austrian military establishment came to about 430,000, but in 1792 losses incurred during the Turkish War had not been made good. The army was expensive, about 45 percent of the total revenues went towards its upkeep, and finances were in poor shape. As a result some regiments had been run down and overall ranks were depleted so that at the outbreak of hostilities there were but 250,000 effectives, raised to about 300,000 the following year.

With minor modifications, the Austrian army operated until 1807 according to the *Generals-Reglement* of 1769. This manual, compiled by Field-marshal Moritz Count Lacy, combined standing orders, field service regulations, and staff instructions. It stressed drill and linear tactics, and emphasized a cautious strategy based on magazines and secure communications. Together with the increasingly close supervision exercised by the bureaucratic *Hofkriegsrat*, the Court War Council in Vienna, a mixed military civilian body constituting the highest command agency in the empire, Lacy's manual tended to make the Austrian military system extremely cumbersome.

The shortcomings of the system, especially its tactical and strategic rigidity, became apparent during the early campaigns. In war the tactical units of horse and foot were the squadron and the battalion, the latter commonly six companies strong. Grenadier companies, two in each regiment, were formed into separate elite battalions to be used at the most decisive point in battle. At Stockach, Aspern, and Wagram, grenadiers took the brunt of the shock and led the counter-attack. The majority of the field pieces, including the effective 6-pounders, were distributed as 'line guns' to the battalions. The remainder, forming mixed batteries of 6-, 12-, and even some 18-pounders, was formed into the batteries of the so-called reserve artillery. There also existed since 1778 a number of 'cavalry batteries', equipped with 6-pounders, and with the crew riding on elongated caissons. Overall, the Austrian artillery enjoyed a well-deserved reputation. Its officers and senior non-commissioned officers were serious professionals, trained at special artillery schools and in the *Bombardeur Corps*. All enlisted personnel was selected by strict standards. Only Austrian subjects, unmarried, healthy, and able to read and write were admitted. Marshal Masséna who encountered the Austrians' guns in Italy declared that the artillery 'left nothing to be desired'.[4]

The Austrian infantry of the line was renowned for its solid bravery, while the cavalry was still considered among the best in the world. Its 32 regiments had the usual division into heavy, medium, and light. Nine regiments of Cuirassiers, 2 of Carabineers, 7 Dragoons, 4 Chevauxlégers, 9 Hussar, and 1 Lancer. By 1792 the Cuirassiers had discarded their iron helmets and back-plates, but together with the Carabineers and the Dragoons, retained their primary shock function. The Chevauxlégers, sometimes termed Light Dragoons, and the Hussars had a fine reputation for dash and the quality of their mounts.

Austrian commanders, however, were not well prepared for the new warfare. Although the old or elderly generals have been underrated – many were competent and energetic – their training and outlook were out of date. Their strategy was tied to their communications and their tactics overrated the value of the controlled volley and the cohesive line. They discounted the effectiveness of skirmishers and during the War of the First Coalition made little effort to cover their white-coated lines by skirmishing screens. 'Regular, trained, and solid infantry,' the regulations of 1796 maintained, 'if it advances in closed ranks with rapid steps, supported by its guns, cannot be held up by scattered skirmishers . . . It should close with the enemy as rapidly and orderly as possible to drive him back and decide the action quickly. This is the method that saves lives; firing and skirmishing cost casualties and decide nothing.'[5] At the same time, however, the instructions permitted a battalion commander to deploy several of his companies into skirmish lines, and by 1798 the Austrian army had learned to fight in open order, supported by closed formations. Skirmishers also were provided by a considerable number of Free Corps, raised in many of the lands of the Habsburg Empire, and after 1801 a special regiment of rifle-armed Tyrolean *Jäger* was formed.

In the campaign of 1799 the Austrians, in fact, were able to achieve a number of victories over the French, in part also due to the generalship of Archduke Charles, the brother of Emperor Francis II, sometimes considered

Austria's greatest captain since the time of Eugene, and thought by Wellington to be the outstanding commander on the Allied side.[6] Frequently at odds
both with his brother and the Court War Council, Charles had been relieved
of his command after he quarrelled with the allied Russians, but after
Hohenlinden he was recalled and managed to hold out in Bohemia until peace
was made.

Charles was unpopular with the ruling circles, but he was Austria's best
commander and the troops admired him. In January 1801 the emperor
reluctantly appointed him president of the Court War Council and later that
year, following a general reshuffling of the government, Charles also assumed
the office of War and Navy minister. Three weary years followed during
which the archduke fought for reform against the entrenched interests and
the suspicions of his imperial brother. He made but little progress. He did
manage to reform the administration of the Military Border and, more importantly perhaps, reorganized the administration of the Court War Council.
The council now was divided into three major departments. Department I,
the Military Department, became responsible for overall direction, engineering, artillery, and the Military Border; Department II, the Political-
Administrative Department dealt with recruiting and remounts, equipment,
supply, pay, and medical arrangements, while Department III, Justice,
administered courts martial and other disciplinary matters. Except for
Department I, the departments, as well as many sub-sections, were headed
by civilian administrators with senior officers as expert advisers. The change
did not produce much greater efficiency, and as late as 1809, General Joseph
Count Radetzky grumbled that there was 'too much administration'. For
operational planning and execution, Charles instituted for the first time a
permanent staff organization, the Quartermaster General Staff. Until then
such an organization had only been activated in time of war. In 1801, however,
the position of Chief of the Quartermaster General Staff became permanent
and Feldmarschall Leutnant Peter Baron Duka became the first incumbent.
His duties, however, were not clearly prescribed until on 1 September 1805
new regulations, superceding Lacy's manual, clarified his position. The
Quartermaster General Staff, both in Vienna and with the field armies,
assumed primarily responsibility for the preparation of operational plans,
though administrative and personnel affairs, more properly belonging to an
Adjutant General, remained among its responsibilities. Another complication
was that the Chief of the Quartermaster General Staff still had to obtain
authorization for his plans from the president of the Court War Council, a
process which slowed down decision making.[7]

Still, this was progress. By contrast, Charles had no success in his attempt
to modify recruitment. The Hungarian Diet refused to accept conscription
and Charles's plans to make military service more popular by drastically short-
ening the terms of enlistment failed. In 1802, he succeeded in reducing the
term to 10 years in the infantry, 12 years in the cavalry, and 14 years in the artillery and technical troops, but his efforts to reduce the term of service to a
uniform eight years in all the branches failed. Discharged soldiers, he was told,

might contribute expert leadership for popular revolts. The state of the Austrian treasury helped to frustrate his efforts. In 1801 military expenditure still amounted to 87 million gulden, the next year they were cut to 45 million, and in 1804 they were reduced to 35 million.[8]

Curiously, while army reform was slowing down, the faction seeking another trial with France was gaining the upper hand in Vienna. Leading the hawks were two civilian ministers, Counts Cobenzl and Colloredo, with Mack as their chief military spokesman. By April 1805 the emperor openly sided with the war faction and appointed Mack as Quartermaster General. War came in October. Mack, now commanding the advanced Austrian Army in Bavaria, found himself surrounded, cut off, and forced to capitulate, while Charles, shunted off to the secondary Italian theatre managed to hold his own. He was marching north to join the combined Austro–Russian Armies in Bohemia, but before his arrival the battle of Austerlitz sealed the outcome of the war for Austria. Charles, who consistently had opposed the war, arguing that the army was not prepared to renew hostilities, was restored to his former offices and additionally invested with the unique title of Generalissimo of the Armies.

The Austrian army and the Great Reforms: 1805–1809

The disasters of 1805 provided an opportunity for general reform, but once again the results were fragmentary. In part this was because, despite his exalted position, the archduke still encountered considerable opposition. Even his brother, who, like all Habsburg rulers since the days of Wallenstein, feared concentrating military power in one hand, did not fully support him. Moreover, Charles essentially was an old-fashioned soldier, opposed to the new concepts of war aiming at the annihilation of the enemy. War, he wrote in 1806, was 'the greatest evil a state or nation can experience', and though personally courageous, he lacked the driving will necessary to get the last ounce out of his troops. He was cautious, rather than enterprizing, and never prepared to risk total defeat to achieve total victory. In part this was due to his belief that the army was the ultimate guarantor of the dynasty which had to be preserved, but it also was due to his strategic concepts, basically grounded in the *ancien régime*. He advocated greater mobility, but rejected living off the land. Magazines and an improved wagon train, he believed, were sufficient. 'A service,' a recent historian observed, 'whose most influential reformer was a conservative contending against soundly entrenched reactionaries could never become fully reconciled to the techniques and to the energy and activity demanded of modern war.'[10]

Still, there were reforms. Between 1805 and 1809 Charles improved the combat performance of the army. He dismissed poor generals and strengthened the Quartermaster General Staff. He introduced higher tactical formations, brigades and corps, but not divisions. An Austrian corps was rather small; in 1809 there were nine, each with 20–30 battalions, 16–24 squadrons, and 70–90 guns. Charles favoured concentrating artillery and abolished many of the battalion pieces. He improved the status of the Military Train and in

1809 its officers were granted recognition as commissioned personnel. Strengthened by former battalion pieces and new production, the Austrian artillery reserves in 1809 matched those of the French.[11]

Charles used concentrated cavalry as a striking force, his regulations establishing the line two deep for the charge, and the massed Austrian cavalry reserve distinguished itself in a countercharge against the French Cuirassiers at Austerlitz and again at Leipzig.

In infantry tactics, however, Charles was more conservative. 'The line,' he maintained, 'was the proper formation for infantry, permitting the best use of its weapons, that is the musket for fighting at long range and the bayonet for close-in'. He did, nonetheless, prescribe that infantry charges, delivered in line, be covered by skirmishers, either companies detached from the line regiments or by *Jäger* units, increased to nine and eventually 13 battalions. His regulation prescribed that the line, screened by skirmishers, was to advance at the normal slow pace to within 150 yards, then the pace was to be accelerated, and at a distance of 60 paces from the enemy the drummers were to beat the charge. At this point the skirmishers retired, while the line charged forward with the bayonet. Charles recognized the value of columns, especially for moving troops rapidly, and he also developed a curious variant formation, the 'mass', designed to allow infantry to move and also to fight off charging cavalry.

Charles believed that shallow, three-line deep squares were vulnerable and where infantry had to manoeuvre in the open under cavalry threat, he favoured the mass formation. Besides battalion masses, Charles prescribed a smaller formation, the 'division mass', two companies closed up one behind the other. Within a mass the men were placed in immediate physical contact, while the intervals between division masses were set at 54 paces. Although clumsy looking and seemingly vulnerable, at Aspern and Wagram these formations manoeuvred in an open plain despite the presence of strong hostile cavalry. As Jomini observed, even 'the brave cavalry of Bessières could make no impression upon these small masses'.[13]

Taken as a whole, the changes improved the fighting posture of the Austrian army, but they were based essentially on precepts of the eighteenth century. Even so, tactical improvements and the courage of his troops would gain Charles his victory at Aspern in 1809, but at the same time his lack of will and drive would limit his success to a tactical and not a strategic victory.

And on the fundamental issue of whether the army should develop into a national mass army or remain a dynastic instrument, Charles sided with the conservatives. Although his new army regulations, issued in 1807, humanized discipline and, for the first time, appealed to the common soldier's sense of honour, he continued to oppose the establishment of a popular national militia, an idea which had been advocated as early as 1793 and was revived after Austerlitz. In the spring of 1808, Charles reluctantly accepted this idea, but only because such a militia was cheaper than expanding the regular army, now about 325,000 and because with the treasury depleted this was the only way to 'remedy after fifteen years of fighting and fifteen years of misfortune the paucity of our resources'. At heart, Charles always considered popular levies as temporary and essentially undesirable expedients which, by engaging popular passions, would escalate the level of conflict. It was an attitude shared by other senior officers. 'I am,' wrote Fieldmarshal Karl Philip Prince Schwarzenberg, 'the sworn enemy of all popular levies (*Landwehr*), though I am quite willing to have a few well-organized militia battalions reinforce the regular army.'

For that matter Emperor Francis too remained sceptical of the wisdom of creating a militia, but Napoleon's removal of the Bourbons in Spain persuaded him to increase his forces and that such a step could no longer be avoided. On 8 June 1808 an imperial decree established the *Landwehr*, a popular militia enrolling all men not serving in the army. Original and optimistic estimates held that Austria and Bohemia would raise 180,000 and Hungary 50,000 men, but the nature of the Habsburg Empire, above all national dissensions and fears of revolt, prevented full exploitation of the manpower potential. Some 70 battalions were mustered in the spring of 1809 and dressed in simple grey smocks, a large black hat, and armed with a variety of muskets, performed useful service. Only some 15,000, however, saw action. The so-called volunteer battalions, the elite formations of the *Landwehr* performed with distinction in the encounters at Ebelsberg and in the battles at Aspern and Wagram. The commander of a Bohemian battalion, Major Ferdinand Prince Kinsky, was decorated with the Maria Theresa Cross, Austria's highest decoration.[14]

The *Landwehr* was part of the great effort made by Austria in 1809. That year saw a considerable army raised, though official estimates of 600,000 did not materialize. Actual field strength amounted to some 265,000 effectives, including 15,000 *Landwehr*. Major combat elements included 35 regiments of cavalry, 78 regiments of infantry, 9 *Jäger* battalions, and 4 regiments of field artillery. During the campaign, Austria was, in fact, slightly superior to the French in the number of guns, though not in the weight of its fire.[15] It was a considerable effort and for the first time in history words like 'fatherland', and 'liberty' were used to animate the spirits of the army. The troops fought exceedingly well, but after Aspern Charles lost his nerve, while patriotic zeal evaporated after Wagram. Accused by the emperor of entertaining devious schemes, Charles was abruptly dismissed and thereafter kept from command while, despite its gallant performance, the *Landwehr* was deactivated. Neither the Emperor Francis nor Prince Metternich, who assumed considerable influence after 1809, relished the idea of an armed populace. The emperor resolved to undertake no further military adventures, with which he connected the *Landwehr*, but placed his faith in the regular military establishment and though some 50 *Landwehr* battalions were brought back to service in 1813, they served only as fillers. Regulars fought the battles of 1813–14.

In October 1809, Austria had to sign the Treaty of Schönbrunn which deprived her of much territory, imposed a heavy indemnity, and limited her armed strength to 150,000 men. With Charles out of the way, the Court War Council reassumed control over the military establishment and this time at least did rather well. The revived Council faced enormous difficulties. Great stocks of arms, including some 800 pieces of artillery, had been captured by the French, state finances were in a truly catastrophic position, and many regiments had to be reduced to cadres. Even a relatively small enterprise – the dispatch of an auxiliary corps against Russia in 1812 – severely strained resources. Despite all shortages, and by employing every possible subterfuge, the Court War Council managed to prepare the framework for a much larger army. The opportunity came in the summer of 1813. When Austria offered her armed mediation she was able to back up her position with two large armies, 138,000 men and 394 guns in Bohemia, about 85,000 in Italy. And when Austria actually entered the war against Napoleon, the army had increased to 300,000 combat troops and a grand total of 480,000, raised by the winter of 1813 to 550,000 men.

Command of this army, and eventually the position as allied supreme commander, went to Prince Schwarzenberg, ably assisted by Joseph Count Radetzky, perhaps the country's ablest strategist, and Chief of the Quartermaster General Staff since 1809. This time the Austrians revealed that they had learned the lessons of Napoleonic warfare. Under Radetzky's direction the army adopted new methods for operating on the battlefield – attack columns screened by skirmishers and massed artillery support during an assault. To be sure, both Schwarzenberg and Radetzky have been faulted for an over-cautious strategy, especially in 1814, but it must be remembered that Schwarzenberg was operating in accordance with the instructions of his political superiors who still sought for an accommodation with Napoleon.[16]

Moreover, although compared with Prussia, Austria did not mobilize as large a percentage of her total population, her resources were stretched to the utmost. An English observer, Colonel Charles Stewart, described the Austrian army. He praised its fine quality and discipline and the serious professionalism of its officers. At the same time, however, he noted that the troops lacked overcoats, packs, and even boots, and that the artillery looked shabby.[17]

Despite these handicaps, the Austrians fought with spirit and tenacity, and proved by their performance that the corporate spirit of a professional force was still to be reckoned with. By the end of the Napoleonic Wars the Habsburg army had adopted Napoleonic strategy and tactics, but retained its old dynastic character. Although this was an anachronism and contrary to the spirit of the age, it emerged from the French Wars with increased prestige and confidence.

The British army during the age of Napoleon: general observations

The army which ultimately earned the admiration and respect of Europe for its leader and its men had entered the conflict totally unprepared. A contemporary description has become famous. 'Our army,' it went, 'was lax in its discipline, entirely without system, and very weak in numbers. Each colonel of a regiment managed it according to his own notions, or neglected it altogether; professional pride was rare; professional knowledge even more so. Never was a kingdom less prepared for a stern and arduous conflict.' And during the first operations in the West Indies, Sir John Moore observed that 'with blockheads at the heads of regiments, and the bad condition of officers, the Army has degenerated to such a degree that we shall lose very soon even our character for spirit'. Still, the army showed remarkable improvement. British troops fought well in Egypt in 1801 and in southern Italy in 1806. After Maida, young John Colborne, commanding the light infantry of the 20th of Foot, could boast that 'I now begin to think, as our ancestors did, that one Englishman is equal to two Frenchmen'.[18] And during the Peninsular campaign the army made such progress that General Bell could later assert that 'we had the bravest, the best, the finest disciplined and well-seasoned army in the world'.[19]

The great changes in the performance of the British army were all the more remarkable because it essentially retained its eighteenth century character. Officers were neither skilled professionals nor, with rare exceptions, dedicated idealists; they were representatives of the English upper classes, a curious blend of landed or mercantile wealth, talent, birth, connection, and favour. At the same time, the rank and file did not represent a cross section of the population. It was composed of long-service volunteers, mostly uneducated, and contained a good proportion of social misfits. Above all, it remained small, its main field force rarely mustering 40,000 effectives. Throughout the conflict, the problems of overseas supply, the needs of industry, and Parliament's refusal to enact conscription set tight limits on British military manpower.

Also persisting throughout the period was the near chaotic administration of the army at the highest level, perpetuated because Parliament regarded it as the surest way to safeguard its supremacy. At the cabinet level there was the Secretary of State for War and Colonies and one step below, and not normally in the cabinet, the Secretary-at-War. His main function was at the War Office directing the stationing and routing of troops, controlling finances, and also certain personnel matters. The army proper, that is the cavalry and the infantry, was the responsibility of the Commander-in-Chief, a nearly defunct office revived in 1793 under the aged Lord Amherst and held after 1795 by the Duke of York, who had not distinguished himself in the field, but patiently carried out a series of important reforms until he lost office because of the conduct of his mistress. The Commander-in-Chief exercised his will through the Horse Guards where the Adjutant General was responsible for personnel, discipline and training, while the Quartermaster General originally dealt with quarters, camps, and movements, but eventually assumed certain operational functions, including intelligence. But the Commander-in-Chief did not control the entire army. Until the Union of 1801 there existed a completely separate military establishment in Ireland, some 20,000 horse and foot, generally not of good quality. More important was the fact that the Master-General of Ordnance and the Board of Ordnance continued to be responsible not only for the weapons and ammunition of the land forces, but also for the personnel of the artillery and engineering branches. In addition, a number of other agencies and individuals also had a say in military affairs. These included the Treasury controlling the Commissariat and the Home Secretary who supervised the various auxiliary forces – the Militia, Yeomanry, Volunteers, and Fencibles. And finally there were separate boards dealing, not always efficiently, with medical affairs and stores.

On service abroad the troops came under the direction of the Secretary of State for War and Colonies, but representatives, military and civilian, of the various agencies functioned at the headquarters of the field commander. Thus Wellington's staff (the word does not necessarily connotate present-day operational functions) not only duplicated the arrangements at the Horse Guards, but also had to deal with representatives of the Master-General of Ordnance, the Treasury and numerous other civil servants. It required a strong personality and much of Wellington's limited supply of patience to impose a sense of common purpose on this mixed military-civilian array. Much of his time was spent trying to adapt War Office and Treasury regulations to a situation for which they had never been designed, but he refused to struggle against them needlessly. An eminently practical man, he realized that the ministers too had to deal with an often refractory Parliament and he refused to demand more from them than the system could provide.[20] Even so, the delay, inefficiency, and shifting of responsibility of the British military administration contributed heavily to failures and created unnecessary suffering for officers and men.

Officers and men of the British army

Wellington was the product of the purchase system which enabled him to become a lieutenant-colonel at 24 and a lieutenant-general at 39 years of age. And when he became a lieutenant-colonel, Wellington had spent almost all of his six years' service as aide-de-camp to the Lord Lieutenant of Ireland. Wellington, of course, has been held up as an example of the potential of the purchase system, but in general the results of the anarchic and highly aristocratic manner by which the British army obtained and promoted its officers were not always as happy.

There were four different ways for entry and promotion in the commissioned ranks – purchase, promotion by brevet, rank by recruiting, and selection for a vacancy by merit. Rank by recruiting was obtained when the Crown wished to raise new units and promised a certain rank to an officer for assembling the required number of men. It was the subject of many abuses and gradually fell into disuse. Selection for merit was also relatively rare. In the Peninsula, so Wellington claimed, 'I believe that . . . I gave every commission I had to give away either to gentlemen volunteers or to non-commissioned officers'. But these instances were rare and in many regiments an officer without private means was shunned. As Wellington admitted, very few of these men had remained in the army. 'They are not persons that can be borne in the society of the officers in the Army.'[21] General Bell was more candid. 'Many brave men,' he remembered, 'were driven out of the service by tyrannical injustice. They could not brook the system of being passed by and purchased over by boys from the nursery.'[22] Even soldiers in the ranks resented it. Private Morris of the 73rd remarked that the French promoted their officers from the ranks up so 'that every man had a strong incentive to good conduct', while in the British army 'as soon as vacancies occur in a regiment they are filled up by mere boys just from school'.[23]

Promotion by brevet, also rare, involved across-the-board advancement of an entire rank. Although it did not always provide command or increased pay, it was a valuable step for future progress. But purchase, accounting for well over three-quarters of all commissions, was the single most important route for the entry and promotion of officers. Except for the Royal Artillery and the Engineers, all commissions, from ensign to lieutenant-colonel, were for sale. Money and the approval of the colonel of the regiment were the only qualifications required. From the rank of colonel up, promotions went by seniority, but below money could buy higher rank. As Bell observed bitterly, this meant that veteran officers found themselves under the command of 'boys from the nursery who stayed at home and never smelled powder'. The Duke of York, to be sure, tried to mitigate the worst abuses. A scale setting the price for each rank was published in 1766, new regulations established lower age limits and stipulated the minimum amount of time to be served in each grade. Ensigns had to be at least 16 years of age, and no one could purchase a captaincy until he had six years of service.[24] Experience produced capable officers, often exceedingly brave, but essentially the British officer remained an amateur, regarding war as a sport and not as a science. There was little sense of subordination or attention to administrative detail. During the 1793–5 campaigns officers openly disregarded orders, went over the heads of their commanders, and absented themselves from duty. And Wellington complained that 'Nobody in the British Army ever reads a regulation or an order as if it were to be a guide for his conduct . . . every gentleman proceeds according to his fancy.' After Vittoria he wrote that the British army was unrivalled in battle, but that indiscipline remained a serious problem. 'The cause of their defects is want of habits of obedience and attention to orders by the inferior officers, and indeed by all. They never attend to an order with an intention to obey it.'[25]

The complaint was, of course, exaggerated. The Duke was quite capable of enforcing obedience among his officers when necessary and he strongly defended the purchase system. The excellence of the British Army, he later declared, derived from the fact that the officers were gentlemen, who paid for their commissions, and only gentlemen he believed, made good officers. For all that, as the scope of operations expanded, it became clear that trained officers and not gifted amateurs were needed for staff duties and in 1799 and in 1802 the Duke of York founded military academies at High Wycombe and Great Marlowe. The senior department at High Wycombe was designed to train staff officers and entrants had to be at least 19 years old and have two years of service. But the two departments combined turned out few officers. By 1815, it was calculated, out of 276 students in the senior department, 114 had served or were serving as staff officers, while the junior department had provided 651 line officers.[26]

Finally, there were the officers of the Royal Artillery and the Engineers, serious professionals who trained since 1741 at Woolwich. Completion of technical training was a prerequisite for commissioning and promotions in these two corps went entirely by seniority. Ordnance commissions could not be sold, and lacking a pension system, officers clung to their rank until they died. As a result, gunners and engineers usually held a much lower rank than their contemporaries in the infantry and cavalry. Wellington disliked this army within an army, with its own promotion roster and medical services, and its control by a Master-General who sometimes challenged the field commander's authority. Although he valued the expertise of his gunners, he often was annoyed by these middle-class technicians. The antipathy was quite mutual. Captain Mercer of the Horse Artillery, for instance, was placed under arrest for a minor mishap during a parade, but, secure in his status, he commented in his diary that 'I snap my fingers at the disgrace'.[27]

Whatever his rank, origin, or method of entry, the British officer was a world apart from the enlisted men who were recruited almost exclusively from the lowest classes of British society, enlisting to escape trouble at home, for the bounty rising to 18 guineas in the later part of the war, and for pay fixed at 1s per day in 1797. Wellington later asserted that most soldiers enlisted for drink. 'That is the plain fact,' he maintained, 'they have all enlisted for drink.' But these words were spoken in a fit of anger. A few days before Waterloo, the Duke made a fairer assessment. He pointed to a scarlet-coated British infantry private and told his friend Mr Creevey, 'there, it all depends upon that article whether we do the business or not. Give me enough of it and I am sure.'[28]

There were, however, not many of 'that article'. The deep-seated dislike of a standing army had caused Parliament to keep the establishment as low as possible and the total effectives available at the outbreak of war in the United Kingdom barely exceeded 17,000, the regiments reduced to skeletons with a cadre of regular officers and a rank and file of ragged and ill-trained recruits. The rest of the army, about 30,000 more, was scattered about the empire, mostly in remote and unhealthy stations which constantly required reinforcements. Hiring German troops permitted a rapid build-up. The King's hereditary Electorate of Hanover agreed to send some 14,000 horse, foot, and artillery, and the government, not without haggling, also negotiated treaties with some other German princes. By the late summer of 1793 there were more than 17,000 German and only 6,500 British soldiers with the army in Flanders. But as the war continued, the government was obliged to fall back on national manpower. The French thrust into Germany forced many princes to withdraw their contingents and by 1798 there were less than 5,000 foreign troops on the payroll. Meanwhile the total strength of the army had increased to 120,000 in 1795, 160,000 in 1801, and 200,000 in 1809. Over half of the total, however, were deployed in the West Indies, Ceylon, India, and other minor stations and the main field force never mustered troops, both complete foreign units and individual fillers, were used. There were the fine regiments of the King's German Legion and the British trained and officered Portuguese units, and by 1812 individual Spaniards were enlisted in British regiments. After suffering considerable losses and getting few replacements, the 95th, Costello recounts, 'found it necessary at last to incorporate some of the Spaniards'. Recruiting sergeants set out and 'in a short time we were joined by a sufficient number of Spaniards to give ten or twelve men to each company'. The Spaniards fought bravely, accompanied the regiment on its march into France where they were discharged in 1814 when the unit returned to England.[29] This pattern of a small field force, supported by foreign auxiliaries, continued until the very end. When Wellington faced Napoleon on the plateau of Mont Saint Jean, only half of his approximately 67,000 troops were British.

Throughout the war Parliament shrank from introducing conscription and troops had to be obtained by voluntary enlistment. There were 15 recruiting districts in England, four in Scotland, and five in Ireland, but the pickings were slim. The war had relieved much of the unemployment which had previously driven men into the ranks, though there always were some desperate souls, while in Ireland destitution was so great that the bounty and the prospect of rations were a powerful inducement. Even so, to procure enough men, the government reluctantly had to allow recruiting from the Militia, a territorial levy of landowners and peasants who turned out each year for a few days of perfunctory exercises. Militia service had long ceased to be universal, but it had survived for home defence. The force was commanded by the Lord-Lieutenants of the counties; officers were drawn from the country gentlemen. Each year Parliament fixed a quota for each county and men were chosen by ballot. Those who were drawn could pay for a substitute, a practice which in turn forced the government gradually to increase its own rate for regular enlistment. Various acts, the Army Reserve Acts, passed between 1802 and 1811, encouraged militiamen to volunteer for general service and produced a fair number of enlistments, 9,000 in 1805, 28,492 in 1809, and 11,453 in 1811. The militia, Lord Fitzwilliam complained, had become a training establishment for the line 'a recruiting or . . . a crimping fund for the supply of the regular army'.[30]

The various regiments competed against each other for militia volunteers and recruiting sergeants, so Rifleman Harris tells, tried 'to make as gallant a show as they could'. The sergeant-major, he tells 'had a sling belt to his sword like a field officer, a tremendous green feather in his cap, a flaring sash, his whistle and powder flask displayed, an officer's pelisse over one shoulder, and a double allowance of ribbons in his cap'. Thus decked out he and Harris went to Hastings where the volunteering of the Leicester Militia had begun. They found that 'one-hundred and twenty-five men and two officers had given their names to the 7th Fusiliers'. Sergeant-Major Adams and Harris worked hard to change their minds and 'the appearance of our Rifle uniform and a little of Sergeant Adam's blarney so took the fancy of the volunteers that we got everyone for the Rifle Corps'. But it was hard work. 'For three days and nights we kept up the dance and the drunken riot,' until the recruits had been examined, attested, and marched off to join their regiment.[31]

Overall, the militia introduced better than average men into the ranks and gradually, despite the protests of many old-fashioned officers, this brought about some amelioration in the ferocious methods by which discipline was enforced. It would, of course, be idle to pretend that the British army had no disciplinary problems. The behaviour of his men was one of Wellington's constant complaints. In battle the army had no rival, but it was difficult to handle in victory and in defeat. During the great retreats in Spain, after the storming of Badajoz, and in the aftermath of the great victory at Vittoria the army dissolved into a mob. During these occasions brutal punishment, meted out on the spot, was perhaps necessary, but it is questionable that, as many contemporaries and even some modern historians insist, with an army containing a considerable number of rough, even bad elements, any relaxation of discipline, and in particular the abolition or reduction of flogging, would have been fatal.[32] For instance, the argument that during Crauford's retreat to Corunna, 'if he flogged two, he saved hundreds from death', stands up only in part.[33]. Many were too tired and too dispirited to move, and even the bayonets of the rearguard could not move them. At Astorga, Sir John Moore could not wait for some 400 to sober up and they were left behind as were another 1,000 men at Bembibre; for days after Badajoz fell Wellington was unable to restore order, and neither was he able to control his army after Vittoria. Corporal punishments degraded men; it brutalized the offenders, and seldom had much effect on the remainder. 'I have seen men suffer 500 to 700 lashes before being taken down, the blood running down into their shoes and their backs flayed like raw red-chopped sausages,' General Bell remembered, and he added that while there were some very bad characters in the ranks, 'such punishment was inhuman'.[34]

For that matter the highly disciplined King's German Legion did not flog. When a British soldier on detached duty with the Hanoverians was sentenced to a flogging by his British superiors, the Hanoverian commander informed him that 'we do not flog in my country, so I shall not flog you, it no being the manner of my people'.[35] Flogging was opposed by humanitarians in England, while abroad it often aroused local citizens to protest. While the 73rd was stationed at Courtrai in 1814, the punishments carried out on the Esplanade caused 'much horror and disgust among the citizenry and protests were made'.[36] The Duke of York did his best to mitigate the worst excesses, and in 1811–12, courts martial were empowered to impose sentences of solitary confinement and extra-guards, instead of being limited to the lash. For desertion, robbery, and a variety of other offences the death penalty was inflicted. Whenever possible executions were carried out by firing-squads and in the presence of troops to set an example. In the field, however, the provost parties would hang culprits without ceremony on the nearest tree.[37]

Some enlightened officers, Sir John Moore foremost, insisted on a more humane approach to the common soldier. Officers should lead rather than command by fear. At Shorncliffe Camp and elsewhere he put his ideas into practice and even after he died, bonds between officers and men were closer in the Rifle regiments than in other units. In peacetime and garrison British officers usually kept their distance from the troops, leaving the daily routine to the sergeants. In the field, however, most of the battalion and squadron officers had closer relations with their men, sharing their dangers and privations. The men clearly perceived who was a good and was a bad leader. 'Our men,' Costello of the 95th wrote, 'divided the officers into two classes: the "come on" and the "go on"; for as Tom Plunkett in action once observed to an officer, "The words 'go on' don't befit a leader, Sir!"'[38] Eventually, the army threw up combat leaders equal or better than the finest on the continent and by 1814 officers and men considered themselves members of the best army in the world. A French historian noted that even the lowliest private was, 'in very truth an aristocrat among the soldiers of the other European armies'.[39] And a French officer observed that the British soldier 'has no superior in the world; fortunately there are only a few of him'. All this was a proud achievement for an army despised and defeated but a decade earlier.

Weapons and organization of infantry, cavalry, and artillery
Musket- and bayonet-armed infantry, famed for its steadiness in battle, remained the mainstay of the British army throughout this period. Its standard weapon, also supplied to many of its auxiliaries and allies, was the British Land Pattern musket, superseded in 1797 by the shorter barrelled India Pattern. Various other muskets with slight variations were also in use, while after a number of trials, the two rifle-armed regiments of the British army, as well as those of the King's German Legion, were issued the Baker rifle, highly accurate at ranges between 200–300 paces.

At first, England was short of weapons. In 1793, excluding weapons in the hands of the troops, there were only 60,000 muskets in reserve, not enough to meet the needs of the expanding army. Although Great Britain, already far advanced into the Industrial Revolution should have outstripped French production, rearmament encountered great difficulties initially. The principle of interchangeable parts was known, but could not as yet be applied to musket production. Attempts to purchase substantial quantities abroad in Germany and Belgium failed, while at home the industry, still relying on hand work with rough grinding only done by water-powered wheels, was slow to go into mass production. The main bottleneck was the assembly of parts procured from various subcontractors. Utilization of the extensive stock held by the East India Company and issue of foreign weapons of suitable calibre alleviated the situation. By 1804 the Board of Ordnance achieved control over manufacturing and also established assembly plants, first in the Tower and later at Lewisham. One other problem, matching the outside of the barrel with the bayonet was resolved after 1812 when the government took over the small-arms factory at Enfield to make barrels.[40]

After 1808 arms production hit full stride. That year it had been difficult to find 200,000 pieces for Spain and Portugal but by 1813, Great Britain not only filled its own needs but supplied over 1,000,000 muskets to its various allies.[41] Ammunition, with high-quality saltpetre provided by the East India Company, was produced in two government powder mills and made into cartridges at government laboratories and arsenals. Woolwich produced both small arms and artillery rounds, while at Plymouth and Portsmouth, only small-arms ammunition was manufactured.

It was much the same story with artillery. At the outbreak of war the English field artillery had a mixture of calibres and designs, 3-, 6-, 9-, and 12-pounder guns and various types of howitzers, iron and bronze. The light 6-pounder was considered the most useful.[42] Artillery was cast in government arsenals, though production of heavy iron guns was often let to private manufacturers. The Carron Company in Scotland enjoyed much of the business and their heavy iron siege pieces and howitzers were among Wellington's favourites.[43] Throughout the campaigns, the British artillery tended to be inferior in numbers to the French and at first some of its materiel was poorly designed. Research conducted at Woolwich remedied many of the shortcomings; carriages, limbers, ammunition wagons, and harness were improved. The introduction of a block trail in 1792 reduced weight and increased mobility. In addition, British artillery pioneered in the development of new weapons and projectiles. By 1802 the battalion guns were withdrawn and field batteries, designated as brigades in the foot and troops in the Horse Artillery, were commonly equipped with five guns, 6–12-pounders, and one light 5.5-inch howitzer. Wellington usually was short of artillery, mainly due to the lack of trained crews and he augmented his field artillery with Portuguese batteries. Until 1813 he was also short of modern siege pieces and during the siege of Badajoz he was forced to employ some ancient Portuguese 24-pounders and some 18-pounder naval guns.[44] In 1813–14, the field artillery was partially re-equipped with the more effective 9-pounders replacing the light 6-pounder guns.

British swords were adequate. The heavy cavalry used a straight sword, commonly the 1796 pattern, with a 35-inch blade, while light cavalry used a pattern designed by Major John G. McMarchant and introduced in 1797. Production of cut-and-thrust weapons for the mounted service was more than adequate and among a list of supplies furnished by Great Britain to Russia, Prussia, and Sweden in 1813, there were 34,443 swords and lances.[45] Besides its pistols, the British heavy cavalry carried a rather cumbersome 26-inch barrel carbine, while the light cavalry carbine, with a 16-inch barrel, was more suitable for mounted action. Known as the Paget carbine, after Lord Uxbridge who secured its introduction, its major improvement was a flexible link connecting the ramrod with the barrel, preventing loss of the rod while loading. But firearms mattered little; the British cavalry, light or heavy was orientated exclusively to the charge, sword in hand.

* * *

The organization of the British army during this period continued to fluctuate. Because of its relatively small size, forces were assigned by infantry battalion, cavalry regiment, 'brigade' or troop of artillery to form temporary brigades for specific enterprizes and it was not until 1809 that Wellington organized divisions in the Peninsula. Divisions remained the highest formation until 1815 when the Duke formed his combined British–Allied forces into three infantry and one cavalry corps.

Although the basic administrative unit of infantry was the regiment (except for the three regiments of Foot Guards) units were raised and disbanded in bewildering fashion, numbers appeared and disappeared, and there was no uniformity in the number of battalions per regiment. Until 1803 nearly all line battalions had but one regiment, though a few had two. Later many were authorized to raise second battalions, and a few even more. Normally the first battalions went on active service abroad while the second, often little more than a recruiting party, was also used for home defence. A few second battalions, however, were recruited to strength and some served in the Peninsula.

A British battalion consisted of 10 companies, of which one was the Light and the other the Grenadier Company. The strength of the battalions varied, but rarely exceeded 500 effectives in the field. In 1793 the British infantry numbered six battalions of Guards and 86 of line infantry, raised to eight and 186 in 1809, and to eight and 210 by 1813. Some confusion continued because of the varying number of foreign units on the payroll.

The regiments of foot were numbered consecutively and although basically similar, there were a number of distinctions. Certain regiments, the 7th, 21st, and 23rd were designated as Fusiliers and considered elite units, as were the Highlanders of the 42nd, 71st, 78th, 79th, and 93rd Regiments. Also in the elite category was the Light Infantry. Its origins dated back to the wars in America, but credit for their introduction in Europe belongs to the diligent Duke of York who, as early as 1798, directed the creation of some provisional formations. Between 1802–4 three regiments, the 52nd, 43rd, and the 95th, were trained as Light Infantry by Sir John Moore, and by 1809 the 68th, 71st, 85th, and 90th were added to the roster. After competitive trials in 1801, the 95th was armed with the Baker rifle and received a second battalion in 1805 and a third in 1810.[46] The other light regiments retained the regulation musket, albeit slightly modified. The real importance of British Light Infantry was not in its armament, but in its training which enabled them to become all-purpose infantry, able to fight as individual skirmishers, in small groups, or in line. Riflemen and light infantry usually fought in open order ahead and on the flanks of the army, often firing the first and last shots in a battle. When needed, however, they could and did fight in line. Formed as the Light Division in the Peninsula they became Wellington's *corps d'élite*, and at Waterloo the 52nd, changing front at the double, flung itself against the assault columns of the Imperial Guard and shattered them with controlled volleys.

British cavalry of the period came under various designations – Horse Guards, Life Guards, Dragoon Guards, Light Dragoons – though basically the distinction was between heavy and light regiments. By 1808 the army had two regiments of Life Guard Cavalry, one regiment of Horse Guards, seven regiments of Dragoon Guards, five heavy and 11 regiments of Light Dragoons. The Dragoon Guards, despite their title, were not part of the Household troops, and none of the dragoon regiments had a dismounted function.

The usual organization for cavalry regiments was four squadrons, each with two troops of 80 men each, but on foreign service the difficulty of transporting horses and losses from action and disease often reduced strength to two or three squadrons, with each troop having only 50 to 60 men. British cavalry fought according to the *Rules and Regulations for Cavalry*, also devised by Dundas and introduced in 1805. Wellington, however, was disappointed in his cavalry. Although superbly mounted and brave, officers and men lacked field training and experience. Lord Paget's mounted troops performed well covering Moore's retreat, but generally commanders handled the horse poorly. All authorities agree that British horse once launched could not be controlled and showed a distressing talent for charging everything, including ambushes, ravines, and imaginary targets. Except for the superb regiments of the King's German Legion, Hanoverian rather than British, their record in the Peninsula was poor. The only significant exception was the great charge at Salamanca where General LeMarchant handled his heavy regiments with great skill, but was killed in the battle.

Finally, British artillery was highly competent, though the French were always superior in the number of pieces and the weight of metal. Perhaps the best unit within this branch was the Royal Horse Artillery, first raised in 1793 and organized in four troops the following year. By 1812 it had 12 troops, each commanded by a captain, assisted by a second-captain. Each troop could be subdivided into three divisions, each with two guns, 6- and later 9-pounder cannon and one $5\frac{1}{2}$-inch howitzer. The troops were organized as independent units with their own farriers, drivers, and other specialists so that they could operate independently. The Royal Artillery in general was inventive; it pioneered spherical case shot, 'Shrapnel' and rockets. Drivers for its limbers were furnished by the Royal Corps of Artillery Drivers, formed in 1794 by the Duke of Richmond, then Master-General of Ordnance. The conduct of this corps, however, both in Flanders and in the Peninsula was less than satisfactory.[47]

British tactics and field supply

Fundamentally tactics rested on infantry firepower. The threat of the French column was parried not by abolishing the line but by improving it. By forming into two instead of three ranks they brought more muskets into play along a broader front, though in considering the relative firepower of a column and an opposing line one must remember that the short range of the muskets limited the number of files that could actually engage the enemy. But, even with this reservation, the firepower developed by a line, usually supplemented by guns placed in direct support and firing canister, was far superior to that of a column. From the simple encounter at Maida, Wellington went on to

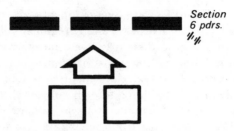

FIG. 17. This diagram demonstrates the fire superiority of the line over the column and also the deeper target presented by this formation. Wellington's habit of attaching a battery or section of light guns, usually 6-pounders, to his line added additional fire weight. *Top* : a British line, three battalions at field strength of 600 men each, of 175 yards frontage, all muskets bearing to the front face, *below* : French attack columns, two 8-company battalions in division formation each 80 men wide and 12 deep with 160 muskets bearing to the front.

refine this tactic in the Peninsula. He trained his troops to select positions where a low ridge protected them from the massive bombardment which covered the initial stages of the advance, and to move up to the ridge only when the closeness of the enemy masked the covering fire. Wellington countered the skirmishers which preceeded the column by developing a skirmisher screen heavier than that of the French; ultimately an Anglo–Portuguese division of 11 battalions would have 18 companies of skirmishers, while a French division of about the same size would have only 11 companies.

Wellington always tried to conceal his position, not only to protect his troops from fire, but also because it gave him the chance of a tactical surprise. The French generals could rarely discover exactly where his line was positioned. In several battles they pushed their columns forward in the belief that they were outflanking him, and suffered the consequences. Only when absolutely compelled did Wellington expose his troops to long-range artillery fire, the best known instances being at Talavera where no cover was available for the centre of his line[48] and at Waterloo where the Inniskillings stood long hours under bombardment. When possible, positions were prepared to offer the best position. At Bussaco, for instance, a path running all along the reverse slope was carefully widened at his orders to allow faster movement along the firing line. The ultimate refinement of his tactics was at Waterloo, where the line was further protected by fortified outposts and strong batteries. The 'thin red line tipped with steel' had become a formidable barrier inviting self-destroying attacks.[49]

A thin line was possible only with steady troops; the Duke placed his weaker elements, Dutch and Belgians, into column formation. Moreover, though he gained much of his reputation as a defensive general, he was capable of operating on the offensive. Except for an assault against a breach, the British army used the line offensively as well as defensively, and tried to execute its battlefield advance as a combined-arms attack.

Although most historians have rated Wellington below Napoleon as a strategist, he was a far better administrator in the field. Having seen at first hand the breakdown of logistics in Flanders, he paid great attention to the details of providing the necessary supplies. 'It is very necessary,' he observed, 'to attend to detail, and to trace a biscuit from Lisbon into a man's mouth at the frontier, and to provide for its removal from place to place, by land or by water, or no military operation can be carried on'. An army without supplies and starving, he wrote to his brother, 'is actually worse than none. The soldiers lose their disciplined spirit'.[50] Supply functions were in the hands of the Commissary, a branch of the Treasury, although uniformed and given assimilated rank by 1810. Some 700 commissaries, from Commissary General to Assistant Commissaries, served with the forces in the Peninsula and ranged from excellent to scandalous. The Commissary was supported by the Royal Wagon Train, resplendent in red jackets, yellow cuffs, and blue breeches, but the reputation and performance of this unit was mixed and it always remained inadequate in number. As late as the Waterloo campaign, only 162 military wagoners were available.

Wagons, in any case, would have been of only limited use on the narrow, twisting cart tracks which substituted for roads in most of Portugal and Spain. Pack-mules provided the answer. 'In Spain,' Captain Jones remarked, 'mule carriage was undoubtedly a principal cause of the efficiency of the army.'[51] And Bell agreed. The Spanish muleteers, he wrote, 'were the very life and sustenance of the Peninsular War; we could not have existed without them. Everything was conveyed by them for the army – provisions, ammunition, rum, etc. Their patience, hardiness, and fidelity to the British army were remarkable.'[52] Here Wellington's insistence that the troops took nothing for which they did not pay in hard cash produced results. Without the support of the Spanish muledrivers and in some cases the population which helped to drag, carry, or otherwise shift supplies forward, he would have been unable to campaign in that hard and barren land.

British allied and auxiliary forces

British soldiers, then as later, had mixed emotions about their allies. They disliked the Spaniards, cursed the Portuguese, did not care much for the Russians, and thought little of the Dutch. They did, however, admire and respect the sturdy regiments of the King's German Legion and they got along with the Prussians. As for the Austrians they saw but little of them after 1794. These feelings emerged as early as the first campaign in Flanders. As for the Dutch, one staff officer wrote, 'from such friends and allies may the Lord deliver us'. In fact, he continued with the true disdain of an English gentleman, most of the allies were a rather rum lot, especially some of the Austrian light troops. 'The drawings which Captain Cook brought back from the South Sea are nothing to some of our friends.'[53] And the English encounter with the Russian soldiers and sailors during the abortive expedition to North Holland in 1799 produced equally bizarre impressions.

Relations between allied troops are often strained, and British insularity and continental resentments did nothing to soften the impact. Except for the

Hanoverians and the Spaniards and Portuguese on the Peninsula, the next occasion the British served again alongside Allied contingents was during the Waterloo campaign and their dislike had remained unabated. By this time, of course, many of these troops had just served Napoleon and their allegiance was suspect. Captain Mercer complained that a 'Belgic' battery sent to support his troop was 'beastly drunk', and that during the advance on Paris Belgian and Nassau troops behaved so rudely that 'I feared every minute we would come to blows'. Overall, he observed, 'our allies are by no means an amiable set, nor very cordial with us'. The Prussians he thought better. They were the 'most soldier-like looking fellows I have ever seen', but he disapproved of their wanton destructions.[54]

But it was in the Peninsular campaign that the British came into the most intimate contact with foreign allies and auxiliaries and relations here were tense most of the time. Both Moore and Wellington were bitter about the deficiencies of the Spaniards and officers and men shared the feeling. Rifleman Costello remembered the Spanish General Cuestas as a 'deformed-looking lump of pride, ignorance and treachery', and his troops as a 'disorganized crew'.[55] And Bell, then a lieutenant, claimed that the Spaniards were 'never to be relied upon in the moment of trial and danger'. They murdered English soldiers, often by order of their officers, and on one occasion, he related, a 'Spanish officer wantonly stabbed at a rifleman, who shot him at once'.[56] And yet, British sentiments were only partially justified. The Spanish army of 1809, cobbled together from remnants of the old regime and local militia, could put in a good day's fighting. At Albuera the regular battalions fought stubbornly; at Ciudad Rodrigo a Spanish garrison cost Masséna more than a month's siege. Above all the Spaniards never forgot Baylen where in the summer of 1808 a rag-tag force had cut off and destroyed a French corps. These were achievements too often overlooked, but at the same time, the arrogance and xenophobia of the Spanish officers and men was also a fact, and a highly counterproductive one.

Relations were better with the Portuguese. In 1807 this army, 24 infantry, 12 cavalry, and 4 field artillery regiments, supported by 43 regiments of militia, had been corrupt and inefficient and had scattered before Junot's ragged battalions. A small remnant had been evacuated and constituted the Loyal Lusitanian Legion, three battalions of foot, a weak regiment of dragoons, and one battery which, led by British officers, returned to Portugal in September 1808. The Legion fought well and in June it was incorporated into the Anglo–Portuguese main force serving as *Caçadores*, light infantry.

After consultation with the Portuguese government-in-exile, the British government in 1809 sent Major-General Beresford to reorganize the Portuguese army. Assuming marshal's rank and assisted by a British cadre he soon 'brought the Portuguese army to its present state of discipline and organization'.[57] Its 24 regiments, formed into brigades of two regiments each, its *Cacadores* battalions, and its four regiments of cavalry and 12 batteries fought alongside, and after 1810 were brigaded with, the British divisions. At Busaco the Portuguese line regiments were perfectly steady, and the knowledge that he could rely on them nearly doubled Wellington's fighting power. The French, too, thought well of the Portuguese; Marbot declared them 'the equal of British troops'.[58]

Within Portugal, British operations were supported by levies of the militia and the *Ordenanza*, the latter a general levy of all male inhabitants with Portuguese and British officers. These irregulars harried the French, attacked stragglers, pickets, and did not spare the wounded. In turn the French granted them no quarter and grisly attrocities were committed by both sides. Although appalled, Wellington claimed that it was the French who had started this mutual slaughter.[59] In any case, the *Ordenanza*, often armed with no more than pikes or farm implements, contributed greatly to Masséna's discomfiture before Lisbon and complicated his eventual retreat into Spain.

The most congenial of the British allied units, however, was the King's German Legion, formed from Hanoverian soldiers who had escaped after their country's army had been forced to capitulate to the French in the Convention of Lauenburg on 5 July 1803.[60] Starting out with one weak regiment, the King's Germans, raised by Baron Decken at Lymington, soon numbered 8,000 of all arms, one cavalry, one light and two line infantry brigade, as well as artillery and engineers. Uniformed and equipped as British troops, they used English manuals and commands, though internal administration continued to be in German.[61] The King's German Legion (KGL) was considered as good as the best British troops and their light cavalry the best in the army as a whole. As Costello remarked, they took better care of their mounts than the British and 'we never saw a German vedette or express galloping furiously, that we did not immediately know there was work for someone to do'.[62]

The KGL took part in every British expedition to the continent during the Napoleonic Wars, serving at Copenhagen, and Flushing, in Pomerania, Sweden, Sicily, and returning to their own country during the abortive Weser operations in 1805. Although this expedition ended in failure and re-embarkation, the KGL was able to find enough recruits so that its strength was brought up to 18,000 effectives.[63] Its main employment, however, was in the Peninsula where it fought with great distinction at Talavera and other battles. It continued in the framework of the British army until 1816 when it was returned to the Hanoverian service.[64] By contrast, the regular Hanoverian army revived in 1813 did not do as well at Waterloo, and the British also had mixed feelings about the Brunswick troops, a few of whom, the Brunswick-Oels *Jäger* Corps served as detached sharpshooter companies in Spain. Finally, throughout the wars the British raised and disbanded a great number of foreign units. French emigrés, Sicilians, Maltese, Greeks and others, whose record generally was undistinguished and had little effect on the course of events.

The Prussian army, 1792–1806
The death of Frederick II in 1786, though received with gloom in the army,

produced little change in a system that had become ossified during the last decade of his reign. There was a slight let-up in discipline and better provisions for old and disabled soldiers, but attempts to overhaul the recruitment system failed. The *Kanton-Reglement* of 1792 reaffirmed the principle that all subjects were obliged to serve the state, but it preserved and even extended exemptions for certain classes and regions. Over 500,000 men of military age were exempted and foreigners continued to make up well over one half of the army's strength, around 200,000 during the 1790's.

Combat doctrine and methods remained Frederician. The infantry stressed the three-rank linear formation, controlled volleys, and a steady advance, while the cavalry retained its faith in the massed charge. The artillery, both horse and foot, was good, though many of its pieces were too heavy for mobility. Tactically the most important change was the formation of 12 independent Fusilier battalions in 1787, designed for skirmishing or fighting in two ranks, and trained to allow more initiative. Also, 10 selected men from each line company were trained as sharpshooters, *Schützen*, and like the independent Fusiliers were equipped with a lighter and more accurate version of the standard musket. Musketry training, however, remained sketchy; in fact, the entire army was poorly trained because of the practice of furloughing natives for the greater part of the year. Moreover, the army had little combat experience and there was considerable confusion in the highest command agencies of the army where the Military Department of the General Directory, a civil service agency, the governors of the Major-Generals, the Inspector-Generals, and the Adjutant-General, each exercised their various and overlapping functions. For that matter, the officer corps was no longer as dedicated or efficient as it had been under Frederick II. The flower of the corps had been killed off in the Seven Years' War, while the rigid exclusion of bourgeois officers deprived it of much needed talent. Commissions given to noble foreigners brought in men of considerable merit, including Gerhard Johann von Scharnhorst, a Hanoverian, but they also made the corps less homogeneous.

And the new king, Frederick William II, had but little interest in the army. Warm, impulsive, childish and coarse, his great interest was women. In any case, the Prussian ruling class was divided between those who saw the main threat from the French Revolution and those who wanted to use the opportunity to destroy Poland. The war against France was pursued half-heartedly, while the Prussian invasion of Poland suffered serious set-backs at the hands of half-armed and ill-trained patriots. In 1795, nonetheless, Poland was partitioned and Prussia agreed to peace and neutrality with France. The 11 years of peace that followed gave Prussia a great opportunity for military reform, but the time was wasted.

In 1795 a commission, the *Immediat-Militär Organisationskommission*, was created to 'investigate and ameliorate the defects that had appeared', though in the end few fundamental changes were made. A new command agency, the *Oberkriegskollegium*, was to oversee the others, but being made up of the heads of the various agencies, it naturally did nothing. The same year the

numbers of light infantry were raised slightly; the number of Fusilier
battalions eventually reached 24 and the number of *Schützen* in each battalion
was doubled. Moreover the new king, Frederick William III who ascended
the throne in 1797, was a military enthusiast, though overly concerned with
the minutiae of regimental organization, uniforms and drill. He supported
both the antiquated linear tactics and the rapid unaimed volleys, but he also
supported the more rapid deployment of infantry by substituting the fast
pace of 108 instead of 78 paces per minute during combat evolutions. In
addition, there were improvements in staff organization and some discussion
regarding the potential of universal military service.[65]

But the reformers were opposed by the old soldiers who had fought with
Frederick the Great, and who only grudgingly conceded introduction of
minor reforms, and by regimental officers who were obsessed with making
money out of their commands and wanted no part in abolishing the Canton
System. By 1806 of the 142 generals in the army four were over the age of 80,
13 were over 70, and 60 were over 60, while fully a quarter of the regimental
and battalion commanders were over 60 too. And out of about 8,000 officers
in the Prussian Army in 1806, less than one-tenth were non-noble, and these
were for the most part isolated in the artillery and technical branches.[66]

Even so, as war against Napoleon drew nearer, there were some last minute
attempts to make, in the king's words, 'our army more like the French'. In
October 1805 the king sanctioned the abolition of the third rank in the line
and its formation into additional light battalion, but the general mobilization
prevented implementation of this scheme. There also were attempts to reduce
the amount of baggage the Prussian army dragged around with it and to make
the artillery more mobile, but little enough came of it. And the most important innovation, the formation of divisions, was made only when the army
was already on the road to Jena. The divisions were to consist of 2 brigades of
infantry each with 4 or 5 battalions, a cavalry brigade of 10 to 15 squadrons,
and 2 batteries of artillery. In addition, each division was to have a light
infantry battalion and 5–10 squadrons of light horse.

The new system was far from perfect. The divisions had too little artillery
and the cavalry was too scattered to use the shock tactics for which it was
trained. Moreover, none of the over-aged generals had any experience or
training in the command of combined arms. All in all, the introduction of
divisional formations at this stage only added to the confusion.[67]

In 1806 the Prussian army took the field entirely over-confident; even men
like Scharnhorst and General Blücher who knew that the army was defective,
pressed for war. On paper it looked imposing: 2 regiments of Foot Guards, 57
regiments of Musketeers (line), 29 battalions of Grenadiers, 24 of Fusiliers,
3 battalions and 1 mounted squadron of *Jäger*, 4 regiments of foot and 1 of
horse artillery, 13 regiments Cuirassiers, 14 regiments Dragoons, 9 regiments
of Hussars, and 1 regiment of Lancers.

The artillery too was powerful. Each infantry battalion was assigned a
6-pounder, though the fusiliers left theirs at home. In addition each of the
4 foot artillery regiments had 9 batteries, each of six 12-pounder guns and

two 10-pounder howitzers. The horse artillery regiment had 20 batteries of six 6-pounders and two 7-pounder howitzers. Line infantry battalions, three in each regiment, commonly had 5 companies, with an authorized strength of 174 men, including 16 sharpshooters and 4 gunners; the fusilier battalions comprised 4 companies, and 165 men each. The heavy cavalry was formed in five squadrons per regiment; the light cavalry commonly had 10, though there were exceptions. But mobilization was disorderly and incomplete. Forces in East Prussia were not called and against Napoleon's 160,000, Prussia brought only 128,000, commanded by the aged Duke of Brunswick.

On 10 October 1809, Napoleon drove in the Prussian advance guard and compelled Brunswick to fall back on his lines of communications. The divided Prussian Army promptly was overwhelmed in the twin battles at Jena and Auerstädt. The first was no disgrace to the Prussians who were out-numbered almost two to one and in the second the Prussian grenadiers stood bravely against the murderous French fire until their morale cracked. The real disgrace was the collapse of the army and state in the days after the defeat; the panic, the surrender of strong fortresses, the abject servility of the civil servants towards the conquerors. To be sure, some few formations and fortresses held out, but all too many capitulated without a shot. Beyond the Oder, reserve elements escaped the contagion, and during the winter gave a good account of themselves. But little consolation could be found in these exceptions. The state of Frederick II had collapsed.

Prussian army reforms: 1807–13
The débâcle of 1806 demonstrated beyond doubt that a drastic overhaul of Prussian society and army could no longer be denied. In Prussia perhaps more than in most states, civil and military change were linked. Deprived by the Treaty of Tilsit of her richest provinces, reduced to a population of 4½ million, burdened with the costs of a French occupation and a heavy indemnity, Prussia's only hope for regaining military strength and eventual independence lay in harnessing the entire social and economic resources still remaining. Military reforms, therefore, had to proceed hand-in-hand with reform of the body politic. Feudal privileges and serfdom had to be liquidated, and military service had to become, in theory at least, truly universal. Every citizen should be able to aspire to a commission, while service in the ranks had to become acceptable to all classes, not a hated burden but a citizen's proud privilege. As early as 1796, Scharnhorst, who now emerged as the leader of the military reformers, had asserted that 'we shall be victorious when one learns to appeal, like the Jacobins, to the spirit of the people'. Such views, of course, were strong medicine and even after Tilsit, conservative opposition and repeated French intervention prevented their full implementation. The reforms achieved by 1813 still fell short of the goal of a people in arms. Nevertheless, when the Prussian army took the field again that year, it was animated by a new spirit, led by new commanders, and fought according to new combat doctrines.

The Treaty of Tilsit had not included any military provisions, but the following year the Convention of Paris limited the Prussian Army to 42,000 men and prohibited all militia and reserve formations. The need to reduce the army, combined with the requirements of economy, army reform and accountability, resulted in a purge of the officer corps. Military reform in general was being carried out by the Military Reorganization Commission headed by Scharnhorst (just promoted to major-general); the task of purging the officer corps was delegated to a Superior Investigating Commission with the inquiry into the conduct of individual officers in 1806, largely left to the regiments.

By 1809 out of 142 generals in 1806, 17 had been cashiered, 86 honourably dismissed, and only 22, including Blücher, retained on active duty. And out of 885 staff officers, a term denoting an officer with the grade of major or above, 50 were cashiered, 584 were dismissed, and 185 retained. And out of some 6,000 junior officers, 4,000 resigned, 141 were cashiered, and only 1,584 retained on active duty. The lot of the released officers, usually without private funds, was grim. 'Their misery,' wrote Gneisenau, a man whose sympathies were with the reforms, 'is indescribable.'[68]

However, despite regulations passed in August and November 1808 abolishing promotion by seniority only and opening the commissioned ranks to all citizens having the required educational and moral qualifications, the officer corps did not become a middle-class stronghold. Due to the limitations in the size of the army and due to the system of the officers in every regiment voting on the admission of officer candidates, the aristocratic element remained strong, even dominant, in the officer corps.[69] Still, the character of the service changed. New regulations also passed in 1808 abolished corporal punishment and did away with the old 'company economy', under which a captain received a lump sum for each man in his unit and furnished him with equipment and rations. This system, an incentive to granting liberal furloughs, was ended, reducing the income of a company commander from some 1,500 thalers to about 800 a year. Pay, equipment, and subsistence were now provided by the state.

But the most important developments were in higher army administration and in the Prussian general staff concepts. On the first count, imitating the French model, the Military Reorganization Committee centralized administration in a war ministry. The king, however, feared that this might challenge his authority and for that reason the two separate bodies making up this ministry, the General War Department and the Administrative Department, did not have a single head until in 1814 General Boyen was appointed war minister. For the time being, Scharnhorst acted as head of the Administrative Department as well as Chief of the General Staff. Prussia, of course, had a general staff – the Quartermaster General Staff – before 1806. Instructions approved by the king on 12 November 1803 had expanded its competence, but it had remained an advisory body. Scharnhorst, for instance, detailed to act as Brunswick's chief of staff, was completely ignored during the campaign. He wrote: 'What ought to be done, I know only too well; what is going to be done, only the gods know.'[70]

After 1806, however, the reformer hoped to develop a general staff system in which collective intelligence would offset the individual genius of Napoleon. Success depended on highly trained staff officers and in his overhaul of the army educational system, besides three new schools for junior officers, he also established in 1810 a special staff school, the Military School for Officers, later the War Academy, in Berlin, where 50 promising officers received instruction. For immediate use, Scharnhorst issued new regulations which, in contrast to other armies, made the chief of staff a full partner in command decisions. In 1813 general staff officers were for the first time assigned to all commanding generals. The most famous of these dual command teams was that of Blücher and Gneisenau, combining a brave, charismatic, but impatient leader, with a cool, methodical, yet courageous and determined, chief of staff. In contrast to the relationship between Napoleon and Berthier, Gneisenau made the plans and Blücher saw that they were executed. Although not without friction, this dual command pattern was to become the hallmark of the Prussian, and later German, command system.[71]

But before the new system could be tried in the field, Prussia had to strengthen her army, replace arms and equipment lost to the French, and develop new tactics. On the first point, French restrictions as well as the king's aversion to the introduction of a popular militia created great difficulties. A partial remedy was the *Krümpersystem*. From 1809 on, the army enrolled a few supernumeraries in each company and released them after a few weeks training. Prussian nationalist historiography created the legend that this enabled Prussia to train vast reserves; in fact, the total number of men trained under the system was small. With reserves the army numbered 53,523 in 1807 and only 65,675 when war was declared early in 1813. The system, however, helped to offset wastage and replace losses incurred during the Prussian operations in Russia, besides providing for a small increase in actual strength.[72]

Replacing weapons and equipment also presented formidable difficulties. As Clausewitz, then a staff officer, wrote in late 1807, 'we lack all war materiel and supplies and during the next five to six years we have no expectation of being able to support a considerable army from our own resources'.[73] Most regulation muskets had been lost to the French who used them to arm the Confederation of the Rhine. Remaining was a mixture of modern, obsolete, and damaged small arms. Workshops to repair or modify these were established in the major garrisons, Neisse, Glatz, Graudenz, Berlin, and Königsberg, while the main factory at Spandau was expanded. Modification, however, was a slow process and the introduction of a new simplified model, the so-called 'new Prussian Model', reverting to a straight butt and a larger calibre to utilize both stocks of obsolete and foreign ammunition, produced but 55,000 weapons by 1813. Artillery was even more difficult to procure and many expedients were used: for example gunners trained on obsolete pieces to save wear and tear on the few remaining guns, and in 1813 the army went to war with only 236 guns, including some dating back to Frederick the

Great, a few batteries provided by Russia, and some French pieces captured in transit.[74]

Most of the weaponry to re-equip the Prussian army in the late spring of 1813, came from England. The Prussians received at least 100,000 stands of arms, considerable quantities of powder, and flint and even Austria contributed some field pieces and muskets.[75] The result was an extraordinary mixture of weapons and calibres, a supply officer's nightmare, only partially remedied when, during the summer armistice, regiments exchanged weapons to achieve uniformity within a formation. Even then the newly raised militia, the *Landwehr*, was not fully armed. Rearmament of Prussia was only completed after Leipzig.

The Prussian reformers also introduced permanent higher tactical formations, but in accordance with their new staff doctrine aiming at uniformity, and in contrast to France where divisions varied in size, they wished to have units of equal strength. Because the reduced establishment did not permit the formation of divisions, mixed brigades of all arms became the basic tactical units. In wartime, two brigades formed a corps. Basically each brigade consisted of two regiments of infantry, each with one battalion of fusiliers and two of musketeers, one elite grenadier battalion, and 10–14 squadrons of cavalry. Artillery (12- and 6-pounder cannon, 7- and 10-pounder howitzers) was organized into mixed batteries of six cannon and two howitzers. In peacetime they constituted separate artillery brigades, but on mobilization one light foot and one horse battery were allocated to each brigade. The remaining artillery formed the corps and army reserve.

In practice, brigade strength tended to differ; the Brandenburg Brigade, for instance, was over-strength. Initially six brigades were formed, the East Prussian, West Prussian, Brandenburg, Lower Silesian, Upper Silesian, and Pomeranian, each recruited and stationed in a particular region whilst localization made mobilization faster and increased unit cohesion.

After considerable experimentation a new field manual, the Regulations of 1812, were adopted. Engels, normally a harsh critic of the Prussian military, described them as 'the best in the world. Simple, logical, based on the principles of sound human understanding, they leave little to be desired.'[76] Based on the brigade structure, the regulations called for infantry to carry the main combat with a combination of skirmishers, columns, and lines. Differences between line and light troops were obscured. In the field all movements were to be made at the fast 108 pace. Half of each regiment, the fusilier battalion and the third rank of the two musketeer battalions, were to act primarily as skirmishers, but all elements were trained to deploy, advance and withdraw under fire, and to form skirmish screens, fire lines, or columns as the occasion required. Cavalry, once Prussia's main strike force, assumed a subordinate role both in the infantry brigade structure and also in the new tactical regulations for cavalry brigades which appeared in 1812. The cavalry regulations stressed the charge in column, but emphasized the need for cooperation with the infantry. Finally, there were new artillery regulations which abolished the battalion guns and called for greater fire concentration.

But, the infantry was the mainstay of the new tactics and assumed a dominant role.

Infantry tactics were aggressive and called for a gradual escalation of pressure against the enemy by a brigade ranged in considerable depth. In battle, the brigade deployed its two fusilier battalions partly in skirmish line, partly as support detachments, *soutiens*, about 150 paces behind. Then, another 300 paces back, came the first major combat element, three musketeer battalions, normally in attack columns some 40 men wide, and accompanied by two half batteries. In turn, another 200 paces behind, came the second major combat element, the elite grenadier battalion and the fourth musketeer battalion. These, if necessary, would reinforce the first element. Finally, and usually kept in reserve or on the flanks, was the cavalry, accompanied by the horse battery if one was available. The skirmishers opened the firefight and were thickened by the *soutiens*. Then, as their fire took effect, the fusiliers withdrew, while the battalions of the main combat elements passed through to attack with the bayonet or, if necessary, form fire-lines. Meanwhile the fusiliers regrouped and returned to the fight. In this fashion units were committed gradually retaining a high degree of flexibility.[77] This sophisticated tactical system gave greater responsibilities to company and battalion commanders, and demanded a very high standard of training, courage, discipline, and initiative if it was to be effective in battle. Officers, non-commissioned officers, and soldiers, line and light infantry, horse and foot, all had to form a single entity. Only the best troops were equal to the initiative required by the new system and the Prussian generals in 1813 often preferred to keep their less well-trained troops, especially the *Landwehr* in its early stages a poorly trained and not always enthusiastic militia, in massed column formations.

The Prussians at war, 1813–15

When war resumed against France in early 1813, the army was hastily increased by volunteer and militia conscripts. On 3 February 1813 an edict called for the formation of volunteer *Jäger* detachments and on 9 February a national militia, the *Landwehr*, was established, calling upon all men between the ages of 17 and 40 years of age to join local units.

Landwehr strength was set at 120,000 and if there were fewer than that number of volunteers, men could be drafted. On 21 April, finally, the king reluctantly called for the formation of the *Landsturm*, a homeguard without uniforms, to fight by sabotage, sniping, and scorched-earth tactics against enemy invaders. Perhaps fortunately the *Landsturm*, arousing great misgivings among conservatives, was never called into action, while both the volunteer *Jäger* and the *Landwehr* have been much idealized by patriotic German historians.

The *Jäger* were recruited from young men able to pay for their own equipment and uniforms and came predominantly from the middle and upper classes. As Treitschke pointed out 'it simply was impossible to enroll the sons of the higher classes as ordinary rankers'.[78] Originally these detachments,

about 12,000 strong overall, were conceived by Scharnhorst as model formations for a future army where discipline was to be based on moral imperatives.
But by the late summer of 1813 their original character was largely diluted
and as many *Jäger* were commissioned in the line or the *Landwehr*.

In contrast to the well-equipped *Jäger*, the *Landwehr* suffered from all
kinds of shortages. Raised jointly by the provincial and royal authorities, its
units were formed on a local or regional basis, with the provincial colours on
their cap bands and flags and the Maltese cross as their cap insignia. Up to the
rank of captain, officers were elected whilst the higher grades were proposed
by the estates and appointed by the king. At first the *Landwehr* lacked officers
and equipment. Muskets were in short supply and pikes had to be issued to
many of the troops. Overcoats, blankets, and packs were lacking, and some
units were barefoot. As late as October 1813, one regiment, poor weavers
from Hirschberg in Silesia, had no boots. Even so, the militia fought with
unexpected élan during the 1813 campaign, though, like the early levies of the
French Revolution, the militiamen were indisciplined, given to sudden panics
and desertion. And like the French levies, they eventually learned to fight by
fighting and to march by marching.[79]

After the summer armistice, its units having reached their projected
strength of 109,000 foot and 11,000 horse, were brigaded with the regular
army, then comprising 72,000 infantry, 12,000 cavalry, and 13,000 artillery
and engineers. Added to this were the volunteer *Jäger*, by this time some
5,000 foot, 3,000 mounted men, and 500 gunners. Late in 1813 the field
army was formed into four army corps, the Guard, and a small independent
field force under General Wallmoden. Each corps had four brigades, *Landwehr* and regulars mixed, while IV Corps was composed almost entirely of
Landwehr units. By this time differences in efficiency between *Landwehr* and
line were slight. In 1814 the army was demobilized, but reassembled when
Napoleon returned from Elba.

Basically the Prussia army of 1813 continued to be dominated by the
regulars, though its appearance and above all its morale was quite different
from that of 1806. The ponderous train had been sharply reduced, most
officers losing their personal and pack horses. There were no tents and with
equipment continuing in short supply, the blanket roll over the shoulder, the
haversack, ammunition pouch, and water bottle became standard marching
order even in the regular units. More important, of course, were attitudes and
morale. In 1806 the typical Prussian soldier had been a mercenary or a
reluctant conscript, now he was animated both by patriotism and by a deep
and even savage hatred of the French. The first expressed itself, as it had in
the days of Frederick, by religion. As the Prussian infantry saw the French
retreating the evening of Waterloo, the fusiliers began to sing the old Lutheran
hymn, *A mighty Fortress is our God*, the same hymn their forefathers had sung
on the field at Leuthen and Kunersdorf. Hatred of the French expressed itself
in bitter fighting and in the ability to rally after initial defeat. At the Katzbach,
Landwehr regiments of Blücher's corps attacked the enemy in a pelting rain
and, advancing in close column, fought with clubbed musket and bayonet,

giving no quarter. And at Lützen, when the intervention of the Imperial Guard finally decided the issue, the Prussians retreated, but later that night a furious charge by nine Prussian squadrons dissuaded the French from any further pursuit. Napoleon rather ungraciously conceded that these were not the Prussians of 1806. 'These beasts,' he remarked, 'have learnt something.' The Russian Count Nesselrode was more impressed and he reported that they 'have once more become the Prussians of Frederick'.[80]

The Russian army : general observations

It is a commonplace observation that modern Russian history was characterized by a constant struggle between the 'westernizers', trying to recast this vast state in a new mould, and those who want to preserve and strengthen the peculiar, eastern and Slavic ways of 'Holy Russia'. And Russian military developments in the late eighteenth and the early part of the nineteenth century reflected this conflict. 'Military developments under the tsars,' an English historian summed up, 'can be seen as a kind of dialogue between two conflicting influences: on the one hand the mind-crushing, goose-stepping discipline of the Potsdam drill square, and on the other a brand of inspirational leadership capable of summoning up reserves of elemental force from the mass of the Russian nation.'[81] There is some overstatement in this summation. The rise of Russian power and its expansion against Turks, Poles, Swedes, and into Siberia owed much to the adoption of western military methods and, except for a few short episodes, these continued to predominate in the military establishment throughout this period. Yet, it is also true that beneath the surface there always remained a number of peculiar Russian traits, above all then and later the high fighting qualities of the common Russian soldier.

Although there were considerable alterations in the structure of the army during this period, both in response to the French challenge and by the whims and prejudices of the different rulers, the individual Russian soldier changed little; he just fought for a different sovereign. He was always noted for his tenacity and ability to suffer hardships. His methods, usually a reflection of a leadership which held human life in little regard, were clumsy. In the attack, a British officer noted, the Russian soldier 'is fearless, disdains the protection of ground, is not intimidated by casualties'.[82] And Marbot reported that during an encounter in Poland in 1807, 'our soldiers fired at the enemy at 25 paces but he continued to march without a sound'.[83] The Russians were equally, perhaps even better on the defence, especially in fixed positions. It has been claimed that they lacked instruction in how to retreat, and though this is untrue, the Russians always fought best with their backs to the wall.

The enlisted ranks were filled by conscripted serfs, periodically selected by the local authorities to meet government-imposed quotas. Until 1793 enlistment was for life, then Catherine II changed it to a 25-year term. In practice, it changed very little. Even if the recruit survived, and this was highly problematical, he would never return to his native village. Unable to read and write, without leave and stationed far from home, he lost all contact with his former life. Therefore, the day recruits were selected was a day of mourning, but shorn of his beard and long hair, he was feasted, given presents, and was considered of having commenced a new life 'as the glorious defender of his sovereign and Holy Russia'.[84]

In peacetime, soldiers were allowed to marry, but their children were subject to conscription and drilled and indoctrinated from an early age. Wilson, somewhat over-enthusiastic, pictured Russian peasant soldiers as physically fit, inured to hardships, bad weather and little food, capable of long marches and hard work, 'ferocious, but disciplined, obstinately brave, and susceptible of enthusiastic excitements; devoted to their sovereign, their chief, and their country'. Religion was a powerful motivating force and played an important part in military life. Before battle holy icons were paraded before the assembled masses and priests, cross in hand, inspired soldiers as they charged against the enemy – infidel, Moslem, heretic, or atheist.

For all that, discipline in the Russian army was brutal and erratic; beatings with a stick or the knout were common and considered as corrections, not punishment. For graver offences there was flogging, running the gauntlet, execution, or exile to punishment companies in Siberia. The serf-soldiers, of course, were accustomed to physical abuses, but foreigners were appalled. The Westphalian gunner Wesemann was amazed at the frequent beatings and corporal punishments from which not even officers were immune. In 1815, Captain Mercer was absolutely thunderstruck when, during a review in France, a very senior and much decorated Russian officer was threatened with a cane by a general who chased him from the field.[85]

This incident reflected perhaps the serious divisions within the Russian officer corps, comprised of several distinct and often hostile elements, Russian and foreign. Generally it was recruited from the Russian upper classes, gentry and nobility, but also contained a significant foreign element, especially in the staff. The great majority of officers came from the provincial gentry and started their military careers as non-commissioned officers. They were poorly educated, often hardly literate, and usually spent their lives as obscure infantry or artillery officers. Wilson, the English gentleman, and generally given to favourable judgment on the Russian army, found this a deplorable practice. He described these officers as hardy, devoted, and loyal, but felt that they had absorbed too many bad habits during their enlisted service and therefore were unable to impart discipline. 'The want of regimental officers,' he wrote, 'is more felt in this army than in any other in Europe.'[86] And Tarle, a Soviet historian and not always a reliable source, described them as 'imprudent, negligent, and incapable of a quick decision in an emergency'.[87]

The nobility entered the army through various cadet schools and later took up appointments in the Guards or in elite mounted regiments like the Cuirassiers. They were cultured, though not well educated, and lacked competence in administration and staff work. Nonetheless, especially if well connected, they frequently found their way into general headquarters where, as Colonel Campbell scornfully commented, they 'spent their time drinking, gambling, or sleeping'. Napoleon is supposed to have said that a French private took more interest in the planning and conduct of a battle than senior Russian officers – plainly an unjustified slur on men like Suvorov or Kutuzov – but applicable enough to the many young aristocrats who crowded the tsar's entourage and, though without experience or training, constantly pushed their views.[88] Before Austerlitz, they were over-confident, brash, boastful, under-estimated their opponents and blamed all previous set-backs on the alleged cowardice of their Austrian allies; attitudes which contributed to their defeat.

The conduct of Russian administrative and staff work, especially at the highest levels, often fell to officers of foreign extraction, or even foreign nationals. Sometimes these were highly qualified men, especially after 1808, but some were incompetents hiding their shortcomings under a cloud of pretentious erudition and paperwork. There were so many reports, returns, accounts, that Wilson commented 'if regularity of manuscript could organize an army, the Russians long ago would have attained excellence'.[89] The nationalist reaction of 1812 eliminated Barclay de Tolly from supreme command, but foreigners like Jomini, Schubert, and others continued to do much of the staff work.

Since the days of Ivan the Terrible artillery had played a prominent role in the Russian army, and this remained true in this period. 'No other army,' commented Wilson after 1807, 'moves with so many guns'. At the same time, however, the artillery officers were not necessarily highly qualified, though reform brought improvement and high artillery command often went to a non-specialist but aristocratic officer.[90]

A peculiar Russian institution, and a special component of the Russian army was the Cossacks, not a race or a nation, but originally an anarchic group of frontiersmen in southern Russia. By this time they constituted an irregular cavalry which, commanded by its own chieftain or *ataman*, was mobilized for specific campaigns, during which they received no pay but were compensated by booty. Wilson believed that discipline would have greatly improved their combat performance, but doubted that Russia had the resources to change the age-old system. As it was, the Cossacks were often counterproductive, 'frequently scourges of terror and desolation, more fatal to friend than foes'. Private Morris, whose regiment was joined by some Cossacks on campaign in 1813, described them as a 'set of barbarians, inspiring as much terror in our ranks as in those of the enemy'. For all that, Wilson wrote that their 'military virtues are splendid' and that they revealed a natural aptitude for light cavalry work. Their shaggy horses, ill-conditioned but well-bred, had great endurance and armed with lance, pistol, and sabre, they excelled in single combat, even routing French Cuirassiers.[91] The French, however, were less impressed and regarded them mainly as a nuisance, rarely if ever prepared to press an attack against a formed unit, afraid of artillery, and unwilling to engage unless the odds were heavily in their favour.

Cossacks were often brigaded with Calmucks and Bashkirs, Mongol tribesmen from Asia, brave but with obsolete arms. The Calmucks had lances and the Bashkirs wore pointed helmets, chainmail, and their main weapon was a bow. 'Our soldiers,' Parquin relates, 'called them the "Cupids" . . . I did not think these soldiers could have successfully measured up to ours.'[92]

As the conflict continued, Russia mobilized increasing numbers of this cheap manpower. In 1812 there were some 20 regiments, about 600 men each, of Cossacks, the vast majority commanded by the legendary Platov. In 1813 they participated in the Leipzig campaign and the next year fought in France.

Overall, though tough, numerous, and formidable in defence of their own country or in fighting its traditional enemies, the Russian army was ill-equipped for operations in areas far away from its own centre of power. The troops Paul I dispatched to aid the Austrians in Italy were weak and poorly equipped and arrived with no administrative or logistic support. And the Russian expedition sent to cooperate with the British in operations against the Dutch coast was equally badly equipped and poorly led to boot. With bad staff work, the Russians moved too slowly in 1805 and 1806, and poor planning and dispositions were also evident during the early stages of the 1812 campaign. The advance of the Russians into Central Europe in 1813 was slow and beset with many logistic troubles. One British observer, Major General Campbell, commented that the Russians were encumbered with an enormous, but inefficient, train, 'resembling a horde of Asiatics'. There were innumerable wagons, carts, tumbrils, and senior officers had as many as 20 or more orderlies. 'This is the ruin of that army, for by those encumbrances the resources of the country are exhausted, while the Army is impeded.'[93] All through the wars, administrative shortcomings allowed the Russians to mobilize and concentrate only a part of their huge armies and even in 1812 they were inferior in strength in several key battles.

These shortcomings were accompanied by conservative fighting methods. Until late in the Napoleonic Wars the Russians fought much as their grandfathers had done, and although new regulations tried to modernize tactics, most commanders continued to rely on the solid column and the bayonet. They also employed the firing line of the linear order, but line and column together were rarely used nor was there little cooperation between the three major combat arms.

The Russian army under Paul I

The army had made an impressive showing during the Seven Years' War, though its record was less good during the wars against the Turks in 1768–74 and 1787–92, the Swedes in 1788–90, and the Poles in 1794–5. Under Catherine II, it assumed many old Russian characteristics, symbolized by the adoption of a uniform patterned after the national costume replacing Prussian-style uniforms. By the end of Catherine's reign the army had many virtues, but also much corruption. Although 400,000 strong on paper, it actually had but half that number of effectives. Many soldiers were employed as servants or in the private business affairs of their officers; many regiments were under strength and poorly equipped, in large part due to the unpredictable whims of Catherine who, on the one hand, supported Suvorov, but on the other also elevated many incompetent favourites to high command.

When Catherine died in November 1796, her son Paul returned the army to the Prussian pattern. The new ruler had a considerable, though shallow, interest in military affairs, limited, as Tauentzien, the Prussian envoy in St Petersburg put it, to a 'superficial acquaintance with the Prussian system and a passion for minute detail'. Beyond that, he wanted to undo all aspects of his mother's regime and put his own stamp on the army. At Gatchina, his estate, he had trained a small model force on Prussian lines and when these troops entered the capital, Prince Czartoryski noted that the population marvelled at the appearance of these soldiers, 'so different from those it had been accustomed to see'. Now the entire army reverted to the uncomfortable and obsolete Prussian uniforms and the refinements of Prussian drill, 'nothing could be more important than a foot raised too soon on the march or a coat badly buttoned on parade'.[94]

How far, away from the capital, these new regulations were enforced was another matter. The troops sent to Italy in 1799 were ill-uniformed, loosely organized, and fought pretty much in small columns. There was little system in the army. The tsar, an unstable and erratic personality, tried to run the army in person. Officers were arbitrarily promoted or punished and Suvorov, who had protested against the new army regulations, poor copies of the Prussian, was retired, but recalled to command the corps sent to aid the Austrians. Army administration was handled by 12 territorial districts, the inspections (nine European and three Asian), with the number of troops in each district varying according to the economic conditions.

There existed no higher tactical formations and units were assigned by regiment, squadron, or battery to the field commanders who formed them into columns as he saw fit. The army was divided into three major components – the Guard, the line, and the Cossacks. The Guard formed a special corps of all branches, while the line was large and numerous. Its most important branch was the infantry, designated as grenadiers, musketeers, fusiliers, and *Jäger*. These distinctions, however, were mainly nominal. The grenadiers were often considered elite units, but the *Jäger* had little in common with their German counterparts. Their morale was high but, except for some sharpshooters, they were musket armed and their skirmishing skill not equal to the British, French, or Prussian light troops.[95] The Russian artillery at this stage was numerous, but the pieces were heavy and the gunners showed little skill in 1805. Calibres included 3-, 6-, 8-, and 12-pounder cannon, and there also were some 9- and 18-pounder licornes, special howitzers designed by General Shuvalov in the 1750s to fire shells over a longer-than-average range in a flat trajectory.

In 1801 Paul, who had alienated many soldiers, was assassinated by a group of Guard officers which left an uncertain military legacy for his son and successor Alexander I.

The Russian army under Alexander I: 1801–8

Following his accession, Alexander I began to reform the Russian army and to suppress some of the abuses introduced by his father and many of his early reforms were copied from the French. In 1802 he created a Ministry of Landforces (renamed the Ministry of War in 1808) essentially an administrative agency with no command function. He also reorganized the regiments and by 1805 the army comprised the Guard with 3 infantry regiments, 1 *Jäger* battalion, 2 Cuirassier, 1 Hussar, 1 Cossock regiment, and 1 battery of horse artillery. The line consisted of 13 Grenadier, 83 Musketeer, 22 *Jäger*, 6 Cuirassier, 30 Dragoon, 8 Hussar, 3 Uhlan, 1 Lithuanian Tartar, 11 artillery, 1 pioneer, and 1 pontoonier regiments. Almost all regiments were formed with three battalions, with an official strength of 738 men each. The light cavalry regiments each had 10 squadrons (a squadron = approx. 150 riders), while the heavy cavalry regiments had 5 squadrons each. The artillery was organized into three types of batteries: heavy position with 8 guns and 6 howitzers; light batteries with the same number of pieces but lighter calibres, and horse artillery with light guns only. To provide better army administration, Alexander organized a special staff course, though foreign officers continued to have considerable influence.[96]

Having regarded themselves as invincible, the Russians were forced by the disaster of Austerlitz to increase the army. The Guard added one Uhlan and one Dragoon regiment and a second battalion to the *Jäger*. The line also received substantial augmentation, 14 regiments of foot and seven of horse. At the same time, except for the Asian districts, the inspections were abolished and divisions, initially 12 and later raised to 18, were formed. Each division comprised 18 battalions, 20 squadrons and 82 guns.[97] However, when the tsar decided to support Prussia in 1806 he mobilized too late and in the end was left to face Napoleon alone. Even so, the Russians fought stubbornly at Eylau and Friedland, and in the end made a fairly acceptable settlement at Tilsit. While the sovereigns negotiated, the troops fraternized. The Imperial Guard was instructed to hold a banquet for their Russian counterparts which went off well, although Coignet was taken somewhat aback when the tsar's warriors swallowed huge goblets of wine at one gulp, tore off large pieces of meat, and when they found that they could not finish everything on the table, made themselves vomit and then started all over again. 'They thus made,' he recorded, 'three meals at one dinner.'[98]

More importantly, after 1808, the Russians undertook a large-scale reform of their army.

The Russian army under Alexander I: 1808–15

The reforms were implemented primarily by two men, Alexei Arakcheev, Inspector-General of Artillery and Minister of War from 1808–10, and his more genial successor as minister, Barclay de Tolly. Although much disliked for his brutality and reactionary sentiments, Arakcheev was a good artillerist and soon after Austerlitz, where the Russian artillery had done extremely poorly, he began to introduce a new range of weapons – the System of 1805. It was comprised of 6- and 12-pounder cannons, and 10- and 20-pounder howitzers, unicorns, with reduced chambering and a long range. The System of 1805 featured modern screw-elevating mechanisms instead of the old wedges and also had an improved sighting apparatus. Russia possessed more than adequate iron-ore deposits and a fair technology and was able to produce between 500 and 800 pieces a year. By 1808 there were 139 batteries with 1,550 guns, increased to 133 batteries and 1,699 guns by 1812. In 1811, Tolly organized the artillery into 27 field, 10 reserve, and 4 depot brigades. Each field battery had three companies, one heavy and two light, each with 12 pieces. The Guard Artillery, 64 pieces, was a separate unit.[99] Russian artillery tactics were defined by General Kutusov's *General Rules for Field Artillery in Field Action*, called for massed gunfire both in attack and defence. Suvorov had already stressed that it was no disgrace to lose guns if they were lost firing and the new regulations re-emphasized this.

The reform of infantry was mainly Barclay's achievement. An unusual soldier, having served 14 years in the ranks, he tried to improve the soldiers' condition. He played down parade-ground drill and issued instructions stressing marksmanship training. Duffy considered his methods of instruction excellent, but the results were limited. For one thing, Russian muskets were poorly made, and although some 100,000 were turned out yearly by factories in Tula and elsewhere, these clumsy weapons were never reduced to a uniform calibre. In 1811 the Russian army still had 28 different calibres, not counting weapons obtained from England and for this reason much emphasis was placed on the bayonet charge as against the fire-fight.

In fact by 1812 Barclay had developed a sophisticated tactical deployment based on the division with three infantry brigades. Behind a screen of *Jäger*, the first brigade deployed in line, with the two other brigades, essentially in *ordre mixte* in support. The artillery brigade took up positions with one big battery each at the wings and in the centre, and the divisional cavalry formed a reserve, two lines deep behind this array. But the system was not always well understood or executed. At Borodino, where Barclay had been superceded in command by Kutuzov, the Russian formations were too densely packed and fully exposed to French long-range fire.

There was then a considerable gap between the new theories, as outlined in Barclay's field manual, *Code on the Conduct of Major Military Operations*, the 'Yellow Book', and the actual capabilities of the army. By 1812 the army comprised 6 regiments of the Guard Infantry and 6 of Guard Cavalry, while the line numbered 13 Grenadier, 96 Line, and 32 *Jäger* regiments. Except for the guard, always at three battalion strength, each infantry regiment consisted of three battalions, two field and one depot. Line cavalry mustered 8 Cuirasier, 36 Dragoon, 11 Hussar and 5 Uhlan regiments, supported by some 15,000 Cossacks, Calmucks, and Bashkirs. The artillery had increased to 44 heavy, 58 Light, and 22 horse batteries, supplemented by a number of cavalry batteries, light 3-pounders designed to steady the Cossack swarms. Guard artillery had increased to 80 pieces.

Field forces numbered only about 210,000 and troops were needed to watch the Caucasus, the Turks, and newly conquered Finland whilst others were in depot, training, or garrison. Shortly before the French invasion,

Barclay introduced the corps system into the First and Second West Armies, basically two infantry divisions, some mounted troops, and some artillery. To increase striking power, he formed the grenadiers into separate divisions and he also introduced cavalry divisions. The two Cuirassier divisions were exclusively composed of armoured heavy horse, the other eight cavalry divisions mixed Dragoons and light cavalry, Hussars or Uhlans. But despite this new divisional structure, Russian cavalry was seldom committed in the large shock formations utilized by the French. In fact, Barclay's reorganization was clearly patterned on the French model, but the Russian army of 1812–13 did not compare in flexibility, speed, or concentration to the corps and divisional system of the *Grande Armée*.

The reasons for this included the relative low level of training on the part of most of the officers and men, the continued problems with the staff, and rivalries and intrigues within the Russian high command. The first is, of course, obvious. As for the staff, little had been done. The introduction of some staff courses by Alexander was a beginning, but it could not produce senior staff officers in a few years. Under Catherine, the Russian system was based on the Prussian Quartermaster-General establishment, but under Paul the operational and planning function had been transferred to a personal staff, the 'Suite of His Majesty for the Duties of Quartermaster'. This arrangement continued under Alexander, with a complement of officers rising to 151 by 1811.[101] Alexander's Chief of Staff was Prince Volkonsky, an amiable nonentity, whose chief adviser was the elderly Ernst von Phull, a Prussian who believed he had a scientific system for making war. And among the officers were men like Major Schubert, serving on Barclay's staff, who regretted the passing of the magazine system because bivouacs affected the appearance of the troops, whereas in regular fixed camps all could be kept clean and shiny.[102] To make matters worse, within the Emperor's entourage the so-called 'German' faction was opposed by the Russian faction, and after initial setbacks, Alexander replaced Barclay the 'German' with Kutuzov, a native Russian. And though Kutuzov was a charismatic leader, he had little patience with the modern ways introduced by Barclay. Kutuzov was a fighter, though his tactical reliance on deep formations caused unnecessarily high casualties at Borodino.

In the end, Russian victories over Napoleon in 1812 were due above all to the weather and the strategic depth, both exploited by Kutuzov, and the unexpected determination of Alexander to resist. A contributing factor also was the fiercely 'national' character of the war. While some Russian troops, especially Lithuanians deserted, the great majority remained steadfast and a hastily mustered militia, the *opolchenie*, showed surprising fighting spirit and was useful in harassing French and allied detachments. In addition, organized bands of partisans, like those of Colonel Davidov, achieved some good results against Napoleon's line of communications, though they received but little encouragement from the military who feared that armed serfs would in turn rise against their landlords. Even so, the war of 1812 took on the character of a national war.[103]

After Napoleon's retreat from Moscow, however, the Russians were hesitant in following up their victory. Political considerations were a factor here, but by the spring of 1813 the army was also in very poor shape. It had used up much of its equipment, stores and ammunition and Kutuzov was uneasy about fighting Napoleon on the central German plain. By 1813, nonetheless, the Russian army had clearly become one of the four major armies in the fight against Napoleon and would continue as one of the great military powers in Europe.

Each of the four main armies opposing Napoleon emerged from the campaigns of 1812–15 with considerable reasons for satisfaction. Austria, shattered at Ulm and Austerlitz, and barely defeated at Aspern and Wagram, in the end played a decisive role in the campaigns which liberated Germany and were to end in Paris itself. Prussia had reorganized her state and the new Prussian army had fought well in Germany and under Blücher had a spectacular role in the advance on Paris. The Russian ruler also had reason for self-congratulation. Eylau, Friedland and Borodino had been Napoleon's most costly and hardest-fought victories, and Russian resistance in 1812 had turned the tide against the French. And England, too, could look with satisfaction on her army. After the initial disasters, it had fought its way from Lisbon to Toulouse and it had stubbornly and victoriously held its lines at Waterloo. Ironically, these successes were due, in part, to adoptions and adaptations of the Napoleonic system – a system which remained valid until the middle of the nineteenth century.

NOTES

1. Karl v. Clausewitz, 'Über das Leben . . . von Scharnhorst', cited by Paret, *op cit.*, 217. See also by the same author *Clausewitz and the State*, Oxford University Press, 1967, 56–7 and *passim*.
2. Some of the material in this section appeared previously in my article, 'The Habsburg Army in the Napoleonic Wars', *Military Affairs*, XXXVII, February 1973, 1–5.
3. C. Falls, *The Art of War from the Age of Napoleon to the Present Day*, Oxford University Press, 1961, 34.
4. Marshal A. Massena, *Mémoires*, vol. II, Pauline Lechevalier, Paris, 1848, 15–17; Dolleczek, *op cit.*, 362–3.
5. Cited in Paret, *Yorck*, 73–4.
6. Falls, *op cit.*, 35.
7. O. Regele, *Generalstabschefs aus vier Jahrhunderten*, Herold, Vienna, 1966, 26–7.
8. H. Ommen, *Die Kriegsführung des Erzherzogs Karl*, E. Ebering, Berlin, 1900, 29–31, 34; Delbrück, *op cit.*, vol. IV, 503–4.
9. K. Peball, 'Zum Kriegsbild der österreichischen Armee und seiner geschichtlichen Bedeutung in den Kriegen gegen die Französische Revolution and Napoleon I in den Jahren von 1792 bis 1815,' in W. v. Groote and K.J. Müller, eds., *Napoleon I und das Militärwesen seiner Zeit*, Rombach, Freiberg, 1968, 149–51, 160.
10. Paret, *Yorck*, 199.
11. Ommen, *op cit.*, 83–6; Lauerma, *op cit.*, 307.
12. Ommen, *op cit.*, 77.

13. *Ibid.*, 81–6; Jomini, *op cit.*, 269.
14. F. Strobl v. Ravelsberg, *Die Landwehr Anno Neun*, Stern, Vienna, 1909, *passim*.
15. Peball, *op cit.*, 153.
16. *Ibid.*, 160.
17. Brett-James, *Leipzig*, 83–4.
18. S.H.F. Johnston, *British Soldiers*, William Collins, 1944, 22–4. Moore cited in Carola Oman, *Sir John Moore*, Hodder & Stoughton, 1953, 153.
19. Bell, *op cit.*, vol. I, 165.
20. Sir A. Bryant, *The Years of Victory*, Collins Sons & Co., 1944, 335–6. Cf. J.D. Hittle, *The Military Staff. Its History and Development*, Stackpole, Harrisburg Pa., 1961, 144–5.
21. Cited in E. Halévy, *England in 1815*, Ernest Benn Ltd, 1949, 78, n. 2.
22. Bell, *op cit.*, vol. I, 115.
23. Morris, *op cit.*, 50.
24. Glover, *op cit.*, 153.
25. Cited in M. Howard, 'Wellington and the British Army', in *Studies in War and Peace*. Viking, New York, 1970, 52–5.
26. Halévy, *op cit.*, 84.
27. Mercer, *op cit.*, 336.
28. Longford, *op cit.*, 404.
29. Costello, *op cit.*, 117, 125–6, 149.
30. Halévy, *op cit.*, 76.
31. Harris, *op cit.*, 166–7.
32. Details in Glover, *op cit.*, 177–8.
33. Harris, *op cit.*, 138.
34. Bell, *op cit.*, vol. I, 121.
35. Costello, *op cit.*, 24.
36. *Ibid.*, 85–6; Harris, *op cit.*, 57.
37. Bell, *op cit.*, vol. I, 37; Harris, *op cit.*, 3–5.
38. Costello, *op cit.*, 82.
39. Halévy, *op cit.*, 83.
40. Glover, *op cit.*, 47; C.J. Ffoulkes, *Arms and Armament : A Historical Survey of the Weapons of the British Army*, Harrap & Co., 1945, 24.
41. J.M. Sherwig, *Guineas and Gun Powder : British Foreign Aid in the Wars with France, 1793–1815*, Harvard University Press, Cambridge, Mass., 1969, 288.
42. Lauerma, *op cit.*, 22.
43. Longford, *op cit.*, 260.
44. Glover, *op cit.*, 101–2.
45. Brett-James, *Leipzig*, 77–8, report of Colonel Stewart.
46. Glover, *op cit.*, 128–32.
47. *Ibid.*, 87–8; Phipps, *op cit.*, vol. I, 305.
48. Charles Oman, *Studies in the Napoleonic Wars*, Charles Scribners, New York, 1929, 39–62, 101.
49. J. Weller, *Wellington at Waterloo*, Thomos Crowell & Co., New York, 1967, 77–82.
50. E.B. Hamley, *The Operations of War Explained and Illustrated*, W. Blackwood & Sons, 1907, 18–19.
51. J.T. Jones, *Journals of the Sieges carried on by the Army Under the Duke of Wellington in Spain during the Years 1811 to 1814 ; with Notes and Additions : Also Memoranda Relative to the Lines Thrown up to Cover Lisbon in 1810*, ed. H.D. Jones, 3rd edition, John Weale, 1846, vol. II, 37.

52. Bell, *op cit.*, vol. I, 37.
53. H. Calvert, *Journals and Correspondence of General Sir Harry Calvert*, Hurst & Blackett, 1853, 80.
54. Mercer, *op cit.*, 180, 204, 242–3.
55. Costello, *op cit.*, 20–1.
56. Bell, *op cit.*, vol. I, 78–123.
57. A. Halliday, *Observations on the Present State of the Portuguese Army as Organized by Sir William Carr Beresford, K.B.*, John Murray, 1811, 5. Cf. Bell, *op cit.*, vol. I, 126.
58. Marbot, *op cit.*, vol. I, 485.
59. Halliday, *op cit.*, 50–6; Pelet, *op cit.*, 155.
60. N.L. Beamish, *Geschichte der Königlich Deutschen Legion*, Hahn, Hanover, 1832, vol. I, 25–31, 38–62, 74–9.
61. *Ibid.*, 91–6. For a list of all KGL units see *Listen und Nachweisungen welche sich auf den Dienst der Königlich Deutschen Legion von Errichtung derselben bis zu ihrer Auflösung beziehen*, Gebr. Janecke, Hanover, 1832.
62. Costello, *op cit.*, 24–5.
63. Beamish, *op cit.*, vol. I, 90–3.
64. *Ibid.*, 322–6.
65. Paret, *Yorck*, 60–1, 101–2.
66. M. Kitchen, *A Military History of Germany from the Eighteenth Century to the Present Day*, Weidenfeld and Nicolson, 1975, 28–35.
67. W.O. Shanahan, *Prussian Military Reforms, 1786–1813*, Columbia University Press, New York, 1945, 85–6.
68. *Ibid.*, 104–9.
69. Kitchen, *op cit.*, 42–3.
70. Hittle, *op cit.*, 63–5.
71. *Ibid.*, 66–7.
72. Kitchen, *op cit.*, 48–9; Shanahan, *op cit.*, 159–78.
73. *Carl v. Clausewitz-Schriften-Aufsätze-Studien-Briefe*, ed. W. Hahlweg, Vandenhoeck & Ruprecht, Göttingen, 1966, vol. I, 74.
74. Marbot, *op cit.*, vol. III, 238.
75. Shanahan, *op cit.*, 211.
76. F. Engels, *Ausgewählte Militärische Schriften*, Verlag des Ministeriums für Nationale Verteidigung, E. Berlin, 1958, vol. I, 434.
77. Paret, *Yorck*, 186–9.
78. H. Treitschke, *History of Germany in the Nineteenth Century*, trs. E. and C. Paul, McBride, Nast, & Co., New York, 1915, vol. I, 515.
79. Kitchen, *op cit.*, 54–5. Cf. D. Showalter, 'The Prussian *Landwehr* and its Critics, 1813–1819', *Central European History*, IV (1971), no. 1, 14–16.
80. Gerhard Ritter, *The Prussian Tradition, 1740–1890*, vol. I of *The Sword and the Scepter*, trs. H. Norden, University of Miami Press, Corat Gables, Fla., 1969, 82–9.
81. C. Duffy, *Borodino and the War of 1812*, Seeley, Service, & Co., 1972, 36.
82. Wilson, *op cit.*, 1.
83. Marbot, *op cit.*, vol. I, 327.
84. Wilson, *op cit.*, 10–11.
85. Mercer, *op cit.*, 306.
86. Wilson, *op cit.*, 44.
87. E. Tarle, *Napoleon's Invasion of Russia, 1812*, Oxford University Press, 1942, 97. Cf. Petre, *op cit.*, 35.
88. Cited in Brett-James, *Leipzig*, 67; Schubert, *op cit.*, 102.

89. Wilson, *op cit.*, 49–50.
90. *Ibid.*, 20–1.
91. *Ibid.*, 27–9, 31; Morris, *op cit.*, 22.
92. Marbot, *op cit.*, vol. III, 122–4; Parquin, *op cit.*, 65, 75–6; Duffy, Borodino, 45.
93. Cited in Brett-James, *Leipzig*, 67.
94. *Memoirs of Prince Adam Czartoryski*, ed. A. Gielgud, Remington & Co., 1888, vol. 1, 243.
95. Paret, *Yorck*, 202–4.
96. Schubert, *op cit.*, 46–8.
97. Petrie, *op cit.*, 37.
98. Coignet, *op cit.*, 155.
99. Duffy, *Borodino*, 41, 45–7; Tarle, *op cit.*, 76.
100. Duffy, *Borodino*, 86–7.
101. Hittle, *op cit.*, 230, 235–6.
102. Schubert, *op cit.*, 154–5.
103. Tarle, *op cit.*, 346–8.

7

Staff Problems, Fortifications and Medical Services

The dramatic increase in the number of men engaged was one of the most significant developments in the warfare of this age. But the increase was a mixed blessing. To direct and supply such vast numbers required sophisticated staff and administrative services and, despite their improvement, the technical and logistical problems overmatched their capabilities. Although roads had been improved, at least in western Europe, they still had only limited capacity to sustain the movement of large numbers and heavy-wheeled traffic. Control of major roads, their junctions, bridges, and terminals became of vital importance. All these points, as well as ports, capitals, and other centres, were defended either by permanent or field fortifications, and though the era is considered one of mobile warfare, sieges were as numerous, and perhaps even more ferociously contested, than in any other age. Finally, the very large number of men engaged, concentrated in crowded camps and cantonments, with campaigns pressed in many climates and in all seasons, resulted in casualties and a disease rate with which the medical services were not equipped to cope. Disease, of course, killed or disabled more men than did battles and physicians at the time estimated that for every combat death there were ten from disease. This figure was far too high, but epidemics decided several campaigns and in the end influenced the outcome of the entire conflict.

General staffs and their problems
Even prior to 1792 the larger and more advanced European armies, the French, Prussian, and Austrian, had started to transform the commander's personal assistants, the staff, into organized bodies of trained officers capable of handling the details of marches, quartering, engineering, topographic, supply, and reconnaissance duties required by the general. The officer in charge of these assistants was commonly called by the French term *maréchal général des logis*, the origin of the word logistics, which translated into the German *Quartiermeister*. At the end of the Seven Years' War, the French staff was not disbanded but became a permanent organization with its own

training college at Grenoble. In 1769 the Austrians followed suit, though their staff was still activated only at the outset of a campaign. But its duties now were detailed in the *Generals-Reglement* which differentiated between operational and personnel functions and carefully enumerated the duties of each officer and official on the staff. In Prussia, finally, Frederick II acted as his own operations officer and depended little on his *General Quartiermeister*. In fact, during the last years of his reign the duties of the Quartermaster-General and the Adjutant-General were combined and handled by one officer, the infamous Wilhelmi Anhalt, a brutal and incompetent martinet. Still, even Frederick needed adjutants to prepare and distribute orders and do his detail work, and he systematically trained promising young officers, the *Quartiermeisterlieutenants*, in the engineering, supply, and intelligence duties required for staff work. Prussia, however, had no permanent staff organization until in 1803, Generals Lecoq and Massenbach provided for a continued existence and a more precise definition of the duties of the Quartermaster-General and his staff.

At the end of the *ancien régime*, France held a clear lead in staff organization and doctrine, the latter elaborated by Pierre Bourcet, then teaching at Grenoble, and described by Wilkinson as the 'greatest staff officer of the French army of the eighteenth century'.[1] In 1790 the National Assembly abolished the ancient title of *maréchal des logis* and replaced it with that of adjutant general. In 1792 one adjutant general was appointed to duty as chief of staff with each of the field armies. For the first year the minister of war assumed the central direction, but after the crisis of 1793, Carnot's rather informal *bureau topographique* handled overall strategy and logistics. At the same time, with generals selected largely for their personal and political qualities, the professional services of the chiefs of staff at the army lever became more important. In 1796, Berthier described the composition and duties of an army field staff in his *Document sur le service de l'état-major-général a l'armée des Alpes*. His division of the staff into four major departments, the first handling personnel, records and discipline, the second logistics and engineering, the third intelligence and operations, and the fourth dealing with the internal administration of the staff, was retained when Berthier became chief of staff to Napoleon. With certain important deviations they also formed the basis for the staff organization of the various armies, corps, and divisions. A detailed manual on staff procedures was produced in 1800 by Colonel Paul Thiebault and was circulated widely in the French and foreign armies.

Under Napoleon, of course, staff organization at the level of the Grand Army changed radically. The emperor was head of state and the actual supreme commander of his forces. At Imperial Headquarters Napoleon's personal staff, the *maison*, became a staff within a staff. Its military department, the *cabinet*, comprised intelligence, topographic, and secretarial sections. Even before a campaign opened, Napoleon made every effort to collect information about the enemy, his dispositions, the nature of the country, and anything else of importance. An effective espionage apparatus and the aggressive use of cavalry reconnaissance supplemented the information and often gave the French an edge in operations. All intelligence went directly to the *cabinet* and Napoleon alone made his decisions. Berthier's role was purely technical, he did not have advisory functions, but merely translated the imperial orders into practice. Still, he was a highly skilled technician and his arrangement for simultaneously passing 150,000 men over the Danube bridges at Aspern was a masterpiece of detailed planning. Although the emperor often raged at Berthier, he was well served by him and when he was forced to substitute Soult in 1815 the result was considerable confusion and some faulty transmission of orders. At Waterloo, Napoleon is supposed to have exclaimed 'if only Berthier was here, then my orders would have been carried out'.[2]

Although Napoleon has been faulted for his over-centralized command style, French staff work remained superior to that of his opponents until 1812. Austrian, Prussian, and Russian staff work was poor for most of the period, though in 1813, largely due to the introduction of the command teams, it reached the level of Napoleonic strategy. The problems of the allied planners were complicated by the appearance of the various monarchs in the field, usually surrounded by a vast array of their own private advisers. Although the monarchs normally refrained from exercising their authority over the nominal command, they had to be briefed on plans, their objections countered, and even their advisers had to receive a hearing. And on occasion, such as at Austerlitz, they did take an active role in the dispositions of the army. At Leipzig the presence of no less than three monarchs, the Austrian emperor, the Russian tsar, and the Prussian king, together with their numerous advisers and retinue, moved even the politic Schwarzenberg to complain that 'it really is inhuman what I must tolerate and bear, surrounded as I am by feeble-minded people, eccentric projectors, intriguers, asses, babblers, and niggling critics'.[3]

In this respect, Wellington was more fortunate. Though he had to contend with a frequently unresponsive home government and its party politics, he was spared royal interference in the field. Only during the Waterloo campaign did he suffer interference and had to put up with the Prince of Orange, a brave but incompetent young man. On the other hand, with an army built up from regiments and batteries, there existed no British field staff and he was forced to develop his own organization. His headquarters in the Peninsula was composed of his personal staff, aide-de-camp and military secretary, and two major military departments, the Quartermaster-General and the Adjutant-General. In addition there were other important officers and officials, the Commanding Officer of Artillery and the Chief of Engineers, the Commissary-General, and the Inspector of Hospitals, and a host of other functionaries. Unlike Napoleon or Blücher, Wellington dispensed with a chief of staff whose duties were shared among the military secretary, the Adjutant-General, and the Quartermaster-General. Wellington developed a particularly close relationship with Quartermaster-General Murray who attended not only to troop movements and encampments, but also assumed responsibility for topographical intelligence and assisted Wellington in his operational planning.

The greater role of the staff aroused sharp jealousies among line officers. Service on the staff provided an avenue for fast promotions and it was resented by line officers. Napoleon's great Imperial Headquarters was beset by many intrigues and all was far from serene on Wellington's staff. The lower-ranking officers, the civilian Deputy Judge Advocate General observed, 'are sharp-set, hungry and anxious to get on and make the most of everything . . . there is much obsequious time-serving conduct to anyone who is in office'.[4] No doubt, similar conditions prevailed in every army.

Staff work throughout the period was hampered by technical limitations. Communications remained slow, largely dependent on the speed of man and horse. Long range visual signalling devices, such as the Chappe telegraph, were unreliable; messages could be delayed or garbled. The most famous mistake occurred when Berthier, sent ahead by Napoleon to set up head-quarters at Strasbourg, actually left the city and did not receive a message sent by Napoleon on 10 April 1809 until the 16th of the month. Meanwhile, he disposed the corps in so absurd a fashion that the marshals were amazed and only the timely arrival of the emperor and the slow reaction of the Austrians saved the army from potential disaster.

Maps were another source of complication. During his advance into Portugal, Masséna was misled by maps which showed the contours much lower than they actually were. The Austrians, though they had a topographic section since 1764, did not have any maps for the Russian campaigns of 1809 or 1812, and the British were no better off. During the Egyptian campaign Lieutenant-Colonel Robert Wilson complained that there was a 'total want of information . . . not a map to depend on could be procured', and matters stood little better at first in the Peninsula. Wellington had adequate maps for the area around Lisbon, but little information on the interior. For that matter, though the British had been fighting in the Low Countries for over a century, no detailed maps were available. As late as the Waterloo campaign officers complained that they could not locate their assigned position on any map and Captain Mercer recalled that his troop had to rely on local guides.[5] Napoleon's topographic section was one of his most important assets, and its head, Bacler d'Albe, has been described as 'probably the most indispensable of all Napoleon's aides'.[6] D'Albe worked hard to procure large-scale, up-to-date maps. Collections in captured cities were ransacked; officers were sent out to purchase maps everywhere, and in 1809, Napoleon established a separate corps of topographical engineers. French agents even managed to smuggle out plates of the newest Russian maps for the invasion of 1812.[7] But despite all efforts, there never were enough maps and their accuracy left much to be desired.

Topographical reconnaissance remained important for all commanders. Wellington often performed this by himself, and Napoleon considered the ability to judge ground one of the all-important requirements for a successful general. Normally, however, topographical reconnaissance was the duty of light cavalry. The French were well served by their light cavalry screen, but when, as in Spain and Portugal, the presence of hostile guerrilla elements prevented their movement, they sometimes had to move blind. Although it seems unlikely that Masséna had no indication of the lines before Lisbon, faulty maps, false information, and inadequate reconnaissance, concealed their true nature. On occasion, the French blundered into British positions, such as the ridge at Bussaco. In contrast, Wellington had an excellent field intelligence service. Cavalry patrols and individual officers were sent forward daily to examine the ground and report enemy dispositions; guerrilla bands and intelligence officers like Colonel Colqhoun Grant provided additional information.[8]

Even the best intelligence and maps could only alleviate one problem, the still inadequate road network. Roads had improved and stone-faced highways connected major centres of western and central Europe. Napoleon often based his strategic calculations on the existence of these major avenues, and also made great efforts to build new roads throughout his empire. Still, outside of France there were but few major roads and secondary roads were liable to become difficult in bad weather.

In Spain roads, where they existed were bad, virtually impassable for wheeled transport in the mountains. In eastern Europe conditions were worse. Bad weather turned roads into mud paths where even infantry could only move at a snail's pace. Soldiers would tie their boots to their ankles with rope, but would still lose them in the mud.[9] Russian roads were no better. Here the 'corduroy' roads often disintegrated as the planks laid over the mud rotted away. But Russian staff officers considered road conditions in Poland the worst they encountered.[10] Even in the Low Countries, heavy vehicles and artillery encountered trouble on secondary roads. On his way to Waterloo, Mercer and his troops had to traverse stretches of secondary road which were flooded out, and difficult to traverse even for his light 9-pounder guns. The movement of large numbers of men, guns, and supplies over an inadequate road network created considerable difficulties for all general-staff planning during this period.

Fortifications and siegecraft

The wars of the French Revolution and Napoleon are usually depicted as wars of movement. Compared to the deliberate pace of the eighteenth century campaigns this is true, but throughout this period the French as well as their adversaries made extensive use of fortifications, both field and permanent, to reinforce positions during battle, to guard lines of communications, base areas and supply ports, to protect bridgeheads and major road junctions. To be sure, fortresses no longer were as all important. In 1800, though the Austrians still held many of the North Italian fortresses, the victory at Marengo decided the issue. In 1806 the Elbe fortresses did not prevent Napoleon from penetrating beyond the Oder and in 1813–14, neither the French-occupied Prussian fortresses nor the chain of fortresses along the French eastern frontier prevented the Allies from advancing to the Rhine and then on to

Paris. With armies no longer totally dependent on magazines, fortresses could be masked while the main army marched on to its target. On the other hand, when such detours were not possible, as in Spain, or when possession of a supply port or a road junction was important, sieges became necessary. Danzig in 1807, Badajoz and Ciudad Rodrigo in Spain, and Lisbon, Wellington's main supply port, provide examples. Then too, fortresses often had influence on field armies. In 1792–3 the fortresses of north-eastern France helped to rally the French armies; the surrender of Charleroi contributed to the Allied defeat at Fleurus; the Italian campaign of 1796–7 centred around Mantua, while the sieges of Maastricht, Mayence and Luxembourg were important for the campaigns on the Rhine and in Holland. In 1800, Masséna's tenacious defence of Genoa helped the Army of the Reserve to cross the Alps. Neither the poorly defended Prussian or Spanish fortresses prevented the French from penetrating into the interior, but the exceptional instances of protracted resistance, Kolberg on the Baltic and Saragossa on the Ebro, served as rallying points and symbols for national sentiment.

French doctrine, as expounded in the text used at the *École polytechnique*, maintained that 'although an offensive war, may, strictly speaking, be carried on without the use of fortifications', temporary fieldworks were useful for an army's tactical defence. And in a defensive war, the text continued, 'fortresses become essential'.[11] Napoleon observed this doctrine closely. Basically an offensive-minded commander, he fully appreciated the tactical value of entrenched positions and field fortifications. 'In a war of marching and manoeuvring', his seventeenth maxim read, 'to avoid battle against superior forces, it is necessary to entrench every night and to occupy always a good position of defence.'[12] In practice, however, the Grand Army rarely resorted to the shovel and the pick until the last stages of the conflict. Napoleon also recognized the value of permanent fortifications and constructed or rebuilt fortresses throughout Europe. 'Alexandria, Antwerp, Juliers – and five hundred more places,' General Foy recorded, had been 'constructed, restored, or augmented. . . . All Europe has been covered by our redoubts and entrenchments.'[13] And when Napoleon finally was forced on the defensive in 1813, he threw considerable forces into the Prussian Elbe and Oder fortresses, he recaptured and fortified Hamburg, and converted Dresden into a fortified camp. His hopes for using these places as manoeuvre bases for his reconstituted Grand Army failed and some commentators have claimed that this was a mistake. The troops blockaded in these places might have aided his manoeuvrable strength decisively. Even so, in 1814, Napoleon again used the fortresses of eastern France to delay allied invasion and this time they allowed him to operate more freely against a numerically greatly superior enemy.

Fortresses old and new
Most fortresses during this era were still built along the principles developed first in the sixteenth century and elaborated by Vauban and Coehorn at the

close of the seventeenth. Basically this called for a wall, the *enceinte*, enclosing
the area to be defended, with triangular or pentagonal bastions protruding
from the *enceinte* to provide interlocking fields of fire interdicting approach
to the main wall. The basic trace, or design, was called a star trace. To protect
the walls and bastions from the effect of hard shots, the stone walls were
partially dug into the ground and shielded on the exterior side by sloping
earth ramparts presenting a low profile. Artillery was mounted both on the
bastion and on the walls between. A wide ditch, its side revetted with masonry,
encircled the entire trace. Its inner face was called the scarp, the outer face the
counterscarp, in front of which a second, lower wall was constructed. On the
reverse side of this outer wall was a walk and a firing step, and the front of this
wall was also protected with earth sloping gradually into level ground, the
glacis, providing a clear field of fire for the defenders. As artillery achieved
greater range and power, it became important for the defenders to keep the
enemy as far away from the main fortifications as possible and outworks were
constructed in front of the line. These *lunettes* or ravelins tended to become
stronger and eventually constituted semi-independent outer strong-points.

FIG. 18.   Vauban fortifications

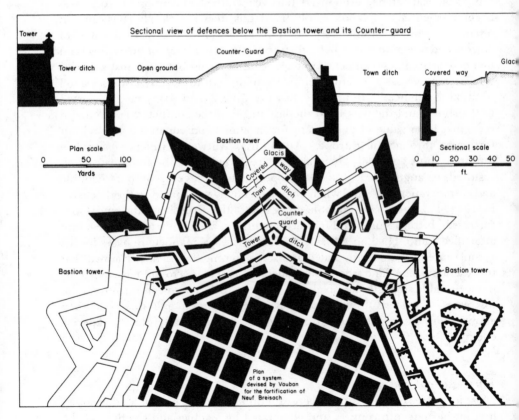

Vauban's fame did not merely rest on his achievements as a fortress builder, he was even more famous for his system of besieging fortresses. To do this he developed a system of entrenchments, the parallels, by which siege artillery was moved slowly forward in a gradually narrowing network of trenches dug parallel to the defence lines, until the breaching batteries were emplaced at the rim of the counterscarp. Once this was accomplished, it was generally assumed that a fortress was lost. To impede the steady advance of the saps, zigzag approaches, and parallels, Frederick of Prussia began the practice of elaborating the outworks into a ring of detached forts, a practice which became common in the next century. Detached forts and strong outworks delayed a besieger and forced him to deal with them prior to undertaking the main siege, either by a preliminary siege, or by a sudden surprise attack – an escalade.

For close-in defence the Marquis de Montalembert, a French engineer, devised a new system of fortification based on a polygonal rather than a star trace, backed up by increased defensive fire delivered from multi-tiered 'perpendicular' enclosed batteries. He revived the use of the *tenaille* trace, already employed in a number of forts, a design in which a series of triangular bastion or redans, meeting at right angles presented a continuous saw-edged outer front. He backed up this defence by successive fortified lines and with double-tiered round towers mounting heavy guns. Montalembert felt that open gun emplacements on the walls and bastions were too vulnerable, and he advocated that all guns should be casemated, that is given overhead protection and fire through embrasures with minimum exposure. In 1777 he refined his system by adding *caponiers*, structures three storeys high connecting the outer defences with the main line at a right angle, and able to enfilade the ditch with fire. Carnot continued Montalembert's work, stressing close-in defence even more. He proposed a defence based on the close-range fire of casemated guns placed to cover the field between the angles of the redans, with strong *caponiers* covering the rear of the successive fortified lines. Ideally, he maintained, all works should be capable of all-round defence.[14]

These new ideas, especially the multi-gun towers and the *caponiers*, became very popular with engineers in the era of the French Revolution and Napoleon, though the expenses involved prevented the total reconstruction of most of the older fortifications. Instead, where practicable, older works were modified with additional strongpoints, gun towers, and protected batteries. Gun towers, for instance the famous Martello towers in England, were also employed as separate coastal defence batteries. But even without such additions, fortifications dating back several hundred years, could, when resolutely defended, constitute serious obstacles to attackers. And this was particularly true when armies moved lightly and rarely had anything heavier than a 12-pounder battery. The medieval walls of Smolensk, for instance, 25 feet high and 10 wide, provided with a moat and a glacis, could not be stormed by the French and the 12-pounders made little impression against them.[15] Similar difficulties were encountered both by the French and British during the sieges in Spain and Portugal, though both managed sometimes to sweep across ramparts in sudden escalades.

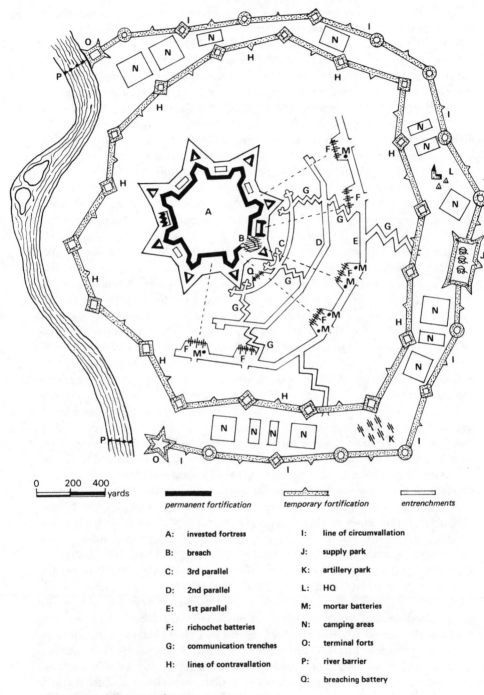

0   200   400
yards

permanent fortification   temporary fortification   entrenchments

A:	invested fortress	I:	line of circumvallation
B:	breach	J:	supply park
C:	3rd parallel	K:	artillery park
D:	2nd parallel	L:	HQ
E:	1st parallel	M:	mortar batteries
F:	richochet batteries	N:	camping areas
G:	communication trenches	O:	terminal forts
H:	lines of contravallation	P:	river barrier
		Q:	breaching battery

The siege of an 18th century fortress

FIG. 19

Another type of fortification, fortified camps, capable of sheltering an entire army, played an important role in the strategic thinking of this era. To be effective, however, they had to be sited in a strategic location that also was highly defensible, considerations which the great Russian camp at Drissa in 1812 lacked. By contrast, Wellington's famous Lines of Torres Vedras not only had great natural strength, but they also protected his major port and, if necessary, evacuation beach.[16] The origin of these lines dated back to the early winter of 1809–10, when it appeared that Napoleon, just having defeated Austria, might return in massive strength to finish off the British expeditionary force in Spain. Even by October 1809 Wellington had ordered his Chief of Engineers, Lieutenant-Colonel Fletcher, to begin construction and when Wellington fell back on Lisbon in September 1810 his entire base area was protected by a formidable belt of fortifications.

These lines were not mere field entrenchments, but solid all round defensible works, carefully located to provide mutual support and to minimize the artillery fire that could be brought against them. There were three lines of echelons in depth. The first two, stretching from the Tagus to the Atlantic, were 29 and 22 miles long respectively, supported on either flank by the British navy. In the first line there were 69 works, armed with 319 guns, while the second line had the same number of works and 215 guns. Behind these belt lines there was a third and final defensive perimeter, covering an evacuation beach on the Tagus, 'perhaps the strongest . . . and least likely to be forced'.[17] Although the lines were strong, they were not considered impregnable, and Wellington manned them with Portuguese troops, militia and artillery retaining his British units as a mobile force to seal off any penetration. The all-important factor, according to Jones, were the British troops, 'giving them strength and efficiency in exact proportion to their own . . . a successful defence of the lines depended on the vigilance and rapid movement of the defenders'.[18]

In the event, Masséna finding himself in the middle of an unfriendly area with most supplies destroyed and harassed in the rear by Portuguese and Spanish guerrillas, did not choose to test their strength. Although it seems unlikely that he was totally surprised by the lines as Marbot maintained, he had not taken the reports he had received seriously. The maps indicated that the terrain was flat, in reality it was covered by steep hills, and he had not considered the lines serious obstacles. But, as one of his staff officers observed 'everything was different. . . . The lines were of such extraordinary nature that I dare say there was no other position in the world that could be compared to them.' Behind steep hills, supported on the one side by the ocean and on the other by a wide river, was a great port, an arsenal and supply depot, protected by numerous batteries, considerable manpower, and with open sea communications. 'We could,' he concluded, 'achieve nothing after piercing the first line. Moreover, these works were not of a nature to fall after being outflanked.' And finally, even if the first line was pierced, there was the second line and the field army.[19]

The observation that these works would not fall after being outflanked, pointed out the great weakness of field fortifications. During this period they were generally nothing more than simple earthworks, occasionally gun pits, incapable of all-around defence. The great Russian redoubt at Borodino actually was far more elaborate than most. Originally a simple V-shaped earth rampart, with a large battery behind a parapet, it had been strengthened by wolf pits dug some 100 paces in front of its ditch, and was protected by breastworks extending laterally in its rear. In addition, a double row of palisades was erected across the back, providing additional protection.[20] By contrast most fieldworks, redoubts, *flêches*, or batteries, were at most simple earthworks, with guns placed in embrasures formed of wicker baskets, the *gabions*, a ditch, sometimes with a cleared field of fire in front, but always open to the rear. These fortifications had little means of resistance once the troops defending their flanks had been driven away and fell easily.

Assaults, bombardments, sieges

Attacks on strongly fortified places were bloody affairs, costly to the assailant, often as costly to the defenders, and sometimes, as happened in Spain, civilian casualties outnumbered those suffered by the military. Moreover, because armies during this period did not move with the huge siege trains required for a proper siege according to the Vauban method, they often had to rely on a more rough and ready approach. Sometimes, depending on the character of the commander, strong places surrendered on a mere summons – Gaeta in 1799, Stettin and Magdeburg in 1806 – were examples. Sometimes a place could be rushed in a surprise attack or taken by a ruse. In 1808, their presence on Spanish territory covered by an agreement with the weak government, a French brigade at Pampeluna rushed the gates of the citadel after challenging the garrison to a snowball fight; at Figueras, the French smuggled troops into the fortress in a convoy of allegedly sick men, and similar acts of treachery occurred at San Sebastian and Barcelona.

Lacking either the time or the necessary equipment for a prolonged siege, the attacker sometimes attempted to frighten the garrison into surrender by a short, violent bombardment. Rockets and mortars, the latter often of large size, 10-inch or more, drove the garrisons into their 'bombproof' casements, and if the fortress had not been provided with casemented guns, and most were not, they made the gun emplacements on the ramparts and bastions untenable. Mortar bombs and rockets, however, were extremely erratic and tended to create as much damage among civilian as among military targets. Essentially they provided an 'area bombardment' pattern. In 1807 the British bombarded Copenhagen for three days with mortars, rockets and guns, set fire to half the city and forced the commandant to surrender. But at Flushing the same year, the French commandant was more stubborn and had little regard for the sufferings of the Dutch civilians. Wellington did not care much for this type of assault which alienated potentially friendly populations.

If the attacker had ample time, or merely wanted to contain the garrison, he could settle down to a lengthy blockade. One of the most prolonged sieges of this type was that of Genoa in 1800 where Masséna, besieged by land and sea by the Austrians and British, held on as his supplies ran out. Then his garrison went hungry while civilians died in the streets, about 400–600 daily, and Austrian prisoners starved on their prison barges in the harbour. In the end, Masséna hung on until the French under Napoleon crossed the Alps and on 4 June 1800 he capitulated, marching out the remnants of his garrison with the full honour of war.[21]

By contrast, the siege of Danzig in 1807 was conducted along the classic lines laid down by Vauban. Such an approach took time. Outlying forts had to be reduced, materials for building parallels and batteries had to be brought up, approaches had to be surveyed. Only when these preliminaries were complete could the besiegers open their first parallel. This was done at night by a working party of infantry supervised by engineers. Speed and secrecy were required here to prevent the besieged from bringing down a concentration of fire while the work was in progress. Communication trenches, either zigzag or at an angle avoiding enfilade had to be cut back to some suitable piece of ground in the second stage, while at the same time saps would be dug forward to the second and third parallel. During this process thousands of *gabions*, sandbags, planks and other materials had to be carried forward and the heavy guns had to be moved at night and emplaced before daylight.

The third stage opened when these batteries had been positioned at the crest of the glacis, no further than 500–700 yards from the main fortifications. Their fire would dismantle the enemy batteries and eventually bring down enough of the wall in ruins so that assault troops could go forward across the rubble while the sappers blew in the counterscarp to fill the ditch. For making a breach, engineers considered the 24-pounder the most useful calibre whilst the 18-pounders, effective in dismantling the enemy guns, had far less striking power. All this took much time and effort, but it saved lives. 'The method of attack by skill and industry,' the French manual declared, 'requires indeed a considerable length of time, but it spares the blood of the assailants.'[22]

Danzig, defended by some 14,400 Prussians under General Kalkreuth, was taken by such an approach. To take the fortress, considered essential as a supply port by Napoleon, Marshal Lefevre assembled the best engineers, 45,000 troops, and almost 100 heavy guns and mortars. Siege operations began on 18 March 1807; the first trench was opened during the night of 1 April, the second on 14 April, and the third parallel was completed on 29 April. Kalkreuth, an able if conventional soldier, did his duty. He made a number of sorties, stoutly defended his outworks, but after the main French breaching batteries were established and a major Russian attempt to reinforce the fortress failed, he considered that he had done all he could. Moreover, Napoleon, anxious to gain possession of the port was willing to grant liberal terms. On 27 May the garrison marched out with the honours of war, bayonets, fixed, drums beating and flags flying, not as prisoners of war, though bound by agreement not to fight against the French for one year.[24]

Things were different at Saragossa. Most of the Spanish fortresses were old-fashioned, but many had been strengthened by additional redans, outworks and batteries, and often buildings behind the *enceinte* had been converted into strongpoints forming an additional defence perimeter. An attacker had to fight through the streets, take house after house, and unable to bring cannon to bear would instead have to rely on demolition explosives. Such a siege took place at Saragossa from 19 December 1808 to 20 February 1809. In July 1808, the inhabitants and garrison of Saragossa had joined in beating back a French attack that had already penetrated the *enceinte*, but the French returned in December, pitting some 50,000 troops against an equal number of Spanish military and civilian defenders, including monks, priests, women and even children. After opening the siege it took the besiegers 29 days to break through the main line, only to find themselves confronted by a ring of fortified convents, public buildings, churches and houses. When the attack stalled, one of Napoleon's toughest commanders, Jean Lannes, took over in the third week of January 1809. Facing heavy odds, French engineers bridged the Ebro, dug trenches, and destroyed the town by mines and bombs. Small Coehorn mortars, already obsolete but useful in the narrow streets and alleys were brought in in great numbers, though tunnelling and mining was more effective against the major defended buildings. 'Six new galleries,' General Lejeune remembered, 'had now reached the other side of the Corso, one under the Law Courts, known as La Audienca, another beneath the theatre, and the other four beneath the biggest hotels. Each chamber had been charged . . . with 3,000 pounds of powder.' Yet, even after these were exploded bringing down the targets in ruin, resistance continued. Lannes was appalled. 'This,' he reported to Napoleon, 'is unlike any other war; it fills me with horror.' Meanwhile, with the dead unburied, typhoid raged in the city and hundreds were dying daily. Finally, on 20 February 1809, the Spanish commander, Count Palafox, agreed to an armistice. After promising favourable terms, a promise broken when the garrison was taken prisoner, the French made their entry four days later. It had taken 58 days of bitter fighting; two-thirds of the city was totally destroyed. Losses among the defenders were estimated at over 54,000, while the French admitted to 60,000 killed in action, including three generals, and another 6,000 felled by disease.[24]

Although long sieges like those of Genoa and Saragossa were bitter and inflicted enormous casualties, some of the old conventions remained alive and if a city capitulated, the conqueror generally maintained order. But if a fortress was taken by a storm, the result could be a horrifying sack, an orgy of looting, rape and murder.

For the British the five major sieges in the Peninsula, the two sieges of Badajoz, the storming of Ciudad Rodrigo, the failure before Burgos, and the capture of San Sebastian – were costly operations. They were troubled by recriminations and on three occasions success was compromised by atrocities that were a stain on the reputation of Wellington's normally well-disciplined army. Except during the last of these operations, the assault on San Sebastian in 1813, the British efforts were hampered by a lack of adequate siege artillery and a shortage of trained engineers and sappers. Moreover, in four cases apprehensions about the approach of strong relief forces caused the attacks to be pressed more rapidly than perhaps was desirable, with storming parties sent forward when the breaches were barely 'practicable', resulting in heavy losses among the attackers.

The first, and unsuccessful, siege of Badajoz, less well known perhaps than the others, provides a good illustration. When Beresford broke ground before the fortress in May 1811, it was the first major siege operation undertaken by the British since their failure before Dunkirk in 1793. The fortress was rather old-fashioned, but powerful nonetheless, with strong outworks and garrisoned by good French troops. A great amount of engineering supplies had been brought forward for this enterprise – 40 gun platforms, 15 mortar platforms, 1,200 shovels, 1,200 pick-axes, 50 earth rammers, 200 miner's picks, 80,000 bushel-sandbags, as well as tarpaulins, crowbars, spare helves, spades, hammers, broad-axes and other implements. The siege artillery, however, was weak. Its mainstay were ancient 24-pounders, with some of the pieces dating back to the sixteenth century, and a few obsolete howitzers, all gathered up from the Portuguese arsenals, were of limited use. 'The ordnance employed at this siege,' Jones of the Royal Engineers commented, 'besides being of an excessively bad quality, was also totally inadequate in quantity.' The guns, he continued, 'were of brass, false in their bore and already worn by previous service; and the shot were of all shape and diameters, giving a windage from one-tenth to half an inch. The howitzers used as mortars were equally defective with the guns.' Inaccurate, with little striking power, the old guns also could not sustain prolonged rapid fire. After about 10 shots their muzzles began to droop and they had to be restricted to about 80 discharges a day.[25]

In any case, before the siege had much progress, Beresford had to march to repel a relief force at Albuera on 16 May 1811, and when Wellington arrived to resume the attack towards the end of the month he faced the problem of concentrating sufficient strength to besiege the fortress and fend off attempts to relieve it without dangerously weakening any part of his army. Wellington not only had inadequate artillery, but he also lacked trained sappers to prepare a way for his infantry. There were only 25 Royal Military Artificers, as the engineer troops were called, in the entire Peninsula.[26] When on 6 June, a week after reopening his trenches, a storming party went forward, 92 out of 180 were lost. A second equally vain attempt three days later cost 140 casualties, half of them fatal. Two hundred more were killed or wounded by enemy fire in the shallow trenches.

Such assaults on a breach, usually made at night to reduce casualties, were led by a 'forlorn hope', usually a subaltern, two sergeants, and about 25 men. After these had established a toehold, the main attack force moved forward in column, with men carrying ladders, bags stuffed with grass or leaves to fill up the ditch, and axes to cut down obstacles.

The defenders, of course, did their best to seal off the breach. If time permitted the ditch would be cleared of rubble, a palisade would be erected in the breach, *chevaux de frise* (huge beams with blades stuck into them) defensive mines, and other obstacles were placed in the path of the attackers. When the storming-parties came up they were showered with hand grenades, exploding shells and even powder-barrels with lit fuses were rolled down against them. The darkness was illuminated by fireballs, burning bales of wool dipped in oil, and anything else that ingenuity could devise. And in the breach, and on the sides and ramparts adjoining the narrow gap, picked men, often issued with several double-shotted muskets, kept up a heavy fire on the troops attempting to work their way up through the rubble, obstacles, and explosions. Often enough it was suicidal business, yet, as Rifleman Costello complained, unlike the French who rewarded survivors of forlorn hopes with commissions and the Legion of Honour, the greatest reward British troops received was a laurel arm badge (issued only to the 95th; other regiments received no recognition at all).[27]

After his two attempts to storm the fortress failed, and with Marshal Soult again approaching in great strength, Wellington raised the siege and retired on 16 June. In his report, he praised the conduct of all ranks and blamed the inadequacy of his siege artillery for the repulse. But in a later comment he added that 'I believe the failure in the attack is . . . to be attributed to the want of experience in the British army'. The breaching batteries, he maintained, ought to have been placed on the crest of the glacis and care should have been taken to prevent the enemy from strengthening the breach by keeping up a continued fire.[28] He repeated these sentiments the following year after the successful attack on Badajoz, complaining to Quartermaster-General Murray, that he hoped that in the future 'armies will be equipped for sieges with the people necessary to carry them on as they ought to be', and that in particular the engineers would learn how to site their guns properly and learn how to blow in the counterscarp, instead of leaving the 'poor officers and troops to get in and across the ditch as they can'. This, of course, aroused controversy in later years, with Jones of the Royal Engineers asserting that the guns had been properly placed, but that there had been not enough ammunition to keep up fire on the breaches to prevent the enemy from fortifying them with obstacles.[29]

In any case, when Wellington assailed Ciudad Rodrigo in January 1812, he had a battering train of 34 iron 24-pounders, though in April at Badajoz, he had to rely on the loan of 18-pounders from the Royal Navy. Later in 1812, following his victory at Salamanca, he unwisely attempted to storm Burgos with little artillery, only three 18-pounders and five howitzers, and a crippling shortage of ammunition and engineers. Only at San Sebastian, in July and August of 1813, did he have a really strong siege artillery, almost 100 heavy iron pieces. At Badajoz, Ciudad Rodrigo, and San Sebastian, however, the storming was followed by an orgy of drunken rape and murder. At Ciudad Rodrigo the troops, Bell wrote, were 'really mad with excitement, furious, intoxication, disorder, and tumult everywhere prevailed; discipline and restraint were disregarded, the troops committed the most terrible deeds'. And at Badajoz, a bloody assault costing the British–Portuguese forces over 1,000 dead and over 6,000 wounded, Bell remembered that 'for two days the town was in possession of the victorious and it may be well to draw a veil over the misdeeds of men stained with the blood of their comrades. . . . The scenes that took place in the town were frightful, not fit to be recorded.'[30] Until the third day, Wellington either could or would not, the evidence here is contradictory, halt the disorders. And then he only brought the troops under control by ordering the provost's men in with their gallows.

The storming of San Sebastian on 31 August 1813 again resulted in horrors, both accidental and deliberate, 'a sack', Lady Longford concluded, 'more murderous than Badajoz'.[31] It is only fair to record that this was the first time the British army had so disgraced itself since Cromwell had taken Wexford and that the French did not do better at Cordova and Oporto, or the Russians in Warsaw. Modern writers claim that long and murderous sieges create a psychotic state, finding release in murder, rape and indiscriminate bloodshed after a climactic assault.

Street-fighting under any conditions was detested by the troops and always was bloody. The narrow streets, burning houses, and total confusion were characteristic of all such encounters. The small engagement in Ebelslerg in Carinthia, on 3 May 1809, during which the town was partially incinerated, cost the Austrians and French each over 1,000 killed, half of whom were miserably burned to death in the houses. Two days later, when Henri Beyle, better known as Stendhal, then a French staff officer, rode through the town he noted that the streets still were lined with charred and partially burned corpses. It was, he recorded, like a scene out of hell.[32] And in Toulouse in 1814 the French, fighting a rearguard action against the British, deliberately fired houses as they slowly retreated before pressure. Bell commented that such fighting was 'ugly, dangerous work . . . so many holes and corners, hiding places and loopholes, where one may be picked off by an unseen enemy'.[33]

Engineers, sappers and miners
Although sieges, investments, bridging operations, demolitions, and other activities required a considerable number of technical troops – engineers, sappers, miners and pontooneers – only the French had an adequate establishment. Every army, to be sure, had corps of engineers, but these were officers-only bodies, charged with the design and construction of permanent works, bridges, and the supervision of sieges. At best, commissioned personnel numbered a few hundred. Napoleon always tried to increase the number and already on 30 November 1799 ordered that the quota of students in the engineering school be raised from 20 to 30 and that engineers and gunners be given the same training. Eventually, he was training several hundred engineers annually. The same method was followed in England where engineers and gunners took the same courses at the Royal Military Academy at Woolwich. Originally each class had between 80–90 students, but after 1803 the number increased to over 150 annually. The curriculum emphasized what today would be called physics, mathematics, chemistry, and architectural drawing.[34]

Other armies during the period proceeded along very similar lines, though none had sufficient engineers for their needs. The shortage was aggravated by the fact that casualties among engineer officers were often heavy; at Saragossa, for instance, 27 out of 40 engineers present, including their commander, General Lacoste, were either killed or wounded. Despite the shared risks, there existed animosity between engineer and line officer, who resented the fact that for most physical work, digging, tunnelling, and carrying, working parties had to be furnished by the infantry. Captain Blaze, perhaps not a totally reliable witness, tells that when an engineer reproached some grenadiers for slowing down digging entrenchments before Wagram, their captain immediately challenged him to a duel.

As for enlisted personnel, the French had by far the most, about 10,000 men. Under the Republic, such units had been in short supply, but during the Empire there existed between six to nine battalions, supplemented by labour units made up from prisoners of war. Technical troops included the miners, previously attached to the artillery, but transferred at Carnot's insistence to the control of the engineers. After 1809, each corps had a battalion of enlisted engineers and a company of miners, well supplied with tools, including 1,700 pick-axes, 170 miner's picks, 1,700 shovels, 680 felling axes, and other implements. In addition, each unit carried demolition stores, field forges, and other materials, transported in 35 wagons.[35] The scale and quality of the French equipment was envied by the British. Wellington repeatedly complained about the shoddy 'cutlery' supplied to his troops, while Bell remembered the 'useless and most disgraceful tools furnished by the Storekeeper-General's office in England', and concluded that the 'sieges carried on by the British in Spain were a succession of butcheries, because the commonest materials and the means necessary for their art, were denied the engineers'.[36] It is rather hard to judge the validity of this claim; soldiers always tend to prefer the enemy's equipment – and the same complaints were heard in both World Wars. Still, whenever possible, the British re-equipped themselves with captured French tools and in 1812, Wellington provided a field pack of 25 mules carrying engineer stores for each of his divisions.

Under the Empire, pontooneers and their bridging train remained part of the artillery, though the engineers also had bridge-building capacity; for instance, it was engineers who constructed the boat-bridges over the Danube in 1809 and repaired them when they were destroyed by floating Austrian barges. They were assisted on this occasion by the Marines of the Imperial Guard.[37] The finest hour of the pontooneers came during the crossing of the Beresina, but on this occasion there were quarrels between them and the engineers over who was to build the two bridges, resolved only by Napoleon who ordered that each organization should build one and that they should get on with it.[38] In the end, there was glory enough for all, and even Lieutenant Chevalier of the *Garde Chasseurs* had to admire their devotion as they worked in the icy water, and he conceded that their death from exhaustion and exposure was no less glorious than that on the battlefield.[39]

In the other armies technical troops were available only in small numbers. By 1810, Austria had four battalions of sappers and miners and one of pontooneers; Prussia mustered two of engineers, and Russia fielded about the same number. The British army, however, managed to have two separate corps under different jurisdictions. The Board of Ordnance was responsible for engineers and in the period following the American Revolution raised a body of enlisted men, the Royal Military Artificers, craftsmen for work on permanent fortifications and other installations both at home and abroad. Stationed usually for long periods in one location, these units often were undisciplined, overrun with women, children, and domestic animals. There were only about 600 of these men, and during the war they did not receive good replacements. Above all, however, the Board of Ordnance greatly cherished its independent status and even in wartime was not necessarily prepared to cooperate with field commanders. In 1799, therefore, the Duke of York established a separate engineer corps of his own, the Royal Staff Corps, consisting of five companies, four officers and 50 men each. In the Peninsula the corps was attached to the Quartermaster-General and carried out the usual engineering duties. Wellington had units from both corps under his command and there was surprisingly little friction. As the campaigns continued, the Royal Military Artificers became more of a field force, attaining a maximum strength of 32 companies in four battalions, and in 1813 were retitled the Royal Sappers and Miners.

Medical Services

The medical history of the campaigns of the French Revolution and Napoleon is often neglected in military accounts.[40] But the importance of the medical services cannot be overestimated. The novel methods of warfare, emphasizing battle, seeking quick victory and pressing operations regardless of season, demanded drastic improvements in the organization and practice of all military medicine. But, except for minor modifications, this did not happen. Compared to the attention given to tactics, strategy, and technology, relatively little thought was given to the treatment of casualties, battlefield evacuation, the administration of hospitals, and the training of medical personnel. With primitive techniques and little support from high authorities, medical services everywhere found themselves outmatched by the greatly accelerated pace of operations, the unprecedented number of casualties, and high disease rates.

When the wars began in 1792 the state of military medicine had barely changed in a century. Medical services in all armies remained compartmentalized with sharp distinctions and often much conflict between physicians, surgeons, and apothecaries, reflecting the same distinctions in civilian life.[41] To coordinate efforts, there usually existed at the highest level the officer of Physician-General, Surgeon-General, and Apothecary-General, sometimes combined in one board. In peacetime permanent military hospitals were maintained in large garrisons; on campaigns field, also called 'flying' or 'marching' hospitals, followed the army. In theory at least, a surgeon, sometimes with an assistant, was attached to each regiment. Arrangements for handling battlefield casualties remained primitive with hospitals normally set up several miles to the rear to which the wounded either dragged themselves or were helped by their comrades. The severely wounded would remain on the field, to be collected after action ceased, hours or even days later during which time sepsis, peritonitis and dehydration took their toll. At the hospital surgeons, working under severe pressure, unclean conditions, and with primitive instruments often performed considerable feats of timing and dexterity, but suffering was great and the mortality rate high. Operative procedures were limited to the amputation of shattered limbs, though if there was time, surgeons might probe for and extract bullets, shell fragments, and other foreign objects. The surgeons usually worked alone, while his assistants held the limb to be amputated and restrained the patient. Ligatures and tourniquets came into use early during the eighteenth century and were a great bonus for operations on the extremities.[42] If the patient survived the shock and the infection following this procedure, he found himself in a hospital where various contagious fevers decimated the population. In fact, even if there was little action (and in the eighteenth century generals tried to avoid them) diseases, their origin still not understood, compounded by poor sanitation, an unsatisfactory diet, unsuitable uniforms and physical exhaustion, caused a very high sick rate, 10 and 12 percent by the end of a campaigning season.

By the middle of the century Sir John Pringle, an army physician and later a baronet and physician to George III laid down rules for hospital and camp hygiene, ventilation, diet, adequate latrines and drainage. He was also the first to suggest that hospitals should be regarded as neutral ground. His work was continued by Dr John Monro who offered practical suggestions on the preservation of the health of the common soldier during campaigns. But implementation of these sensible recommendations was quite another matter. On the practical level responsibility for the treatment of casualties, the care of the sick, and the supervision of troop hygiene fell to the regimental surgeons, usually men of humble origin and little education, barely removed from their demeaning association with barbers. On campaigns, in small garrisons, and isolated stations these men often were the only medical officers and acting by necessity as physicians, they did their best to convince hostile or sceptical commanders of the need for preventive medicine, sanitation and a proper diet. Their task was made difficult by the fact that although nominally ranked as officers, they occupied a lowly position in the army hiearchy and generally were neither considered soldiers nor gentlemen. But very slowly the humble army surgeon was emerging as an all round medical officer, as Sir John Hunter, Surgeon-General of the British army from 1790–3 put it, he was the 'fittest to take care of the soldier in his accumulated state'.[43]

The outbreak of conflict in 1792, with 23 years of almost constant campaigning did much to continue this development; on the other hand, with casualties and sick lists mounting, medical services in all armies remained inadequate. Progress was made in battlefield surgery by such men as Larrey, Percy, and Guthrie, and there were innovations in casualty evacuation, but with rising numbers of men, surgeons were scarce, neither hygiene or sanitation could be enforced, and many generals considered medical arrangements an expensive luxury.

French medical services, 1792–5

The French medical service, especially under Napoleon, is often described as the best and most progressive of all the armies. This was true, though by 1813 Wellington's medical arrangements in the Peninsula matched the French in efficiency. But even at its best, the French medical service was inadequate. One recent writer has suggested that under the Convention medical service was of a high quality, and that it deteriorated only under the autocratic Napoleonic regime. This judgment is backed up by a history of the French medical service which asserts: 'The Empire scorned humanity . . . the abandonment and disdain of the wounded was the rule in its armies. The decadence of the medical service is one of its major faults.'[44] But these conclusions must be regarded as tainted by political leanings, an overly strong faith in the 'humanitarianism' of the Jacobins, and by a refusal to recognize that the Directory already had dismantled the medical service. For that matter, arrangements were none too good even under the Jacobins.

By the end of the *ancien régime* the military hospitals that had been fairly well organized under Louis XIV had been broken up. Attempts to modernize the medical service in 1772 and 1788 had dismantled most of the old structure, but nothing had been put in its place. At the outbreak of the Revolution the French army's medical service was in a state of near chaos. The National Assembly reorganized it provisionally in 1790 and when war broke out there were about 4,000 physicians, surgeons, apothecaries and assistants. Of this number about 800 were surgeons. Their utilization, however, was limited, and surgeons with the armies complained of a lack of medicines, bandages and beds. Moreover, most of the medical personnel was stationed at the permanent hospitals originally built by Vauban and in the field, rapid troop movement made it impossible for the hospitals to follow the soldiers. Finally, during the first 18 months of the war, over 600 doctors were lost in battle whilst many others disappeared in the revolutionary turmoil. In 1792 the National Assembly passed a series of laws aiming to provide greater autonomy and independence for medical officers in the field and freeing them from the direct supervision of field commanders. This new approach, combined with the genuine national enthusiasm of that year attracted many volunteers and by January 1793 there were some 2,750 surgeons and physicians with the armies. But with the rapid growth of armies later that year, the Committee of Public Safety issued a decree in August, making all physicians, surgeons, medical students, and pharmacists between the ages of 18 and 40 liable for military service. The same month, however, acting in an excess of egalitarian zeal, the Convention closed down all universities, colleges and academies in France, including 18 faculties of medicine and 15 colleges of surgery, thus preventing the training of more military physicians.[45]

To replace doctors, the Convention authorized the training of assistant surgeons in military hospitals at Strasbourg, Lille, Metz, and Toulon, all within the immediate zone of operations. This clearly would not produce many new surgeons. Instead, anyone with even the slightest knowledge of medicine was appointed as a military surgeon and by the end of 1793 the number of medical officers with the Republican armies had risen to 4,000. In addition, the Convention ordered the foundation of three National Schools of Health, at Strasbourg, Paris, and Montpelier where, until discontinued in 1798, 550 students annually, chosen for their revolutionary sentiments as much as for their talents, 'hastily memorized many facts, learned some technical skills, and then were sent off to complete their apprenticeship on the battlefield'.[46] Medical training was very much like the process by which recruits learned their trade on the battlefield and it yielded similar results. By 1794, though their proficiency left much to be desired, the number of medical men in the armies, including physicians, surgeons, assistant surgeons, pharmacists, and the new *officiers de santé*, reached an imposing 9,000 men.

The quality of medical care varied according to the qualification and the dedication of medical officers and the availability of medical supplies. In general, hospitals were still unable to keep up with mobile operations and many base hospitals were in a deplorable condition. On taking command of the Army of the Eastern Pyrenees in 1794, General Dugommier declared that the hospitals could ruin the most robust health. Soldiers dreaded them and did their best to avoid them.[47] But the Revolution also permitted two outstanding battlefield surgeons and innovators – Pierre-François Percy, a former royal army surgeon, and Dominique-Jean Larrey, a former naval surgeon – to develop new medical procedures and methods. Both became famous under the Empire. Larrey's fame, in fact, was world wide. Wellington and Blücher respected him whilst Napoleon pronounced him the 'most virtuous man I have ever known'.

Larrey, a front-line soldier who, by the end of his career, had altogether been in 60 battles and almost 400 engagements, was convinced that the wounded should be treated during and not after battle. Rapid treatment, he was sure, improved recovery chances manifold. This required a speedy and systematic casualty evacuation, and also bringing the surgical stations closer to the battle line. While serving with the Army of the Rhine in late 1792, Larrey conceived 'flying hospitals', the term *ambulances volantes* applying both to the forward surgical stations and to casualty evacuation vehicles. At first Larrey organized teams of three mounted surgeons and one orderly with extra horses carrying surgical instruments, bandages, and other litters for the transport of the wounded. But the litters were found impracticable and while serving with the Army of Italy in 1796, Larrey perfected the prototype of his casualty evacuation vehicle – light, enclosed wagons with strong springs in which the stretchers were suspended. One side of the wagon could be completely opened so that a seriously wounded man could be placed and removed in a horizontal position without having to be shifted. Bandages and medicaments were carried in special compartments and side pockets of these wagons. Eventually two- and four-wheeled models were developed, the first capable of carrying two stretchers, the other four. Larrey's invention became the basis for the French medical evacuation vehicles during the Empire.[48]

Larrey accompanied Napoleon on his expedition to Egypt, but Percy continued his work with the Army of the Rhine. By 1792 he had organized the first units of stretcher bearers whose task it was to collect the wounded on the battlefield. His next innovation was the modification of artillery caissons, the Wurst wagons, into makeshift medical vehicles. These were not used for transporting the wounded, but to bring up medical supplies and dressing, each converted caisson carrying sufficient dressings for 1,200 casualties. Mounted male attendants accompanied the caissons, while nine surgeons rode astride the wagons.

Percy, however, ran into unexpected opposition. In Paris the Directory was remaining in power solely with the goodwill of the army, and the army now had become more professional and much more under the control of its officers who had never really accepted the army surgeons and health officers as equals and resented the legislative acts of 1792–4 that had tried to make them so. In 1798, therefore, the Directory abrogated the authority of medical officers to make independent decisions in the field and in an exercise of pettiness also deprived them of their horses, making them march alongside their regiments. This measure aroused Percy's violent opposition, but to no avail.[49] Military commanders also opposed the introduction of new ambulances. 'Some thought,' Percy wrote in anger, 'that it might have been a dangerous spectacle to see medical officers ride, since a system of ill-will, oppression, and humiliation had long condemned them to walk . . . they should walk and be miserable, otherwise, some administrators said they would become too cocky.'[50] Going one step further, in March 1799 the Directory established an administrative board of non-medical officers and generals to supervise the medical services.

This was the situation when Napoleon returned from Egypt and assumed full powers in December 1799. During his expedition in the East he had been confronted by new disease, opthalmia and the bubonic plague, the latter assuming serious proportions during his advance into Palestine. In confronting these problems, Napoleon had given his full backing to Larrey and had fearlessly visited the plague victims and during the retreat from Acre he had ordered that all horses be utilized to evacuate the wounded, dismounting himself and marching on foot. But these gestures were carefully calculated to maintain troop morale; basically Napoleon disliked dictors, distrusted medication and his attitude towards the medical service, as towards so much else, was governed by expediency. In his later years, when he had more troops than in Egypt, he was prepared to accept greater casualties rather than to encumber the movement of his armies with elaborate and costly medical arrangements. He would also listen to Larrey and Percy whom he personally respected; he would make promises to them which he usually failed to make good.

As First Consul, Napoleon had the opportunity to reorganize the medical service along with the rest of the army, but he gave it a very low priority. In fact, soon after the Treaty of Lunéville he began to discharge hundreds of medical officers. Between 1801 and 1804 the number of medical officers declined from 210 physicians and 1,655 surgeons to 62 physicians and 842 surgeons. At the same time, a number of military hospitals were abolished and even the so-called teaching hospitals were dissolved. Napoleon did not consider the medical officers as an integral part of his army. 'The army medical service,' he decreed in 1802, 'is based on temporary commissions only . . . strictly speaking, there is no medical corps.'[51] This attitude is difficult to explain. It has been suggested that Napoleon expected a long period of peace after the Treaty of Amiens, but the evidence also shows that he expected a renewal of hostilities, at least against England, in the near future. In any case, his miscalculation would exact a heavy toll during his subsequent campaigns.

When hostilities on land began again in 1805 his medical services were, inevitably, inadequate and demoralized. Denied regular status within the military organization, the doctors were now administered by a narrow-minded bureaucracy and at the same time subject to the demands of the field commanders who, like their master, often assigned a very low priority to medical needs. During the 1805 campaign the troops were fresh and initially casualties were low, but after Austerlitz, only the utilization of civilian facilities saved the army from medical disaster. For the campaign against Prussia in 1806, Larrey organized six flying ambulance detachments, each with its own transport and evacuation vehicles, one detachment to each corps. But these detachments never reached their full establishment and the heaviest burden continued to be carried by the regimental surgeons.

There was, to be sure, an increase in numbers. In 1804, the medical faculties and colleges had been reopened and new military surgeons, not always the most dedicated men Larrey complained, were recruited. By 1806, 1,051 surgeons were available, but Napoleon still would not admit them to fully equality within the army. After Eylau, Percy suggested to the emperor the creation of a permanent surgical corps, and although Napoleon showed some interest, he never followed up on this proposal. He continued to honour Percy and Larrey, but he also continued to mistrust doctors in general. 'The inexperience of surgeons,' he complained in 1812, 'does more harm to the army than the enemy's batteries.'[52] This complaint, made after Borodino where medical services broke down, was unjustified. The emperor had made inadequate medical preparations for the campaign. Although there now were 11 medical companies, that is flying hospital detachments, they could not cope with the enormous number of casualties. Over 400,000 men crossed the Niemen, but even before the first great battle, Smolensk, the army had lost most of its horses and medical vehicles were among the first to be abandoned. One commentator, Clausewitz, held that Napoleon's medical and sanitation preparations were totally inadequate and that the lack of food, supplies and medicaments were the most important factors in the destruction of the Grand Army.[53]

The one corps in Napoleon's army with an excellent medical service was the Imperial Guard. It had its own physicians and surgeons, its own hospitals, ambulances and trained attendants. As for the entire Guard, the pay for medical officer was much higher than in the rest of the army. The chief physician, surgeon, and apothecary of the Guard were paid 9,690 francs a year, over three times the salary of any other army doctor. On the battlefield, Guard casualties received priority attention, they were given special care in hospitals and, better fed and clothed than other troops, they had a much higher recovery rate. But even this privileged medical service broke down in Russia. A surgeon of the Imperial Guard complained that there was 'a drastic lack of transportation, food, medical supplies and drugs. Several days after a battle one could still find wounded men who had not been helped. They would die of hunger rather than of their wounds.'[54]

Austrian, Prussian, Russian and British medical services
For all its shortcomings the French medical service was the envy of other armies whose arrangements remained, by and large, even more lamentable. The Austrian medical service had an excellent and highly learned training school, the Medical-Surgical Academy, also called the *Josephinium*, established in 1795 in Vienna. Its head, Anton Beinl Edler v. Bienenburg, also served as chief medical officer of the army. There were about 120 staff-physicians and a surgeon or an assistant surgeon was attached to each regiment. Military surgeons were trained at a special school established at the Military hospital in Gumpendorf in 1781. In addition, there was a special Military Pharmacy Department with some 20 apothecaries. Medical officers were assisted by a special corps of orderlies, but were rated as military officials rather than as officers, and in the army list, the *Militär-Schematismus*, they appeared at the very bottom, just above the Commissariat.

Its performance in the field was mediocre at best. There never was a full complement of surgeons, while the senior staff-physicians were described as scared of contagion and refused to come close to their patients.[55]. The service was saved from total collapse by the devoted care given to Austrian wounded by civilian institutions, above all religious nursing orders.

The Prussian medical service was perhaps even worse. Frederick the Great had been little concerned with severely wounded soldiers and rumour had it that surgeons had been instructed to let patients die if they were unlikely to return to active duty. As in most other armies, the medical service was directed by Surgeon-General, *General-Chirugus*, and the Physician-General, *General-Stabs-Medicus*, and there was also a small pharmaceutical department. At the regimental level there were *Feldscher*, surgeons, who in theory had to be graduates of an accredited medical school, and at the outset of a campaign received a lump sum to hire assistants. On paper then, the Prussian medical service was much like that in other armies, but it had done poorly in the Seven Years' War and been neglected in the last years of Frederick's reign.

In 1795 Surgeon-General Johann Goercke founded a Medical-Surgical Institute, the so-called *Pepiniere* in Berlin, to provide a better educated and a more adequate supply of regimental surgeons. In 1806 every regiment or independent battalion was to have a surgeon or at least an assistant-surgeon, with two packhorses to carry his supplies, but in practice there never were enough. During the long retreat medical arrangements broke down and many thousands perished in 1806–7 from want of attention. As in Austria, civilian facilities afforded some relief, and the hospitals of Konigsberg, a university town, were reputed to be excellent.

The Prussian military reformers have some attention to improving military medicine, but shortages of funds and materiel forced them to rely on civilian support. By August 1813, however, the Prussian army had three general hospitals with 1,200 beds each, nine field hospitals with 200 beds each, and a considerable back-up capacity in various civilian hospitals established in major towns. But battlefield arrangements were poor; in 1813 there only were three ambulance vehicles for the entire army.

In Russia, medical services were based on the Prussian pattern and, if anything, were even more rudimentary. In 1798, Paul I had founded an Academy of Military Medicine in St Petersburg, but its output of physicians and surgeons was small. In the field, the Russian troops were accompanied by poorly trained *Feldschers*, the word like so many other military terms, borrowed from the German. Most of the higher-ranking medical officers and many others were foreigners, referred to as 'Germans' by the troops and disliked by the Russians who did not trust doctors or their medications. Suvorov had warned his men against 'German medicines and hospitals', and Platov, the Cossack leader, felt the same. When asked by the tsar if he needed additional surgeons for his troops, he is reported to have replied ' 'God and your Majesty forbid, the fire of the enemy is not half as fatal as one drug'.[56]

During the 1805–7 campaigns, Russian hospitals were atrocious. On one occasion soldiers at Riga approached the tsar and complained that their wounds had not been dressed for over two weeks and that they had not received any food for days. Wilson recorded that the tsar listened graciously to their pleas, but he does not tell whether anything was done. Most likely not. The Russians were callous towards their wounded; at Friedland, Wilson was shocked to hear a senior officer remark that 'a cannon ball was the best doctor for men without limbs'.[57]

The reforms of 1810 did not alleviate the medical situation, especially the shortage of doctors and supplies. During the fighting at Jakubovo (30 July to 1 August 1812) where 23,000 Russians were engaged, suffering 4,300 casualties, only two surgeons were available to treat the wounded. Even the Russian Minister of the Interior, Kozodavlev was appalled. 'There is a complete shortage of medicine and bandages,' he reported to the tsar, 'and the worms are eating many of the wounded alive.'[58] It was the same after Borodino where the abbey at Kolotskoye was filled with wounded and sick, and no bandages, food or medicine. But, as always, there were exceptions. Gunner Wesemann of the 1st Westphalian Artillery, taken prisoner at the Beresina, recounts that near Velikije Luki he was put in a hospital run by a German doctor where there were 'beds for everyone, with fresh linen and good food', and that most of the patients recovered.[59]

The British medical service, finally, was the least centralized and even by contemporary standards most archaically administered. Yet, under Wellington's constant prodding, and with the assistance of able men like Drs McGrigor and Guthrie, it became at long last, in the Peninsula at least, also one of the most efficient. Since 1793 it was under the supervision of a Medical Board composed of the Physician-General, the Surgeon-General, and the Inspector-Generals of Hospitals, elderly worthies, who spent most of their time with their private practice, quarrelled with each other, and gave little attention to military affairs. Their mishandling of medical arrangements during and after the evacuation from Corunna caused angry recriminations from medical officers and a parliamentary investigation. But the next year, when a British army was dying from disease on Walcheren, not one of the Board members saw fit to make a personal visit to the scene. The government, nearly brought down by a parliamentary vote over the outcome of this expedition, now dismissed the three incumbents and early in 1810 appointed three army doctors to a new board.[60]. New regulations improved the functioning of this body, but it still remained less than responsive to the requirements of the field army. When Wellington complained about it from Portugal, the Duke of York's military secretary replied that the commander in chief agreed, 'the Medical Board is the torment of his life', but that little could be done about it.[61]

The Board was responsible only for personnel. Supply was handled by two other officials, the Purveyor-General and the Apothecary-General who supplied surgical equipment, medicaments, and other such items to the hospitals. Regimental surgeons, however, had to furnish their own separate medical service, subject to most of the same limitations.

At the working level, medical officers were divided into two major categories. Staff surgeons and physicians were in charge of medical arrangements for armies or large base hospitals; the soldiers' immediate care was in the hand of the regimental surgeons and assistant surgeons, since 1751 commissioned officers. Regimental surgeons ranked as captains and assistant surgeons as lieutenants. Until 1793, the appointment of regimental surgeons was in the hands of the colonels and purchase was not rare; thereafter it became a responsibility of the Medical Board. In theory the qualifications of the surgeons had to be attested either by the Physician or Surgeon General, or the London College of Physicians and Surgeons, but with the demand far outrunning supply, standards were relaxed. Sometimes surgeon's mates were promoted; more often placards at the college gates at Dublin, Edinburgh, and Glasgow offered commissions to any student who could pass a cursory examination. In 1811, the Medical Board admitted to Dr Franck, then Wellington's inspector of hospitals, that 'the urgent demands lately made for hospital assistance have compelled us to receive into the Service, several who under other circumstances would not have been admitted'.[63] The troops suspected as much. In his reminiscences Private James Donaldson of the 94th, a man of some education, offered the opinion that the new surgeons 'were chiefly, I believed, composed of apothecary boys, who, having studied a session or two, were thrust into the army'.

Conditions improved slowly. Unlike Napoleon, Wellington realized that he could not draw upon unlimited manpower and he tried to prevent wastage of men due to the lack of medical attention. After Talavera, he pointed out to Lord Liverpool, the Secretary of State for War and Colonies, that among the reasons that had compelled him to fall back rather than to continue his advance was the 'want of surgeons with the army', so acute that 'if we had an action, we should not have been able to dress our wounded'. And for the next two years he continued to plead with higher authorities for more and better medical personnel, at the same time constantly reminding his subordinate commanders of the need to preserve the health of their men.[64]

But his efforts achieved little. Dr Franck was not a man to take any initiative and only after he was replaced in January 1812 by Dr James McGrigor, an experienced and contentious Scot, was there major improvement in the medical services in the Peninsula. McGrigor improved hospitals, diet, and set up a system for keeping medical statistics. He was greatly concerned with speedier evacuation of casualties, though his proposal for adopting French-style ambulances was rejected by Wellington. He did, however, succeed in obtaining prefabricated hospitals from England and during the great advance in 1813 he set up a chain of efficiently run hospitals to the French frontier.[65] Although he occasionally clashed with Wellington, he won his reluctant admiration and on his insistence the work of army doctors was mentioned for the first time in dispatches. In January 1814, Wellington wrote to his brother, Sir Henry Wellesley, that 'I can only say that during the five years that I have commanded the army, I have never known it so healthy as it is, and has been since the month May last'.[66] Although death from disease still remained greater than fatalities incurred in combat – about three to one – McGrigor had achieved much. He was rewarded by appointment as Director-General of the Medical Board, and unhappily was absent during the Waterloo campaign where there was again a shortage of regimental surgeons and of medical evacuation vehicles.

The practice of surgery on the battlefield

The exertions by Larrey, Percy, McGrigor and others to alleviate the miseries of war by bringing prompt relief to the wounded on the battlefield were great humanitarian ventures, but in practice the number of surgeons and other facilities were far too limited to have much effect. In most battles the severely wounded, friend or foe alike, still remained unattended for hours, even days. Hardened campaigners like Coignet, Costello, or Harris remembered their agonized cries throughout the long night, and usually could not offer any assistance. And this was true from the very first to the last battle. At Waterloo, Morris comforted wounded men as best he could as long as daylight lasted, but with his canteen empty he could give them nothing to quench their terrible thirst. Then he and the wounded had to wait until daylight when carts arrived to take the survivors to Brussels.[67]

There always were only a very few of Larrey's new ambulances and wagons, carts, even wheelbarrows were pressed into service. At Leipzig both French and Allied medical preparations were totally inadequate. 'Neither stretchers nor wagons had been provided for carrying away these mutilated men,' one horrified eyewitness recorded.[68] In Spain, lumbering unsprung oxcarts and even mules were used to evacuate casualties. 'The only conveyance for these poor cripples with broken arms and legs,' Bell wrote, 'were some mules sent up by the commissary. Two men were placed on each mule, with their broken limbs bandaged up in a way and dangling down.' Only a few survived this particular trip to a base hospital.[69]

The walking wounded staggered or dragged themselves into the house, barn, church, or courtyard used as forward surgery stations. On occasion they were assisted by friends, but since this withdrew men from the battleline it was expressly forbidden. 'The wounded who cannot move themselves,' Napoleon ordered after Wagram, 'will stay on the field. In the name of honour, it is forbidden to quit the battlefield to help casualties to the rear.' At the surgical stations surgeons wielded knife, bone-saw, and probe among a foul mess of blood, rags, dirt and amputated limbs. Private Harris described such a scene in a graveyard near Vimeiro. 'Two long tables had been procured from some houses near and were placed end to end among the graves, and upon them were laid the men whose limbs it was found necessary to amputate. Both French and English were constantly lifted on and off these tables . . . and the surgeons, with their sleeves turned up, and their hands and arms covered with blood, looking like butchers in the shambles.' Morris recalled a similar scene in a church in 1813 when he was detailed to assist the surgeons. 'We carried the wounded to the operating table, holding them while the operation was performed and then depositing them on the floor . . . and occasionally, carrying away such of them as had died. . . . In the morning there was a stack of amputated limbs besides the altar.'[70]

On occasion surgeons operated under fire, and almost always worked under immense pressure. At Talavera, for instance, George J. Guthrie, sometimes called the 'English Larrey', had to take care of over 3,000 casualties, with only the surgeons' personal kits carried in the mule panniers. From necessity then, surgical procedures had to be fast and simple. To operate, surgeons had only a limited number of instruments, typically knives and scalpels, saws, tourniquets, forceps, probes, elevators, and various straight and curved needles. In addition they had a supply of lint, sponges, linen, adhesive plaster, pins, thread, wax, sometimes a little opium and a canteen of spirits or wine.[70] In order to speed up operations, a procedure advocated by Larrey and Guthrie, surgeons commonly amputated the limb at the joint above the injured region, avoiding the time consuming and agonizing probing for balls, fragments, and other foreign objects. New techniques, the use of the tourniquet and the extraction of foreign bodies through counter-incision became common and if time permitted wounds were closed by ligation. There were, of course, no anaesthetics, and no antiseptics except vinegar, sometimes an extract of turpentine. Under the knife men struggled, but usually they submitted with remarkable composure. A French surgeon noted a trooper of the Old Guard sitting on his horse watching calmly. He asked the man what he was doing and the trooper turned his mount to reveal a shattered leg. He was waiting for his turn to be amputated.[71] And such calmness and composure was frequent.

Post-surgery recovery varied enormously, depending on the location of the injury, the condition of the patient, and the quality of the care. Larrey maintained that if a casualty was treated within 24 hours his chances for recovery were almost 75 per cent. But this was a far too optimistic estimate. In general, the chances hovered around 50 percent, though the privileged Imperial Guard did in fact do better. Of 1,200 guardsmen operated on after Wagram, 600 returned to duty within several days, 254 including 38 amputees, were evacuated to France, 145 died of their wounds, 80 recovered completely after a few months, and 150 lived but had to be pensioned off. Proper food and care raised the rate. Figures for a British general hospital during the ten weeks after the end of hostilities in 1814 show that amputations of the extremities had a very low death rate, abdominal surgery had a poor chance, and wounds of the spine and compound fracture had little chance at all. Still, out of 1,242 patients only 146 died under the optimal conditions prevailing here.[72] But this rate of recovery was possible only in a well supplied and managed base hospital. In the field, especially for the common soldier who naturally got less attention than senior officers, the fatality rate was much higher, probably one in two.

Diseases and the conduct of war

Throughout history disease often decided the outcome of campaigns and also had a great, perhaps decisive, influence on the outcome of this conflict. It is, of course, impossible to make an accurate computation of the losses incurred in the 23 years from Valmy to Waterloo, but attempts have been made. One historian of military medicine estimated that of the '4½ million soldiers engaged in the Revolutionary and Napoleonic Armies . . . about 2½ million died in the hospitals and 150,000 were killed in action.[73] The figure seems open to challenge. France alone certainly did not suffer that many fatalities, though the total number for all combatants certainly approached this figure. Then too, the deaths in the hospitals, included post-operative cases. Still, there is no doubt that infectious diseases, the 'ague' and the 'fever', both favourite terms of contemporary medical men covering a wide spectrum of infectious diseases, influenza and malaria, typhus and typhoid fever, yellow fever, and dysentery killed more men than enemy action.

In the West Indies, the 'fever islands', both French and British armies were wiped out. From 1793–6, the British army there lost 40,000 dead, more than the total losses from all causes sustained by Wellington in the Peninsula.[74] But disease decimated armies in Europe too. During the Valmy campaign the Prussians lost several hundred men a day from dysentery; one-third of the Prussian army in Poland in 1794–5 died in the hospitals. Campaigning in the malarial regions of southern Italy in 1806 sent 9,000 men to hospitals, and almost 4,000 died. And in the Peninsula, British fatalities from disease, including a particularly violent form of syphilis, the 'black lion', far exceeded battle casualties. Out of a total of 61,511 troops, 8,889 died from combat-related injuries and 24,930 from sickness.[75] Sometimes the contrast was even more pronounced. Of the 39,214 men sent to Walcheren in April 1809, only 4,000 remained fit for duty when the army was withdrawn in December. There were but 106 battle casualties, but 4,175 died from the 'Walcheren fever', probably a species of malaria. 'Disease, not the bullets or bayonets of the enemy had destroyed an entire army.'[76]

The most spectacular and substantial results of disease during this period was the decimation of Napoleon's Grand Army in Russia. The army, totalling upward of half a million men assembled in cantonments from northern Germany to Italy. Until the main body entered Lithuania and Poland there was little sickness, then the situation deteriorated rapidly. The summer of 1812 was unusually hot, water scarce and bad, and the disease rate for typhus, typhoid, dysentery, and enteric fever reached epidemic proportions. In the first five weeks, Napoleon lost over a third of his troops. Several battle losses compounded the situation, and during the retreat exhaustion and pneumonia added their toll and finished off the army. But this was not all. When Napoleon raised a new army in 1813, the young recruits were particularly susceptible to infection and by the time he stood at Leipzig, preliminary battles and disease had reduced his force to little over 170,000 men against 200,000 allied troops. One estimate is that 105,000 were lost through combat and 219,000 to disease in the months before Leipzig.[77]

French losses to disease in Russia were due to a progressive collapse of the supply arrangements and also to a grave shortage in medications. The army set out with short medical supplies in 1812, perhaps in part due to Napoleon's distrust of medicine. In his earlier directives he always had stressed that the health of troops should be preserved through preventive hygiene and sanitation. In 1811, for instance, he had warned Bertrand not to station French troops in the unhealthy Adriatic littoral. Local troops, Napoleon held, were good enough for such assignments.[78] But in Russia such measures could not be taken. The need to keep his army concentrated for a massive blow against the enemy forced a concentration along a major axis and this heavy congestion spread infections throughout all corps and units.

Other armies failed equally to deal with infectious diseases. Quinine, then called Peruvian bark, was recognized as a valuable medication against fever, but France could not import it, and even the English did not have adequate quantities either in Spain or on Walcheren.[79] Some doctors used a most pragmatic and simple treatment for fever, 'throwing cold water from canteens or mess kettles as often as possible over the bodies of patients'. This, of course, lowered the temperature and often was beneficial. Costello ascribed his recovery to this treatment.[80] But more often nothing was done. Bell reports that when he had the fever the surgeon visited him daily to see if he was still alive. 'He had nothing to give me but a kind and encouraging word.'[81] At that Bell was better off than the fever patients described by Chevalier in a hospital in Calabria. 'The poor patients,' he wrote, 'were all laid on the bare floors, without blankets, water, and without hope. Three hundred died the first day, sixty-five every day thereafter, and it was not until the sixth day that some emetics, purgations, and infusions were administered.'[82] This French hospital was not an isolated exception; one French historian characterized hospitals as the 'tombs of the Grand Army'.[88] Nor were hospitals in other armies much better. The filth, neglect, and general inefficiency which some 40 years later shocked Florence Nightingale were an integral part of military life during this era.

NOTES

1. Wilkinson, *op cit.*, 33; Hittle, *op cit.*, 59–61, 91–8, 104–10.
2. On Berthler and the staff in Italy see M. Reinhard, *Avec Bonaparte en Italie*, Hachette, Paris, 1945, 58–79; Lejeune, *op cit.*, vol. II, 142.
3. O. Regele, *Fieldmarshall Radetzky*, Herold, Vienna, 1957, 136.
4. *The Private Journal of F. Seymour Larpent*, ed. Sir G. Larpent, R. Bentley, 1853, vol. I, 110–11.
5. Pelet, *op cit.*, 168.
6. Chandler, *op cit.*, 371.
7. J.W. Thompson and S.K. Padover, *Secret Diplomacy*, F. Ungar, New York, 1965, 223–45 *passim*.
8. *Ibid.*, 224–6; Pelet, *op cit.*, 223.
9. Coignet, *op cit.*, 138; Chevalier, *op cit.*, 182; Marbot, *op cit.*, vol. I, 315.
10. Schuster, *op cit.*, 99.
11. Gay de Vernon, *op cit.*, vol. II, 242.
12. L.E. Henry, *Napoleon's War Maxims*, Gale & Polden, 1899, 57.
13. Chandler, *op cit.*, 365.
14. Gay de Vernon, *op cit.*, vol. II, 218–19, 223–4; Q. Hughes, *Military Architecture*, St Martin's Press, New York, 1974, 137–41.
15. Fezensac, *op cit.*, 23–4.
16. Jomini, *op cit.*, 141.
17. Jones, *op cit.*, vol. III, 43, 90, 92–6, 99.
18. *Ibid.*, 48.
19. Pelet, *op cit.*, 223, 228, 242.
20. Duffy, *Borodino*, 72, 92.
21. Marbot, *op cit.*, vol. I, 95–8, 110–11.
22. Gay de Vernon, *op cit.*, vol. II, 74, 100.
23. Chandler, *op cit.*, 560–4.
24. Lejeune, *op cit.*, vol. I, 166, 193; Marbot, *op cit.*, vol. II, 99, 101–2.
25. Jones, *op cit.*, vol. I, 71, 345, 352.
26. J.W. Fortescue, *History of the British Army*, Macmillan, 1902, vol. IV, 417.
27. Costello, *op cit.*, 133–4.
28. Jones, *op cit.*, vol. I, 73, 76–80.
29. *Ibid.*, 223–6.
30. Bell, *op cit.*, vol. I, 22–3, 33–5.
31. Longford, *op cit.*, 332.
32. R.W. Litschel, *Das Gefecht bei Ebelsberg am 3. Mai 1809*, Herresgeschichtliches Museum, Vienna, 1968, 18–19.

33. Bell, *op cit.*, vol. I, 165.
34. Glover, *op cit.*, 187–90.
35. Jones, *op cit.*, vol. II, 385–6.
36. Bell, *op cit.*, vol. I, 24, 35.
37. Lejeune, *op cit.*, vol. I, 263–4, 285.
38. Marbot, *op cit.*, vol. III, 195–6.
39. Chevalier, *op cit.*, 232–3.
40. D.B. Weiner, 'French Doctors face War, 1792–1815), in C.K. Warner ed., *From the Ancient Regime to the Popular Press*, Columbia University Press, New York, 1969, 52.
41. L.S. King, *The Medical World of the Eighteenth Century*, University of Chicago Press, 1958, 4–7.
42. O.H. Wangenstern, J. Smith, and S.D. Wangensterm, 'Some Highlights in the History of Amputations Reflecting Lessons in Wound Healing', *Bulletin of the History of Medicine*, vol. XLI, 1967, no. 2, March–April, 102–3.
43. Cited in L.G. Stevenson, 'John Hunter, Surgeon-General, 1790–1793', *Journal of the History of Medicine*, vol. XIX, 1964, 254.
44. Weiner, *op cit.*, 56, 71.
45. A.G. Chevalier, 'The Physicians and Medical Services of the Revolutionary Armies', *Ciba Symposia*, vol. VII, nr. 11, February 1964, 251–2.
46. D.M. Vees, 'The Collapse and Revival of Medical Education in France: A Consequence of Revolution and War, 1789–1795', *History of Education Quarterly*, vol. VII, no. 1, 1967, 77–81; the quotation is in Weiner, *op cit.*, 59.
47. Phipps, *op cit.*, vol. III, 137.
48. Chevalier, 'The Physicians', 252–3; R.L. Blanco, *Wellington's Surgeon General: Sir James McGrigor*, Duke University Press, Durham, NC., 1974, 113.
49. Phipps, *op cit.*, vol. V, 61.
50. Cited in Weiner, *op cit.*, 61.
51. *Ibid.*, 69; A.G. Chevalier, 'Hygiene Problems of the Napoleonic Armies', *Ciba Symposia*, vol. III, no. 6, September, 1941, 974–5.
52. Picard, *op cit.*, 157.
53. C.V. Clausewitz, *The Campaign of 1812 in Russia*, reprint of 1843, London ed., intro. by F.A. Miller, Academic International, Hattiesberg, Miss., 1970, 97–8. Cf. Fezensac, *op cit.*, 20.
54. Weiner, *op cit.*, 68, 70.
55. Phipps, *op cit.*, vol. IV, 154.
56. Wilson, *op cit.*, 53.
57. *Ibid.*, 53–4.
58. Tarle, *op cit.*, 100–2.
59. Wesemann, *op cit.*, 86–7.
60. Blanco, *op cit.*, 89–91, 101–3, 110–11.
61. Glover, 'Doctors', 233.
62. *Ibid.*, 235; Blanco, *op cit.*, 115.
63. *Ibid.*, 115.
64. *Ibid.*, 117–18.
65. *Ibid.*, 114, 120–43; Longford, *op cit.*, 303.
66. Blanco, *op cit.*, 141.
67. Morris, *op cit.*, 81–2.
68. Brett-James, *Leipzig*, 149.
69. Bell, *op cit.*, vol. I, 101.
70. Harris, *op cit.*, 61–2; Morris, *op cit.*, 23.

71. Glover, 'Doctors', 235; Blanco, *op cit.*, 18.
72. Phipps, *op cit.*, vol. I, 29.
73. F.H. Garrison, *Notes on the History of Military Medicine,* Association of Military Surgeons, Washington, DC., 1922, 169–70. For a general discussion see H. Zinsser, *Rats, Lice, and History,* Little, Brown & Co., Boston, 1935, 150–65.
74. Fortescue, *op cit.*, vol. IV, 496.
75. Blanco, *op cit.*, 100–7.
76. *Ibid.*, 142.
77. Zinsser, *op cit.*, 161–4; Clausewitz, *Invasion,* 85.
78. Rothenberg, *Military Border,* 115.
79. Beamish, *op cit.*, vol. I, 77.
80. Costello, *op cit.*, 22.
81. Bell, *op cit.*, vol. I, 77.
82. Chevalier, *Souvenirs,* 85.
83. Morvan, *op cit.*, vol. II, 366.

Epilogue

This book has tried to describe and explain the major changes in the conduct of war and the nature of the major armies from the last decades of the *ancien régime* to Napoleon's final defeat at Waterloo. It now becomes necessary to ask 'and what became of it at last?' The answer is that the Revolutionary and Napoleonic wars left a mixed military legacy. By the end of the period most armies had adopted some forms of Napoleonic strategy and tactics, and these were retained. On the other hand, as soon as the conflict ended all governments, even the Prussian, realizing that radical innovations in the military sphere were closely linked to changes in the political, social and economic framework, returned as much as they could to military establishments resembling those of the pre-revolutionary period.

When the *ancien régime* had vanished and the state had become a nation, there had been a departure from the older traditions of dynastic wars with limited participation. Resting on conscription and patriotic fervour, and with war nourishing war, the new French armies were larger and more mobile than those of the eighteenth century. At the same time new methods of organization, divisions and later corps, and new tactics, skirmishing and charging in columns, not only could be taught more easily than linear evolutions, but they also proved highly effective To fight the French the other European powers had to adopt similar methods and organizations; as Frederick William III of Prussia said, it was necessary to 'make our army more like the French'.[1]

Yet, in the end, the reforms adopted were limited and partial. Generally speaking, French military organization, strategy, and tactics were adopted. Armies manoeuvred in corps, divisions and brigades, and fought in columns and skirmish lines supported by massed batteries of mobile field artillery. But on the question of whether armies should become 'national', that is whether they should be constituted by citizens with rights and obligations, or whether the traditional forms of officers procured from the upper classes in society and a rank and file enlisted from the opposite end of the social spectrum should be continued, the powers, except for Prussia proved extremely conservative. England had always continued the system of raising troops by voluntary enlistment; there also had been no change in the Russian army.

Austria, to be sure, had experimented with the *Landwehr* concept in 1809, but had discarded it by 1813. Only Prussia, keenly aware of her manpower weakness compared to the other powers, had in 1814–15 introduced universal conscription legislation preserving the *Landwehr* as a permanent part of her military establishment.

The tendency to retain, or revert to, the traditional pattern was reinforced by the international situation. The fall of Napoleon ushered in a period of relative stability in Europe, based primarily on the balance of power established by the treaties of 1815 and the rigorous suppression of all domestic disorder. Except for a continuing suspicion of French designs, the armies of the great continental powers were designed primarily for use against nationalist and liberal uprisings and not for use against each other. Governments after 1815 feared that the ghost of revolution had only been inadequately banished and they believed that Jacobinism, nationalism, and the nation in arms were interlocking revolutionary concepts. Therefore even where changes in the military establishment had been made, the governments returned as soon as possible to the spirit and forms of the eighteenth century.

Even where extensive changes had occurred, there was a determined effort to insulate soldiers once again from the political, social, and economic problems around them. In France the restored Bourbons returned as soon as they could to a professional long-service army, though retaining conscription on paper. And in Prussia, too, the reformers, regarded as military Jacobins by the reactionaries, first scaled down their hopes and then almost became reactionaries themselves. In any case, most of these professional officers had been uneasy about the idea of a 'people's army' and the citizen-soldiers. As one of Gneisenau's assistants wrote even before the army had been withdrawn from France, 'it was quite proper to use them as *piqueurs* who, with the moral hunting-whip, drove the lazy dogs as long as the hunt lasted. But when they sat down to dine with the hunting society . . . it became time to show them the door'.[2] By 1819, most of the radical officers associated with the innovations of the Scharnhorst period either had recanted or had been driven from office.

In tactics, however, there was considerable continuity between those of the Napoleonic era and the second quarter of the nineteenth century and beyond. To be sure, the British clung to their refined linear system, in many ways the ultimate perfection of eighteenth century warfare. But in the other armies combat methods evolved by the end of the Napoleonic wars remained in use, even though new technological developments rapidly diminished their effectiveness. This in part was due to the prevailing conservatism in ruling circles, but also due to the fact that all military establishments were dominated by men who had gained their experience, and sometimes fame, in the Napoleonic wars. In France there were Soult, Marmont, and St Cyr; in England Wellington, and in Austria Radetzky. And while Scharnhorst had died in 1813 and Blücher in 1819, Prussian tactical methods continued to be dominated by Gneisenau and Clausewitz, and after them by men like Wrangel and others. And in Russia, finally, Paskievich, promoted to Lieutenant-General at Leipzig, dominated the military scene into the Crimean War. None of these men were disposed to abandon the tried and true methods and they did not encourage their subordinates to question them. As a result, tactics became ossified and the manoeuvres of the wars in the mid-nineteenth century in Europe, and for that matter those of the Civil War in America, would have been perfectly familiar to any Napoleonic general. Indeed, the European commanders during these wars had seen their last active service in 1813–15.

There was, in fact, some regression. Emphasis on squadrons of glittering cavalry and long lines of infantry wheeling with precision on the parade ground became common in all armies. The economic exhaustion following the long war played a role here. Mechanical drill, the manual of arms, and parade-ground exhibitions were less expensive than realistic training and also more in line with the return of the concept of the officer as gentleman or aristocrat and not a professional.

Except for Prussia, and even here there was a marked decline, the general staff was neglected. Everywhere there was a resurgence of the old antagonisms between the 'quill-pushers' and the men of the sword, many of whom retained an essentially pre-industrial conception of the army, distrusting all scientific and technological developments likely to upset the status quo. Emperor Francis Joseph of Austria put this feeling into words. 'The quality of my army,' he remarked, 'does not depend on learned officers, but on brave and chivalrous men.'[3] Loyalty, unquestioning obedience, literal observance of regulations, and above all personal courage were considered the most essential soldierly qualities.

As a result there was little progress in military theory, though there now arose a considerable literature attempting to interpret the lessons of the Napoleonic past. Baron Jomini, who had served on Ney's staff before deserting to the Russians, became the most influential interpreter until the 1860's. His many writings, prescribed readings in most military academies, provided little more than a clear and schematic exposition of Napoleonic strategy, culminating in the elaboration of 10 major maxims and three general combinations emphasizing mass, mobility, and pressure against the decisive strategic point. Jomini was completely silent on the issue of motives and political objectives, and he frequently confused the categories of strategy and tactics. In fact, he said little about tactics, though when he did, he emphasized the attack. By contrast, Clausewitz's writings, especially his uncompleted work *On War*, were far more sophisticated and complex. He did not believe in the validity of rigid systems and dogmas, but stressed instead the interaction of war, politics and society. He described war as 'an act of force to compel our enemy to do our will', and since war was the continuation of state policy by other means, it was subject to certain limitations. Nonetheless, Clausewitz scorned the thought that there was 'some ingenious way to disarm or defeat an enemy without too much bloodshed', and while he warned against escalating the level of force beyond that required to attain the political aim, he also felt that battle, an act of will and moral force as much as that of skilled generalship and manoeuvre, was the decisive act.[3]

Although Clausewitz's work soon became accepted as authoritative in Prussia, translated into French by 1849 and into English by 1873, it was not always clearly understood. Most military men read his sentiments not as a subordination of warfare to state policy, but as an ideological superstructure for their profession. And as far as tactics went, Clausewitz too was but little removed from the Napoleonic era. When he did his writing, all armies had achieved an approximately equal technological level and therefore he concluded that 'superiority in numbers becomes every day more decisive, and that the principle of assembling the greatest possible numbers may therefore be regarded as more important than ever'.[4]

On the operational level, therefore, despite his profound socio-political insights which became more important than ever in the twentieth century, Clausewitz had only limited impact. All military commentators were agreed on the importance of morale, though Clausewitz, to be sure, extended this morale factor from the private in the rear ranks to the commanding general and from the lowest civilian to the head of state. But the immediate military revolution on the operational level came through the perfection first of efficient and relatively cheap percussion rifle-muskets, later breech-loaders, and rifled artillery, together with the development of dense railroad and telegraph networks. Although these innovations were accepted by the military everywhere in the 1850s, there was no realization that they created a dichotomy between firepower and the existing tactics. Despite the fact that massed charges yielded constantly diminishing returns against the new weapons, faith in the mass attack remained constant until the 1870s and beyond. At the same time, there was some hesitation to adopt the new strategic mobility conferred on armies by railroads and telegraph, and much preoccupation with secure operational bases, good positions, and safe lines of communications. This, of course, represented a regression to the eighteenth century, but generals commanding old-fashioned armies were unprepared for the new, and revolutionary, implications in strategy and tactics created by the new weaponry and communications.[5]

The Prussian general staff, directed since 1857 by Helmuth v. Moltke, was perhaps the first to realize that the forces unleashed by the Industrial Revolution provided the means to mobilize, equip, and direct huge armies, and that this required both a complex and highly professional staff and the support of the entire sociopolitical potential of the nation. But, with conscription becoming once again universal in Prussia in the 1850s, and with an all pervasive and effective state controlled educational system, for the first time Clausewitz's conception of the national will could be transmitted to the entire population. Meanwhile, realizing the potentialities of rail transportation, Moltke developed new strategies which demonstrated, and on an even larger scale, the Napoleonic principle of forcing a quick and decisive battle within a few weeks after the outbreak of war.

Prussia's surprising victories in 1866 and 1870–1 induced all continental armies to adopt the Prussian, and now German, system of mass mobilization through conscription, professional staffs, strategic railroads, and extensive telegraphic communications. Yet, although he had promoted the adoption of a breech-loader – the famous needle gun – into the Prussian army, achieving a decisive fire-superiority over the Austrians in 1866, Moltke, too, did not fully comprehend the necessity to adopt tactics suited to the radically changed circumstances. In fact, there was little realization of the growing gap between weapons and tactics, and between tactics and strategy in all European countries. All of the 1914 war plans of the continental general staffs were offensive and based on the expectation of achieving a quick and decisive decision on the Napoleonic–Moltkean pattern. All of these schemes failed, creating a bloody stalemate, a war of attrition and not a war of quick annihilation of the opposing forces.

The development of new tactics, and especially the rise of air and armour, seemed to revive the possibilities for quick decisions. During the Second World War, and in the smaller conventional wars of the post-war period, there was a revival of Napoleonic strategy – feints, penetrations, flank attacks, and envelopments, conducted by armoured and motorized armies under the cover of air umbrellas. But at the same time, the emergence of nuclear arsenals and missile-delivery system seems to have undercut the viability of conventional wars and Napoleonic strategy. Instead some writers suggest that the guerrilla warfare which plagued the French in the Vendée, the Tyrol, and above all in Spain, may well dominate the spectrum of future conflict. To be sure, there are others who disagree. They argue that while military planners in the past often made the mistake of underestimating the guerrilla, the danger now is that this type of warfare will be overrated and be considered a military panacea. Guerrilla wars, they maintain, remain only one form of conflict and they believe that there will be future wars in which Napoleonic doctrines, suitably adapted to modern conditions, still retain validity. The issue remains unresolved.

Whatever the outcome, it seems likely that as long as soldiers survive and men follow the profession of arms, Napoleon will continue to exert a powerful attraction and his achievements will continue to be studied. Few understood as well as he did the possibilities and limitations of time and space, and few commanders had his ability to inspire devotion and courage amidst peril and confusion. In recognizing and honouring these qualities, one also recognizes the qualities of his adversaries.

NOTES

1. Shanahan, *op cit.*, 84.
2. Cited in A. Vagts, *A History of Militarism*, W.W. Norton, New York, 1937, 175–6.
3. Paret, *Clausewitz*, 204–5, 382–95. Cf. Vagts, *op cit.*, 192–6.
4. *Ibid.*, 195.
5. W. McElwee, *The Art of War from Waterloo to Mons*, Weidenfeld and Nicolson, 1974, 1–69 *passim*.

Notes to the Appendices

The following two appendices contain a brief selection of representative battles and engagements, sieges, assaults, blockades, and capitulations during the period 1792–1815. According to Bodart no fewer than 644 major combats took place during this period, while the number of smaller encounters cannot be computed. For instance in 1794, a relatively quiet year, the Austrian army during the period from 6 January to 26 March, recorded no less than 45 encounters, ambuscades, and incidents, though the total number of casualties was insignificant, about 200 in all.

This selection has tried to provide an overview of major battles and sieges, illustrating the wide swings in combat performance, casualty rates, victories by inferior over superior numbers, and the like. Data are mainly based on Bodart, though modified in the light of more recent scholarship. The numbers are usually rounded off and like all combat data not wholly reliable. When a '?' follows a number it means that the data are particularly suspect.

Abbreviations: k + w = killed and wounded
               m = missing
               des. = deserted
               pw = prisoners of war
               Austr. = Austrians
               Bav. = Bavarians
               civils. = civilians
               Engl. = English, incl. King's German Legion
               Hanov. = Hanoverians
               Port. = Portuguese
               Pruss. = Prussians
               Russ. = Russians
               Span. = Spaniards

APPENDIX I: *Selected Battles 1792–1815*

Name	*Date*	VICTORIOUS Combatants (*a*)	DEFEATED Combatants (*b*)	VICTOR Losses (*a*)	DEFEATED Losses (*b*)
Valmy	20.9.1792	Dumouriez, Kellermann, 59,000 French	Brunswick, 35,000 Pruss.	300 k+w	200 k+w
Jemappes	6.11.1792	Dumouriez, 45,000 French	Duke Albert, 13,200 Austr.	2,000 k+w	1,000 k+w, 500, pw, 8 guns
Neerwinden	18.3.1793	Coburg, 43,000 Austr.	Dumouriez, 41,000 French	2,600 k+w, 400 m	3,000 k+w, 1,000 m+pw
Hondschoote	8.9.1793	Houchard, 24,000 French	Freytag, 16,000 Allies: Eng., Dutch, Hanov., Austr.	3,000 k+w	1,600 k+w 1,400 pw
Wattignies	16.10.1793	Jourdan, 45,000 French	Coburg, 30,000 Allies	5,000 k+w	2,500 k+w 500 pw
Tourcoing	18.5.1794	Souham, 70,000 French	Coburg, 74,000 Allies	3,000 k+w 7 guns	4,000 k+w 1,500 pw, 60 guns
Tournai	22.5.1794	Coburg, 50,000 Allies	Pichegru, 45,000 French	3,000 k+w	5,500 k+w 500 pw, 7 guns
Fleurus	26.6.1794	Jourdan, 81,000 French	Coburg, 46,000 Austr., Dutch	5,000 k+w	5,000 k+w?
Warsaw [Praga]	4.11.1794	Suvorov, 22,000 Russ. storms suburb	Wawrzecki, 28,000 Poles	4,000 k+w?	8,000 k+w? 12,000 inhab.
Quiberon	16.7.1795	Hoche, 13,000 French	d'Hervilly, 17,000 French Royalists and Engl.	500 k+w	1,700 k+w 6,500 pw
Mayence	29.10.1795	Clerfayt, 36,000 Austr.	Schaal, 33,000 French	1,600 k+w 200 pw+m	3,000 k+w 1,800 pw, 138 guns
Montenotte	11.4.1796	Bonaparte, 10,000 French	Argenteau, 4,500 Austr.	880 k+w	2,500 mainly pw, 12 guns

Selected battles 1792–1815 (cont.)

Name	Date	VICTORIOUS Combatants (a)	DEFEATED Combatants (b)	VICTOR Losses (a)	DEFEATED Losses (b)
Millesimo	13.4.1796	Bonaparte, 9,000 French	Provera, Austr., Sardinians	700 k+w	2–3,000 mainly pw, 18 guns
Mondovi	22.4.1796	Bonaparte, 17,500 French	Colli, 13,000 Sardinians	600 k+w	1,600 k+w and pw, 8 guns
Lodi	10.5.1796	Bonaparte, 17,500 French	Beaulieu, 9,500 Austr.	900 k+w	400 k+w, 1,700 pw, 14 guns
Lonato	4.8.1796	Bonaparte, 20,000 French	Quosdanovich, 15,000 Austr.	2,000 k+w	3,000 k+w, 20 guns
Castiglione	5.8.1796	Bonaparte, 30,000 French	Wurmser, 30,000 Austr.	1,500 k+w	3,000 k+w?, 20 guns
Neresheim	11.8.1796	Moreau, 50,000 French	Charles, 48,000 Austr.	1,200 k+w, 1,200 pw	1,100 k+w, 900 pw?
Amberg	24.8.1796	Charles, 46,000 Austr.	Jourdan, 34,000 French	500 k+w	1,200 k+w, 800 pw
Würzburg	3.9.1796	Charles, 44,000 Austr.	Jourdan, 30,000 French	1,200 k+w, 300 pw	2,000 k+w, 1,000 pw, 7 guns
Arcola	15–17.11.1796	Bonaparte, 20,000 French	Alvinczy, 24,000 Austr.	3,500 k+w, 1,300 pw+m	2,200 k+w, 4,000 pw, 11 guns
Rivoli	14–15.1.1797	Bonaparte, 22,000 French	Alvinczy, 28,000 Austr.	2,200 k+w, 1,000 pw	4,000 k+w, 8,000 pw, 8 guns
Pyramids	21.7.1798	Bonaparte, 23,000 French	Murad Bey, 6,000 Mameluks, 54,000 Egyptians	300 k+w	2,000 Mameluks, 2 Egyptians?, 20 guns
Stockach	25–26.3.1799	Charles, 46,000 Austr.	Jourdan, 38,000 French	2,900 k+w, 3,100 pw	2,000 k+w, 2,000 pw
Magnano	5.4.1799	Kray, 46,000 Austr.	Schérer, 41,000 French	4,000 k+w, 2,000 pw	3,500 k+w, 4,500 pw

Name	Date	Combatants (a)	Losses (a)	Combatants (b)	Losses (b)
Zurich	4.6.1799	Charles, 55,000 Austr.	2,200 k+w 1,200 pw	Masséna, 45,000 French	1,300 k+w 300 pw, 28 guns in battle, 150 guns in Zurich
Trebbia	17–20.6.1799	Suvorov, 20,000 Austr., 17,000 Russ.	5,000 k+w 500 pw	Macdonald, 33,000 French	9,500 k+w 7,000 pw
Novi	15.8.1799	Suvorov, 16,000 Russ., 34,000 Austr.	7,000 k+w 2,000 m or pw	Joubert, 35,000 French	7,000 k+w 4,000 pw or m, 37 guns
Zurich	25–26.9.1799	Masséna, 33,500 French	4,000 k+w	Korsakov, 23,000 Russ.	6,000 k+w 2,000 pw, 100 guns
Stockach	3.5.1800	Moreau, 84,000 French	3,000 k+w	Kray, 72,000 Austr.	3,000 k+w 4,000 pw, 17 guns
Marengo	14.6.1800	Napoleon, 28,000 French	6,500 k+w 1,500 pw	Melas, 31,000 Austr.	7,000 k+w 4,000 pw, 13 guns
Hohenlinden	3.12.1800	Moreau, 55,000 French	2,500 k+w	John, 52,000 Austr., 5,000 Bav.	5,500 k+w 8,500 pw, 24 guns
Mincio	25–26.12.1800	Brune, 66,000 French	4,000 k+w	Bellegarde, 50,000 Austr.	4,100 k+w 4,300 pw, 40 guns
Aboukir	21.3.1800	Abercromby, 12,000 Engl.	1,500 k+w	Menou, 10,000 French	3,000 k+w? 500 pw, 2 guns
Ulm	17.10.1805	Napoleon, 80,000 French	—	Mack, 29,000 Austr.	capitulation 59 field guns
Caldiero	29–31.10.1805	Charles, 49,000 Austr.	5,700 k+w	Masséna, 46,000 French	6,300 k+w 1,700 pw
Austerlitz	2.12.1805	Napoleon, 65,000 French	10,000 k+w	Kutuzov, 67,000 Russ., 16,000 Austr.	16,000 k+w 20,000 pw, 186 guns
Jena	14.10.1805	Napoleon, 96,000 French [54,000 in action]	6,000 k+w?	Hohenlohe, 47,000 Pruss., 17,000 Sax.	12,000 k+w 15,000 pw, 112 guns
Maida	4.7.1806	Stuart, 4,800 Engl. and Neapolitans	300 k+w	Reynier, 4,300 French	1,700 k+w

Selected battles 1792–1815 (cont.)

Name	Date	VICTORIOUS Combatants (a)	DEFEATED Combatants (b)	VICTOR Losses (a)	DEFEATED Losses (b)
Auerstädt	14.10.1806	Davout, 27,300 French	Brunswick, 50,000 Pruss.	7,100 k+w	10,000 k+w? 3,000 pw, 115 guns
Erfurt	15.10.1806	Murat, —?	Orange, 10,000 Pruss.	—	capitulation 65 guns
Prenzlau	28.10.1806	Murat, —?	Hohenlohe, 10,000 Pruss.	—	capitulation 64 guns
Pultusk	26.12.1806	Lannes, 26,000 French	Bennigsen, 44,000 Russ.	3,300 k+w 700 pw	3,500 k+w 12 guns
Eylau	7–8.2.1807	Napoleon, 75,000 French	Bennigsen, 74,500 Russ., 8,500 Pruss.	22,000 k+w	23,000 k+w 3,000 pw, 24 guns
Heilsberg	10.6.1807	Napoleon, 65,000 French (49,000 in combat)	Bennigsen, 92,000 Russ., 3,000 Pruss. [53,000 in action]	1,000 pw+m 12,500 k+w	9,000 k+w
Friedland	14.6.1807	Napoleon, 80,000 French	Bennigsen, 61,000 Russ., about 20,000 more in vicinity	12,000 k+w	20,000 k+w 10 guns
Bailen	19.7.1808	Castannos, 32,000 Span.	Dupont, 22,000 French, some allies	1,000 k+w 1,000 pw	3,000 k+w 1,000 des.
	22.7.1808	Dupont and remainder of force capitulated			
Vimiero	21.8.1808	Wellesley, 17,000 Engl., 2,000 Port.	Junot, 13,000 French	750 k+w	1,500 k+w, 300 pw, 12 guns
Corunna	16.1.1809	Moore, 15,000 Engl.	Soult, 20,000 French	90 k+w 110 pw	1,500 k+w? 100 pw
Eckmühl	22.4.1809	Napoleon, 66,000 French and Bav.	Charles, 74,000 Austr.	3,000 k+w?	6,000 k+w 5,000 pw, 12 guns
Ratisbon	23.4.1809	Napoleon, 72,000	Charles, 78,000 Austr.	2,000 k+w	2,000 k+w

Name	Date	VICTORIOUS Combatants (a)	VICTOR Losses (a)	DEFEATED Combatants (b)	DEFEATED Losses (b)
Aspern-Essling	21–22.5.1809	Charles, 99,000 Austr., 264 guns	21,500 k+w 1,500 pw	Napoleon, 66,000 French, 150 guns	23,000 k+w 2,000 pw
Wagram	5–6.7.1809	Napoleon, 160,000 French 500 guns	30,000 k+w? 7,000 pw	Charles, 130,000 Austr. 450 guns	19,000 k+w 7,000 pw
Talavera	27–28.7.1809	Wellesley, 20,000 Engl., 34,000 Span.	6,000 k+w 700 pw	Joseph, 47,000 French	7,100 k+w 200 pw and m
Bussaco	27.9.1810	Wellesley, 32,000 Engl. and Port.	1,300 k+w	Masséna, 58,000 French	4,500 k+w
Fuentes de Onoro	3–5.5.1811	Wellesley, 35,000 Engl. and Port.	1,500 k+w 300 pw	Masséna, 45,000 French	2,700 k+w
Albuera	16.5.1811	Beresford, 32,000 Engl. Port. and Span.	7,000 k+w 500 pw	Soult, 18,000 French	8,000 k+w
Salamanca	22.7.1812	Wellington, 47,000 Engl. and Port, 60 guns	5,200 k+w	Marmont, 42,000 French, 74 guns	10,000 k+w 7,000 pw
Smolensk	17–18.8.1812	Napoleon, 180,000 French [45,000 in action]	10,000 k+w?	de Tolly, 120,000 Russ. [30,000 in action]	6,000 k+w?
Borodino	7.9.1812	Napoleon, 124,000 French and Allies, 587 guns	28,000 k+w	Kutuzov, 122,000 Russ., 640 guns	50,000 k+w or m? 40 guns
Maloyaroslavets	24.10.1812	Napoleon, 24,000 French and Italians	6,000 k+w	Kutuzov, 24,000 Russ.	8,000 k+w
Beresina	26–28.11.1812	Napoleon, 33,000 French and Allies	20,000 k+w? 10,000 pw	Kutuzov, 60–64,000	8,000 k+w 2,000 pw
Lutzen (Gross-Görschen)	2.5.1813	Napoleon, 144,000 [78,000 in action], 240 guns	19,200 k+w 3,000 pw and m	Wittgenstein, 37,000 Pruss., 56,000 Russ., 407 guns	12,000 k+w
Bautzen	20–21.5.1813	Napoleon, 167,000 French and Allies, 530 guns	21,200 k+w 3,000 m, 800 pw	Wittgenstein, 66,000 Russ., 31,000 Pruss., 639 guns	11,000 k+w
Vittoria	21.6.1813	Wellington, 42,000 Engl., 25,000 Port., 23,000 Span.	4,900 k+w 300 m	Joseph, 60,000 French and Allies	6,000 k+w 800 pw, 143 guns

Appendix I

Selected battles 1792–1815 (cont.)

Name	Date	VICTORIOUS Combatants (a)	DEFEATED Combatants (b)	VICTOR Losses (a)	DEFEATED Losses (b)
Katzbach	26.8.1813	Blücher, 80,000 Pruss. and Russ.	Macdonald, 60,000 French	4,000 k+w	12,000 k+w; 18,000 pw, 170 guns
Dresden	26–27.8.1813	Napoleon, 100,000 French and Allies	Schwarzenberg, 200,000 Austr. and Russ.	10,000 k+w	14,000 k+w; 24,000 m and pw
Kulm	29–30.8.1813	de Tolly, 103,000 Russ., Pruss., Austr. 228 guns	Vandamme, 37,000 French, 81 guns	11,000 k+w	9,000 k+w; 8,000 pw
Bidassoa	7–9.10.1813	Wellington, 42,000 Engl. Port., Span. [32,000 in action]	Soult, 32,000 French and Allies [14,000 in action]	1,600 k+w	1,100 k+w; 600 pw
Leipzig	16–19.10.1813	Schwarzenberg, 122,000 Russ., 105,000 Austr., 80,000 Pruss., 18,000 Swedes, 1,384 guns	Napoleon, 175,000 French and Allies [7,100 desert during battle], 717 guns	75,000 k+w; 5,000 pw	45,000 k+w; 15,000 pw, 325 guns
Hanau	29–30.10.1813	Napoleon, 60,000 French, 140 guns	Wrede, 23,000 Austr., 17,000 Bav., 138 guns	6,000 k+w; 4,000 m or pw	5,000 k+w; 5,000 m or pw
Nivelle	10.11.1813	Wellington, 90,000 Engl. Span., Port. [45,000 in action]	Soult, 50,000 French [18,000 in action]	5,300 k+w	3,200 k+w; 1,300 pw
Brienne	29.1.1814	Napoleon, 36,000 French	Blücher, 30,000 Pruss. and Russ.	3,000 k+w	3,000 k+w
La Rothière	1.2.1814	Blücher, 45,000 Austr., 39,000 Russ., 8,000 Pruss., 17,000 Bav. and 14,000 other [80,000 in action]	Napoleon, 41,000 French	6,000 k+w	3,000 k+w; 3,000 pw
Toulouse	10.4.1814	Wellington, 60,000 Engl., Port., Span., 64 guns	Soult, 32,000 French, 56 guns	6,700 k+w	4,000 k+w; 9 guns
Quatre-Bras	16.6.1815	Wellington, 32,000 Engl. and Allies, 42 guns	Ney 24,000, 90 guns	4,800 k+w; 600 m or pw	4,400 k+w

Name	Date	Combatants (a)	Losses (a)	Combatants (b)	Losses (b)
Ligny	16.6.1815	Napoleon, 71,000 French 210 guns	12,000 k + w	Blücher, 84,000 Pruss., 224 guns	16,000 k + w 21 guns
Waterloo	18.6.1815	Wellington, Blücher, 67,000 Engl. and Allies, 53,000 Pruss., 288 guns	19,000 k + w 4,000 m	Napoleon, 72,000 French, 246 guns	25,000 k + w 7,000 m, 10,000 pw, 216 guns

Appendix II

APPENDIX II: Selected sieges, assaults, blockades 1792–1815

Name	Date	Assailant (a)	Defender (b)	Losses (a)	Losses (b)	Result
Longwy	23.8.1792	Brunswick, 60,000 Austr. and Pruss.	Lavergne, 6,000 French	—	71 guns	capitulation on summons.
Mayence	21.10.1792	Custine, 12,000 French	German, Imperials, 2,900	—	237 guns	capitulation on summons.
Dunkirk	24.8.–8.9.1792	Souham, 10,000 French	Freytag, 21,000 Allies	1,000 k+w incl. sick	2,000 k+w incl. sick	siege raised after French victory.
Charleroi	19.6.–25.6.1794	Hatry, 11,000 French	Reinach, 3,000 Austr.	?	?	garrison capitulates.
Mantua	27.8.1796–2.2.97	Bonaparte, up to 40,000 French	Wurmser, 28,000 Austr.	?	7,000 k, 6,000 sick	garrison capitulates. Wurmser and staff paroled.
Acre	17.3.–21.5.1799	Bonaparte, 12,000 French	Djezzar Pasha, 12,000 Turks, asst. by Engl. naval squadron	2,000 k+w	4,000 k+w and sick	siege lifted.
Genoa	19.4.–4.6.1800	Ott, 24,000 Austr. asst. by Engl. squadron	Masséna, 12,000 French	2,500 k+w 3,500 pw	4,000 k+w 15,000 civils.	allowed free evacuation.
Gaeta	4.3.–18.7.1806	Masséna, 12,000 French, 94 guns	Hesse–Philippsthal, 4,000	1,000 k+w	1,000 k+w 171 guns	garrison allowed free evacuation.
Stettin	29.10.1806	Lasalle, 800 French cavalry	Romberg, 5,300 Pruss., 281 guns	—	—	fort surrenders on summons, officers paroled, garrison pw.
Küstrin	1.11.1806	Gauther, 1,500 French	Ingersleben, 2,400 Pruss.	—	—	surrender on summons.
Magdeburg	29.10–8.11.1806	Ney, 16,000 French	Kleist, 24,000 Pruss.	—	92 guns	surrender, all men and guns.
Kolberg	20.3.–2.7.1807	Mortier, 14,000 French and allies	Gneisenau, 6,000 Pruss., 230 guns	5,000 k+w?	3,000 k+w? 3,000 pw	defence holds out until peace.

Name	Date	Assailant (a)	Defender (b)	Losses (a)	Losses (b)	Result
Saragossa	15.6–14.8.1808	Verdier, 15,500 French, 500 guns	Palafox, 6,000 Span., 7,000 armed civils.	3,500 k+w	3,000 k+w	siege lifted.
Saragossa	19.12.1808–20.2.1809	Lannes, 50,000 French, 50 hvy guns	Palafox, 30,000 Span. troops and civils.	6,000 k+w 6,000 k. by disease	18,000 k+w 12,000 pw 34,000 civils.	capitulation after bitter resistance, garrison pw.
Gerona	6.6–10.12.1809	Verdier, 18,000 French	Alvarez, 9,000 Span., 168 guns	15,000 about one half to disease	5,200 k+w or sick, 4,200 pw	capitulation following stiff resistance.
Ciudad Rodrigo	7.1–20.1.1812	Wellington, 36,000 Engl.–Port.	Barrié, 2,000 French, 173 guns	1,350 k+w	900 k+w 1,100 pw	assault after short bombardment.
Badajoz	17.3–9.4.1812	Wellington, 51,000 Engl.–Port.	Philippon, 5,000 French	1,850 k 6,650 w	1,300 k+w 3,700 pw	taken by assault.
Burgos	19.9–21.10.1812	Wellington, 32,000 Engl.–Port., 42 guns	Dubreton, 2,000 French, 26 guns	550 k 1,550 w	200 k 450 w	5 assaults repulsed.
Riga	24.7–18.12.1812	MacDonald, 32,500 French and Allies, 130 hvy guns	Essen, 17,000–25,000 Russ.	—	—	withstood siege.
Danzig	16.1–29.11.1813	Alexander of Württenberg, 4,000 Russ., Pruss. with Engl., Russ., fleet, 150 hvy guns	Rapp, 36,000 French and Allies	—	6,000 k+w 16,000 pw 6,000 sick 8,000 desert	blockaded and forced to capitulate for lack of food and ammunition.
Hamburg	24.12.1813–12.5.1814	Bennigsen, 56,000 Russ.	Davout, 40,000 French	6,000 k+w 8,000 k? by disease	6,000 k+w 10,000 k by disease	succ. defence until peace.
Magdeburg	15.9.1813–14.5.1814	Wobeser, 30,000 Pruss.	Lemarois, 20,000 French	—	1,200 k+w	blockaded but held out until peace.
Hüningen	25.6–26.8.1815	John, 15,000 Austr., Bav., others	Barbanègre, 3,000 French, about 1/2 Natl. Guard	—	1,100 desert	capitulated on terms; troops repatriated.

Select Bibliography

This bibliography repeats only the most important works cited in the notes. Included, however, are books not previously mentioned and considered most valuable for further reading. The citations are grouped in functional categories, though, inevitably, there is some overlap.

CAMPAIGNS AND BATTLES:

Adlow, E., *Napoleon in Italy, 1796–1797,* W.J. Rochfort, Boston, 1948.

Alombert, P.C. and Colin, J., *La campagne de 1805 en Allemagne,* 4 vols, R. Chapelot & Cie., Paris, 1902.

Balagny, D.E.P., *Campagne de l'empéreur Napoléon en Espagne (1808–1809),* 7 vols, Berger-Levrault, Paris, 1902–7.

Becke, Captain A.F., *Napoleon and Waterloo: The Emperor's Campaign with the Armée du Nord,* Routledge & Kegan Paul, 1914.

Belmas, J. ed., *Journaux des sièges faits ou soutenus par les Français dans la Peninsule de 1807 a 1814,* 4 vols, Didot Frères, Paris, 1836–7.

Berthier, L.A., *Campagne d'Égypte,* Baudouin Frères, Paris, 1827.

Burton, Brigadier General R.G., *Napoleon's Campaigns in Italy, 1796–1797 and 1800,* George Allen & Unwin Ltd., 1912.

Chandler, D.G., *The Campaigns of Napoleon,* Macmillan, New York, 1966.

Clausewitz, General C. v., *Nachrichten über Preussen in seiner grossen Katastrophe,* vol. X of Germany, Grosser Generalstab, *Kriegsgeschichtliche Einzelschriften,* Mittler & Sohn, Berlin, 1888.

Clausewitz, General C. v., *The Campaign of 1812 in Russia,* 1843 London ed., reissued with intr. by F.A. Miller, Academic International, Hattiesburg, Miss., 1970.

Criste, O., *Kriege unter Kaiser Josef II,* Seidel & Sohn, Vienna, 1904.

Cugnac, G.J.M.R. de, *Campagne de Marengo,* Chapelot, Paris, 1904.

Davout, Marshal L.N., *Opérations du 3ᵉ Corps, 1806–1807: Rapport du Maréchal Davout, Duc d'Auerstaedt,* C. Levy, Paris, 1904.

Delderfield, R.F., *The Retreat from Moscow,* Athenaeum, New York, 1967.

Driault, E., *Austerlitz, la fin du Saint-Empire,* F. Alcan, Paris, 1912.

Duffy, C., *Borodino and the War of 1812,* Scribner's, New York, 1973.

Dumoulin, M., *Précis d'histoire militaire, Revolution et Empire,* 3 vols, Maison Andriveau-Gujon, Paris, 1906.

Dupuy, Colonel T.N., *The Battle of Austerlitz,* Macmillan, New York, 1968.

Elgood, P.G., *Bonaparte's Adventure in Egypt,* Oxford University Press, 1931.

Fabry, G.J., *Campagne en Russie 1812,* 5 vols, Lucien Gougy, Paris, 1900–12.

Fézensac, General M.R.A.P. de, *The Russian Campaign 1812,* trs. L. Kennett, University of Georgia Press, Athens, Ga., 1970.

Foy, General M.S., *Histoire de la guerre dans la Peninsule sous Napoléon,* 4 vols., Baudouin Freres, Paris, 1827.

Friedrich, Major R., *Geschichte des Herbstfeldzuges 1813,* 3 vols, Mittler & Sohn, Berlin, 1903–6.

Friedrich, Major Rudolf, *Die Befreiungskriege 1813–1815,* 4 vols, Mittler & Sohn, Berlin, 1911–13.

Germany, General Staff, Historical Section, *1806. Das Preussische Offizierskorps und die Untersuchung der Kriegsereignisse,* Mittler & Sohn, Berlin, 1906.

Gieraths, G., *Die Kampfhandlungen der Brandenburgisch-Preussischen Armee 1626–1807, ein Quellenhaddbuch,* vol. VIII of *Veröffentlichungen der Historischen Kommission zu Berlin,* W. de Gruyter, 1964.

Glover, M., *Wellington's Peninsular Victories,* Macmillan, New York, 1962.

Glover, R.G., *Britain at Bay; Defence against Bonaparte 1803–1814,* Allen & Unwin, 1973.

Goltz, General C. v., *Jena to Eylau: The Disgrace and Redemption of the Old Prussian Army,* tr. C.F. Atkinson, Dutton, New York, 1913.

Henke, C., *Davout und die Festung Hamburg, 1813–1814,* Mittler & Sohn, Berlin, 1911.

Heriot, A., *The French in Italy, 1796–1799,* Chatto & Windus, 1957.

Herold, J.C., *Bonaparte in Egypt,* Harper, New York, 1962.

Houssaye, H., *1814,* Didier, Paris, 1888.

Houssaye, H., *1815 – Waterloo,* Didier, Paris, 1893.

Houssaye, H., *Jena et la campagne de 1806,* Perrin, Paris, 1912.

Jackson, W., *Attack in the West; Napoleon's first Campaign re-read today,* Eyre & Spotiswoode, 1953.

Janson, Lieutenant General R. v., *Geschichte des Feldzuges 1814 in Frankreich,* 2 vols, Mittler & Sohn, Berlin, 1903.

Jones, Colonel J.T., *Journals of the Sieges carried on by the Army under the Duke of Wellington in Spain during the Years 1811 to 1814,* ed. H.D. Jones, 2 vols, J. Weale, London, 3rd ed., 1846.

Jonquière, C.E. de la, *L'expédition d'Égypte,* 5 vols, H.C. Lavauzelle, Paris, 1889–1902.

Keegan, John, *The Face of Battle,* Cape, 1976.

Kennedy, General Sir J., *Notes on the Battle of Waterloo,* John Murray, 1865.

Lachouque, Commandant H., *The Last Days of Napoleon's Empire,* trs. L.F. Edwards, Orion Press, New York, 1967.

Lloyd, C., *The Nile Campaign: Nelson and Napoleon in Egypt,* Barnes & Noble, New York, 1973.

Lloyd, Major General H., *The History of the Late War in Germany,* 2 vols, S. Hooper, London, 1781.

Manceron, C., *Austerlitz,* trs. G. Unwin, Norton, New York, 1966.

Maude, Major General F.N., *The Jena Campaign of 1806,* Swan & Sonneschein, London, 1909.

Maude, Major General F.N., *The Ulm Campaign 1805,* George Allen, 1912.

Napier, Major General W.F.P., *War in the Peninsula and in the South of France,* 5 vols, A.C. Armstrong & Sons, New York, 1882.

Naylor, J., *Waterloo,* Batsford, 1960.

Oman, C.W.C., *A History of the Peninsular War,* 7 vols, Clarendon Press, Oxford, 1902–30.
Palmer, A., *Napoleon in Russia: The 1812 Campaign,* Simon & Schuster, New York, 1967.
Parker, W.T., *Three Napoleonic Battles,* Duke University Press, Durham, N.C., 1944.
Pelet, J.J., *The French Campaign in Portugal, 1810–1811,* ed., trs., and annot. D.D. Howard, University of Minnesota Press, Minneapolis, Minn., 1973.
Petre, F.L., *Napoleon's Conquest of Prussia,* John Lane, 1906.
Petre, F.L., *Napoleon's Campaign in Poland, 1806–1807,* John Lane, 1907.
Petre, F.L., *Napoleon and the Archduke Charles,* John Lane, 1909.
Petre, F.L., *Napoleon at bay, 1814,* John Lane, 1914.
Quistorp, B. v., *Geschichte der Nord-Armee im Jahre 1813,* 3 vols, Mittler & Sohn, Berlin, 1894.
Reinhard, M., *Avec Bonaparte en Italie d'après les lettres inédites de son aide de camp Joseph Sulkowski,* Hachette, Paris, 1946.
Rodger, A.B., *The War of the Second Coalition, 1798–1801,* Clarendon Press, Oxford, 1964.
Saski, C.G.L., *Campagne de 1809 en Allemagne et Autriche,* 3 vols, Berger-Levrault, Paris, 1899.
Segur, General P.P. de, *Napoleon's Russian Campaign,* ed. J.B. Townsend, Houghton Mifflin, Boston, 1958.
Siborne, H.T. Maj.-Gen., ed., *Waterloo Letters,* Cassell, 1891.
Sporschil, J., *Feldzug der Oesterreicher in Illyrien und Italien in den Jahren 1813 und 1814,* G. Westermann, Breisach, 1844.
Tarle, E., *Napoleon's Invasion of Russia, 1812,* Oxford University Press, 1942.
Thiry, J., *Leipzig, 30 juin–7 novembre 1813,* Berger-Levrault, Paris, 1972.
Tournes, R., *La campagne de printemps en 1813: Lützen,* Charles-Lavauzelle, Paris, 1931.
Veltzé, Colonel A., ed., *1813–1815. Osterreich in den Befreiungskriegen,* 10 vols, Seidel & Sohn, Vienna, 1911–14.
Weller, J., *Wellington in the Peninsula, 1808–1814,* Nicholas Vane, 1963.
Weller, J., *Wellington at Waterloo,* Thomas Y. Crowell, New York, 1967.
Wilson, Major General Sir R., *Narrative of Events during the Invasion of Russia by Napoleon Bonaparte and the Retreat of the French Army 1812,* John Murray, London, 1860.
Woinovich, General E., *et. al., Das Kriegsjahr 1809 in Einzeldarstellungen,* 11 vols, Stern, Vienna, 1905–10.

MILITARY ORGANIZATION, ARMS, AND SERVICES:

Beamish, N.L., *Geschichte der Königlich Deutschen Legion,* 2 vols, Hahn Hofbuchhand- lung, Hanover, 1832.
Boppe, Commandant P., *La Légion Portugaise (1807–1813),* Berger-Levrault, Paris, 1897.
Boppe, Commandant P., *Les Espagnols à la Grande Armée,* Berger-Levrault, Paris, 1899.
Boppe, Commandant P., *La Croatie militaire,* Berger-Levrault, Paris, 1900.
Cooper, L., *British Regular Cavalry, 1644–1914,* Chapman & Hall, 1964.
Corvisier, *L'armée française de la fin du XVIIᵉ siècle au ministère de Choiseul,* Presses Universitaires, Paris, 1964.
Dalton, C., *George the First's Army,* 2 vols, Eyre & Spottiswoode, 1910–12.

Davies, G., *Wellington and his Army*, B. Blackwell, Oxford, 1954.

Duffy, C., *The Army of Frederick the Great*, Hippocrene Books, New York, 1974.

Fallou, L., *La Garde Impériale (1804–1815)*, Olmes, Krefeld, 1975.

Fortescue, J.W., *History of the British Army*, 13 vols, Macmillan, 1899–1930.

Germany, Great General Staff, Historical Section, *Das preussiche Heer der Befreiungs-kriege*, 2 vols, Mittler & Sohn, Berlin, 1912–14.

Glover, R.G., *Peninsular Preparation: the Reform of the British Army, 1795–1809*, Cambridge University Press, 1963.

Halliday, A., *Observations on the Present State of the Portuguese Army as organized by Sir William Carr Beresford*, K.B., John Murray, London, 1811.

Jany, General C., *Geschichte der königlich-preussichen Armee*, 4 vols, K. Sigismund, Berlin, 1928–33.

Jedlicka, L. ed., *Unser Heer. 300 Jahre österreichisches Soldatentum in Krieg und Frieden*, Fürlinger, Vienna, 1963.

Kennett, L., *The French Armies in the Seven Years' War: a Study in Military Organization and Administration*, Duke University Press, Chapel Hill, N.C., 1967.

Kunisch, J., *Der kleine Krieg. Studien zum Heerwesen des Absolutismus*, Stein, Wiesbaden, 1973.

Meynert, H., *Geschichte der k.k. Armee*, 4 vols, Vienna, 1852–4.

Oman, C.W.C., *Wellington's Army, 1809–1814*, Edward Arnold, 1913.

Phipps, Colonel R.W., *The Armies of the First French Republic*, 5 vols, Oxford University Press, 1926–39.

Picard, L.M.E., *La cavalerie dans les guerres de la Révolution et de l'Empire*, Librairie militaire, Saumur, 1895.

Regele, O., *Der österreichische Hofkriegsrat*, Österreichische Staatsdruckerei, Vienna, 1949.

Rothenberg, G.E., *The Military Border in Croatia, 1740–1881*, University of Chicago Press, 1966.

Shanahan, W.O., *Prussian Military Reforms, 1786–1813*, Columbia University Press, New York, 1945.

Ward, S.P.G., *Wellington's Headquarters: a Study of Administrative Problems in the Peninsula, 1809–1814*, Oxford University Press, 1957.

Weygand, General M., *Histoire de l'armée française*, Flammarion, Paris, 1961.

Wilkinson, S., *The French Army before Napoleon*, Clarendon Press, Oxford, 1915.

Wilson, Major General R., *Brief remarks on the character and composition of the Russian army*, Egerton, London, 1810.

Wohlfeil, R., *Vom stehenden Heer des Absolutismus zur Allgemeinen Wehrpflicht (1789–1814)*, vol. II of *Handbuch zur deutschen Militärgeschichte*, Bernard & Graefe, Frankfurt, 1964.

Wood, General Sir E., *Cavalry in the Waterloo Campaign*, Roberts Brothers, Boston, 1896.

Wrede, Colonel A.v., *Geschichte der k.u.k. Wehrmacht*, 5 vols, Seidel & Sohn, Vienna, 1898–1903.

Zimmermann, J., *Militärverwaltung und Heeresaufbringung in Österreich bis 1806*, vol. III of *Handbuch zur deutschen Militärgeschichte*, Bernard & Graefe, Frankfurt, 1965.

MILITARY THEORY, STRATEGY, TACTICS, AND WEAPONRY:

Blackmore, H.L., *British military firearms, 1650–1850*, Herbert Jenkins, 1962.

Bonnal, H.G., *L'esprit de la guerre moderne de Rosbach a Ulm*, Chapelot, Paris, 1903.

Camon, General H., *La bataille Napoléonienne,* Chapelot, Paris, 1899.

Charles, Archduke, *Ausgewählte Schriften,* 6 vols, ed. F. Malcher, Braumüller, Vienna–Leipzig, 1893–4.

Clausewitz, General C. v., *On War,* trs. M. Jolles, Infantry Journal Press, Washington, D.C., 1950.

Colin, J.L.A., *The Transformation of War,* tr. L.H.R. Pope-Hennessy, H. Rees, London, 1912.

Dolleczek, Captain A., *Geschichte der österreichischen Artillerie,* the author, Vienna, 1887.

Eckhardt, W. and Morawietz, O., *Die Handwaffen des brandenburg preussisch-deutschen Heeres, 1640–1945,* 2nd rev. ed., Schultz, Hamburg, 1973.

Frauenholz, E. v., *Das Gesicht der Schlacht: Taktik in der deutschen Kriegsgeschichte,* Union Deutsche Verlagsgesellschaft, Stuttgart, 1937.

Fuller, Major-General, J.F.C., *Sir John Moore's System of Training,* Hutchinson & Co., 1924.

Frederick II, King of Prussia, *The Instructions of Frederick the Great for his Generals, 1758,* trs. T.R. Philips, Stackpole Press, Harrisburg, Pa., 1960.

Goltz, General C. v., *Von Rossbach bis Jena und Auerstädt,* 2nd ed., Mittler & Sohn, Berlin, 1906.

Hittle, Colonel J.D., *The Military Staff. Its history and Development,* Stackpole Press, Harrisburg, Pa., 1952.

Hughes, Major General B.P., *Firepower, Weapons Effectiveness on the Battlefield, 1630–1850,* Charles Scribner's Sons, New York, 1974.

Hughes, Q., *Military Architecture,* St Martin's Press, New York, 1974.

Jähns, Captain M., *Geschichte der Kriegswissenschaften vornehmlich in Deutschland,* 3 vols, Historische Kommission bei der kgl. Akademie d. Wissenschaften, Munich, 1891.

Jany, General C., *Die Gefechtsausbildung der preussischen Infanterie von 1806,* vol. V of Germany, Great General Staff, Historical Section, Mittler & Sohn, Berlin, 1903.

Jomini, Baron de, *The Art of War,* trs. G.H. Mendell and W.P. Craighill, Lippincott, Philadelphia, Pa., 1862.

Lauerma, M., *L'artillérie de campagne française pendant les guerres de la Révolution,* Soumalainen Tiedeakatemiaf Helsinki, 1958.

Lorenz, R., *Volksbewaffnung und Staatsidee in Österreich (1792–1797),* Österreichischer Bundesverlag fur Unterricht, Wissenschaft, und Kunst, Vienna, 1926.

Marshall-Cornwall, General Sir J., *Napoleon as a Military Commander,* Batsford, 1967.

Napoleon I, *Préceptes et jugements de Napoléon,* ed. E. Picard, Berger-Levrault, Paris, 1913.

Monge, G., *Description de l'art de fabriquer les canons,* Imprimerie du Comité de Salut Publique, Paris, 1794.

Müller, H., *Geschichte des Festungskrieges seit allgemeiner Einführung der Feuwerwaffen,* 2nd rev. ed., Mittler & Sohn, Berlin, 1892.

Oman, C.W.C., *Studies in the Napoleonic Wars,* Scribner's, New York, 1930.

Paret, P., *Yorck and the Era of Prussia Reform, 1807–1815,* Princeton University Press, Princeton, N.J., 1966.

Paret, P., *Clausewitz and the State,* Oxford University Press, 1976.

Quimby, R.S., *The Background of Napoleonic Warfare,* Columbia University Press, New York, 1957.

Rüstow, W., *Die Feldherrnkunst des neunzehnten Jahrhunderts, 1792–1815,* Schultheiss, Zurich, 1898.

Shadwell, L., *Mountain Warfare : Illustrated by the Campaign of 1799 in Switzerland,* H.S. King, London, 1875.

Vernon, Colonel Gay de, *Treatise on the Science of War and Fortifications,* 2 vols, trs. J.M. O'Connor, Seymour, New York, 1817.

Yorck v. Wartenburg, General, *Napoleon as a General,* 2 vols, Kegan Paul, 1902.

Zastow, A. v., *Geschichte der beständigen Befestigung,* A. Winter, Leipzig, 1854.

BIOGRAPHIES AND MEMOIRS:

Aldington, R., *The Duke : being an account of the life and achievements of Arthur Wellesley, 1st Duke of Wellington,* Viking, New York, 1943.

Bell, General Sir G., *Rough Notes of an old Soldier during fifty Years' Service,* 2 vols, Day & Son, 1867.

Beresford, Lieutenant General Lord, *Peninsula Cavalry Journal (1811–1813) of Lieutenant General R.B. Long, Lord Beresford,* ed., T.H. McGuffie, George G. Harrap & Co., 1951.

Blakeney, R., *A Boy in the Peninsular War,* ed. J. Sturgis, J. Murray, 1899.

Blanco, R.L., *Wellington's Surgeon General : Sir James McGrigor,* Duke University Press, Durham, N.C., 1974.

Blaze, Captain E., *Recollections of an Officer of Napoleon's Army,* trs. E.J. Meras, Sturgis & Walton, New York, 1911.

Bonnal, H.G., *La vie militaire du Maréchal Ney, Duc d'Elchingen, Prince de la Moskawa,* 3 vols, Chapelot, Paris, 1910–14.

Bourgogne, A., *Mémoires du Sergeant Bourgogne, 1812–1813,* Hachette, Paris, 1909.

Bricard, M., *Journal du cannonier Bricard,* Hachette, Paris, 1894.

Browning, B., *The Life and Letters of Sir John Moore,* Oxford University Press, 1923.

Burne, A.H., *The Noble Duke of York : The Military Life of Frederick, Duke of York and Albany,* Staples Press, London and New York, 1949.

Caulaincourt, A.A.L., *Mémoires,* 2 vols, Cassels, 1935–8.

Chevalier, Lieutenant, *Souvenirs des guerres napoliénnes,* ed. J. Mistler and H. Michaud, Hachette, Paris, 1970.

Chevillet, J., *Ma vie militaire, 1800–1810,* Hachette, Paris, 1906.

Coignet, Captain J., *The Narrative of Captain Coignet,* ed. L. Larchey, trs. M. Carey, Thomas Y. Crowell & Co., New York, 1890.

Costello, E., *Military Memoirs. The Peninsula and Waterloo Campaigns,* ed. A. Brett-James, Archon Books, Camden, Conn., 1968.

Cotton, E., *A Voice from Waterloo ; a History of the Battle fought on the 18th June 1815,* B. Green, 1877.

Criste, O. *Erzherzog Carl von Österreich,* 3 vols, Braumüller, Vienna–Leipzig, 1912.

Delbrück, H., *Das Leben des Feldmarschalls Graf Reinhardt von Gneisenau,* 2 vols, 3rd ed., Georg Stilke, Berlin, 1902.

Delderfield, R.F., *The March of the Twenty-Six,* Hodder & Stoughton, 1962.

Dible, J.H., *Napoleon's Surgeon,* Heinemann, 1970.

Dodge, Captain T.A., *Napoleon,* 4 vols, Houghton Mifflin, Boston and New York, 1904.

Dupuy, V., *Souvenirs militaires de Victor Dupuy, 1794–1815,* C. Levy, Paris, 1892.

Gallaher, John G., *The Iron Marshal : A Biography of Louis N. Davout,* Southern Illinois University Press, Carbondale, 1976.

Gleig, G.R., *The Subaltern : a Chronicle of the Peninsular War,* L. Cooper, 1969.

Grattam, W., *Adventures with the Connaught Rangers,* ed. C. Oman, London, 1902.

Harris, Rifleman, *Recollections of Rifleman Harris,* ed. H. Curling, R.M. McBride, New York, 1929.

Haswell, J., *The First Respectable Spy,* Hamish Hamilton, 1969.

Henderson, E.F., *Blücher and the Uprising of Prussia against Napoleon, 1806–1815,* G.P. Putnam's Sons, New York, 1911.

Huard, A., *Connaissez-vous Cambronne?,* Bloudet & Gay, Paris, 1959.

Humble, R., *Napoleon's Peninsular Marshals,* Macdonald, 1973.

James, J.H., *Surgeon James's Journal,* 1815, ed. J. Vansittart, Cassel, 1964.

Jomini, H. Baron, *Life of Napoleon,* Nostrand, New York, 1854.

Jonnès, Moreau de, *Adventures in the Revolution and under the Consulate,* trsl. C. Hammond, intro. M. Glover, Praeger, New York, 1970.

Kincaid, Captain Sir J., *Adventures in the Rifle Brigade,* Peter Davies, 1929.

Larrey, D.J., *Memoir of Baron Larrey, Surgeon in Chief of the Grande Armée,* Henry Renshaw, London, 1862.

Lefebvre, G., *Napoleon,* Routledge & Kegan Paul, 1969.

Lehmann, M., *Scharnhorst,* 2 vols, S. Hirzel, Leipzig, 1886–7.

Lejeune, General L.F. de, *Memoirs of Baron Lejeune,* 2 vols, trs. and ed. A. Bell, Longmans, Green & Co., 1897.

Longford, E., *Wellington: The Years of the Sword,* Harper & Row, New York, 1969.

Longworth, P., *The Art of Victory. The Life and Achievements of Field-Marshal Suvorov,* Holt, Rinehart, & Winston, New York, 1965.

MacDonald, Marshal J.E.J.A., *Souvenirs du Maréchal Macdonald, Duc de Tarente,* Plon, Paris, 1892.

MacDonnel, A.G., *Napoleon and his Marshals,* Macmillan, 1934.

Marbot, General M. de, *Mémoires du Général Baron de Marbot,* 3rd ed., 3 vols, Plon, Paris, 1891.

Marmont, Marshal A.F.L.V., *Mémoires du Maréchal Marmont, Duc de Raguse,* 9 vols, Perrotine, Paris, 1857.

Marshall-Cornwall, General Sir J., *Marshall Masséna,* Oxford University Press, 1965.

Masséna, Marshal A., *Mémoires de Masséna,* 7 vols, ed. General J.B.F. Koch, Paulin & Lechevalier, Paris, 1848–50.

Mercer, Captain C., *Journal of the Waterloo Campaign,* intro. M. Glover, Praeger, New York, 1970.

Morris, T., Private, *Memoirs of a Soldier in the 73rd Infantry Regiment,* ed. J. Selby, Archon Books, Camden, Conn., 1967.

Morton, J.B., *Marshal Ney,* Barker, 1958.

Muffling, General Baron F.C. v., *Passages from my Life together with Memoirs of the Campaigns of 1813 and 1814,* 2nd ed., trs. P. Yorke, Bentley, London, 1853.

Ney, Marshal M., *Memoirs of Marshal Ney,* Bull & Churton, London, 1833.

Odeleben, E. de, *Rélation de la campagne de 1813,* Delauney, Paris, 1817.

Ompteda, Colonel Baron C., *In the King's German Legion,* Grevel, London, 1894.

Parquin, Captain D.C., *Napoleon's Army,* trs. and ed. B.T. Jones, Archon Books, Camden, Conn., 1969.

Regele, O., *Feldmarschall Radetzky: Leben, Leistung, Erbe,* Herold, Vienna–Leipzig, 1957.

Reichel, D., *Davout et l'art de la guerre,* Delachaus & Niestlé, Paris, 1975.

Schubert, General F. v., *Unter dem Doppeladler. Erinnerungen eines Deutschen im Russischen Offiziersdienst, 1789–1814,* Kohler, Stuttgart, 1962.

Schwarzenberg, Prince K., *Feldmarschall Fürst Schwarzenberg,* Herold, Vienna–Munich, 1964.

Suchet, Marshal L.G., *Mémoires du Maréchal Suchet, Duc d'Albufera sur ses campagnes en Espagne*, Anselin, Paris, 1834.

Thadden, F.L.v., *Feldmarschall Daun*, Herold, Vienna–Munich, 1967.

Ward, S.P.G., *Wellington*, Batsford, 1963.

Watson, S.J., *By Command of the Emperor*, The Bodley Head, 1957.

Wesemann, J.H.C., *Kanonier des Kaisers. Kriegstagebuch des Heinrich Wesemann, 1808–1814*, ed. H.O. Wesemann, Verlag Wissenschaft und Politik, Cologne, 1971.

Wheeler, Private, *The Letters of Private Wheeler*, ed. B.H. Liddell Hart, Houghton Mifflin, Boston, 1952.

Wilkinson, S., *The Rise of General Bonaparte*, Clarendon Press, Oxford, 1930.

Young, Major General P., *Napoleon's Marshals*, Hippocrene Books, New York, 1973.

MILITARY LIFE AND CONDITIONS OF SERVICE:

Bell, D.H., *Wellington's Officers*, Collins, London, 1938.

Baldet, M., *La vie quotidienne dans les armées de Napoléon*, Hachette, Paris, 1964.

Büsch, O., *Militärsystem und Soziallleben im alten Preussen, 1713–1807*, vol. 7 of *Veröffentlichenungen der Berliner Historischen Kommission*, W. de Gruyter, Berlin, 1962.

Choury, M., *Les grognards et Napoléon*, Librairie academique, Perrin, 1968.

Demeter, K., *The German Officer Corps in Society and State, 1750–1945*, trs. A. Malcolm, F.A. Praeger, 1965.

Dupont, M., *Napoléon et ses grognards*, Hachette, Paris, 1945.

Holden, M., *The British Soldier*, Wayland, 1974.

Lachouque, H. and Brown, A.S.K., *The Anatomy of Glory: Napoleon and his Guard*, Brown University Press, Providence, R.I., 1962.

McGuffie, T., *Rank and File: the Common Soldier in Peace and War, 1642–1914*, Hutchinson, 1964.

Morvan, J., *Le soldat impérial (1800–1814)*, 2 vols, Plon, Paris, 1904.

Richards, D.S., *The Peninsular Veterans*, Macdonald & Jane's, 1975.

Watteville, Colonel H. de, *The British Soldier: His Daily Life frum Tudor to Modern Times*, Dent, 1954.

MISCELLANEOUS AND REFERENCE WORKS:

Bodart, G., *Militär-historisches Kriegs-Lexikon*, Stern, Vienna and Leipzig, 1908.

Brett-James, A., ed., *Wellington at War, 1794–1815*, Macmillan, 1961.

——, *The Hundred Days*, St Martin's Press, New York, 1964.

——, *1812. Eyewitness Accounts of Napoleon's Defeat in Russia*, St Martin's Press, New York, 1966.

——, *Europe against Napoleon. The Leipzig Campaign, 1813, from Eyewitness Accounts*, Macmillan, 1970.

Connelly, O., *Napoleon's Satellite Kingdoms*, Free Press, New York, 1965.

Craig, G.A., *The Politics of the Prussian Army, 1640–1945*, Oxford University Press, 1964.

Delbrück, H., *Neuzeit*, vol. IV of *Geschichte der Kriegskunst im Rahmen der politischen Geschichte*, G. Stilke, Berlin, 1920.

Earle, E.M., ed., *Makers of Modern Strategy*, Princeton University Press, Princeton, N.J., 1948.

Esposito, Brigadier General V.J., and Elting, Colonel J.R., *A Military History and Atlas of the Napoleonic Wars*, Praeger, New York, 1964.

Fuller, Major General J.F.C., *Decisive Battles. Their Influence on History and Civilization*, Charles Scribner's Sons, New York, 1940.

——, *The Conduct of War, 1789–1961*, Rutgers University Press, New Brunswick, N.J, 1961.

Garrison, F.H., *Notes on the History of Military Medicine*, Association of Military Surgeons, Washington, D.C., 1922.

Groote, W. v. and Müller, K.J., eds., *Napoleon I und das Militärwesen seiner Zeit*, Rombach, Freiburg, 1968.

Gurwood, Lieutenant Colonel, J., *The General Orders of the Duke of Wellington in Portugal, Spain, and France from 1809 to 1814 and in the Low Countries and France, 1815*, W. Clowes, 1832.

Higham, R., ed., *Guide to Sources of British Military History*, University of California Press, Berkeley–Los Angeles, 1971.

Horsetzky, General A. v., *A Short History of the Chief Campaigns in Europe since 1792*, J. Murray, 1909.

Hoyt, Captain E., *Practical Instructions for Military Officers*, John Denio, Greenfield, Conn., 1811.

Laffin, J., *Surgeons in the Field*, Dent, 1970.

Ropp, T., *War in the Modern World*, Duke University Press, Durham, N.C., 1959.

Scharfenort, G. v., *Quellenbuch der Kriegswissenschaften für den Zeitraum 1740–1910*, Mittler & Sohn, Berlin, 1910.

Sherwig, J.M., *Guineas and Gunpowder. British Foreign Aid in the Wars with France, 1793–1815*, Harvard University Press, Cambridge, Mass., 1969.

Six, G., *Dictionnaire biographique des géneraux et amiraux de la Révolution et de l'Empire (1792–1814)*, 2 vols, G. Saffroy, Paris, 1934.

Vagts, A., *A History of Militarism*, Norton, New York, 1937.

Index

Officers are listed with the highest rank reached.